"Here are the clarion voices that are crystallin
our day. This scholarly work with pastoral p
issue. I encourage every pastor to read this boo.

—Mac Brunson, senior pastor, First Baptist Church, Jacksonville,

"Exploring issues from a biblical, historical, philosophical, and theological perspective, the contributors to *Whosoever Will* have put forward an alternative to the Calvinist model of the doctrine of salvation within Baptist life."

—David S. Dockery, president, Union University, Jackson, Tennessee

"We took a large group of our staff members to the John 3:16 Conference, and we found it to be scripturally based, scholarly, fair, and on target. With the resurgence of Calvinism in the SBC, every Baptist should read this book."

—Steve Gaines, pastor of Bellevue Baptist Church, Memphis, Tennessee

"All who wish to consider seriously the role of Calvinism in Baptist life today can find stimulation in these pages, which in turn invite further discussion and dialogue."

—James Leo Garrett, Distinguished Professor of Theology, Emeritus
Southwestern Baptist Theological Seminary Fort Worth, Texas

"I believe that you will see the spirit of Christ from page to page . . . this book . . . was never intended to bash those of a different persuasion, but rather be part of an ongoing Southern Baptist dialogue that is building bridges."

—Johnny Hunt, pastor, FBC Woodstock, Georgia, and
President, Southern Baptist Convention

"*Whosoever Will* is an excellent introduction to those who wonder from where the Southern Baptist passion for evangelism and missions came and why a concern for the integrity of God's Word and the necessity of the atonement were major forces driving the Conservative Resurgence."

—Chuck Kelley, president, New Orleans Baptist Theological Seminary,
New Orleans, Louisiana

"A much needed corrective to the contemporary rise of Calvinism especially among young Christians; it presents a scholarly, biblically accurate, and reasonable case against radical Reformed theology."

—Roger E. Olson, professor of Theology, George W. Truett Theological Seminary,
Baylor University, Waco, Texas

"There is no more important message in all the world than that contained in John 3:16. The contents of this book will encourage everyone who reads it to keep the balance in proclaiming this verse's majestic truth."

—R. Philip Roberts, president, Midwestern Baptist Theological Seminary,
Kansas City, Missouri

"These stimulating essays provide thoughtful and provocative reflection, both pastoral and academic, from the Baptist *via media* tradition between Arminianism and Calvinism. Though I would differ with some of the contributors' perspectives (for example, their approach to perseverance), this book is a must read for all those interested in the current healthy exchange over Arminianism and Calvinism in the evangelical community."

—Matthew Pinson, President, Free Will Baptist Bible College, Nashville, Tennessee

{ Acknowledgments }

We would like to express our appreciation to Dr. Jerry Vines and his staff for allowing us to publish this book based on the presentations given at the John 3:16 Conference. We appreciate each scholar who contributed a chapter to the book, as well as Dr. Johnny Hunt for his foreword and Dr. James Leo Garrett Jr. for his preface. The editors and staff at B&H Academic have been of superb assistance, particularly Dr. Terry Wilder, Jim Baird, Dean Richardson, and Emily Cheney. We were also greatly assisted in the manuscript editing by Christopher Black, Bob Littlefield, Rhyne Putman, Kristin White, Carol Lemke, and Pam Cole at New Orleans Baptist Theological Seminary. And thanks to the many Baptists who have been encouraging us to write such a volume. We hope that it accomplishes its purpose and glorifies the Lord.

David L. Allen
Southwestern Baptist Theological Seminary
Fort Worth, Texas

Steve Lemke
New Orleans Baptist Theological Seminary
New Orleans, Louisiana

A Biblical-Theological Critique of Five-Point Calvinism

WHOSOEVER WILL

Edited by

DAVID L. ALLEN and STEVE W. LEMKE

{ REFLECTIONS FROM
THE JOHN 3:16 CONFERENCE }

ACADEMIC

NASHVILLE, TENNESSEE

{ Table of Contents }

Part One

Part Two

{ Foreword }

A s I contemplated writing the foreword for this book, the phrase that captured my heart as I consider the subject of Reformed and non-Reformed theology is just this: differing views—unified spirit. I can honestly confess that the Lord has placed people in my life whom I deeply love who have made incredible contributions to my life and who are on both sides of the fence. What I have come to love most about theology is the capacity to agree to disagree but to do it in the spirit of Christ. With that being said, I really believe that you will be a better student of God's Word having read this wonderful book.

As Baptists, we all know that we have Calvinists and non-Calvinists within our ranks. I believe that the Lord Jesus Christ is highly exalted when we can acknowledge our differences but join hands around a gospel-centered message to proclaim its truth to the nations. I also confess that, having studied the subject of Calvinism and its doctrines, I am a better student of God's Word. As most everyone who knows me personally is aware, I do not adhere to the five points of Calvinism. However, as a student of God's Word, by becoming better informed by hearing the heart of my friends and reading recommended volumes, I have a better love for and greater understanding of soteriology. One thing is for sure: I will never get beyond the day that God stepped out of heaven in the person of the Lord Jesus Christ and saved me. Since that day I am so grateful for the men and women who have been used by God to help shape my life as well as my theology.

The essays you will read in this book are from some of the most influential men I have known. As you read a simple yet profound message by Dr. Jerry Vines, you will be reminded that God really does love the world, and He gave the ultimate gift. Few men have touched my life like Dr. Paige Patterson by the way he has reached out and loved me from the first day I met him, and few men have more encouraged me to be a better student of God's Word.

As you continue to read, you will be grateful for such a great mind and heart as Dr. David Allen. He, along with the other authors, will lead us through this step-by-step process of taking a look at the subject of Calvinism. Obviously, this book is written from a non-Calvinistic perspective. However, you will see the spirit of Christ from page to page because it was never intended to bash those of a different persuasion. Rather, the book is part of an ongoing Southern Baptist dialogue of building bridges. I, for one, have sensed an incredible progression in the relationship of Calvinists and non-Calvinists. My prayer is that we would take the soteriology we have embraced and make it known to those who are the least and the lost in this nation and the nations of the world.

I trust that you will be greatly blessed, informed, and encouraged by this book and that you will feel impressed to recommend it and pass it on to others. Also, I pray you will seek to be the best student, and better yet, the best Christian you can be in a way that God would indeed be glorified and others would be drawn to Him.

> Blessings on you as you read.
> Johnny Hunt, Pastor
> First Baptist Church Woodstock, Georgia
> President, Southern Baptist Convention

{ Preface }

JAMES LEO GARRETT JR.

Although Christian preachers for centuries have sought to honor the Pauline testimony as to proclaiming "the whole will of God" (NIV), "the whole purpose of God" (NASB), or "the whole plan of God" (HCSB) (Acts 20:27), at times certain Christian doctrines, teachings, or issues have received attention or emphasis not accorded to other teachings. In the fourth century, when Arius was teaching that Jesus was a creature of the one God and thus not the Son of God and not God, the doctrines of the Trinity and of the person of Jesus Christ were a major concern. In the sixteenth century, when Martin Luther heralded the doctrine of justification by God's grace alone through faith alone and Anabaptists were stressing the new birth, questions about how human beings are saved were paramount. In the seventeenth century, when little-known John Smyth constituted a congregation of English exiles in Amsterdam on the basis of believer's baptism, the issue of believer's baptism versus infant baptism came to be greatly controverted.

So also the doctrines set forth by the Synod of Dort (1618–1619) in the Netherlands in opposition to the teachings of the Arminians have been high on the agenda of the Reformed expression of Christianity and at times of major importance to Baptists. For the first two centuries of Baptist history—the seventeenth and the eighteenth—the issues that distinguished the Arminians and Dort were the principal differentiating standard between General and Particular Baptists in England and between Regular and Free Will Baptists in America. But for most of the nineteenth and twentieth centuries those historic differences were less sharply drawn[1] and less central to Baptist theology and the life of Baptists churches.

When I was a youth in the church which B. H. Carroll had once served as pastor for 29 years, I was not made aware of the Calvinist-Arminian issues; they were simply not on our radar. A similar assessment can be made of the classrooms of Southwestern Baptist Theological Seminary during 1945–1948, when, as I recall, only church history professor W. W. Barnes specifically alluded to these issues in his course in Baptist history. For faculty and students these were not contemporary issues. Only when I began (1950) to develop a course in the history of Baptist theology did I discover the great significance of these issues for early Baptists, and only when I became a colleague of Dale Moody (1959) did the perseverance-apostasy question move to the front burner.

But issues that have lain fallow can come to life again. So with the Dortian-Arminian debate. The neo-Calvinist movement among Southern Baptists began to take on significance during the 1980s, and now perhaps one third of the recent SBC seminary graduates who are active in church ministry consider themselves to be five-point or Dortian Calvinists.[2] How is such a trend to be explained? The present author has suggested that it is a basic swing of the pendulum away from movement toward human accountability and activity and back toward divine sovereignty and activity.[3] Others have argued that Christians today are seeking greater security and some fixity in a time of anxiety and great change. Baptist Calvinists may contend that they have read their Bibles more closely and thus have come to Calvinist conclusions or that young Southern Baptists are discovering and adopting their earlier Calvinistic Baptist heritage.

What do we mean by "Calvinism"? There are several answers. First, it can mean the entirety of the teaching of John Calvin (1509–1564). This would include his teaching on infant baptism, presbyterial polity, the linkage of church and state, and the state's punishment of dissident believers. Second, it could refer to the entire Reformed theological tradition. Although such usage hardly does justice to the work of Ulrich Zwingli and others,

---

[1] Most, though not all, of the General and the Particular Baptists in England united in 1891.

[2] Ed Stetzer, "Calvinism, Evangelism, and SBC Leadership," in *Calvinism: A Southern Baptist Dialogue*, ed. E. Ray Clendenen and Brad J. Waggoner (Nashville: B&H Academic, 2008), 17.

[3] James Leo Garrett, "What Are the Alternatives to Dortian Calvinism?" *The Alabama Baptist*, 2 August 2007, 12.

such usage does exist. Richard A. Muller, a major Reformed theologian, has argued that one cannot rightly separate the teachings of Dort from the rest of Reformed teaching or regard Dort as the "sole" or "absolutely primary" indicator of Calvinism.[4] Third, Calvinism can be used to identify the teachings of the Synod of Dort. Fourth, the term can be used to refer to the elements of the Reformed heritage that have been retained and affirmed by some Baptists. This is what Malcolm B. Yarnell calls "Baptist Calvinism."[5] Fifth, there is also the term "Hyper-Calvinism." Although it has today come again into the Baptist vocabulary, it is most properly used to refer to the views of certain Anglican, Congregationalist, and Particular Baptist theologians in eighteenth-century England.[6]

We must indeed acknowledge that there has been a major strand of Calvinism in Baptist life, that is, Baptist Calvinism, despite the efforts of some to downplay such.[7] What was the precise nature of that strand, and is it supportable by a fair, accurate, and comprehensive reading of the New Testament? These questions have been addressed by those who made presentations at the John 3:16 Conference and by those who have prepared supplemental papers. Hence they are the burden of this book. Such issues need to be approached in a reflective and irenic spirit, not in a hostile, polemical fashion. The contributors to this volume have sought to do this.

---

[4] "How Many Points?" *Calvin Theological Journal* 28 (November 1993): 426. For Muller, John Gill, despite his embrace of the five points of Dort, was not a true Calvinist, and Muller's indictment of "a personal relationship with Jesus" implies a discrediting of the ministry of Billy Graham.

[5] Malcolm B. Yarnell III, "Calvinism: Cause for Rejoicing, Cause for Concern," in *Calvinism*, 77–81.

[6] The present author has identified five marks of Hyper-Calvinism: supralapsarianism; an eternal covenant among the Father, the Son, and the Spirit; eternal justification that is only manifested in time; no general offers of grace in preaching; and antinomianism. *Baptist Theology: A Four-Century Study* (Macon, GA: Mercer University Press, 2009), 89. Nathan Finn, "Southern Baptist Calvinism: Setting the Record Straight," in *Calvinism*, 182, has challenged the inclusion of two of these marks, i. e., "unconditional election" and the eternal "covenant of redemption," based on Garrett, "Calvinism: What Does It Mean?" *The Alabama Baptist*, 2 (August 2007): 7. First, I did not cite "unconditional election" in the sense that election was not based on God's foreknowing who would repent and believe but rather supralapsarianism with its doctrine of double predestination, including reprobation of the non-elect, not mere preterition—a teaching not embraced by the First or Second London confessions of Particular Baptists. Second, my use of the term "distinctive teachings" in reference to those marks—a debatable usage not repeated in *Baptist Theology*—was intended to mean "distinctive" from the five points of Dort, not "distinctive" from the entire Reformed heritage or from the entire history of Christian doctrine. Hence Finn was correct in noting that Calvinists other than Hyper-Calvinists have taught the eternal covenant of redemption.

[7] F. Humphreys and P. E. Robertson, *God So Loved the World: Traditional Baptists and Calvinism* (New Orleans: Insight Press, 2000); Humphreys, "Traditional Baptists and Calvinism," *Baptist History and Heritage* 39 (Spring 2004): 56–60.

Nevertheless, some heavy artillery has been put in place, especially by David Allen and Steve Lemke in their detailed studies of limited atonement and of irresistible grace (or effectual calling). Allen has gathered evidence that many Reformed theologians did not embrace limited atonement, and Lemke's chapter is replete with biblical texts and theological critique. Richard Land has offered an alternative to unconditional election that will likely send his more scholarly readers in pursuit of whether it is *sui generis* or has an earlier advocate in the history of Christian doctrine. Kenneth Keathley has reassessed assurance so as to conclude that it is based on justification, not sanctification, and is of the essence of faith, and he proposes a modified form of the evidence of genuineness view of perseverance. Paige Patterson's treatment of total depravity, hardly a refutation of Dort, may serve to support the present author's contention that the crucial difference was not total depravity but repentance and faith.[8] Kevin Kennedy supplements Allen by laying out the evidence that Calvin himself did not teach limited atonement, whereas Malcolm Yarnell focuses on the potential dangers of Calvinism for today's Baptist congregations, and Alan Streett deals with practice of the public invitation, or altar call. Jeremy Evans probes the compatibilism that seeks to combine determinism and human freedom over against a preferred libertarian freedom amid the rejection of effectual calling, and Bruce Little examines the problem of evil and suffering with a "simple sovereignty"—what God allows and what God ordains—and without two divine wills, the revealed and the secret. Jerry Vines introduces the volume with an engaging sermon on the great text that provides the title for the volume.

All who wish to consider seriously the role of Calvinism in Baptist life today can find stimulation in these pages, which in turn invite further discussion and dialogue.

James Leo Garrett Jr.
Distinguished Professor of Theology, Emeritus
Southwestern Baptist Theological Seminary

---

[8] *Baptist Theology*, 27.

{ Contributors }

David L. Allen, professor of Preaching, director of the Southwestern Center for Expository Preaching, George W. Truett Chair of Ministry, and dean of the School of Theology, Southwestern Baptist Theological Seminary, Fort Worth, Texas

Jeremy A. Evans, assistant professor of Christian Philosophy, Southeastern Baptist Theological Seminary, Wake Forest, North Carolina

Kenneth D. Keathley, professor of Theology and dean of Graduate Studies, Southeastern Baptist Theological Seminary, Wake Forest, North Carolina

Kevin Kennedy, assistant professor of Theology, Southwestern Baptist Theological Seminary, Fort Worth, Texas

Richard Land, president of the Ethics and Religious Liberty Commission of the Southern Baptist Convention, Nashville, Tennessee

Steve W. Lemke, provost and professor of Philosophy and Ethics, New Orleans Baptist Theological Seminary, New Orleans, Louisiana

Bruce A. Little, professor of Philosophy and director of the Bush Center for Faith and Culture, Southeastern Baptist Theological Seminary, Wake Forest, North Carolina

Paige Patterson, president, professor of Theology and L. R. Scarborough Chair of Evangelism, Southwestern Baptist Theological Seminary, Fort Worth, Texas

R. Alan Streett, W. A. Criswell Chair of Expository Preaching, Criswell College, Dallas, Texas

Jerry Vines, president of Jerry Vines Ministries, Inc. and pastor emeritus of First Baptist Church, Jacksonville, Florida

Malcolm B. Yarnell III, associate professor of Systematic Theology and director of the Center for Theological Research, Southwestern Baptist Theological Seminary, Fort Worth, Texas

{ Introduction }

DAVID L. ALLEN AND STEVE W. LEMKE

The Resurgence of Interest in Calvinism

The issue of Calvinism has garnered significant interest in recent years. In the September 2006 issue of *Christianity Today*, Collin Hansen wrote the cover-page article titled "Young, Restless, and Reformed: Calvinism Is Making a Comeback—and Shaking Up the Church," which dealt with two trends among younger evangelical ministers, including those within the Southern Baptist Convention (SBC).[1] This widely circulated issue also featured a cover picture depicting a young theologian wearing a T-shirt emblazoned with the words "Jonathan Edwards Is My Homeboy." The issue primarily focused on the Calvinistic turn of many young Baptist ministers toward Reformed theology.

---

[1] C. Hansen, "Young, Restless, and Reformed: Calvinism Is Making a Comeback—and Shaking Up the Church," *Christianity Today*, 50, no. 9 (September 22, 2006), http://www.christianitytoday.com/ct/2006/september/42.32.html. Using the same title, Hansen later published an expanded version of this article in his book, *Young, Restless, Reformed: A Journalist's Journey with the New Calvinists* (Wheaton: Crossway, 2008).

Several recent meetings have exhibited interest in Calvinism. The conference called "Together for the Gospel" has been held biennially in Louisville, Kentucky, since 2006, with Calvinistic Baptist and Presbyterian speakers drawing several thousand attendees. The leaders of the 2006 conference crafted a document titled "Together for the Gospel," which emphasizes shared beliefs of Calvinistic Baptists and Presbyterians. Then in November 2007, a conference titled "Building Bridges: Southern Baptists and Calvinism," hosted by LifeWay Christian Resources and sponsored by the Founders Ministries and Southeastern Baptist Theological Seminary, was held at the Ridgecrest Assembly Center in Black Mountain, North Carolina. At these conferences the overwhelming majority of the speakers were strong or moderate Calvinists.

On November 6–7, 2008, the John 3:16 Conference was held at First Baptist Church in Woodstock, Georgia. The presenters in the John 3:16 Conference stand in the great Baptist tradition that is neither fully Calvinist nor Arminian but is informed by both of these theological traditions. They believe that the majority of Southern Baptists and many other evangelicals do not fully embrace Calvinism or Reformed theology.[2] Therefore, the John 3:16 Conference was held in part to present their response and offer a perspective differing from that of some of these other meetings. The conference aimed to provide a biblical and theological critique of five-point Calvinism. Jerry Vines Ministries sponsored the conference, but New Orleans Baptist Theological Seminary, Southwestern Baptist Theological Seminary, Midwestern Baptist Theological Seminary, Liberty Baptist Theological Seminary, and Luther Rice Seminary cosponsored the event. The conference attracted a crowd of about 1,000 participants, and CDs and DVDs from the conference have been widely distributed.

The speakers at this conference would not identify themselves as Calvinists (nor as Arminians) but simply as Baptists. The first six chapters in

---

[2] In a 2006 study of 413 Southern Baptist pastors, about 10 percent described themselves as being five-point Calvinists. See L. Lovelace, "10 Percent of SBC Pastors Call Themselves 5-Point Calvinists," *Baptist Press*, September 18, 2006, http://www.bpnews.net/bpnews.asp?ID=23993; accessed 11/1/08. Since the study addressed only full-time pastors, some researchers have suggested that if the large number of bivocational pastors in the SBC had been included in the study, it may have reduced the overall percentage of strongly Calvinistic pastors to about 8 percent. However, a higher proportion of recent SBC seminary graduates (29 percent, according to a 2007 New Millennium Ministers Study conducted by NAMB and LifeWay) affirm five-point Calvinism (see "Calvinism and SBC Leadership: Key Findings and Evangelistic Implications," http://74.125.95.132/search?q=cache:EEC6sv6AHvYJ:www.lifeway.com/common/clickthru/0,1603,Link%3D238092,00.html%3FX%3D/file/%3Fid%3D4492+ed+stetzer+calvinism+study&cd=3&hl=en&ct=clnk&gl=us. In both of these studies, more than 70 percent of Southern Baptist leaders do not affirm five-point Calvinism.

part 1 of this book provide edited versions of the presentations made at the conference, all of them addressing issues concerning Calvinist soteriology. Jerry Vines's "Sermon on John 3:16" is a masterful treatment of that crucial text. Then Paige Patterson addresses "total depravity" and is followed by Richard Land, who focuses on "unconditional election." David L. Allen covers the topic of "limited atonement," and Steve Lemke treats the issue of "irresistible grace." Ken Keathley's treatise, "Perseverance of the Saints," completes part 1 of the book.

In part 2, an additional five chapters deal with other issues arising from Calvinist theology. This part begins with a chapter by Kevin Kennedy titled "Was Calvin a 'Calvinist'? John Calvin on the Extent of the Atonement." Malcolm Yarnell explores Calvinism and the local Baptist church, and Alan Streett provides the article "The Public Invitation and Calvinism." Jeremy Evans offers "Reflections on Determinism and Human Freedom," and Bruce Little rounds out the book with "Evil and God's Sovereignty."

The Debate over Calvinism

The debate about Calvinism is not new. Although the issue of human depravity, important to Calvinism, has incurred debate at least since Augustine, the Dutch Reformed Synod of Dort (AD 1618–1619) most famously addressed the issue in response to concerns voiced by the Remonstrants, who were themselves Dutch Reformed Calvinists. The theologian Jacob Arminius best articulated their views, although he did not live to attend the Synod of Dort. Other Calvinists strongly disagreed with the Arminian Remonstrants. In preparation for the Synod to discuss these issues, some of these Calvinists wrote down their views on human depravity:

> That man has not saving grace of himself, nor of the energy of his free will, inasmuch as he, in the state of apostasy and sin, can of and by himself neither think, will, nor do any thing that is truly good (such as saving Faith eminently is); but that it is needful that he be born again of God in Christ, through his Holy Spirit, and renewed in understanding, inclination, or will, and all his powers, in order that he may rightly understand, think, will, and effect what is truly good, according to the Word of Christ, John 15:5, "Without me ye can do nothing."
> That this grace of God is the beginning, continuance, and accomplishment of all good even to this extent, that the regenerate

man himself, without [the grace of God], can neither think, will, nor do good, nor withstand any temptations to evil; so that all good deeds or movements that can be conceived must be ascribed to the grace of God in Christ.[3]

What a strong Calvinist statement of human depravity and our absolute helplessness apart from God to provide for our salvation! It affirms that human beings are so depraved that they cannot think, will, or do anything that is truly good. Furthermore, humans cannot save themselves by their own efforts, faith, or free will because they live "in the state of apostasy and sin." It describes their utter helplessness to think, will, or do good, or to withstand temptations. The only hope for salvation is from God—to be born again and renewed by the Holy Spirit of God. The statement affirms that only God can renew human understanding, thinking, and willing so that humans can do good, for Jesus said that without Him humans can do nothing. Indeed, it affirms that any good deed "that can be conceived" must be ascribed only "to the grace of God in Christ."[4]

One might infer that such a strong Calvinist statement was voicing the opinions of the strong Calvinists who formed the majority at the Synod of Dort (the Remonstrants were systematically excluded from the Synod so that their views had no real representation at the Synod). In fact, this statement is a quote from Articles III and IV of the issues raised by the Remonstrants. Such a strong affirmation of human depravity and the complete inability of humans to save themselves means the Remonstrants cannot responsibly be called Pelagians or even semi-Pelagians. Pelagians and semi-Pelagians affirm that natural human beings can initiate or respond to God completely independent of God's grace.[5] Nothing could be more foreign to the beliefs of these Arminian Remonstrants than the notion that sinful humans could initiate, much less earn, their own salvation. Just as there are different kinds of Calvinists, with many Calvinists bristling at being called hyper-Calvinists, it is totally inappropriate for theologians to describe these Arminian Remonstrants as Pelagian or semi-Pelagian in doctrine. Indeed, the Synod of Dort unfortunately mislabels the Arminian Remonstrants

---

[3] "The Five Arminian Articles," Art. III and IV in *The Creeds of Christendom* (ed. P. Schaff; 6th ed.; Grand Rapids: Baker, 1983), 3:546–47.

[4] Ibid.

[5] R. H. Weaver, *Divine Grace and Human Agency: A Study of the Semi-Pelagian Controversy*, Patristic Monograph Series 15 (Macon: Mercer University Press, 1996), ix–x, 1–14.

as "entirely Pelagian."[6] Some later Arminians do go to that extreme, and they are wrong in doing so. Likewise, some Calvinists became so extreme that they became hyper-Calvinists. But let us abstain from calling them what they are not. The Arminians at Dort were Calvinists—members of Reformed congregations—who had concerns about the extremes to which some Calvinist theologians had taken Calvinism, at points probably further than Calvin himself. Caricaturing the Remonstrants as Pelagians or semi-Pelagians is, therefore, historically inaccurate and inappropriate.

However, despite defending the Arminian Remonstrants from this caricature, none of the authors in this project is Arminian or a defender of Arminianism. None of the authors is a five-point Arminian, a Pelagian, a semi-Pelagian, or a strong Calvinist. All these authors join the long history of the church in affirming that Pelagianism is a heresy that overly exaggerates human potential, overly minimizes human sinfulness, and overly minimizes the necessity of salvation solely through the grace of God. All these contributors support the fight against the "openness of God" perspective about God that places such a high value on human free will that it affirms that God does not have exhaustive foreknowledge of the future, and the contributors have also opposed those who do not believe in the security of the believer. Instead, our contributors try to keep the two more extreme positions in balance, learning from both, counting themselves as being in the mainstream of the Baptist theological tradition. This tradition, however, is broad enough to embrace both poles of this issue. Can Baptists be Calvinists? Yes, but Baptists can be non-Calvinists too. Baptists have always had both Calvinists and non-Calvinists within their ranks. Two extremes must be avoided: (1) Southern Baptists should *never* be Calvinists, and (2) true Southern Baptists *must* be Calvinists.

---

[6] "The Canons of the Synod of Dort," Heads III and IV, Rejection of Errors for Heads 3 and 4, Article VII (in Latin), in Schaff, "The Five Arminian Articles," 3:570. English translations of the Canons can be found in many places, including L. M. Vance, *The Other Side of Calvinism* (rev. ed.; Pensacola: Vance, 1999), Appendix 4, 621–22; or online at http://www.reformed.org/documents/index.html; accessed 11/1/08. The Synod further accuses the Remonstrants of teaching "that grace and free choice are concurrent partial causes which cooperate to initiate conversion, and that grace does not precede—in the order of causality—the effective influence of the will; that is to say, that God does not effectively help man's will to come to conversion before man's will itself motivates and determines itself. For the early church already condemned this doctrine long ago in the Pelagians, on the basis of the words of the apostle: It does not depend on man's willing or running but on God's mercy (Rom. 9:16)." ("The Canons of the Synod of Dort," Rejection of Errors for Heads III and IV, Article IX, in Schaff, "The Five Arminian Articles," 3:570; see 3:588). Clearly, the Remonstrants explicitly denied any human role in initiating salvation, and they affirmed that salvation is initiated by God's grace rather than any kind of human response. The Synod of Dort misrepresented the Remonstrant position in a completely inaccurate way with this *reductio ad Pelagian* caricature.

While both Remonstrants and Dortians agreed that all humans are depraved and totally helpless to save themselves apart from the grace of God, why did the leaders of the Synod of Dort oppose the Remonstrants so bitterly and violently that they persecuted them, forced them out of their churches, arrested and imprisoned them, banished and exiled them, and even beheaded them? In what way did the Remonstrants and the Dortian Calvinists significantly differ? The famous acronym TULIP has provided the distillation of the doctrinal differences between the two theological positions: Total depravity, Unconditional election, Limited atonement, Irresistible grace, and Perseverance of the saints. From the beginning of Baptist life, two theological trajectories somewhat mirrored the two positions at the Synod of Dort. "General Baptists" leaned toward the Remonstrant position, and "Particular Baptists" basically endorsed the Synod's position.

Which Calvinism?

Difficulty in addressing the doctrines of Calvinism accurately stems, in part, from having many Calvinisms rather than one monolithic "Calvinism." Various types of Calvinists differ significantly on a number of issues. For example, saying that *any* Baptist fully endorses Calvinist or Reformed theology is imprecise. A distinction can be drawn between one who is a *Calvinist* or *Reformed* (that is, someone who embraces all or most of the doctrines of Calvinism) and one who is *Calvinistic* (that is, someone who embraces some doctrines of Calvinism). Some Baptists are Calvinistic in their soteriology but not Calvinist in the Reformed sense of the term. Richard A. Muller, as a former member of the Calvin Theological Seminary faculty, holds indisputable Calvinist credentials. He has debunked in *Calvin Theological Journal* the notion that evangelicals such as Baptists who think of themselves as Calvinists can appropriately claim to be Calvinists simply because they believe in the five points of Calvinist soteriology:

> I once met a minister who introduced himself to me as a "five-point
> Calvinist." I later learned that, in addition to being a self-confessed
> five-point Calvinist, he was also an anti-paedobaptist who assumed
> that the church was a voluntary association of adult believers, that the
> sacraments were not means of grace but were merely "ordinances" of
> the church, that there was more than one covenant offering salvation
> in the time between the Fall and the *eschaton*, and that the church

could expect a thousand-year reign on earth after Christ's Second Coming but before the end of the world. He recognized no creeds or confessions of the church as binding in any way. I also found out that he regularly preached on the "five points" in such a way as to indicate the difficulty in finding assurance of salvation: He often taught his congregation that they had to examine their repentance continually in order to determine whether they had exerted themselves enough in renouncing the world and in "accepting" Christ. This view of Christian life was totally in accord with his conception of the church as a visible, voluntary association of "born again" adults who had "a personal relationship with Jesus."

In retrospect, I recognize that I should not have been terribly surprised at the doctrinal context or at the practical application of the famous five points by this minister—although at the time I was astonished. After all, here was a person, proud to be a five-point Calvinist, whose doctrines would have been repudiated by Calvin. In fact, his doctrines would have gotten him tossed out of Geneva had he arrived there with his brand of "Calvinism" at any time during the late sixteenth or the seventeenth century. Perhaps, more to the point, his beliefs stood outside of the theological limits presented by the great confessions of the Reformed churches—whether the Second Helvetic Confession of the Swiss Reformed church or the Belgic Confession and the Heidelberg Catechism of the Dutch Reformed churches or the Westminster standards of the Presbyterian churches. He was, in short, an American evangelical.[7]

Muller disdained "Particular Baptists" such as John Gill because Gill did not embrace the rest of the Calvinist doctrines.[8] To be fully Calvinistic (Reformed) requires much more than the five points often associated with the Synod of Dort. For Muller, to be truly a Calvinist requires the affirmation of other beliefs such as the baptism of infants, the identification of sacraments as means of grace, and an amillennial eschatology.[9] When these additional Calvinist doctrines "are stripped away or forgotten," Muller laments, "the remaining famous five make very little sense."[10] From the perspective of a true Calvinist, Baptists are modified Calvinists at best. Nobody in the SBC measures up to this standard of Calvinism. The SBC has Southern Baptists who are Calvinistic in some aspects of

---

[7] R. A. Muller, "How Many Points?" *Calvin Theological Journal* 28, no. 2 (1993): 425–26.
[8] Ibid., 428.
[9] Of course, many non-Calvinists also embrace amillennialism.
[10] Muller, "How Many Points?," 428.

their soteriology but Southern Baptist Calvinists do not endorse all doctrines of Reformed theology.

Therefore, since these articles quote from and respond to so many
varieties of Calvinism, other Calvinists may object that these arguments
do not address the beliefs of their particular stripe of Calvinism. Although
all of the contributors in this book are Southern Baptists, the subject matter of this book is broader than merely the writings of Calvinistic Baptists.
Since the articles are addressing Calvinism broadly, as opposed to any particular Calvinist thinker, this limitation of quoting Calvinists with whom
other Calvinists disagree is unavoidable. In particular, Calvinistic Baptists
may agree with critiques of statements by more thoroughgoing Calvinists.
The authors welcome their affirmation and agreement against more strin-
gent forms of Calvinism.

As Southern Baptists, all the speakers at the John 3:16 Conference as
well as the other contributors to this book affirm the doctrines of grace
discussed in Article IV on "Salvation" and Article V on "God's Purpose of
Grace," both located in the Baptist Faith and Message 2000,[11] the only
approved doctrinal confession of Southern Baptists. Since reaching the
lost is at the heart of God (Matt 18:14; 1 Tim 2:3–4; 2 Pet 3:9), evangelism and missions are at the heart of the concerns of the authors of
these articles, who gladly join hands with all Christians to discover what it
means to accomplish the Great Commission in this new millennium. The
primary focus of Christians should be to carry out the Great Commission
under the lordship of Jesus Christ according to the guidelines found in the
inerrant Word of God.

Differing Views, Unified Spirit

Addressing an issue such as Calvinism without inflaming emotions is difficult. Therefore, the authors enter into this discussion with some reluctance and yet also with determination. Our reluctance to approach these
issues stems from our desire for unity among Christians and particularly
within the SBC. The goal of unity is well pleasing to God and presents

---

[11] The Baptist Faith and Message 2000 is available online from the Baptist Center for Theology and
Ministry at http://baptistcenter.com/bfm2000.html. Commentary on the confession can be found in
C. S. Kelley Jr., R. Land, and R. A. Mohler Jr., *The Baptist Faith and Message 2000* (Nashville: LifeWay,
2007); and D. Blount and J. Wooddell, *The Baptist Faith and Message 2000: Critical Issues in America's
Largest Protestant Denomination* (New York: Rowman and Littlefield, 2007).

the most positive witness to those who do not know Jesus Christ as their Savior.

So why does this book deal with such a controversial issue? The book does so because it involves the authors' deep convictions concerning what they believe the Bible teaches about who God is and how He works in the world. Clearly, others have different convictions, flowing from their biblical interpretations and views of who God is and how He works in the world. These beliefs matter, for the convictions of the overwhelming majority of Southern Baptists and other evangelical Christians deserve to be heard, and lie at the heart of what Christianity is and what the gospel proclaims. The contributors are not "anti-Calvinist" and therefore are interested in dialogue, not diatribe. We have no desire to sweep the SBC clean of Calvinism. Since it has never been—and should never become—a crime to be a Calvinist in the SBC, any and every agenda to remove Calvinism from the SBC needs to be opposed. On the other hand, Calvinism should not be a major focus in the SBC either. As Nathan Finn said at the Building Bridges Conference:

> Southern Baptists on both sides of the Calvinism discussion must
> be free both to hold their convictions and to seek to persuade other
> Southern Baptists to embrace those convictions. . . . If we are to move
> toward a more cooperative future, we must all be committed to
> defending and commending our particular convictions but not at the
> expense of either our cooperation with one another or our personal
> sanctification.[12]

In that spirit and toward that end, this book is offered.

Baptists have always included those who are Calvinistic and shall continue to do so. Baptists claim Calvinistic believers as fellow believers and work hand in hand with them as they serve the Lord together. However, many Baptists honestly disagree with this theology. Our hope is that disagreement can occur in an irenic Christian spirit, without disagreeableness or harshness. We humbly ask forgiveness when we fail to do so, or when we misunderstand what others have intended. We take our stand on God's Word and challenge our readers to search the Scriptures to discover what the Bible says about these key issues.

---

[12] N. A. Finn, "Southern Baptist Calvinism: Setting the Record Straight," in *Calvinism: A Southern Baptist Dialogue* (ed. E. Ray Clendenen and Brad J. Waggoner; Nashville: B&H, 2008), 192.

{ Part One }

{ Chapter 1 }

Sermon on John 3:16[1]

Jerry Vines

Introduction

In the 1870s archaeologists uncovered a giant, red granite obelisk in the sands of Egypt. The Egyptians named it "Cleopatra's Needle" and gave it to Great Britain. "Cleopatra's Needle" was erected along London's Thames River. At the base of the shaft was a time vault. In it were placed several items of the day: coins, clothing, children's toys, newspapers, and photographs. A committee was appointed to include the greatest single verse in the Bible. The committee unanimously chose to place into the vault John 3:16, which had been translated into the 215 known languages of the day.

John 3:16, perhaps the best known verse in the Bible, is also perhaps both the first verse we learn and the last one we forget.[2] This one verse has brought multitudes to Christ. Herschel Hobbs called it "the Gospel in superlatives." Martin Luther called it "the Bible in miniature."

---

[1] This chapter is a transcribed sermon that was preached on November 6, 2008, by Jerry Vines at the John 3:16 Conference held by Jerry Vines Ministries at the First Baptist Church of Woodstock, Georgia.

[2] Unless otherwise noted, all Bible references in this chapter are from the King James Version (KJV).

A. T. Robertson referred to it as "the Little Gospel." Others have called it "the Mount Everest of Holy Scripture." Still others have called it "the most exquisite flower in the Garden of Holy Scripture." I like to call it "the Gospel in a nutshell." If all the other verses in the Bible were lost but this one, we would nonetheless still have them since all the rest of the verses of the Bible are contained in John 3:16.

John 3:16 addresses a number of "isms." The phrase "For God" responds to atheism, which claims there is no God. The phrase "so loved" responds to fatalism, which asserts God is an impersonal force. The phrase "the world" responds to nationalism, which says God loves only one group of people. The phrase "that He gave" responds to materialism, which says it is more blessed to receive than to give. The phrase "His only begotten Son" responds to Mohammedism, which says God has no Son. The phrase "that whosoever believes" responds to five-point Calvinism, which says Christ died only for the elect. The phrase "in Him" responds to pluralism, which says all religions are equal. The phrase "should not perish" responds to annihilationism, which says there is no hell. The phrase "but have everlasting life" responds to Arminianism, which says God only gives life conditionally. John 3:16 is a simple biblicism which reveals the mind, the heart, and the will of God.

F. W. Boreham called it "everybody's text." Here is a verse so simple a little child can understand it yet so profound that all the scholars of the ages cannot plumb its depths. Furthermore, John 3:16 can receive the designation as the inexhaustible text, as the following story illustrates. D. L. Moody met a young preacher in England named Henry Moorhead and invited him to preach at his Chicago church, should he ever come to America. To his great surprise, he received a telegram from the young man saying, "I have landed in New York. I will be coming to Chicago to preach for you." Moody was going to be away and instructed that Moorhead be allowed to preach one night. When he returned he discovered young Moorhead had preached several nights with growing crowds and many coming to Christ. Even more surprising, Moorhead had used John 3:16 as his text each night. Even more interesting, Henry Moorhead started preaching at age 16 and continued until his death at 33. His text for every sermon he preached was John 3:16. The sermons were different, but the text was the same.

John 3:16 is indeed inexhaustible because it is about the love of God. Who can fully expound the love of God? The task of expounding the love of God can be likened to that of the noted British painter William Morris, who received a commission to paint the portrait of the gorgeous Jane Burden. After quite a while, Morris wrote on the canvas, turning it to her, "I can't paint you, but I love you." Such is the feeling when Christians contemplate the love of God.

F. M. Lehman likewise expresses this sentiment in his hymn, "The Love of God": "Could we with ink the ocean fill / And were the skies of parchment made, / Were every stalk on earth a quill / And every man a scribe by trade, / To write the love of God above / Would drain the ocean dry; / Nor could the scroll contain the whole, / Tho' stretched from sky to sky."[3] This verse may be slick from frequent usage so that without care when reading it, it will roll off the mind without lodging. Instead of approaching it with a sense of competency, A. W. Tozer provides the better way:

> I think my own hesitation to preach from John 3:16 comes down to this—I appreciate it so profoundly that I am frightened by it—I am overwhelmed by John 3:16 to the point of inadequacy, almost of despair. Along with this is my knowledge that if a minister is to try to preach John 3:16, he must be endowed with great sympathy and a genuine love for God and man . . . so I approach it as one who is filled with great fear and yet great fascination. I take off my shoes, my heart shoes, at least, as I come to this declaration that God so loved the world.[4]

In this spirit, analysis of the verse in some detail—hopefully without destroying its beauty, which can occur when overanalyzing the parts of a flower—will proceed by expounding each of its four parts.

I. God's Love Is Global

"For God so loved the world . . ." The load-bearing verb here is "loved." The English word "love" can be used to express very different sentiments: "I love peanut butter. I love my wife. I love football." The Greek language has several words for "love": *eros*, *philos*, and *agapē*. *Eros*, from which we get the word "erotic," suggests a love that desires only to take. It is a sensual love. So odious is this word that it is not one time planted in the sweet soil of New Testament Scripture. Then, there is *philos*, which forms part of the

---

[3] Words from the hymn written in 1917 by F. M. Lehman, "The Love of God," in *Baptist Hymnal* (ed. M. Harland; Nashville: LifeWay Worship, 2008), 111.

[4] A. W. Tozer, *Christ the Eternal Son* (Camp Hill, PA: Wingspread Publishers, 1991), 85–86.

word "Philadelphia," the city of brotherly love. It conveys a give and take kind of love, a social love of mutual friendship and affection. The word here in John 3:16 is *agapē*, spiritual love. This love is a love that desires to give. It is a love not based on the worthiness of the object but on the character of the one loving. It is a love to the highest degree. John uses *agapē* 36 times in his Gospel.

The origin of this spiritual love is "God." Love is traced to its source. A God who loves like this was unheard of in pagan culture. They had all kinds of gods: peaceful gods, fighting gods, lazy gods, lustful gods. There were gods galore. It was "here a god, there a god, everywhere a god, a god." Never would it have occurred to them to say that any of these gods "loved" in this way. The use of the definite article in the Greek text gives definiteness to the term, "The God." Which God? The only God there is! The fundamental assertion about God in the Bible is "God is love" (1 John 4:8). God is omnipresent; He is everywhere. God is omnipotent; He is all powerful. God is omniscient; He knows everything. But, supremely, God is love. First John 3:1 says, "What manner of love the Father hath bestowed upon us." The Greek word for "what manner" can also mean "from what country." We would say even more so, God's love is "out of this world!"

The overflow of this love is expressed by "so loved" (*houtōs ēgapēsen*). The verb is a first aorist, active, indicative verb. More specifically, the verb is not an ingressive aorist, which would suggest a time when God began to love. The verb is also not a cumulative aorist, which would indicate a time when God will decide to love. The verb is, however, a constantive aorist, which emphasizes God's eternal, constant, total love. It means God's love in its entirety.

A young couple left their six-year-old girl with a babysitter. When they returned they found their little girl crying in her bed. "Why are you crying, darling?" "Because the babysitter said if I wasn't good, you wouldn't love me." They quickly assured her that their love was unconditional. God's love is as well, just as the hymn "Jesus Love Me" expresses: "Jesus loves me when I'm good, when I do the things I should. Jesus loves me when I'm bad, though it makes Him very sad."[5]

In Jeremiah 31:3 God says, "I have loved thee with an everlasting love." The Hebrew word for "everlasting" means "beyond the vanishing point." Young people might define it as "God's love is out of sight." My wife Janet

---

[5] A verse from an unknown rendition of the song by A. B. Warner and W. B. Bradbury, "Jesus Loves Me" (public domain).

used to tell our grandchildren, "I loved you before you were born." One night she said that to Ashlyn, still a little girl. Ashlyn cupped her hands under Janet's chin and said, "Memaw, I loved you before you were born!" There was a time when you began to love your mate or your children, but there was never a time when God began to love you. God's love reaches to eternity past, before you were born. Before the earth was created and before the sun, the moon, and stars existed, God loved you. God's love reaches to eternity; there will never be a time when God will cease to love you. When the heavens roll away like a scroll and the stars fall from their sockets like chunks of coal, God will still love you.

Do not overlook that little word "so" (*houtōs*). The Bauer Arndt Gingrich Danker Greek Lexicon says it is a demonstrative adverb.[6] Thayer calls it an adverb of degree. If the former is correct, it could be translated, "in this manner." If Thayer is correct, it could be translated, "to such an infinite degree." According to the MacArthur Study Bible, "so" emphasizes the intensity or greatness of His love. Perhaps we may combine both ideas by translating the verse as "God loved the world in such an intense manner." There are volumes in that little word. God's love is not like a trickling stream; instead it is like a flooding river. It is not like a leaky faucet; instead it is like a bottomless ocean. It is not like a flickering lightning bug; instead it is like a blinding sun. Unlike the Lanier and Allatoona Lakes, which were dangerously low a few summers ago when our area went through a severe drought, God's love is a reservoir that never runs dry!

The object of God's love is "the world." In Greek the word is *kosmos* and is an accusative, masculine, singular direct object. The word occurs 78 times in the Gospel of John and 24 times in 1, 2, and 3 John—over half of its 185 occurrences in the New Testament. Sometimes it refers to a world system organized in antagonism to God, but most often the word refers to the realm where human beings live. Sometimes the emphasis is on the human realm itself; most often it refers to the people who live in that realm. A. T. Robertson says it means "the whole human race."[7] It refers to the sum total of all people. The verse provides no hint here that "world" refers only to the world of the elect. God does not love just the elect; God loves everyone. God does not love just Christians; God loves all people. God does not just love Americans; God loves all nations. God

---

[6] See "houtōs" in *Greek-English Lexicon of the New Testament and Other Early Christian Literature* (ed. W. Bauer, F. W. Danker, W. F. Arndt, and F. W. Gingrich; 3rd ed.; Chicago: University of Chicago Press, 1999).

[7] A. T. Robertson, *Word Pictures in the New Testament*, vol. V: *The Fourth Gospel and the Epistle to the Hebrews* (Nashville: Broadman Press, 1932), 50.

does not love just white people, God loves all races. As in the song sung in Sunday school, God's love is all-embracing: "Jesus loves the little children, / all the children of the world. / Red and yellow, black and white, / they are precious in His sight. / Jesus loves the little children of the world."[8] Is there any child in the world, who attends church, who cannot correctly sing that song or "Jesus Loves Me"? Here is a question for us: If God does not love all the people of the world, why did God create them? In April 2008 the world population reached 6.6 billion. Put all those people in a line and walk them before God. John 3:16 teaches that God would say "I love you" to each one.

What kind of world does God love? In 1 John 5:19, "the whole world lieth in the wickedness." This world is like a precious vessel sunk in a putrid stream. Romans 3:19 teaches that the whole world is guilty before God. Learning about this world comes from observation, by reading the daily newspaper, and by watching the evening news on television: a drunken dad burns off the fingers of his little child, and a live-in boyfriend rapes a six-month-old baby, giving the child AIDS. Learning about this world also comes from the human heart, for "the heart is deceitful above all things, and desperately wicked: who can know it?" (Jer 17:9). The great evangelist Jesse Hendley said, "Only God could love a human being." Only God could love a world of such ugliness, perverseness, and shame. How can God love a sinful world like ours? God's love is not conditioned by the worthiness of its object.

Move this thought closer to you. Perhaps the thought that God loves the world does not move you. Move a little closer by remembering that "Christ loved the church, and gave himself for it" (Eph 5:25). Move a little closer by remembering that "[He] loved me and gave Himself for me" (Gal 2:20). I remember singing this old hymn at my boyhood church: "I am so glad that our Father in heaven / Tells of His love in the book He has giv'n; / Wonderful things in the Bible I see; / This is the dearest, that Jesus loves me."[9] My young heart would overflow as we sang the refrain, "I am so glad that Jesus loves me. Jesus loves me. Jesus loves me. I am so glad that Jesus loves me. Jesus loves even me." He loves you, Bill, Emily, Jason, Jessica. He loves each one individually, personally. He loves you as if there were no one else in the world. Augustine said, "God loves each one of us as if there was only one of us to love." I have a friend who had a lady in his

---

[8] Words from the song written by C. H. Woolston, "Jesus Loves the Little Children," in *Baptist Hymnal* (ed. M. Harland; Nashville: LifeWay Worship, 2008), 651.

[9] Words from the hymn by P. P. Bliss, "I Am So Glad that Our Father" (also known as "Jesus Loves Even Me") in *Baptist Hymnal* (ed. W. H. Sims; Nashville: Convention Press, 1956), 509.

church who had ten children. He asked her: "You have so many children. Do you ever neglect any?" The mother replied, "Oh no, I never forget a one of them, 'cause they're all precious to me." My friend learned something about a mother's heart. A mother's heart does not operate by the laws of division—one mother's heart divided ten ways. A mother's heart operates by the laws of multiplication—one mother's heart multiplied ten ways. Compute that to God's heart. God does not operate by laws of division, with one heart divided many ways, but by laws of multiplication, with one heart multiplied 6.6 billion ways.

A world outside our churches needs to know about this incredible global love. A young college girl approached me during the invitation after a message on the love of God. With tears glistening in her eyes, she asked, "Are you telling me God really loves me?" I responded, "God really loves you." Why church? Why church planting? Why denominations? Why evangelism? Why missions? "For God so loved the world." Whomever you see or meet wherever you go, remember that this is a person loved by God.

II. God's Love Is Sacrificial

"That he gave his only begotten Son." "That" is *hōste*, a consecutive conjunction introducing a result clause. God so intensely loved the world with the result that He gave His Son. Love always gives. It is the nature of fire to burn and of light to shine. It is the nature of love to give. A person can give and not love; a person cannot love and not give.

Love is a decision. Of course, there is an emotional element to love. I used to tell our young people in Jacksonville, "Love's a very funny thing. It's shaped just like a lizard. It wraps its tail around your throat and goes right through your gizzard!" But, primarily, love is a decision. When you marry, you decide to love someone whose hair may fall out, who snores at night, whose teeth must be replaced, who bites his/her toenails in bed, who brings emotional baggage and irritating traits into a relationship. Love is a decision.

God loved the world *definitely*. "He gave." The verb is *edōken*, an aorist active indicative. Again, it is a constantive aorist, emphasizing the totality and definiteness of the giving. It includes the incarnation, crucifixion, resurrection, and exaltation of Christ. First John 4:10 says God "sent his Son," another aorist indicating a definite decision. The word there, *apostellō*, means "to send off or away on a mission." God sent His Son tenderly, wonderfully, lovingly on a mission. I sometimes imagine that God, knowing mankind would sin and need a Savior, surveyed the farthest reaches of heaven. He looked at the cherubim and seraphim. None of them would do. He looked at the archangels and angels. None was good enough. His holy gaze fell upon the Son. In the counsels of the Godhead, it was agreed that the Son would come to be the Savior of the world. Imagine how it was when Jesus left heaven. The angels must have cried, "Don't go down there, Jesus; they will misunderstand and mistreat You." But down He came. As He passed by Jupiter, it said, "Don't go down there, Jesus; they will slap You and beat You." But down, down He came. As He passed by the sun, the sun cried out, "Don't go down there, Jesus; they will thrust a spear in Your side, crush a crown of thorns on Your head, and drive nails into Your hands." But down, down, down He came—all the way from the glory place to the gory place. "Out of the Ivory Palaces, into a world of woe. Only His great, eternal love, made our Saviour go."[10] He came down to this godless globe, to be born in a smelly manger, live in a hick town, work as a carpenter, be rejected by the world, and be nailed to a cross. God gave Him definitely.

God also gave Him *uniquely*. The phrase "only begotten" (*monogenēs*) is interesting and is built on two words: *monos*, which forms part of our words "monopoly" and "monorail," and *genos*, from which we get the words "genetics" and "genes." It is best translated "unique" or "one of a kind." John uses it five times in his writings (1:14,18; 3:16,18; 1 John 4:9). It is used in other places to refer to the son of the widow of Nain (Luke 7:12); Jairus's only daughter (Luke 8:42); the demon-possessed son (Luke 7:38); and Isaac (Heb 11:17). Isaac is called Abraham's "only begotten son," not his only biological son but his uniquely, miraculously born son. Jesus is God's Son in a sense no one else can ever be. He is God's unique Son.

A mystery surrounded Jesus' birth. When I was pastor in Mobile, Alabama, Dr. Mitchell, a gynecologist, was a member of my church. At the time he had delivered over 16,000 babies. I invited him out to lunch and asked him to explain biological birth. When he finished, I was aware that biological birth is a miracle but that no one was ever born as was Jesus. First Timothy 3:16 begins, "Without controversy great is the mystery of godliness: God was manifest in the flesh." When Jesus was born, God was born. The Infinite became an infant, the Creator became a creature, and

---

[10] Words from the 1915 song composed by H. Barraclough, "Ivory Palaces" (public domain).

God was in a cradle. Who can understand that?! The eternal God confined Himself to the narrow dimensions of a woman's womb and a single sperm cell. R. G. Lee used to say, "Jesus was the only One ever born who had a heavenly Father, but no heavenly mother; an earthly mother, but no earthly father. The only One ever born older than His mother and as old as His Father!"

When Jesus was born, there was a "must" about it. Does the virgin birth not matter? It is absolutely essential. Had Jesus not been born of a virgin, He would have had a sinful nature. Thus, He could not have lived a sinless life. Had Jesus not lived a sinless life, His death would not have been a perfect sacrifice for sin. By the virgin birth God short-circuited the sin cycle so that Jesus was never tainted by original sin. The same Holy Spirit, who impregnated the earth and brought forth beauty, impregnated the womb of Mary and brought forth deity.

There was also a magnificence about it. If slick Madison Avenue marketing experts had planned it, how different it would have been! They would have placed Him with a celebrity couple in a Trump Towers condo, but God placed Him with a carpenter and humble Jewish girl. They would have placed Him on the soft satin pillows of a king's palace, but God placed Him on the coarse straw of an animal stable. They would have announced Him to kings and scholars, but God announced Him to common shepherds. Yet the magi came to worship Him; a king feared Him; angels praised Him; and the Father was pleased with Him!

God gave His Son *incredibly*. The word order and the definite article are significant: "The Son the only begotten He gave." Just think of it! He gave His Son—His unique Son. What an incredible sacrifice! Romans 8:32 says God "spared not his own Son, but delivered him up for us all." God not only gave His Son to the world; He gave Him for the world. Oh, what He gave Him up to!

He gave Him up to scourging. The TV miniseries *Roots* helped me realize the severity of scourging. More recently *The Passion of the Christ* brought it vividly home to me. Jesus was not beaten with the Jewish 39 stripes: 13 on each shoulder and 13 on the small of the back. He was beaten with the Roman halfway death. So severe was it that men went raving mad under it; some died. It was all prophesied: "I gave my back to the smiters" (Isa 50:6); "the plowers plowed upon my back; they made long their furrows" (Ps 129:3). It was administered by a Roman lictor, a trained soldier. He used a flagellum, a whip made of wood with strips of leather. Attached were pieces of polished bone and steel. In the hands of the lictor, it became a whistling monster. Imagine the ripping of flesh, the splattering of blood. See the exposed, quivering veins.

God gave Him up to crucifixion. Death by crucifixion was the cruelest punishment ever devised by the depraved minds of men. Some say the Phoenicians got the idea from seeing rats nailed to a wall. They drove Jesus to Calvary. On Skull Hill, amid the screaming and spitting, the filth and gore, they laid the bruised, battered body of the Lord. Nailing Him to the cross, they lifted Him between heaven and earth as if He were fit for neither. As the cross dropped into the hole prepared, the flesh ripped and the lungs heaved. Muscles were pulled; bones were disjointed; tendons were shred; and the heart pumped desperately. Every movement sent pain, with shoes of fire racing over our Lord's nervous system. Oriental insects feasted on His body. The hot oriental sun beat down upon Him. The physical suffering is not enough to explain His sacrifice, for there is a spiritual aspect as well. Martin Luther was said to have spent hours contemplating the statement, "My God, my God, why have you forsaken me?" Luther was overheard to say, "God forsaken of God. Who can understand that?" "None of the ransomed ever knew how deep were the waters crossed. Nor how dark was the night that the Lord passed through 'ere He found His sheep that were lost."

Why such physical and spiritual misery? Why was Jesus dying? For what was He dying? The gospel makes it very clear. "Christ died for our sins according to the scriptures" (1 Cor 15:3). For whose sins did He die? Again, Scripture makes it very clear. "He is the propitiation for our sins: and not for ours only, but also for the sins of the whole world" (1 John 2:2).

In light of the sacrifice Jesus made on the cross, the love of God for the whole world, and the sacrifice made by God's love are beyond doubt. Our hearts can only sing, "What wondrous love is this, O my soul . . . that caused the Lord of bliss to bear the dreadful curse for my soul."[11] God does not love us because Christ died; Christ died because God loves us. Romans 5:8 says, "God commendeth his love toward us, in that, while we were yet sinners, Christ died for us." The word "commend" (*sunistēsin*) means "to exhibit, to prove" and literally means "to

---

[11] Words from the American folk hymn (author unknown), "What Wondrous Love Is This," in *Baptist Hymnal* (ed. M. Harland; Nashville: LifeWay Worship, 2008), 169.

put together." At the cross God put it all together. He proved His love by the sacrifice of His Son.

Remember when you would get a crush on a boy or girl in grade school and wanted so much for him/her to love you? I would get a daisy and begin to pluck the petals, saying, "She loves me. She loves me not." If the last petal was "She loves me," she loved me! That's the way it always came out. Why? I rigged it! On the cross God did not have to rig it. Every drop of our Savior's blood said, "I love you. I love you. I love you."

A world outside our churches needs to know about God's sacrificial love. Romans 3:25 says, "God hath set forth [His Son] to be a propitiation." The word translated "set forth" is *protithēmi*, which also means "to expose to view" and ties to the mercy seat in the Old Testament, which was closed off in a cube-shaped room. God put His love on display on a cross for the whole world to see. You cannot keep God's love confined in a church or in a Christian's life. Sooner or later it has to burst forth.

III. God's Love Is Personal

"That whosoever believeth in him . . ." At this point in the verse, the subject of the verbs changes. God is the subject of "loved" and "gave." Now the verse gets personal: you and I are the subject! We see the beautiful balance in this one verse that we find all over the Bible. Scripture gives the divine side and the human side of salvation. To overemphasize either to the exclusion of the other is to miss the complete message of the Bible. Gerald Borchert says:

> God is the initiator and principal actor in salvation, and we should
> never think salvation originated with us. God, however, has given
> humanity a sense of freedom and requires us to make a choice.
> Accordingly, people are responsible for their believing. It is
> unproductive theological speculation, therefore, to minimize either the
> role of God or humanity in the salvation process. The Bible and John
> 3:16 recognize the roles of both.[12]

The final clause begins with another conjunction, *hina*, which is a subordinate conjunction introducing a purpose clause. What is the purpose of God's giving His unique Son?

---

[12] G. L. Borchert, *John 1–11*, New American Commentary (Nashville: B&H Publishing, 2002), 25b: 184.

Look now at the word "whosoever." The transliteration of the Greek word is *pas*. It is used 1,228 times in the New Testament. It is translated as "whosoever," "all," and "every." It is a pronominal substantival adjective. As an adjective it modifies the participle *pisteuōn* (translated "believes"). As a substantive it fills the noun slot; as a pronominal it functions as a pronoun. It appears with an article and participle eight times in John's Gospel (3:8,15,16,20; 4:13; 6:40; 8:34; 18:37). *Pas* with the participle *pisteuōn* occurs four times in John (3:15,16; 6:40; 12:46). Here it carries the idea of totality. Kittel says it means a totality and an inclusion of all individual parts.[13] *The Dictionary of New Testament Theology* says, "Stress may be laid on each of the many individuals or parts which make up the totality."[14] Herschel Hobbs on the Southern Baptist Peace Committee, often reminding us of the use of *pas* in the phrase "*all* Scripture" in 2 Tim. 3:16, said it meant the whole of Scripture and every part of Scripture is inspired of God. Likewise, here it means God loves the whole world collectively, and He loves and will save "whosoever" individually.

The word is a welcome mat inviting the world to God. The Holy Spirit could have inspired John to say only, "the one believing." Does it just mean that all who believe will be saved? If so, the addition of the word is meaningless. Tell the word "whosoever" to the person in the remotest jungles of Africa, on the snowcapped North Pole, in the finest mansion in your city, or in the poorest shack. This all-embracing adjective is added to emphasize there are no limits on who may believe. David Allen says, "The addition of *pas* before the participle generalizes it to every single person. The best translation is: 'Anyone who believes.' The idea is non-restrictive. The idea is anyone . . . anywhere . . . anytime."[15] To say otherwise is to make a travesty of this verse. It is the design of the sovereign God to make the salvation of all people possible and to secure the salvation of all who believe. What kind of God would not make salvation possible for all?

I'm glad it says "whosoever" rather than saying my name. I received a letter from the Rome, Georgia, water company some years ago, informing me they were going to cut off my water for an unpaid bill, even though I was not using city water. I had my own well. There was another man named

---

[13] B. Reicke, *"pas,"* in *The Theological Dictionary of the New Testament* (ed. G. Kittel and G. Friedrich; Grand Rapids: Eerdmans, 1969), 5:887.

[14] F. Graber, "All, Many," in *The Dictionary of New Testament Theology* (ed. C. Brown; Grand Rapids: Zondervan, 1967), 1:94.

[15] D. Allen, e-mail message to author.

Jerry Vines who was not paying his water bill. It was a case of mistaken identity. This word *pas* removes any question of mistaken identity.

John "Bull" Bramlett was known as the meanest man in the NFL. He was a drinker and carouser. His wife came to Christ in Memphis, Tennessee. She immediately began to pray for John. Two men from Bellevue Baptist Church visited John, sharing the gospel with him. The next day he told his assistant to hold all calls. He began to read his New Testament. Several days later he came to John 3:16. When he read "whosoever," he said, "Whosoever? That could be me!" He knelt and received Christ as his personal Savior. If the word does not refer to every person, no person could ever know he/she is included.

It is fascinating to note how often *pas* occurs in passages about salvation. "He . . . should taste death for every (*pas*) man" (Heb. 2:9). "The Lord . . . is not willing that any should perish, but that all (*pas*) should come to repentance" (2 Pet. 3:9). God "will have all (*pas*) men to be saved, and to come unto the knowledge of the truth" (1 Tim. 2:4). God "is the Savior of all (*pas*) men, specially of those that believe" (1 Tim 4:10).

The next word is the present active participle *pisteuōn* ("believes"). John uses the verb *pisteuō* 96 times, eight times in John 3. He uses the participle with *pas* six times (1:7; 3:15,16; 6:40; 11:48; 12:46). The best translation of the verb is "trust." It is John's way of conveying saving faith. Three basic ideas are involved. First is the *mental* aspect—confidence in the Lord Jesus Christ. That is the idea conveyed in John 20:30–31. The use of *pisteuōn* in 3:15 seems to emphasize the mental aspect of saving faith. Second is the *volitional* aspect—commitment to the Lord Jesus Christ. The preposition *eis* is used in John 3:16 and carries the idea of movement toward. Third is the *emotional* aspect—communion with the Lord Jesus Christ. The use of the active participle and *auton* here suggest a continuing relationship with a living Person.

How does this saving faith come about? A sovereign God has given every person the faculty of faith and a will to exercise it (see Rom 12:3). This does not rob God of His sovereignty. Humans exercise the faculty of faith every day. They trust that their spouse is not poisoning them, so they eat their breakfast. They trust the banker to keep their money safe so they make their deposit. They trust the pilot is capable so they board the plane. As Norman Geisler says about humans' capacity to choose—it has been "effaced, not erased; limited, not lost; damaged, not destroyed." God commands us to believe. In Acts 16:30–31, the Philippian jailer asked

Paul, "What must I do to be saved?" There was nothing he could do to save himself. Christ had already done it by His death on the cross. In John 19:30, when Jesus said, "It is finished," the work was done. The hymn "O Happy Day" conveys this same affirmation: "'Tis done, the great transaction's done!"[16] But Paul said to him, "Believe on the Lord Jesus Christ and thou shalt be saved" (Acts 16:30–31). It would be unreasonable to command someone to do something impossible for them to do. It would be like commanding an armless man to embrace you.

When it comes to saving faith, the faculty of faith is raised to a new level by the conviction of the Holy Spirit. How does this happen? I used to take Billy Baptist with me to the annual meetings of the Southern Baptist Convention. The liberals never could see him. Only the conservatives could! How was Billy saved? He came to church, heard the Word preached ("So then faith cometh by hearing, and hearing by the word of God," Rom 10:17), was convicted by the Holy Spirit ("And when he is come, he will reprove the world of sin, and of righteousness, and of judgment," John 16:8), and believed the truth ("because God hath from the beginning chosen you to salvation through sanctification of the Spirit and belief of the truth," 2 Thess 2:13). And he was saved! Many people around us need to hear that if they will believe on the Lord Jesus Christ, they will be saved.

The result of saving life is eternal life. Attention to context makes this clear. John 3:16 begins with the explanatory conjunction *gar*, which ties it to the preceding verses. In the opening pericope of the chapter, we have the interview of Nicodemus with Jesus, during which the Lord told him he must be born again. The question of how rebirth can occur is raised and is followed with an illustration from the Old Testament. Numbers 21 includes the account of the snakebitten Israelites who could receive new life by looking at the brazen serpent on the pole. In the LXX the word *pas* is used frequently in the passage. What precedes the new life? The look of faith does! Now John 3:16 nails it. When does eternal life come? Eternal life comes upon saving faith. John 1:12 puts it this way: "As many as received him, to them gave he power to become the sons of God, even to them that believe on his name." When does regeneration come? Regeneration comes after saving faith.

---

[16] Words from the hymn written by P. Doddridge, "O Happy Day That Fixed My Choice," in *Baptist Hymnal* (ed. M. Harland; Nashville: LifeWay Worship, 2008), 574.

IV. God's Love Is Eternal

Have you noticed that John 3:16 begins and ends in eternity? It begins with a God who has no beginning and ends with a life that has no ending. Eternity! There was a time when you were not; there will never be a time when you will not be. The issue in the phrase "should not perish, but have everlasting life" is where will humans be in eternity? Perish! A noxious weed is growing in this fresh garden. Pay close attention: you can smell the fire, see the worms crawling, hear the weeping, and see the gnashing of teeth. The word "perish" encapsulates everything about hell.

Jesus had the most tender heart that ever beat in a human breast. Yet He said more about hell than any other person in the Bible. Thirteen percent of all His teaching was about judgment or hell.

The Greek word *apolētai*, translated "perish," is an aorist middle subjunctive. The verbs are now in the subjunctive mood, the mood of potential or possibility. This word is used in two ways: a physical destruction (see "Lord, save us: we perish," Matt 8:25) or a spiritual condition. A. Oepke says it refers to "an eternal plunge into hades and a hopeless destiny of death . . . an everlasting state of torment and death."[17]

The idea of hell is perfectly logical. Hell can be called the garbage dump of the universe or the asylum for the spiritually insane. The use of the aorist tense indicates the final tragedy of a soul. If one is lost, that person is perishing right now. First Corinthians 1:18 uses the present tense ("them that perish") to convey a condition that begins here and now but reaches full and terrible culmination in final condemnation. William Hull paraphrases it, "should not come to a dead end with everything utterly lost."[18] R. O. Yeager says, "The ingressive and cumulative effects of perishing are eternal. The onset of the perishable state (ingressive) results in the culmination of a total state of separation from God (culminative)."[19] It is the final tragedy of the soul.

The same word used to describe eternal life is also used to describe eternal hell. Matthew 25:46 says, "These shall go away into everlasting punishment." Think of it. Once they are in hell, they will always be in hell. To go into hell knowing you will never return is the tragedy of all

---

[17] A. Oepke, "*apollymi*," in *The Theological Dictionary of the New Testament* (ed. G. Kittel and G. Friedrich; Grand Rapids: Eerdmans, 1969), 1:394.

[18] W. E. Hull, *Love in Four Dimensions* (Nashville: Broadman, 1982), 86.

[19] R. O. Yeager, *The Renaissance New Testament*, vol. 4 (Woodbridge, VA: Renaissance Press, 1979), 415.

tragedies. "Let some air in." No air is in hell. "I need a drink of water." No water is in hell. "Turn on some light." No light is in hell. "Let me die." No death occurs in hell.

Then the text says, "But!" This little word introduces a breathtaking reversal in potential and possibility. It is the adversative conjunction *alla*, denoting contrast. Coiled in that little word is the hinge of hope. What changes in thought from agony to ecstasy, from misery to glory, and from hell to heaven occur here!

Come a little closer. Stop, look, and listen. Stop and consider what is possible. Look and see gates of pearl and streets of gold. Listen and hear anthems of angels and shouts of saints! Note the change in the verb tense in the phrase "have everlasting life." The verb is in the present active subjunctive tense. It means "to have now and forever." The phrase "everlasting life" occurs 17 times in John's Gospel. It carries the ideas of qualitative and quantitative life. The idea is of endless and never-ending life and of a difference in quality. This eternal life can be a present possession (see 1 John 5:12) and a hope (see Titus 3:7). So eternal life involves a person and a place! Believe on Him and have Jesus now and heaven someday!

Conclusion

Bennett Cert told the story of a child in an orphans' home. Since the child was somewhat troublesome and difficult, the workers in the home looked for an excuse to move the unwanted child to another home. One day the child was seen stealing across the yard to a tree, climbing to one of the branches, and depositing a note. After the child was gone, the workers hurried to retrieve the note. They opened it and read, "If anybody finds this, I love you."[20] To a world that treats God like an unwanted child in an orphans' home, to a world that does not love Him, in John 3:16 God is saying, "If anyone finds this, I love you."

---

[20] B. Cert cited in *Love in Four Dimensions* (ed. W. E. Hull; Nashville: Broadman, 1982), 10.

Chapter 2

Total Depravity

Paige Patterson

The doctrine of election is generally considered the most hated doctrine in the church. According to some, lack of agreement on exactly what election means makes it a despised doctrine, emphasized by some, neglected by others. Actually, the most hated doctrine is the doctrine of the exclusivity of Christ in salvation. The second most hated doctrine, especially in the postmodern era, is the doctrine of human depravity. The columnist Mike Adams, speaking from a political point of view, suggested that this fact alone is the difference between *conservative and liberal perspectives*: "If there is one thing that separates the conservative from the liberal it is his view of human nature. The conservative sees man as born in a broken state. This tragic view of human nature sees man as selfish and hedonistic by design."[1] Adams continued:

> This tragic view of human nature also explains why conservatives often speak of religion and family values. Given his selfish nature, man must internalize some reason to behave in prosocial ways. That fact that he falls short of these values does not mean he is a hypocrite. The one who

[1] Mike Adams, "The Nature of Conservatism," *Salem Web Network*, May 18, 2009, http://townhall.com/columnists/MikeAdams/2009/05/18/the_nature_of_conservatism; accessed December 1, 2009.

does not even believe what he says is a hypocrite. The one who believes what he says and falls short is merely human.[2]

There are two reasons Jerry Vines asked me to write on the doctrine of total depravity. First, he wanted me to address the most objectionable doctrine. The second reason was somewhat more pointed. When he called and asked me to write this article, he said, "I just could not think of anybody who modeled total depravity as well as you do!"

To address the subject of total depravity, we must go to the Scriptures. Since it is commonly known that I am neither a Calvinist nor Reformed, I can perhaps be permitted this observation. A tragedy exists in the pulpits of most non-Calvinists. Far too many preachers apparently feel no mandate to preach sermons expounding the biblical text. Thankfully, many of our Calvinistic brethren are still proclaiming the Word of God instead of pop psychology. If a preacher is not a Calvinist and yet is not consistently expounding the Word of the Lord, that preacher is not pleasing the God who inspired the Book. No wonder so much depravity is exhibited in churches, considering the fact that preachers are often giving their people no insight into what God's Word really says! Preachers are too busy entertaining their congregants. I commend my Calvinistic friends for consistently teaching the Bible.

The *locus classicus* for the subject of depravity is found in Romans 1–3.

> For the wrath of God is revealed from heaven against all ungodliness and unrighteousness of men, who suppress the truth in unrighteousness, because what may be known of God is manifest in them, for God has shown *it* to them. For since the creation of the world His invisible *attributes* are clearly seen, being understood by the things that are made, *even* His eternal power and Godhead, so that they are without excuse, because, although they knew God, they did not glorify *Him* as God, nor were thankful, but became futile in their thoughts, and their foolish hearts were darkened. Professing to be wise, they became fools, and changed the glory of the incorruptible God into an image made like corruptible man—and birds and four-footed beasts and creeping things. Therefore God also gave them up to uncleanness, in the lusts of their hearts, to dishonor their bodies among themselves, who exchanged the truth of God for the lie, and worshiped and served the creature rather than the Creator, who is blessed forever. Amen. For this reason God

---

[2] Ibid.

gave them up to vile passions. For even their women exchanged the natural use for what is against nature. Likewise also the men, leaving the natural use of the woman, burned in their lust for one another, men with men committing what is shameful, and receiving in themselves the penalty of their error which was due. And even as they did not like to retain God in *their* knowledge, God gave them over to a debased mind, to do those things which are not fitting (Rom 1:18–28 NKJV).[3]

Then a litany of deeds, which are characteristic of the human family, follows:

Being filled with all unrighteousness, sexual immorality, wickedness, covetousness, maliciousness; full of envy, murder, strife, deceit, evil-mindedness; *they are* whisperers, backbiters, haters of God, violent, proud, boasters, inventors of evil things, disobedient to parents, undiscerning, untrustworthy, unloving, unforgiving, unmerciful; who, knowing the righteous judgment of God, that those who practice such things are deserving of death, not only do the same but also approve of those who practice them (Rom 1:29–32).

Paul continues his description of the human condition:

What then? Are we better *than they?* Not at all. For we have previously charged both Jews and Greeks that they are all under sin.
As it is written:

"There is none righteous, no, not one;
There is none who understands;
There is none who seeks after God.
They have all gone out of the way;
They have together become unprofitable;
There is none who does good, no, not one."
"Their throat is an open tomb;
With their tongues they have practiced deceit";
"The poison of asps is under their lips";
"Whose mouth is full of cursing and bitterness."
"Their feet are swift to shed blood;
Destruction and misery are in their ways;
And the way of peace they have not known."
"There is no fear of God before their eyes."

---

[3] Unless otherwise noted, all Scripture passages are from the New King James Version.

Now we know that whatever the law says, it says to those who are under the law, that every mouth may be stopped, and all the world may become guilty before God. Therefore by the deeds of the law no flesh will be justified in His sight, for by the law *is* the knowledge of sin. But now the righteousness of God apart from the law is revealed, being witnessed by the Law and the Prophets, even the righteousness of God, through faith in Jesus Christ to all and on all who believe. For there is no difference; for all have sinned and fall short of the glory of God, being justified freely by His grace through the redemption that is in Christ Jesus, whom God set forth *to be* a propitiation by His blood, through faith, to demonstrate His righteousness, because in His forbearance God had passed over the sins that were previously committed, to demonstrate at the present time His righteousness, that He might be just and the justifier of the one who has faith in Jesus (Rom 3:9–26).

Those passages are seldom read in contemporary churches, and they are expounded even less frequently. Neither the modern mind nor the postmodern mind wants to hear about God's verdict on the human family. Having read the texts, what exactly are Christians to understand about depravity? First, the question, What is depravity? needs to be discussed. Second, a brief discussion about the origin of depravity by exploring the question, How does it happen? needs attention. Finally, an answer to the question, What can a dead man do? must be considered.

The Meaning of Depravity

These verses display several observations concerning the meaning of depravity.

1. "There is none righteous, no, not one" (Rom 3:10). *Depravity means that there is not a single human being on the face of the earth who is right with God.* Prior to the exercise of regeneration and justification, whereby he is made right with God through the blood of Christ, there is not a single person, however religious or ethically moral he may be, who is righteous before God.

2. "There is none who understands" (Rom 3:11). Whatever else is happening in depravity, *intellectual abilities have been adversely*

affected. Rather than being able to see clearly what humans need to see, at the very best, they see truth in a distorted way. That is true even for those who have come to know Christ. As the apostle Paul said, "For now we see through a glass darkly" (1 Cor 13:12 KJV). Christians are looking forward to a time when they shall see with great clarity. If even the redeemed do not see with perfect clarity, what shall be said of those who are still in an unredeemed state? On the one hand, "what may be known of God is manifest in them, for God has shown it to them" (Rom 1:19); but, on the other hand, "the natural man does not receive the things of the Spirit of God, for they are foolishness to him; nor can he know them, because they are spiritually discerned" (1 Cor 2:14). In his state of depravity, a man may know that God exists and that He is overwhelmingly powerful; but he will still fail to understand the nature and truth of God.

3.   That same verse provides a third observation. "There is none who understands. There is none who seeks after God" (Rom 3:11). *The direction of depraved man is away from God.* While he is going away from God, he may go to church because of a sense of obligation; but he is still going away from God. On his way away from God, he may take his coat and, in an act of chivalry, lay it over the puddle of water so that a lady can walk across. It is a good deed, but it does not change the direction in which he is going. He is going away from God because he is depraved.

4.   "They have all gone out of the way; they have become altogether unprofitable" (Rom 3:12). Isaiah echoes this: "All we like sheep have gone astray. We have turned, every one, to his own way" (Isa 53:6). This action has necessitated the Lord's laying upon Christ the iniquity of all humans. *Humans have become unprofitable.* They have turned to their own way; and in going that way, there is no way by which they profit spiritually—they are totally depraved. "There is none who does good, no, not one" (Rom 3:12). Someone may protest that this verse fails to acknowledge the acts of nobility such as frequently attending worship, doing an act of chivalry, giving money to Tsunami victims, or any number of good things. The verse does not mean that a person never does anything good. Rather, one can never do anything that is *counted* as good toward a right standing

with God. "There is none who does good, no, not one" (Rom 3:12). In addition, any good deed, however laudable it may be, is invariably tainted with the contagion of human sinfulness.

5. "Whose mouth is full of cursing and bitterness. Their feet are swift to shed blood. Destruction and misery are in their ways. And the way of peace they have not known" (Rom 3:14–17). *Total depravity means that there is no ultimate peace in the heart.* There may be denial. Someone may insist that he is living a wonderful life and having a good time, but this claim is shallow. Deep inside lies a troubled heart. The presence of war in the world is a continual reminder of total depravity; and that war, which courses over the face of the globe, wherever it may be found, is the same war that is going on in the human heart. There is no peace in the heart. If at no other point, the heart is not at peace because there is enmity toward God and His purposes; humans are totally depraved (Col 1:21). Finally, "There is no fear of God before their eyes" (Rom 3:18). There may be those moments when a man is in a foxhole, the ordinance is falling, and a certain fear is elicited. In that moment he may even cry out to God. But as a matter of the course of his life, he lives in such a way as to show that he does not understand the power of God—let alone the justice and the holiness of the God.

To illustrate God's perspective regarding sin, suppose a person goes to school to become a heart surgeon. He goes to the hospital one morning, prepared to do surgery. He goes by the medical records room and reads over his patient's chart so that he knows exactly what needs to be done. Putting that aside, that physician walks into the preparation area or the scrub room and scrubs himself down. They give him a green beret to cover his hair, put a green robe around him to cover his clothes, and even give him green moccasins for his feet. Then he dons the surgical gloves. He now walks into the operating room.

The patient is on the operating table, and the surgical team has gathered. He asks the nurse to pull the sheet back from the chest of the patient. The nurse reaches over and pulls back the sheet to expose the chest of the patient; and, as she does, three cockroaches race from under the sheet across his chest and onto the floor. What will the surgeon say? "Who is responsible for these conditions in this operating room? My patient will not die of heart problems, nor will he die of a mistake I made. He will die because there is filth in the operating room!"

The revulsion that he would feel as a heart surgeon under those circumstances is one in eight to the six hundredth power how God views sin. One may begin to understand how a holy God feels about one single solitary sinful thought. "There is no fear of God before their eyes" (Rom 3:18).

Total depravity, like *Trinity*, is not a biblical term. Like *Trinity*, the term provides a short form helpful for stating the truths above. The purpose is to demonstrate that man is fallen in every aspect of his being and cannot, without regeneration and the imputed righteousness of Christ, ever please God or be satisfactory to God. Some Calvinists (not all) take the term to mean that in order for a depraved human being to respond to God's redemptive act in Christ, that person must first be regenerated. In other words, God regenerates an individual, thus enabling him to exercise repentance and faith. Except for citing John 6:44, the argument garners little other biblical support but follows the logical demands of the Calvinistic system.

While no one comes to Christ of his own volition ("unless the Father draws him," John 6:44), the Bible also affirms that "I, if I am lifted up from the earth, will draw all peoples unto Myself" (John 12:32). The Father's plan for the Suffering Servant is one way by which appeal is made to every human heart. Calvinist C. H. Spurgeon saw as unscriptural the idea that regeneration preceded faith.

> If I am to preach faith in Christ to a man who is regenerated, then the man being regenerated is saved already, and it is an unnecessary and ridiculous thing for me to preach Christ to him, and bid him to believe in order to be saved when he is saved already, being regenerate. But you will tell me that I ought to preach it only to those who repent of their sins. Very well; but since true repentance of sin is the work of the Spirit, any man who has repentance is most certainly saved, because evangelical repentance never can exist in an unrenewed soul. Where there is repentance there is faith already, for they never can be separated. So, then, I am only to preach faith to those who have it. Absurd, indeed! Is not this waiting till the man is cured and then bringing him the medicine? This is preaching Christ to righteous and not to sinners.[4]

---

[4] C. H. Spurgeon, *C. H. Spurgeon's Sermons: Metropolitan Tabernacle Pulpit* (Pasadena, TX: Pilgrim Publications, 1970), 532.

Therefore, all people, though totally depraved and unable to do anything to save themselves, receive the witness of Christ lifted up in His atoning work to draw them to the Savior. This enablement, together with the witness of the Word of God and the convicting agency of the Holy Spirit, is adequate to elicit faith but may ultimately be resisted by the sinner in his depravity. As Norm Geisler says:

> Extreme Calvinists believe that a totally depraved person is spiritually dead. By 'spiritual death' they mean the elimination of all human ability to understand or respond to God, not just a separation from God. Further, the effects of sin are intensive (destroying the ability to receive salvation).[5]

But this view negates the order of salvific events found throughout the New Testament.

The Origin of Depravity

The depravity of all members of the race must be understood in connection with the rebellion of Adam in Eden. The soteriological message of the Bible is intimately tied to the historicity of the Genesis account of the temptation and fall of Adam. Romans 5:15 and 18 paint the picture.

> But the free gift is not like the offense. For if by the one man's offense many died, much more the grace of God and the gift by the grace of the one Man, Jesus Christ, abounded to many (v. 15).

> Therefore, as through one man's offense judgment came to all men, resulting in condemnation, even so through one Man's righteous act the free gift came to all men, resulting in justification of life (v. 18).

The question to be addressed is the meaning of the word "many" in verse 15. If "many" means that only some of the race were adversely affected by the sin of Adam, then an argument for limited atonement would be possible since the gift of God's grace in Christ abounded only to some. But verse 18 renders that understanding impossible. Through one man's offense, condemnation came to "all men." So through Christ's righteous act, God's gift is made available to all. But the cause of universal human depravity is clear. This is confirmed again in 1 Cor 15:22 when Paul declares, "In Adam all die."

---

[5] N. Geisler, *Chosen but Free* (Minneapolis: Bethany House Publishers, 1999), 56.

In what sense does the whole race die in Adam? Augustus Hopkins Strong delineates several historical theories, but for most evangelicals the choice is between the Federal Theory of the imputation of Adam's sin and the Natural Headship Theory. Strong defines the Federal Theory as follows:

> According to this view, Adam was constituted by God's sovereign appointment the representative of the whole human race. With Adam as their representative, God entered into covenant, agreeing to bestow upon them eternal life on condition of his obedience, but making the penalty of his disobedience to be the corruption and death of all his posterity. In accordance with the terms of this covenant, since Adam sinned, God accounts all his descendants as sinners, and condemns them because of Adam's transgression.[6]

Strong's objections to this theory are well taken. The theory is extra-scriptural, contradicts Scripture, and impugns (even if this is not intended) the justice of God. In addition, the Federal Theory fails to explain adequately the transmission of a sinful nature and does not account for the necessity of the virgin conception of Christ.

Strong defines the Natural Headship Theory that many of the Reformers advanced:

> It holds that God imputes the sin of Adam immediately to all his posterity, in virtue of that organic unity of mankind by which the whole race at the time of Adam's transgression existed, not individually, but seminally, to him as its head. In Adam's free act, the will of the race revolted from God and the nature of the race corrupted itself. The nature which we now possess is the same nature that corrupted itself in Adam—"not the same in kind merely, but the same as flowing to us continuously from him."[7]

This explanation rings true, offering a viable explanation for the effect of Adam's sin upon all subsequent members of the race. Also, it has the advantage of transferring the inherent proclivity to evil from Adam to all subsequent humans but establishing guilt before God as the act or rebellion against God of each individual. By the same token, the virgin conception of Jesus, the second Adam, is necessitated since if Jesus were born with a sinful nature, then He, too, would have been susceptible to sin. As the second Adam, with no sinful nature, He was able to confront

---

[6] A. H. Strong, *Systematic Theology* (Philadelphia: Judson Press, 1907), 612.
[7] Ibid., 619.

temptation, triumph over the overtures of Satan, and remain a spotless, sinless sacrifice for Adam's race.

When our first parents had eaten of the fruit of the tree of the knowledge of good and evil, they immediately began to demonstrate in many ways how sin affects the race. First, they discovered their nakedness and made aprons of fig leaves (Gen 3:7). Once detached from the tree, a fig leaf withers and dies—not a very profitable long-term solution, to say the least. Human solutions to spiritual problems always fail. Our first parents knew it did not work because when the voice of the Lord God was heard when He was walking in the cool of the day, they hid themselves from an omniscient, omnipresent God (Gen. 3:8). Sin never makes people clever. They hid themselves, thereby indicating that they knew the fig leaf solution was inadequate.

Why did Adam and Eve cover their reproductive organs? They knew those were the very organs of their bodies that ought to have been the most treasured because with their reproductive organs they could do something that could not be done in any other way. God has so designed the man and the woman to make it possible for them to join with Him in making a new human being who has the potential, if rightly related to God, to live forever. What a treasure God has given to humanity! But Adam and Eve were mortified about the exposure of those organs because by those organs they were going to perpetuate the memory of their rebellion against God. Every son, every grandson, every great-grandson right on down the line until now—all have been affected by the sin of Adam. All the fig leaf solutions—the human solutions of the world—are not going to suffice. Later, when they discovered the bloody, bludgeoned body of their son Abel, they could only say, "Look what we have done."

Can the Dead Respond?

Are humans born guilty before God? That cannot be demonstrated from Scripture. Humans are born with a sin sickness—a disease that makes certain that humans will sin and rebel against God. Humans are condemned for their own sins. The Bible says this repeatedly (cf. Ezk 18:19–20; Rom 1:32; 3:23). What about Eph 2:5, which says that humans are dead in trespasses of sin? If humans are dead, then they cannot do anything to respond to God. Dead people cannot do anything. When people are dead, they are dead!

As a boy in Southeast Texas, I often hunted in the woods. Rattlesnakes were a favorite prey, and I had only one weapon. I visited the army surplus store and purchased an old bayonet, which I learned to use like a machete. At age nine I was armed to the teeth with a bayonet. My friends and I would find a rattlesnake, and I would chop its head off. One day I was not too accurate, severing the reptile about six inches behind his head. He was dead, and I left him there for a while before touching him to be sure that he was dead. He was such a big rattler that I wanted to take him home and show my father. In a careless moment, I reached out to take his frame, and at that moment the snake's head struck at me and nearly got me. In fact, he did strike the bottom of my blue jeans. I was so glad I was not wearing shorts that day. Its teeth stuck in the bottom of my blue jeans. That was a dead snake!

Actually, being dead does not assure that someone can do nothing. Ephesians 2:1–3 demonstrates this situation:

> And you He made alive, who were dead in trespasses and sins, in which you once walked according to the course of this world, according to the prince of the power of the air, the spirit who now works in the sons of disobedience, among whom also we all once conducted ourselves in the lusts of our flesh, fulfilling the desires of the flesh and of the mind, and were by nature children of wrath, just as the others.

Note that those who were dead in sin *walked* in lust and fulfilled the desires of the flesh and mind. When Adam and Eve first took the fruit of the tree, they died—"The day that you eat of it you shall surely die" (Gen 2:17). They did die then! Yet in another sense they kept on living. Though dead spiritually, they could and did respond to God, preparing for His visit, hiding, talking with Him, and eventually accepting His remedy for their nakedness.

Consider Rom 4:16–22 for what it says about Abraham.

> Therefore it is of faith that it might be according to grace, so that the promise might be sure to all the seed, not only to those who are of the law, but also to those who are of the faith of Abraham, who is the father of all (as it is written, "I have made you a father of many nations") in the presence of Him whom he believed, even God, who gives life to the dead and calls those things which do not exist as though they did; who, contrary to hope, in hope believed, so that he became the father of many nations, according to what was spoken, "So shall your descendants

be." And not being weak in faith, he did not consider his own body, already dead (since he was about a hundred years old), and the deadness of Sarah's womb. He did not waiver at the promise of God through unbelief, but was strengthened in faith, giving glory to God, and being fully convinced of what He had promised, He was also able to perform and therefore "it was accounted unto him for righteousness."

Without straying far from the text, one can imagine what may very possibly have happened: Three men—two of them were angels and one the Angel of Yahweh—came to visit Abraham and Sarah one day under the Terebinth trees at Mamre. They said to Abraham, among other things, "You are going to father a child. As a matter of fact, Sarah your wife is going to bear a child" (cf. Gen 18:10). Sarah was behind in the tent and laughed because she knew it was not possible. The men asked, "Why did Sarah laugh?" "Oh! I did not!" Sarah said (cf. Gen 18:15). Her depravity was apparent. She then lied about it, the visitors went down to Sodom, and the days passed.

One night about eight o'clock, the sun had long since set in the west. They had their lamb kabobs and barley loaves for dinner and maybe a few bitter herbs washed down with goat's milk. They had just brought the camel saddles into the tent and placed a carpet over them. Abraham was leaning against them, working with some leather. One of the camels had died a few months before. They tanned the hide, and now Abraham was making some new sandals for his feet from the hide. Sarah was leaning up against the other camel saddle and making herself a new dress out of the beautiful red fabric that was so characteristic of that part of the world.

While Abraham was working on the sandals, he just looked over at Sarah, and a smile came across his face. Perhaps he was thinking, "She has lost some of that young beauty she once had, but I remember it very well. Did Pharaoh fall for it? He dropped like a rock into placid water! Abimelech nearly got in trouble also. She was a looker, no question about it. He just could not take his eyes off her. He just kept looking at her. She looked at him and said, "What?!" Abraham said, "I did not say anything!" She said, "Yes, but you are looking at me!" And he said, "Well, is that criminal?" "No, but it is just the particular way you are looking at me. I have not seen that in a long time." "Don't worry about it, Honey." He went back to working on that leather sandal, but soon he was looking at her again. She caught him again and said, "What are you thinking?" He said, "Nothing." She said, "That is not true. There is a smirk on your face. I haven't seen that for years. I know what you're thinking!" He said, "Yes, Honey, you know we are going to turn in a little early tonight." Sarah cautioned, "You have lost it!" "Yes," replied the aged patriarch.

Every old man ought to love this passage! The text declares that he did not stop to consider his own body as though it were already dead, since he was, after all, a hundred years old; nor did he consider the deadness of Sarah's womb. All Abraham did was to consider his own faith in the promise of God regarding the birth of Isaac; and sure enough the impossible happened because with man it may be impossible, but with God all things are possible. His faith led to an interesting night. That interesting night led to the promises of God becoming reality.

Sarah's plan to produce a male heir through her servant Hagar not only failed but, with the birth of Ishmael, inaugurated a host of headaches from which the world still suffers. Without God's plan and miracle, human efforts to meet the need inevitably fail (Gen. 16:1–16). Isaac's birth was a miracle of God's hand, but Abraham and Sarah cooperated.

It was October 25, 1944. The U.S.S. St. Lo, along with other ships operating in Filipino waters, was attacked for the first time by *kamikaze* pilots.[8] I once heard a sailor give a report of an incident that happened that day. Even if apocryphal, it demonstrates the point about depravity and inability. According to this veteran, one of the sailors on the St. Lo opened the door and came out onto the bridge just in time to be transfixed where he stood. He could not believe it. Less than 100 feet away, a Japanese suicide bomber was coming right at him. He knew it was going to hit him. He knew he was going to die. At the last second, somehow the plane dropped just a little below the bridge and crashed into the St. Lo with a full load of bombs. The explosion knocked him from his feet, blew out most of his hearing, and immediately engulfed him with a fireball. He knew that he was on fire. The fire was so intense that it blinded his eyes, but he knew he was on fire. He could feel that, and he did the only thing a man would do under those kinds of circumstances. In desperation he thought, "I've got to get the fire out even though I know I am dead," and he just threw himself overboard into the ocean.

When the sailor plunged beneath the waters, the flames, of course, were extinguished. He came back to the surface and could not see anything at all. He began to swim, but after a little while, he realized there

---

[8] See "USS ST LO (CVE 63)," available from http://www.bosamar.com/cve/cve63.html; accessed December 1, 2009.

really was no use—he was far away from shore. About that time the *St. Lo* finally sank beneath the waves; and when it got down to about 50 feet of depth, the depth charges the *St. Lo* was carrying exploded in an unbelievable display of destruction. Water flew into the air, and the sailor felt the full force of the explosion. The explosion rattled him again, but he did not see anything because he was blind. He floated and struggled as long as he could. He later expressed fear that he may have even caused the death of other sailors because as he encountered objects in the water, not knowing what they were, he would struggle to get hold of them, only to have them drift away from him. He only prayed they were not other sailors, but he did everything he could to save himself. Finally, he realized no hope remained.

About that time, though injured and his ears nearly ruined, the sailor heard faintly the whirring sound of the helicopter. As he listened to the sound of the helicopter hovering overhead, he began to shout, "Here I am! Here I am! Save me! Here I am! Save me!" The chopper dropped the collar down to him, but due to his lack of sight and the ocean's rising swells, he could not find the collar and get a hold on it. He was growing weaker by the moment, and at that point the corpsman in the helicopter said to the pilot, "I'm going after him." That corpsman dived into the water and surfaced next to that sailor. He got over to him and reached out to help him, but the sailor was so panicked by then that he actually fought him off as though he thought the corpsman was attempting to take him down. I suppose he may have imagined that he was another one of the sailors who had been hit from the *St. Lo*, and so he actually tried to fight off the one who would be his savior. Finally, the corpsman hung on to him until he could get the collar around him, and then he gave the signal to the helicopter. The wench began to do its work and lifted that sailor into the helicopter. He was eventually delivered to the hospital.

Weeks went by, accompanied by several surgeries. Finally, the doctor told the sailor, "Son, I do not know whether I have been able to save your eyes. We have done everything we can do. We are going to come to the moment of truth and remove the bandages to see if your sight has been saved." The sailor said, "Well, I am ready to live with it either way, but I want to know if I can see." So in a semi-darkened room, the doctor first removed the outer bandages and then gradually the cup bandages closest to the eye. The first visual for the sailor was the face of the corpsman who had jumped into the water, placed the collar around him, and saved him.

The heavenly Father is the Admiral who saw our hopeless condition and sent that helicopter. That helicopter with the whirring blades is like the Word of God. The Lord Jesus is like the corpsman; He came to Earth and leaped into the water to save us even while we resist him. Three years—ages six to nine—were the most miserable of my life. I thought that the invitation hymn, "Just as I Am," had 336 stanzas, and we seemed to sing them all in every service. My father would stand at the front and plead for people to come to Christ. I resisted Jesus and fought with the Holy Spirit; as in my own depravity, I refused to come to Christ. Finally, the Lord Jesus made Himself known to me through the Word of God—through the testimony of the Holy Spirit of God. Some wonderful day I am going to stand in heaven. The scales of all remaining depravity will have been taken away, leaving my glorified body; and the first face I will see is the One who loved me so much that He gave Himself to save me from my sins. We will stand before the Lord Jesus Christ.

If analogies are pressed, they all break down. Analogies do work as illustrations to help understand what is involved in depravity. Humans are all like that sailor. Humans are blind and cannot spiritually hear as they ought. They cannot save themselves. The sharks are closing around them, their strength is dying, and they are going down. Humans are totally depraved. They cannot help themselves. That is what depravity means. Humans are in sin that has come from their father Adam, and now it has been visited upon them. They are helpless and hopeless in that sin, but they can still cry out to God. All the people on the face of the earth can cry out to God. Abraham did not count his body or Sarah's womb dead, even though he was a hundred years of age, but instead he believed God.

Robert Picirilli speaks of preregenerating grace. Of this he pointed out, "By definition, pre-regenerating grace is that work of the Holy Spirit that 'opens the heart' of the unregenerate (to use the words of Acts 16:14) to the truth of the gospel and enables them to respond positively in faith."[9] Further, he stated:

> Theologically, this concept meets the need of the totally depraved sinner. As already acknowledged, the unregenerate person is totally unable to respond positively, by his natural will, to the offer of salvation contained in the gospel. Pre-regenerating grace simply means that the Spirit of God overcomes that inability by a direct work on the heart,

---

[9] R. Picirilli, *Grace, Faith, Free Will: Contrasting Views of Salvation, Calvinism and Arminianism* (Nashville: Randall House, 2002), 154.

a work that is adequate to enable the yet unregenerate person to understand the truth of the gospel, to desire God, and to exercise saving faith.[10]

In brief, the wise Blaise Pascal noted:

> It is dangerous to prove to man too plainly how nearly he is on a level with the brutes without showing him his greatness; it is also dangerous to show him his greatness too clearly apart from his vileness. It is still more dangerous to leave him in ignorance of both. But it is of great advantage to show him both.[11]

Gracious Lord, we are sorry for our sin. We do not know why You ordered things as You did and why we inherited a sin nature, but Lord, we have certainly demonstrated that we have it. We admit that to You openly. Depravity has touched every part of our being. We are not what we ought to be physically; we are not what we ought to be mentally; we are not what we ought to be spiritually. In every way we are totally depraved, but, Lord, I thank God that the Bible's witness, throughout its pages, is that "whosoever calls upon the name of the Lord shall be saved" (Rom 10:13). I believe that You have given us the witness of the Spirit of God, the witness of Holy Scripture, and the witness of countless thousands of missionaries and proclaimers of Your Word who have preached the gospel of Christ to every man. Everyone who hears it and calls out to You will surely be saved. God grant that we be faithful. In Jesus' name, we pray. Amen.

---

[10] Picirilli, *Grace, Faith, Free Will*, 154.

[11] M. A. Molinier, *The Thoughts of Blaise Pascal* (trans. C. K. Paul; London: Kegan Paul, Trench & Co., 1885), 45.

Chapter 3

Congruent Election: Understanding Salvation from an "Eternal Now" Perspective

Richard Land

When preaching God's Word, a preacher might as well aim high. This essay will suggest a conceptual model that I believe provides a better way to understand the scriptural doctrine of election than some other traditional theological models offer.

God's inerrant and holy Word never changes, and this inerrant and infallible Word of God does not contradict itself. However, human understanding of God's Word is not infallible, and, as our Baptist forefathers believed, God always has yet more truth to break forth from His holy Word to those who are receptive to the Holy Spirit's leading.

God's Word is cast in stone, but no human formulation, confession, or doctrine should be. Christians must delve in as deeply and as humbly as they can and pray for as much knowledge, discernment, and insight as the Lord will grant them in their zeal to resolve any apparent difficulties. Christians must always seek an ever deepening and widening grasp of a totality of doctrine that is as congruent with as much of scriptural revelation as is possible. What understanding of a doctrine of election is in accord with the entire body of revealed Scripture—not just with certain proof texts?

Southern Baptist Beginnings: The Birth of a Theological Tradition

My understanding of the doctrine of election as I now conceptualize it comes from my immersion since infancy in the Sandy Creek heritage that permeates the Southern Baptist heritage and tradition. In recent decades some have attempted to abscond with our Southern Baptist history and heritage. Consequently, taking a short excursion into the history of the Baptist movement in the South is advisable in order to understand how in God's providence we have arrived at the present situation.

John Leland, both a product and predominant leader of the Separate Baptist movement that swept across colonial America in the middle decades of the eighteenth century, was a circuit-riding preacher who personally baptized more than 20,000 people during his more than 20-year ministry in Virginia and North Carolina before going back to his native Massachusetts in 1791.[1] Leland, a friend of both Thomas Jefferson and James Madison, played a key role in the First Amendment's inclusion in the United States Constitution.

Why is Leland so important? As the most significant of the Separate Baptist leaders in the South, he had enormous influence because the Separate Baptists overwhelmed the other Baptist groups in the South within just a few years of their North Carolina Sandy Creek revivals in the 1750s.

In 1791, Leland said,

> I conclude that the *eternal purposes* of God and the *freedom of the human will* are both truths, and it is a matter of fact that the preaching that has been most blessed of God and most profitable to men is *the doctrine of sovereign grace in the salvation of souls, mixed with a little of what is called Arminianism.*[2]

---

[1] J. Leland, "A Letter of Valediction on Leaving Virginia, 1791," in *The Writings of the Late Elder John Leland*, ed. Louise F. Green (New York: G. W. Wood, 1845), 172, quoted in S. E. Ahlstrom, *A Religious History of the American People* (New Haven: Yale University Press, 1992), 322.

[2] Ibid., 172.

Leland's statement is as good a short summary of the Baptist Faith and Message's soteriology as you will find. Leland went on to say,

> These two propositions can be tolerably well reconciled together, but the modern misfortunate is [some things never change!] that men often spend too much time in explaining away one or the other, or in fixing the lock-link to join the others together; and by such means have but little time in a sermon to insist on these two great things which God blesses.[3]

Sydney Ahlstrom, the renowned, prize-winning Yale historian, who, as a Lutheran, has no dog in this fight, surveyed the history of eighteenth-century Baptist development in America, particularly the South, and concluded, "The general doctrinal position of the resulting Baptist tradition was distinctly Reformed, a modified version of Westminster."[4] The ultimate result "was a blending of revivalistic and 'orthodox' tendencies, along the lines suggested by John Leland's compromise."[5] With the passage of time, the New Hampshire Confession (1833) "came to express this majority view."[6] The New Hampshire Confession is the progenitor of the Baptist Faith and Message—its most famous and influential descendant.

Prior to the First Great Awakening, Baptists were a small, persecuted sect throughout Colonial America, with the South perhaps the least populated with a Baptist presence. Then came the mighty spiritual wind of the Great Awakening and the miracle of Sandy Creek in North Carolina. The exponential growth of Baptists in the South, resulting from the Great Awakening, and the consequent rise of the Separate Baptist movement numerically overwhelmed the other Baptist traditions. By 1790, as the new nation began, Baptists had become the largest denomination in the South and joined with the Methodists as the largest denominations in the country. They remained so until massive waves of Catholic immigration from Europe in the middle decades of the nineteenth century propelled Catholicism into first place.

Noted Baptist historian William Lumpkin explained how the Separate Baptist Movement, enormous both in size and energy, "greatly advanced the cause of religion in America and shaped the character of Protestantism in the South."[7] The Separate Baptists

---

[3] Ibid.

[4] Ahlstrom, *A Religious History*, 322.

[5] Ibid.

[6] Ibid.

[7] W. L. Lumpkin, *Baptist Foundations in the South: Tracing Through the Separates the Influence of the Great Awakening, 1754–1787* (Nashville: Broadman Press, 1961), 154.

provided the antecedents for the Southern Baptist Convention in such
things as their aggressiveness and evangelical outlook, their centralized
ecclesiology that was influential in 1845 when Southern Baptists chose
their type of organizational structure, and many other aspects, such as
their self-conscious attitudes, their hymnody, their lay leadership, many
ecclesiastical practices, and their strong biblicism.[8]

Robert Baker, the doyen of Southern Baptist historians, surveyed the
historical record of the period and concluded that

> there seems to be a providential element in the mingling of the Separate
> Baptist distinctives with those of the older General and Particular
> Baptists in the South. Taken alone, any one of these three large Baptist
> movements possessed many weaknesses. In the uniting of the three
> movements, Southern Baptists were prepared fundamentally for the
> remarkable development that came in the next two centuries.[9]

"The General Baptists," Baker explained, "provided emphasis on the
necessity for human agency in reaching men with the gospel."[10] They gave
Baptists in the South a deep and abiding commitment to doing the work
of the Great Commission to go to all men with the gospel witness. The
Regular Baptists (the Calvinists) contributed "doctrinal stability and a con-
sciousness of the divine initiative."[11] They were a constant reminder that
men can preach all they want, but if God's Holy Spirit does not convict
and call, men are not going to respond. The Separate Baptists embraced
"some of the best features of both" and emphasized "structural responsibility" and "the necessity of the presence and power of the Holy Spirit."[12]

Ahlstrom, Lumpkin, and Baker all identified in the historical record of
the last half of the eighteenth century the emergence of a clear, discernible
Southern Baptist theological tradition at least a half century before the
Southern Baptist Convention was founded in 1845. This Southern Baptist
theological tradition was characterized by a soteriology that John Leland
best describes as the preaching of "sovereign grace in the salvation of souls,
mixed with a little of what is called Arminianism," for "these two propositions can be tolerably well reconciled together."[13]

---

[8] R. A. Baker summarizes Lumpkin's assessment in *The Southern Baptist Convention and Its People 1607–1972* (Nashville: Broadman Press, 1974), 56–57.

[9] Ibid., 57.

[10] Ibid.

[11] Ibid.

[12] Ibid.

[13] J. Leland, "A Letter of Valediction," 172. The historical record indicates that the Separate Baptists were giving altar calls for people to respond to the gospel preaching from the 1750s onward.

This distinctive Baptist soteriology was neither fully Calvinist nor remotely Arminian. It was, and is, different and distinctive from both. It found confessional expression in the New Hampshire Confession, which first declared under "God's Purpose of Grace" that "election is the gracious purpose of God, according to which he graciously regenerates, sanctifies, and saves sinners; that being perfectly consistent with the free agency of man."[14]

This distinctive Baptist soteriology follows the New Hampshire Confession's declaration that

> we believe that the blessings of salvation are made free to all by the
> Gospel; that it is the immediate duty of all to accept them by a cordial,
> penitent, and obedient faith; and that nothing prevents the salvation
> of the greatest sinner on earth except his own inherent depravity and
> voluntary refusal to submit to the Lord Jesus Christ, which refusal will
> subject him to an aggravated condemnation.[15]

The New Hampshire Confession, adopted by the Baptists of that state in 1833, quickly became widely popular among Baptists, North and South, as it reflected a significant shift away from the more Calvinistic eighteenth-century Philadelphia Confession of Faith. With minor revisions, J. Newton Brown, editorial secretary of the American Baptist Publication Society, published it in *The Baptist Church Manual* in 1853.[16] This publication ensured an even wider distribution and popularity for the New Hampshire Confession, direct progenitor of all three versions of the Baptist Faith and Message—1925, 1963, and 2000.

The fact that the New Hampshire Confession, with its distinctive Separate Baptist-inspired soteriology, became "the confession" among nineteenth- and early twentieth-century Southern Baptists is vividly illustrated by the Southern Baptist Convention's Sunday School Board reproducing that confession in various books.[17] Most notable among these was O. C. S. Wallace's *What Baptists Believe*, first published in 1913. Wallace, pastor of Baltimore's First Baptist Church, wrote an article-by-article exposition of the New Hampshire Confession, which was widely circulated

---

[14] W. L. Lumpkin, "The New Hampshire Confession," in *Baptist Confessions of Faith* (repr.; Valley Forge: Judson Press, 1959), 363.

[15] Ibid., 364.

[16] Ibid., 360–61.

[17] J. E. Carter, "American Baptist Confessions of Faith: A Review of Confessions of Faith Adopted by Major Baptist Bodies in the United States," in *The Lord's Free People in a Free Land: Essays in Baptist History in Honor of Robert A. Baker* (ed. W. R. Estep; Fort Worth: Evans Press, 1976), 59–74.

in thousands of churches as a study course book. It sold 191,118 copies (in a much smaller Convention numerically) before it finally went out of print after the Baptist Faith and Message (1925) became the Convention's confession.[18]

Why did Wallace choose the New Hampshire Confession in 1913? He says it "was chosen . . . because it is the formula of Christian truth most commonly used as a standard in Baptist churches throughout the country, to express what they believe according to the Scriptures."[19] He also pointed out that the recently founded (1908) Southwestern Baptist Theological Seminary had adopted the New Hampshire Confession "as a suitable expression of its doctrinal character and life."[20] Wallace did provide for "helpful comparison and study" Southern Seminary's "Abstract of Principles" as an appendix.[21] He further dedicated *What Baptists Believe* to James P. Boyce, "First President, Southern Baptist Theological Seminary," and B. H. Carroll, "First President, Southwestern Baptist Theological Seminary," both "MIGHTY MEN in the Kingdom of Christian Teaching."[22] Wallace, by selecting the New Hampshire Confession for the *What Baptists Believe*'s confession, acknowledged it as the majority confessional statement of the era, with the "Abstract of Principles" as a minority statement.

Why delve into Southern Baptists' history in such detail? First and foremost, the record must be set straight. Ever since the First Great Awakening, the Separate Baptist Sandy Creek Tradition has been the melody for Southern Baptists, with Charleston and other traditions providing harmony. Southern Baptists are immersed in Sandy Creek. If the average Southern Baptist is "scratched," he or she will bleed Sandy Creek. Separate Baptists are the stock, and the other traditions, the seasoning in the Southern Baptist stew.

The theological model of election I espouse today I partially caught by osmosis growing up in Southern Baptist churches. I learned it by reading my daily Bible readings, studying my Sunday school and Training Union quarterlies and church study course books, participating in the Royal Ambassador program and Bible drills, and going to church camps. I was led to the Lord, nurtured in the faith, and called to preach in the context

---

[18] Ibid., 62.
[19] O. C. S. Wallace, *What Baptists Believe* (Nashville: Sunday School Board, Southern Baptist Convention, 1913), 4.
[20] Ibid.
[21] Ibid., 4, 204–8.
[22] Ibid., 3.

of Southern Baptist church and denominational life. This theology, neither Calvinist nor Arminian, was part of the air I breathed, the water I
drank, and the food I ate as my soul and spirit were fed and nurtured in
our Southern Baptist Zion. I had to leave home and go to college in New
Jersey before I knew that some currently living Southern Baptists believed
some people could not be saved, as well as discovering other Southern
Baptists who believed the Bible had errors and mistakes in it.

So what does this Sandy Creek Southern Baptist believe about election and free will? I believe in election. I do not believe you can put yourself under the authority of Scripture and not believe in election. I further
believe that election "is consistent with the free agency of man."[23] I also
believe that the New Testament reveals God as dealing differently with
the "elect" and the "non-elect."[24]

A Suggested Conceptual Model: Congruent Election

So what is congruent election, and how does it differ from unconditional
election? Why is congruent election a better model?

If our goal is to preach "the whole plan of God" that we may be "innocent of everyone's blood" as the apostle Paul declared to the Ephesian
elders (Acts 20:26–27), then we should be seeking a biblical theology that
is in harmony with all scriptural revelation.

We must seek a conceptual understanding of each doctrine of the faith,
including election, that allows us to preach on every passage of Scripture without contradiction, confusion, or hesitancy, and without ignoring
some "problem" passages in favor of others more easily harmonized with
our particular doctrinal model. The goal should always be "both/and" not
"either/or" when it comes to harmonizing Scripture.

If I am going to seek to emulate the apostle Paul's example to preach
"the whole plan of God" and if literally every individual Scripture verse
is *theopneustos* ("God-breathed" or "God-exhaled," 2 Tim 3:16), then my
doctrinal formulation should ignore no Scripture and seek to harmonize
all revelation.

---

[23] H. Hobbs, "God's Purpose of Grace," in *The Baptist Faith and Message* (Nashville: Convention
Press, 1971), 64; c.f. C. S. Kelley Jr., R. Land, and R. A. Mohler Jr., *The Baptist Faith and Message* (Nashville: LifeWay, 2007), 77.

[24] Rom 8:29–30; Eph 1:3–6; 1 Pet 1:2.

My theology should allow me the freedom to preach from Paul's Epistle to the Romans that those God "foreknew He also predestined to be conformed to the image of His Son . . . and those He predestined, He also called; and those He called, He also justified; and those He justified, He also glorified" (Rom 8:29–30 HCSB). Here the objects of His grace are so secure and certain in their destiny that He can speak of their ultimate heavenly glorification as a past, completed event.

It should also allow me to preach with equal conviction that "God so loved the world that he gave his only begotten Son, that whosoever believeth in him should not perish but have everlasting life" (John 3:16 KJV) and "the Spirit and the bride say, Come. And let him that heareth say, Come. And let him that is athirst come. And whosoever will, let him take the water of life freely" (Rev 22:17 KJV).

My theology should make me equally comfortable preaching Eph 1:3–5 and 1 Tim 2:3–6. Ephesians declares: "Blessed be the God and Father of our Lord Jesus Christ, . . . for He chose us in Him, before the foundation of the world, to be holy and blameless in His sight. In love He predestined us to be adopted through Jesus Christ for Himself, according to His favor and will" (Eph 1:3–5 HCSB). On the other hand, in his first epistle to Timothy, the apostle Paul declares that "God our Savior . . . wants everyone to be saved and to come to the knowledge of the truth" (1 Tim 2:3–4 HCSB). In these verses God's "desire" for everyone to be saved is *thelō*, "speaking of a wish or desire that arises from one's emotions."[25] Wuest explains that the "literal Greek is, 'who willeth all men'" and "marks a determinate purpose."[26] God, Paul reveals, strongly desires that all men be saved and come to an *epignōsis* or "advanced or full knowledge" of the truth.[27] The Timothy passage further declares that Jesus gave Himself as a substitutionary atonement, "a ransom for all" (1 Tim 2:6 HCSB).

How do I harmonize these together? Many years ago, when I was teaching theology full-time, I found that one of the best arguments for the existence of God was the "argument from congruity"—what theory, model, or answer harmonizes the most known facts? The Intelligent Design movement illustrates this argument. When one examines the irreducible complexity and intricate balance and design of even primitive,

---

[25] K. S. Wuest, *The Exegesis of I Timothy*, in *Wuest's Word Studies from the Greek New Testament* (Grand Rapids: Eerdmans, 1973), 2:40.

[26] Ibid., 40–41.

[27] Ibid.

single-cell organisms, an intelligent designer is the answer far more "congruent" with the known facts than the Darwinian theory of evolutionary origins.

Is there a conceptual model for election that fits the entirety of the biblical revelation better than the Calvinist model of unconditional election? I think so—it is "congruent election."

The Congruent Election Model

Understanding congruent election first requires recognizing that Scripture reveals two different types of election—Abrahamic election and salvation election. Abrahamic election explains how God chose the Jews to be His chosen people (Gen 12:1–3). Salvation election pertains to God's elective purpose in how He brings about the eternal salvation of individual human beings, both Jew and Gentile, in both the Old and the New Testaments.

Abrahamic election refers to the status of the Jews as a special, chosen people, not to their salvation. Not all the people of the Abrahamic covenant were saved—only those within the covenant people who were also the objects of salvation election and who understood and appropriated in their souls the saving truths taught in the Old Testament's sacrificial system. These objects of salvation election genuinely looked forward to Christ's substitutionary atonement on the cross in the same way Christians look back to that one-time propitiatory sacrifice by Christ the Great High Priest.

There was always a saved remnant within the covenant nation, the chosen people (Rom 11:1–10). Such individuals, exemplified by Abraham in the Old Testament and the apostle Paul in the New Testament, were the objects both of Abrahamic election and salvation election.

The first significant difference between Abrahamic election and salvation election is that Abrahamic election refers to special status as a people of God and salvation election refers to eternal salvation. The second significant difference between the two, but related to the first, is that Abrahamic election is a corporate action, dealing with an ethnically and genetically defined people ("the seed of Abraham"), while the objects of Salvation election are individuals from "every tribe, and tongue, and nation."

In God's providence He has chosen to explain and reveal His dealings with His people more fully in the New Testament. In doing so, a third difference between Abrahamic (corporate) election and salvation (individual) election has been underscored. As God has chosen to deal with individuals concerning election to eternal salvation in Christ, as opposed to corporate election to the status as a special covenant people, something called "foreknowledge" becomes a prominent factor. God has revealed in the New Testament that salvation election is somehow intertwined with, and connected to, foreknowledge in a significant way (Rom 8:29–30; 1 Pet 1:2).

Indeed, as Paul anticipated Jewish objections to the preaching of the gospel of grace to Gentiles (Romans 9–11), he explained that God always had "a remnant chosen by grace . . . His people whom He foreknew" (Rom 11:1, 5 HCSB)—those such as Abraham in the Old Testament and the apostle Paul in the New Testament, who experienced salvation election as well as Abrahamic election.

I want to suggest as gently as possible (because historically they have understood a lot more correctly than they have understood incorrectly) that the reason Calvinists formulated their doctrine of election incorrectly is they defined their ecclesiology incorrectly. Having failed to discern the distinction between Israel and the church (perceiving Israel as the people of God in the Old Testament and the church as replacing Israel in the New Testament), they were not attuned to the significant differences between the election of Israel (corporate) and the election to salvation (individual) in both the Old and New Testaments. When differences between Abrahamic election (corporate) and salvation election (individual) are as significant as those outlined above, conflating the two differing types of election or assuming they are the same—they are not—is unwise and misleading.

No better illustration can be found of the theological confusion and mayhem caused by confusing Abrahamic election and salvation election than interpretations of Romans 9–11. Whenever objections are raised to the Calvinistic understanding of election, voices are immediately raised, crying, "What about Jacob and Esau?" (cf. Rom 9:11–13). In his *Lectures on the Epistle to the Romans*, H. A. Ironside explains the difference between Abrahamic election and salvation election and how they should be differentiated, not conflated:

> There is no question here of predestination to Heaven or reprobation to hell; in fact, eternal issues do not really come in throughout this chapter, although, of course, they naturally follow as the result of the use or abuse of God-given privileges. But we are not told here, nor anywhere else, that before children are born it is God's purpose to send one to

heaven and another to hell. . . . The passage has entirely to do with privilege here on earth.[28]

I challenge all interested parties to read Romans 9–11 carefully and think about two types of election, Abrahamic (corporate) and salvation (individual), remembering that "not all who are descended from Israel are Israel. Neither are they all children because they are Abraham's descendants" (Rom 9:6–7 HCSB). When you view these chapters from that perspective, previous understandings of election are challenged and changed.

God and "Time"

The key to a new and more comprehensive understanding of salvation election is a deeper and more complete understanding of God's relation to and experience of "time." While God experiences "time" in the linear time-space continuum or chronological sense as a function of His omniscience and omnipresence, He alone is not bound by its constraints or parameters. Unlike man, God has always existed in what C. S. Lewis termed the "Eternal Now."[29]

God has always experienced the totality of time and everything before time (eternity past) and after time (eternity future) as the present. The New Testament scholar Geoffrey Bromiley bases God's foreknowledge on His omniscience: "Past, present, and future are all present to God."[30] Herschel Hobbs explained it this way: "The foreknowledge of God is based upon his omniscience, or all knowledge. Since the Bible views God as present at all times and all places contemporaneously in his universe, he knows all things simultaneously."[31]

Thus God is described as living in the "Eternal Now," the "present," and knowing "all things simultaneously." What if the Bible is telling us in the concept of "foreknowledge" that God does not just know all things

---

[28] H. A. Ironside, *Lectures on the Epistle to the Romans* (Neptune, NJ: Loizeaux Brothers, 1928), 116.

[29] C. S. Lewis, *Miracles* (New York: Macmillan, 1947), in *The Best of C. S. Lewis* (ed. H. Lindsell; Washington, DC: Canon, 1974), 375. J. Cottrell discusses eternal concepts of time in relation to God in his article "The Classical Arminian View of Election," in *Perspectives on Election: Five Views* (ed. C. Brand; Nashville: B&H, 2006), 112–15, but draws significantly different conclusions than the ones proposed in this article.

[30] G. W. Bromiley, "Foreknowledge," in *The Evangelical Dictionary of Theology* (ed. W A. Elwell; Grand Rapids: Baker Book House, 1984), 320.

[31] H. Hobbs, *What Baptists Believe* (Nashville: Broadman, 1964), 24.

that have or will ever happen as if they are the present moment to Him, but that He has, and always has had, the "experience" of all things, events, and people as a punctiliar present moment? That, I believe, is precisely what is suggested by the biblical concept of foreknowledge. From God's perspective there can never have been a single moment when God has not had the totality of His experience (their acceptance and after, or their rejection and after) with each and every human being as part of His "present" (i.e., eternal) experience and knowledge.

Romans 8:29–30 declares that God "foreknew" individual human beings, and these same individuals He "predestined" and "called" and "justified" and "glorified," speaking of the end result (far in the future for at least the first official recipients involved) as a settled, past event—which it always has been for God.

"Foreknowledge" (*prognōsis*, noun; *proginoskō*, verb form) by its New Testament usage "in relationship to God" has "acquired an additional content and meaning."[32] Used as it is in Rom 8:29, Wuest concludes that it "means more here than mere previous knowledge, even though that knowledge be part of the omniscience of God."[33]

If that additional New Testament usage is perceived as "pre-experience with," meaning there is no moment in eternity when the sum total of God's experience with each person was not God's present, then the pieces of salvation election and the Scripture passages upon which that concept is founded fall into place in a most convincing and congruent fashion.

In the old traditional model of unconditional election (fig. 1), the "elect" must be saved because they are the objects of God's irresistible grace, and the "non-elect" cannot be saved because they are only the recipients of a "general call" (which may or may not involve the Holy Spirit, but which is never sufficient for salvation). According to the Reformed view, from eternity past it has been decreed that the elect must be saved and the non-elect cannot be saved, and it will thus unfold in human history just as God has decreed it.

This view has presented problems to many seeking to exegete such passages as 1 Tim 2:1–6; Rev 22:17; and John 3:16. Scripture affirms "that by God's grace He might taste death for everyone" (Heb 2:9 HSCB). Giants of the faith have struggled with how the unconditional election of figure 1

---

[32] Wuest, *Studies in the Vocabulary of the Greek New Testament*, in *Wuest's Word Studies*, 3:35.
[33] Wuest, *Romans in the Greek New Testament*, in *Wuest's Word Studies*, 2:144. See also Wuest, *First Peter in the Greek New Testament*, in *Wuest's Word Studies*, 2:16.

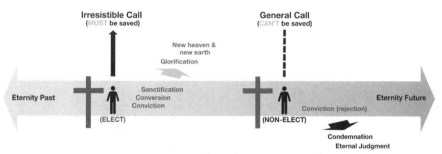

Figure 1

is "consistent with the free agency of man."[34] The great nineteenth-century Baptist preacher Charles Haddon Spurgeon, far less optimistic than John Leland, questioned whether Bible teaching on these subjects could ever be reconciled: "I am not sure that in heaven we shall be able to know where the free agency of man and the sovereignty of God meet, but both are great truths."[35]

However, if one affirms the belief that foreknowledge means "experience with eternally—from before eternity past and into eternity future," then congruency of the biblical passages emerges. In congruent salvation election (fig. 2), you have a vertical emphasis, as opposed to the horizontal figure 1. This is to emphasize the punctiliar, "eternal now" aspect of election within in the larger "Eternal Now" concept. If God lives in the Eternal Now, then He has always had not just the knowledge of but experience with every individual. So there has never been a moment in eternity when God has not had the experience of every elect person being convicted, accepting God's completion of their faith, conversion, sanctification, glorification, and their eternal praise and worship in the new heaven and the new earth.

Conversely, God has always had the experience of the "non-elect"— their rejection of the Spirit's conviction, their rejection of Him, their increasingly hardened heart, and their ultimate condemnation and

---

[34] "The New Hampshire Confession," in Baptist Confessions of Faith, 363; "God's Purpose of Grace," Article 5 in the Baptist Faith and Message 2000, cited in Kelley, Land, and Mohler, *The Baptist Faith and Message*, 77.

[35] C. H. Spurgeon, *The Metropolitan Tabernacle Pulpit* (Pasadena, TX: Pilgrim Publications, 1978), 51: 50, quoted in Kelley, Land, and Mohler, *The Baptist Faith and Message*, 77.

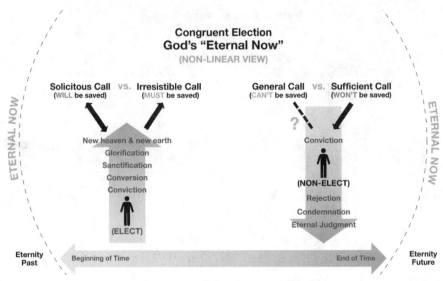

Figure 2

eternal judgment. In the congruent election model, while the vertical model symbolizes the simultaneous nature of the totality of God's experience with the person, elect or non-elect, the linear time represented across the bottom of figure 2 accommodates our need to understand that the events that comprise God's experience with us occur for us across linear time.

I had a conversion experience at age six. I was baptized Easter Sunday, 1953. In the years since, I have grown in grace, responded to a call to full-time ministry; and at some point in the future, I will be called home to be with my heavenly Father to worship and praise Him forever. The entirety of that experience has always been part of God's experience with me while it is still unfolding in space and time.

What an experience it is! Revelation 21:7 reveals God declaring that in the new heaven and the new earth concerning those who belong to Him, "I will be his God, and he will be My son" (HCSB). This is not mere corporate fellowship. This is individual, personal, and intimate relationship with each of us. As His children we will have Him to enjoy and worship personally forever. It lies in the future for us. It has always, eternally been part of God's experience of us. God's experience of my response to, and relationship with, Him has always caused Him to deal differently with me than He does with a person with whom God's eternal life experience has been rebellion and rejection.

Thus, I would posit a distinction between unconditional election's "irresistible call" (one *must* be saved) and congruent election's "solicitous call" (one *will* be saved). There is a similar distinction to be made for unsaved persons between unconditional election's (one *can't* be saved) and congruent election's (one *won't* be saved). I, for one, see a big difference between "must" and "will" and an even bigger difference between "won't" and "can't."

If God had chosen to do it the way Calvinists say He did, He would still be a merciful and gracious God. If God were merely fair, all men would deserve condemnation. However, the congruent model of election harmonizes the largest number of Scripture passages. Congruent election allows its adherents to preach all the Scriptures on the subjects of foreknowledge, calling, election, and whosoever will.

Congruent election maintains the serious, eternal difference between how God deals with the elect and the non-elect. It rejects the woeful underestimation by some Arminians of the ravaging effects of the sinful nature on the human ability to respond to God apart from prevenient, enabling grace. However, in arguing that the solicitous call to the elect and the sufficient Call to the non-elect, while different, are both sufficient and that both are based upon God's eternal experience *with*, not just prior knowledge *of*, individual beings (and not solely on God's decree in eternity past), congruent election gives deeper and fuller meaning to God as "fatherly in His attitude toward all men" as the Baptist Faith and Message declares Him to be.[36]

This, then, is the congruent conceptual model of election. Abrahamic election (corporate) and salvation election (individual) differ from each other in definitive and important ways. Additionally, salvation election, though close to Calvin's unconditional election indeed differs, since it is based on God's eternal (present) experience with each human being. I believe God led me to this understanding of election, and it was but a journey of a small distance to this doctrinal destination for a Sandy Creek Baptist. Some would say it was no distance at all.

---

[36] This quote has been taken from Article 2a of the Baptist Faith and Message 2000, "God the Father," which reads as follows: "God as Father reigns with providential care over His universe, His creatures, and the flow of the stream of human history according to the purposes of His grace. He is all powerful, all loving, and all wise. God is Father in truth to those who become children of God through faith in Jesus Christ. He is fatherly in His attitude toward all men"; cited in Kelley, Land, and Mohler, *The Baptist Faith and Message*, 31.

{ Chapter 4 }

The Atonement:
Limited or Universal?

DAVID L. ALLEN

Introduction

The issue of the extent of the atonement looms large in Baptist history. At the cradle of Baptist origins in the early seventeenth century, it was the line of demarcation. "General Baptists," the earliest Baptists, believed the nature of Christ's satisfaction for sin on the cross extended to every human being. Thus the atonement was universal in scope. "Particular Baptists," for the most part, believed that Christ only suffered for the sins of the elect. The theological and popular term used to describe this latter position is "limited atonement."

This chapter will examine several questions. The key question is whether Scripture teaches limited atonement. Several related questions follow. Have there been and are there today Calvinists who reject limited atonement? Must one hold to limited atonement to be a good Calvinist? What are the implications of limited atonement for evangelism, missions, and preaching?

The goals of this essay are to be firm but fair, simple but substantive, biblical but not bombastic, and to avoid an unbecoming pride of ignorance as well as an arrogant elitism. *All* the options need to be on the table, *and all of them must be rightly represented* before beginning to discern which viewpoint is true biblically. Often in discussions of Calvinism, people use the same vocabulary but define the terms differently. Confusion often reigns over the terminology itself. Consequently, defining the terms used in this chapter is necessary. The following are brief definitions of the terms:

> *Atonement,* in modern usage, refers to the expiatory and propitiatory act of Christ on the cross whereby satisfaction for sin was accomplished. One must be careful to distinguish between the *intent, extent,* and *application* of the atonement.
>
> *Extent of the atonement* answers the question "For whom did Christ die?" or "For whose sins was Christ punished?" There are only two options: for the elect *alone* (*limited atonement*) or for all of humanity (*universal atonement*). The second option may be further divided into (a) Dualists (Christ has an *unequal* will to save all through the death of Christ) and (b) Arminians and non-Calvinists (Christ has an *equal* will to save all through the death of Christ).
>
> According to *limited atonement,* Christ *only* bore the punishment due for the sins of the elect *alone.*[1] Consequently, no one else can or will receive the saving benefits of His death. This term will be used as a synonym for "definite atonement," "particular redemption,"[2] and "strict particularism."

---

[1] While all Calvinists who believe in "definite atonement" believe in a kind of limited imputation of sin to Christ, the majority of them reject "equivalentism"; that is, they do not hold to a quid pro quo (tit for tat) theory of expiation, as if there is a quantum of suffering in Christ that corresponds exactly to the number of sins of those He represents. I am not equating "strict particularism" with "equivalentism." T. Nettles is an example of one who holds the equivalentist view (see his *By His Grace and for His Glory* [Grand Rapids: Baker, 1986], 305–16).

[2] There is variety within the group of people who describe themselves by this label. Dagg wrote: "Other persons who maintain the doctrine of particular redemption, distinguish between redemption and atonement, and because of the adaptedness referred to, consider the death of Christ an atonement for the sins of all men; or as an atonement for sin in the abstract." J. L. Dagg, *Manual of Theology* (Harrisonburg, VA: Gano Books, 1990), 326. Notice that Dagg is affirming there are two particular redemption positions within Calvinism, something which is seldom recognized. Notice also that one of these positions within Calvinism affirms that Christ died for the sins of all men. It is remarkable that when Andrew Fuller modified his views as a result of his interaction with General Baptist Dan Taylor, he explicitly says that he agreed with him on "the universal extent of Christ's death" (*The Complete Works of the Rev. Andrew Fuller, with a Memoir of His Life by the Rev. Andrew Gunton Fuller* [ed. A. G. Fuller; rev. ed. J. Belcher; vol. 2; Harrisonburg, VA: Sprinkle Publications, 1988 (1845)], 550). Moreover, in Fuller's treatment of substitution in his *Six Letters to Dr. Ryland,* he seeks to answer the question of "The persons

According to *universal atonement*, Christ bore the punishment due for the sins of *all* humanity.

Dualism refers to the view that Christ bore the punishment due for the sins of all humanity, but not for all *equally*; that is, He did not do so with the same *intent, design,* or *purpose.* Most Calvinists who reject (or do not espouse) limited atonement in the Owenic sense are dualists.[3]

Particularism, when used in a strict sense (which is the sense I will use it in this chapter), is a synonym for limited atonement or particular redemption.

A *particularist* is someone who holds to particularism, that is, the position of limited atonement.

In *limited imputation,* the sins of the elect *only* were substituted for, atoned for, or imputed to Christ on the cross.

In *unlimited imputation,* the sins of *all* of humanity were substituted for, atoned for, or imputed to Christ on the cross.

Infinite or *universal sufficiency,* when used by strict particularists, means that the death of Christ *could have been* sufficient or able to atone for all the sins of the world *if God had intended for it to do so.* However, since they think God did not intend for the death of Christ to satisfy for all, but only for the elect, it is not *actually* sufficient or able to save any others. When used by Dualists and non-Calvinists, the term means that the death of Christ is of such a nature that it can actually save all men. It is, *in fact* (not hypothetically), a satisfaction for the sins of all humanity. Therefore, if any people perish, it is not for lack of an atonement for their sins.[4] The fault lies *totally* within themselves.

According to *limited sufficiency,* the death of Christ only satisfied for the sins of the elect *alone.* Thus it is *limited in its capacity to save* only those for whom He suffered.

---

for whom Christ was a substitute; whether the *elect only,* or mankind in general." He argues that Christ substituted for mankind in general, but he maintained this in conjunction with his belief that Christ did such with an effectual purpose to save only the elect (*Works,* 2:706–09). Fuller seems to fit Dagg's second type of particular redemptionist.

[3] "Owenic" refers to John Owen's classic treatment of the limited atonement position in his *The Death of Death in the Death of Christ* (Cornwall, England: Diggory Press, 2007).

[4] C. Hodge (concurring with the Synod of Dort) makes this point in his *Systematic Theology* (Grand Rapids: Eerdmans, 1993), 2:556–57. The Puritan S. Charnock also powerfully argues the point in "The Acceptableness of Christ's Death," in *The Works of Stephen Charnock* (Carlisle, PA: Banner of Truth, 1985), 4:563–64.

Intrinsic sufficiency speaks to the atonement's internal or infinite abstract ability to save all men (if God so intended), in such a way that it has no direct reference to the actual extent of the atonement.

Extrinsic Sufficiency speaks to the atonement's actual infinite ability to save all and every human, and this because God, indeed, wills it to be so, such that Christ, *in fact*, made a satisfaction for all humankind. In other words, the sufficiency enables the unlimited satisfaction to be truly adaptable to all humanity. All living people are in a saveable state because there is blood sufficiently shed for them (Heb 9:22).

Three major areas comprise the subject of the atonement: intent, extent, and application. The *intent* of the atonement, since it relates to the differing perspectives on election, answers the question, What was Christ's saving *purpose* in providing an atonement? Did He equally or unequally desire the salvation of every human? Then, consequently, does His intent necessarily have a bearing upon the extent of His satisfaction? A crucial passage in this connection is found in 2 Cor 5:19: "God was in Christ, reconciling the world to himself" (KJV). God's plan in the atonement was to provide a punishment and a satisfaction for sin as a basis for salvation for all humanity and to secure the salvation of all who believe in Christ.[5] High-Calvinists[6] believe in limited atonement and thus interpret the word *world* here to mean the elect[7] and not all humanity. They argue that God's limited saving intent necessarily requires that Christ provided a satisfaction only for the elect[8] and thus to secure salvation only for the elect. Moderate-Calvinists[9], that is, those who reject a strictly limited atonement, believe God's saving *design* in the atonement was dualistic: (1) He sent Christ for the salvation of all humanity so that His death paid the penalty for their sins, and (2) Christ died with the special purpose of ultimately securing the salvation of the elect. The classic Arminian and non-Calvinist view of the intent of the atonement is that Christ died equally

---

[5] See G. Shultz's treatment of 2 Cor 5:18–21 in "A Biblical and Theological Defense of a Multi-Intentioned View of the Extent of the Atonement" (Ph.D. diss., Southern Baptist Theological Seminary, 2008), 125–31. Schultz, a moderate-Calvinist, has an excellent recent article on the extent of the atonement, which is a summary of his dissertation. (G. Schultz, "God's Purposes in the Atonement for the Nonelect," *Bibliotheca Sacra* 165, no. 658 [April-June 2008]: 145–63.) His article identifies the many biblical purposes for the atonement for the non-elect, including "payment of the penalty for all of the sins of every person who has ever lived" (147).

[6] The term "high-Calvinist" is equivalent to "five-point Calvinist."

[7] Here the elect usually refers to the *believing* elect.

[8] Not all Calvinists say that Christ's death only provided for the salvation of the elect since they differ among themselves over the meaning of the sufficiency of Christ's death.

[9] These are sometimes called "four-point Calvinists," but the label is imprecise.

for all men to make salvation possible for all who believe, as well as to secure the salvation of those who do believe (the elect).[10]

The *extent* of the atonement answers the question, For whose sins was Christ punished? There are two possible answers. First, Christ died for the sins of all humanity, either with equal intent (He died for the sins of all as He equally intends their salvation), or with unequal intent (He died for the sins of all but especially intends to save the elect). Second, Christ died for the sins of the elect only (strict particularism) as He only intends their salvation.[11] All Arminians, moderate-Calvinists, and non-Calvinists believe that Jesus died for the sins of all humanity.

The *application* of the atonement answers the question, When is the atonement applied to the sinner? This question has three possible answers: (1) It is applied in the eternal decree of God. Many hyper-Calvinists hold this view. (2) It is applied at the cross to all the elect at the time of Jesus' death. Some hyper-Calvinists and some high-Calvinists hold this position, which is called "justification at the cross." (3) It is applied at the moment the sinner exercises faith in Christ. Most high-Calvinists, all moderate-Calvinists, all Arminians, and all non-Calvinists hold this view, which is the biblical view. The *ultimate cause* of the application is also in dispute since Calvinists want to argue that those who believe in libertarian free will ground the decisive cause of salvation in man's will rather than in God's will.

These three subjects concerning the atonement (intent, extent, and application) cannot and should not be divorced from one another. The focus in this chapter is primarily on the question of the extent of the atonement.

At the outset it is vital to say a word about the popular formula Peter Lombard first explicitly articulated in his *Sentences:*[12] Jesus' death is

---

[10] I am referring here to the classical Arminian position that does not necessarily deny the security of the believer. Modern Arminians deny the security of the believer.

[11] Most in this group do admit, however, that Christ's death results in common grace flowing to all. The important point here is sin bearing. They do *not* admit an unlimited imputation of sin to Christ.

[12] The formulaic section has recently been translated as follows: "He offered himself on the altar of the cross not to the devil, but to the triune God, and he did so for all with regard to the sufficiency of the price, but only for the elect with regard to its efficacy, because he brought about salvation only for the predestined." P. Lombard, *The Sentences–Book 3: On the Incarnation of the Word* (trans. G. Silano; Mediaeval Sources in Translation 45; Canada: Pontifical Institute of Mediaeval Studies, 2008), 86. The *concept*, however, is *at least* as old as Ambrose (AD 338–397). See his *Exposition of the Holy Gospel According to Saint Luke* (trans. T. Tomkinson; Etna: Center for Traditionalist Orthodox Studies, 1998), 201–2. He wrote, "Although Christ suffered for all, yet He suffered for us particularly, because He suffered for the Church."

sufficient for all but efficient only for the elect. The debate over the nature of this sufficiency is *the key debate* in the extent question. Calvinists often state that "the debate is *not* over the sufficiency of the atonement; all agree the atonement was sufficient to atone for the sins of the whole world." The debate is very much about sufficiency. The high-Calvinist position on the atonement entails that Christ's death is only sufficient to save the elect. The non-elect are not savable because Jesus did not die for their sins. Jesus' sufficiency in the strictly limited atonement position is what is called an *intrinsic* sufficiency (or a *bare* sufficiency).[13] The idea is that if God had intended for all the world to be saved, then Jesus' death *could have been*[14] sufficient for all (as it has enough intrinsic merit), but that is not what God intended. The moderate-Calvinist and non-Calvinist position interprets the term "sufficient" to mean Christ actually made satisfaction for the sins of all humanity. Thus, Jesus' death is "extrinsically" or "universally" sufficient in capacity to save all people. Understanding Lombard's formula is fraught with confusion today since those on both sides of the post-Reformation debate have used it to articulate and defend their position, often without the speaker specifying in what sense he is using the term. Whenever the formula is used, the question must always be asked: what is meant by the term "sufficient"?

This essay is going to argue the case for unlimited atonement (an unlimited imputation of sin to Christ) and against limited atonement (a limited imputation of sin to Christ) without ever quoting a single Arminian or non-Calvinist. The best arguments against limited atonement come from Calvinist writers.[15] Five areas will be surveyed in answering the ques-

---

[13] The "intrinsic" or "bare sufficiency" view is discussed and refuted in the writings of several Calvinists, including J. Davenant, *An Exposition of the Epistle of St. Paul to the Colossians: With a Dissertation on the Death of Christ* (2 vols.; London: Hamilton, Adams, and Co., 1831), 401–04; J. Ussher, "An Answer to Some Exceptions," in *The Whole Works of the Most Rev. James Ussher* (Dublin: Hodges, Smith, and Co., 1864), 12:561–71; E. Polhill, "The Divine Will Considered in Its Eternal Decrees," in *The Works of Edward Polhill* (Morgan, PA: Soli Deo Gloria Publications, 1998), 164; and N. Hardy, *The First General Epistle of St. John the Apostle* (Edinburgh: James Nichol, 1865), 140–41.

[14] John Owen was conscious of the fact that he and others were revising the formula of the "schoolmen," and prefers to put it in hypothetical terms: "the blood of Christ was sufficient *to have been made* a price for all" [emphasis mine]. See *The Works of John Owen* (ed. W. H. Goold; New York: Robert Carter and Brothers, 1852), 10:296. Richard Baxter calls Owen's revision of the Lombardian Formula a "new futile evasion" and refutes his position in *Universal Redemption of Mankind by the Lord Jesus Christ* (London: Printed for John Salusbury at the Rising Sun in Cornhill, 1694), 343–45. This revision is also briefly discussed in W. Cunningham, *Historical Theology* (Carlisle, PA: Banner of Truth, 1994), 2:332.

[15] I would like to thank Tony Byrne for his research and writing assistance. Some of the material used in this chapter was originally posted on his blog site TheologicalMeditations.blogspot.com. Tony is a moderate-Calvinist and a former student of mine at The Criswell College. He has far outdistanced his professor on the subject of the extent of the atonement. His Web site has scores of in-context quotations

tion whether the atonement of Christ is limited or unlimited: historical, biblical, logical, theological, and practical.

Historical Considerations

What two things do all these men—John Calvin, Heinrich Bullinger, Thomas Cranmer, Richard Baxter, John Preston, John Bunyan, John Howe, Zacharias Ursinus, David Paraeus, Stephen Charnock, Edward Polhill, Isaac Watts, Jonathan Edwards, David Brainard, Thomas Chalmers, Philip Doddridge, Ralph Wardlaw, Charles Hodge, Robert Dabney, W. G. T. Shedd, J. C. Ryle, A. H. Strong—have in common? All were Calvinists, and all did not teach limited atonement.[16] Such a claim often shocks Calvinists and non-Calvinists alike.

What two things do these names all have in common: John Davenant, Matthias Martinius, Samuel Ward, Thomas Goad, Joseph Hall, Ludwig Crocius, and Johann Heinrich Alsted? All were Calvinists, and all were delegates at Dort who rejected limited atonement. What two things do these names have in common: Edmund Calamy, Henry Scudder, John Arrowsmith, Lazarus Seaman, Richard Vines, Stephen Marshall, and Robert Harris? All were Calvinists, and all were Westminster Divines who rejected limited atonement. All of the above men also affirmed a form of universal atonement.

The issue of the extent of the atonement looms large in Reformation history. It was the single most debated issue at Dort. The final committee modified the language of Dort and deliberately left it ambiguous in order to accommodate those high-Calvinists who believed in limited atonement (strict particularism) *and* those like John Davenant and others from the British and Bremen delegations who rejected strict particularism and believed Jesus' death paid the penalty of the sins of all humanity.[17]

---

from Calvinists on a host of subjects ranging from God's love, God's universal saving will, common grace, the well-meant gospel offer, to the extent of the atonement. Tony has greatly helped to sharpen my own thinking on this subject.

[16] The point here is that they did not teach "limited atonement" in the sense of a limited imputation of sin to Christ, as Owen taught, and as most modern "five-point" Calvinists think. Rather, they held to a form of universal atonement.

[17] See W. Godfrey, "Tensions Within International Calvinism: The Debate on the Atonement at the Synod of Dort, 1618–1619" (Ph.D. diss., Stanford University, 1974), 252–69; and R. Muller, *Post-Reformation Reformed Dogmatics* (Grand Rapids: Baker, 2003), 1:76–77. Muller even says that the same confessional compromises on the language of the extent of the atonement occurred at Westminster so as to allow both views.

In considering the historical data on this question, one should be aware of three things. First, there has been and is significant debate over beliefs concerning the extent of the atonement in Calvinistic history. The same honesty used with interpreting the biblical and systematic data needs to be used with reading the historical data as we seek to be with the biblical and systematic data. Baptists need to be aware of the many Calvinistic stalwarts within the Baptist denomination, including Southern Baptists, who held to a form of universal atonement and rejected limited atonement.

Second, Baptists, whether Calvinistic *or not*, need to be more historically self-aware concerning the extent of the diversity on the point. The primary sources must be consulted. There is a great deal of ignorance in this area. Many contemporary authors from a Calvinistic perspective write as if Calvinists historically propounded only one view on this subject. Since it is unlikely that these authors are unaware of the diversity within their own tradition on the subject of the extent of the atonement, one wonders why only the strict limited position is presented and argued. A cursory glance at many of the blog sites hosted by Calvinists reveals the same lacuna and the need to listen honestly to historical theology. The only way to do this is to read the *primary* sources carefully.

Third, one needs to see the novelty of the Owenic view of limited atonement in church history. It has always been the minority view among Christians[18] even after the Reformation. This unpopular status does not in and of itself make it incorrect, but too many Calvinists operate under the assumption that a strictly limited atonement is and has been the only position within Calvinism.[19] It is not, nor has it ever been.

The first person in church history who explicitly held belief in limited atonement was Gottschalk of Orbais (AD 804–869).[20] Contrary to what some Calvinists think, Augustine did not hold the view of limited

---

[18] But not necessarily among *Reformed* Christians after the Reformation period.

[19] Richard Muller has begun to inform the church about the historical diversity within the Reformed camp. Consult his lectures at Mid-America Reformed Seminary in November 2008, titled "Revising the Predestination Paradigm: An Alternative to Supralapsarianism, Infralapsarianism and Hypothetical Universalism." He considers the following to be "hypothetical universalists" of the non-Amyraldian variety: Musculus, Zanchi, Ursinus, Kimedoncius, Bullinger, Twisse, Ussher, Davenant (and others in the British delegation to Dort), Calamy, Seaman, Vines, Harris, Marshall, Arrowsmith (the latter six were Westminster Divines), Preston, and Bunyan.

[20] G. M. Thomas, *The Extent of the Atonement: A Dilemma for Reformed Theology from Calvin to the Consensus (1536–1675)* (Carlisle: Paternoster, 1997), 5.

atonement.[21] On the other hand, Gottschalk stated that "Christ was not crucified and put to death for the redemption of the whole world, that is, not for the salvation and redemption of all mankind, but only for those who are saved."[22] Three French councils condemned both Gottschalk and his views.

Turning to the Reformation period, Martin Luther clearly held a form of unlimited atonement: "Christ has taken away not only the sins of some men but your sins and those of the whole world. The offering was for the sins of the whole world, even though the whole world does not believe."[23] In another place Luther argued poignantly concerning John 1:29:

> You may say: "Who knows whether Christ also bore my sin? I have no doubt that He bore the sin of St. Peter, St. Paul, and other saints; these were pious people." . . . Don't you hear what St. John says in our text: "This is the Lamb of God, who takes away the sin of the world"? And you cannot deny that you are also a part of this world, for you were born of man and woman. You are not a cow or a pig. It follows that your sins must be included, as well as the sins of St. Peter or St. Paul. . . . Don't you hear? There is nothing missing from the Lamb. He bears all the sins of the world from its inception; this implies that He also bears yours, and offers you grace.[24]

John Calvin likewise held to a form of universal atonement. Consider the following:

> *To bear the sins* means to free those who have sinned from their guilt by his satisfaction. He says many meaning all, as in Rom. 5:15. It is of course certain that not all enjoy the fruits of Christ's death, but this happens because their unbelief hinders them. That question is not dealt

---

[21] C. Daniel, "Hyper-Calvinism and John Gill" (Ph.D. diss., University of Edinburgh, 1983), 497–500. It is clear that Augustine thought that Jesus redeemed Judas. See Augustine, *Exposition of Psalm LXIX*, Section 27 (*Nicene and Post-Nicene Fathers*, Series 1, 8:309). Moreover, Prosper of Aquitaine is historically viewed as the normative interpreter of Augustine (not Gottschalk), and he *very clearly* held to universal redemption. See his *Defense of St. Augustine* (trans. P. De Letter; New York: Newman Press, 1963), 149–51, 159–60, 164.

[22] Quoted in J. Davenant, *An Exposition of the Epistle of St. Paul to the Colossians: With a Dissertation on the Death of Christ* (2 vols.; London: Hamilton, Adams, and Co., 1831), 334. [The 2005 Banner of Truth reprint of Davenant's commentary omits the *Dissertation on the Death of Christ*.] Davenant contrasts Gottschalk's "novelty of doctrines" with scores of quotes from early church fathers, including Augustine and Prosper. See also Daniel, "Hyper-Calvinism and John Gill," 503.

[23] M. Luther, *Lectures on Galatians—1535 Chapters 1–4*, in *Luther's Works* (trans. and ed. J. Pelikan; St. Louis: Concordia, 1963), 26:38.

[24] M. Luther, *Sermons on the Gospel of St. John Chapters 1–4*, in *Luther's Works* (trans. and ed. J. Pelikan; St. Louis: Concordia, 1957), 22:169.

with here because the apostle is not discussing how few or how many benefit from the death of Christ, but means simply that He died for others, not for Himself. He therefore contrasts the many to the one.[25]

Paul makes grace common to all men, not because it in fact extends to all, but because it is offered to all. Although Christ suffered for the sins of the world, and is offered by the goodness of God without distinction to all men, yet not all receive Him.[26]

Such is also the significance of the term "world," which He had used before. For although there is nothing in the world deserving of God's favour, He nevertheless shows He is favourable to the whole world when He calls all without exception to the faith in Christ, which is indeed an entry into life.[27]

We must make every effort to draw everybody to the knowledge of the gospel. For when we see people going to hell who have been created in the image of God and redeemed by the blood of our Lord Jesus Christ, that must indeed stir us to do our duty and instruct them and treat them with all gentleness and kindness as we try to bear fruit this way.[28]

It is, as I have already said, that, seeing that men are created in the image of God and that their souls have been redeemed by the blood of Jesus Christ, we must try in every way available to us to draw them to the knowledge of the gospel.[29]

In Calvin's last will and testament, he clearly affirmed a form of universal atonement:

I testify and declare that as a suppliant I humbly implore of him to grant me to be so washed and purified by the blood of that sovereign Redeemer, shed for the sins of the human race, that I may be permitted to stand before his tribunal in the image of the Redeemer himself.[30]

---

[25] J. Calvin, *The Epistle of Paul the Apostle to the Hebrews and the First and Second Epistles of St. Peter* (ed. D. W. Torrance and T. F. Torrance; trans. W. B. Johnston; Grand Rapids: Eerdmans, 1963), 131.

[26] J. Calvin, *The Epistle of Paul the Apostle to the Romans and to the Thessalonians* (ed. D. W. Torrance and T. F. Torrance; trans. R. Mackenzie; Grand Rapids: Eerdmans, 1960), 117–18.

[27] J. Calvin, *The Gospel According to St. John 1–10* (ed. D. W. Torrance and T. F. Torrance; trans. T. H. L. Parker; Grand Rapids: Eerdmans, 1961), 74.

[28] For J. Calvin's treatment of Acts 7:51, see his "Sermon 41," in *Sermons on Acts 1–7* (Edinburgh: Banner of Truth, 2008), 587–88.

[29] J. Calvin, *Sermons on Acts 1–7*, 593.

[30] J. Calvin, *Letters of John Calvin* (ed. and trans. J. Bonnet; New York, 1858, repr. [Edinburgh: Banner of Truth, 1972]), 4:365–69; See also Beza's *Life of Calvin* in Calvin's *Tracts and Treatises* (ed. T. F. Torrance; trans. H. Beveridge; Grand Rapids: Eerdmans, 1958), 1:cxiii–cxxvii.

Calvin's discussion in both his commentary and his sermon on the use of "all" in Isa 53:6 ("All we like sheep have gone astray . . . and the LORD hath laid on him the iniquity of us all" KJV) clearly makes no distinction in usage. "All" like sheep strayed, and on the Servant was laid the sin of us "all." All without exception had sinned, and the sin of all without exception had been laid on the suffering Servant. Calvin further says: "By adding the term 'each one,' he [the author of Isaiah] descends from a universal statement, in which he included all, to a particular, that each person may consider in his own mind whether it be so . . . he adds this word 'all' to exclude all exceptions . . . even to the last individual . . . all men are included, without any exception."[31] Calvin goes on to say that "many" means "all" in Isa 53:12.

With respect to Calvin's view of the extent of the atonement, Rouwendal's conclusion in a recent article is striking:

> If Calvin taught particular atonement, he would not have used the language [for universal atonement] Clifford has gathered in great number. Thus, the universal propositions in Calvin's works do prove negatively that he did not subscribe to particular atonement, but they do not prove positively that he subscribed to universal atonement. These propositions can be used to falsify the conclusion that Calvin was a particularist, but are not sufficient to prove him a universalist.[32]

Note carefully that Rouwendal himself has concluded that the evidence shows Calvin did not subscribe to limited atonement. Note also he *does not* say Calvin *did not* subscribe to universal atonement; rather he says Calvin's "universal propositions" in his writings "do not prove positively that he subscribed to universal atonement." Frankly, given the clear evidence that Calvin did, indeed, subscribe to a form of universal atonement, Rouwendal's demurral is unnecessary.

Two years after his death, Calvin's biblical universalism was reflected in the Second Helvetic Confession (1566).[33] The last of the great Reformation confessions, it was drawn up by Calvin's friend Heinrich Bullinger (1504–75),[34] Zwingli's successor at Zurich.

---

[31] J. Calvin, *Sermons on Isaiah*, 66, 70, 78–79. See the chapter in this volume by K. Kennedy on Calvin's view of the extent of the atonement.

[32] P. L. Rouwendal, "Calvin's Forgotten Classical Position on the Extent of the Atonement: About Sufficiency, Efficiency, and Anachronism," *Westminster Theological Journal* 70 (2008): 328.

[33] See A. Cochrane, ed., *Reformed Confessions of the Sixteenth Century* (London: SCM Press, 1966), 220–22, 242, 246.

[34] R. Muller acknowledges that Bullinger (like Musculus, Zanchi, and Ursinus) taught a form of "non-speculative hypothetical universalism." See Muller's review of J. Moore's *English Hypothetical Universalism: John Preston and the Softening of Reformed Theology* in *Calvin Theological Journal* 43

Another important reformation document affirming universal atonement is the Heidelberg Catechism (1593). Question 37 says:

> What do you confess when you say that He [Christ] suffered? Answer: During all the time He lived on earth, but especially at the end, Christ bore in body and soul the wrath of God against the sin of the whole human race. Thus, by His suffering, as the only atoning sacrifice, He has redeemed our body and soul from everlasting damnation, and obtained for us the grace of God, righteousness, and eternal life.

Zacharias Ursinus (1534–1583), in his commentary on the Heidelberg Catechism, said:

> Question: If Christ made a satisfaction for all, then all ought to be saved. But all are not saved. Therefore he did not make a perfect satisfaction.
> Answer: Christ satisfied for all, as it respects the sufficiency of the satisfaction which he hath made, but not as it respects the application thereof.[35]

According to Rouwendal, Beza's criticism of the Lombardian formula launched a new stage in the development of the doctrine of limited atonement. Up until his day, Calvin and all the Reformers had accepted the Lombardian formula. Following Beza, other Reformers began to accept Beza's critical approach. Bucanus, who was professor at Lausanne from 1591 to 1603, wrote that Christ's death

> "could have been" (instead of "was") a ransom for the sins of all people. Piscator went even further and called the classic formula of the distinction "contradictory." Others, like Ames and Abbot, were also critical. The trend of restricting the atonement to the elect in every respect began with Beza. It is of great importance to acknowledge that this trend did not begin until 1588, twenty-four years after Calvin had died.[36]

(2008): 149–50. One can also find a Calvinistic form of universal redemption in the writings of Rudolf Gwalther, Bullinger's student and successor. See *A Hundred Threescore and Fifteen Homilies or Sermons upon the Acts of the Apostles* (trans. J. Bridges; imprinted Henrie Denham, dwelling in Pater noster rowe, at the sign of the Starre, 1572), 108; 751–52. Gwalther married Regula Zwingli, the daughter of the Reformer.

[35] Z. Ursinus, *The Commentary of Dr. Zacharias Ursinus on the Heidelberg Catechism* (trans. G.W. Willard; Phillipsburg: P&R, 1994), 215. Again, see Muller's article in *Calvin Theological Journal* in the preceding footnote. He agrees with J. Davenant's historiography on Ursinus.

[36] Rouwendal, "Calvin's Forgotten Classical Position on the Extent of the Atonement," 320.

The early English Reformers all held to universal atonement. For example, Thomas Cranmer clearly affirmed universal atonement in the following quotation:

> This is the honour and glory of this our high priest, wherein he admitteth neither partner nor successor. For by his own oblation *he satisfied his Father for all men's sins*, and reconciled mankind unto his grace and favour. And whosoever deprive him of his honour, and go about to take it to themselves, they be very antichrists, and most arrogant blasphemers against God and against his Son Jesus Christ, whom he hath sent.[37]

In 1571, the Anglican Church adopted the doctrinal statement known as the Thirty-Nine Articles. Article 31 of the Thirty-Nine Articles states: "The offering of Christ once made is the perfect redemption, propitiation and satisfaction for all the sins of the whole world, both original and actual; and there is no other satisfaction for sin, but that alone."[38]

The Westminster Assembly was held from 1643 to 1649 in London. It is sometimes believed that all those who were members of the Westminster Assembly held to limited atonement (strict particularism). They did not. For example, listen to Henry Scudder (1585–1652):

> It must be granted, that Christ gave himself a ransom for all. This ransom may be called general, and for all, in some sense: but how? namely, in respect of the common nature of man, which he took, and of the common cause of mankind, which he undertook; and in itself it was of sufficient price to redeem all men; and because applicable to all, without exception, by the preaching and ministry of the gospel. And it was so intended by Christ, that the plaster should be as large as the sore, and that there should be no defect in the remedy, that is, in the price, or sacrifice of himself offered upon the cross, by which man should be saved, but that all men, and each particular man, might in that respect become salvable by Christ.[39]

In the broader context of this quotation, Scudder discusses the fact that the death of Christ was for all men. He denies the argument that all people

---

[37] T. Cranmer, *The Works of Thomas Cranmer* (Cambridge: University Press, 1844), 1:346 [emphasis mine].

[38] P. Schaff, *The Evangelical Protestant Creeds, with Translations*, vol. 3 in *Creeds of Christendom* (Grand Rapids: Baker, 1966), 507. I have updated the old English spellings to modern English.

[39] H. Scudder, *The Christian's Daily Walk in Security and Peace* (Glasgow: William Collins, 1826), 279–82.

will be saved because Christ ransomed all humankind. Scudder does not deny this by rejecting the premise that Christ ransomed all humankind;[40] rather, he argues that the new covenant of grace is conditional: only those who believe will obtain salvation.[41] Further, in granting that Christ died for the sins of every individual person, he bases that truth on Christ's common humanity. This view is classical Christology in accord with Heb 2:5–14. The sufficiency of which Scudder speaks is an *extrinsic* sufficiency whereby Christ bore the sin of all humanity. Scudder grounds God's universal offer upon the fact of that extrinsic sufficiency. He further associates God's "general and common love to mankind" with Christ's death for all mankind.[42] All men are "salvable" (an archaic word meaning "savable") by virtue of what Christ did on the cross. None are left without a remedy for their sin. Therefore, those who hear the gospel and perish have only themselves to blame.[43] One will also notice that Scudder does not use "world" to connote the elect in his scriptural references and allusions.

Another important Westminster Divine was Edmund Calamy (1600–1666). He said:

> I am far from universal redemption in the Arminian sense; but that that I hold is in the sense of our divines in the Synod of Dort, that Christ did pay a price for all,—absolute intention for the elect, conditional intention for the reprobate in case they do believe,—that all men should be *salvabiles, non obstante lapsu Adami* . . . that Jesus Christ did not only die sufficiently for all, but God did intend, in giving of Christ, and Christ in giving Himself, did intend to put all men in a state of salvation in case they do believe.[44]

> I argue from John 3:16, in which words a ground of God's intention of giving Christ, God's love to the world, a philanthropy the world of elect and reprobate, and not of elect only; it cannot be meant of the elect, because of that "whosoever believeth.". . . If the covenant of grace is to

---

[40] Like those who accept the "double payment" argument. See discussion below.

[41] This was also how Ursinus handled the issue. See *The Commentary of Dr. Zacharias Ursinus on the Heidelberg Catechism*, 215.

[42] This is also true of Charnock. See S. Charnock, "A Discourse of the Subjects of the Lord's Supper," in *The Complete Works of Stephen Charnock* (Edinburgh: James Nichol, 1865), 4:464. Amyraut also frequently made this connection. See L. Proctor, "The Theology of Moise Amyraut Considered as a Reaction Against Seventeenth-Century Calvinism" (Ph.D. diss., University of Leeds, 1952), 200–259.

[43] C. Hodge makes all of these points. See his *Systematic Theology* (Grand Rapids: Eerdmans, 1993), 2:556–57.

[44] A. F. Mitchell and J. P. Struthers, eds. *Minutes of the Sessions of the Westminster Assembly of Divines* (Edinburgh: W. Blackwood and Sons, 1874), 152.

be preached to all, then Christ redeemed, in some sense, all—both elect and reprobate.[45]

One should observe several salient points in these quotations. First, Calamy says that he holds to a form of universal redemption that is distinct from the Arminian view. Second, he sees his view expressed by some at the Synod of Dort. Third, he speaks of an intentional sufficiency, (conditional for the non-elect; absolute for the elect) such that Christ did actually pay a price for all. This objective price paid for all renders all men savable, but they must believe to obtain the benefit. Notice that Calamy uses John 3:16 as a proof of his view, and he argues that "world" cannot mean "the elect only" in that passage. He also argues that a universal proclamation presupposes a form of universal atonement.

In his *Chain of Principles*, Arrowsmith interpreted John 3:16 to refer to "the undeserving world of mankind," not to the "elect world," as Calamy did.[46] Many at Westminster did not affirm limited atonement (strict particularism).[47]

Several of the Puritans likewise held a form of universal atonement. For example, Richard Baxter's position can be summed up, according to Curt Daniel, in the following sentence: "Christ therefore died for all, but not for all equally, or with the same intent, design or purpose."[48] John Bunyan declared that

Christ died for all . . . for if those that perish in the days of the gospel, shall have, at least their damnation heightened, because they have neglected and refused to receive the gospel, it must need be that the gospel was with all faithfulness to be tendered unto them; the which it could not be, unless the death of Christ did extend itself unto them; John 3:16. Heb. 2:3. For the offer of the gospel cannot with God's

---

[45] Ibid., 154.

[46] J. Arrowsmith, *Armilla Catechetica: A Chain of Principles; or an Orderly Concatenation of Theological Aphorism and Exercitations; Wherein, the Chief Heads of Christian Religion Are Asserted and Improved* (Cambridge: Printed by John Field, Printer to the University, 1659), 182. Mitchell and Struthers say that Gataker, Caryl, Burroughs, and Strong concurred with this interpretation of John 3:16. See *Minutes*, lvii.

[47] Mitchell and Struthers, *Minutes*, liv–lxi. P. Schaff also mentions the name of Thomas Gataker in his analysis of the Westminster Confession. See *The Creeds of Christendom* (Grand Rapids: Baker, 1993), 1:770.

[48] Daniel, "Hyper-Calvinism and John Gill," 531; See also R. Baxter, *Catholicke Theologie* (London, Printed by Robert White, for Nevill Simmons at the Princes Arms in St. Paul's Church-yard, 1675), II:53. Baxter appeals to Twisse's universal interpretation of John 3:16 in *Universal Redemption*, 287–88. One may consult J. I. Packer's recently printed doctoral dissertation at Oxford on Baxter for an overview of his redemption theology. See *The Redemption and Restoration of Man in the Thought of Richard Baxter* (Vancouver: Regent College Publishing, 2003), 183–208.

allowance, be offered any further than the death of Jesus Christ doth go; because if that be taken away, there is indeed no gospel, nor grace to be extended.[49]

Turning our attention to America, no one would demure at the claim that Jonathan Edwards was its greatest eighteenth-century theologian. He seldom discussed the subject of the extent of the atonement in his voluminous writings. When he did, he clearly held a form of universalism: "From these things it will inevitably follow, that however Christ in some sense may be said to *die for all*, and to redeem[50] all visible Christians, yea, the whole world, by his death; yet there must be something *particular* in the design of his death, with respect to such as he intended should actually be saved thereby."[51] One can see that Edwards is advocating a form of dualism on the extent of the atonement. Christ may be said to die for all, in that he *redeemed* all, but there is still something particular in His work in the case of the elect, such that he purposes that they alone should obtain the benefit through faith. Redemption *applied* is limited but not redemption *accomplished*. Redemption accomplished is unlimited.

Under the heading "Universal Redemption," Edwards wrote:

UNIVERSAL REDEMPTION. In some sense, redemption is universal of all mankind: all mankind now have an opportunity to be saved otherwise than they would have had if Christ had not died. A door of mercy is in some sort opened for them. This is one benefit actually consequent on Christ's death; but the benefits that are actually consequent on Christ's death and are obtained by Christ's death, doubtless Christ intended to obtain by his death. It was one thing he aimed at by his death; or which is the same thing, he died to obtain it, as it was one end of his death.[52]

---

[49] J. Bunyan, *Reprobation Asserted*, in *Works of John Bunyan* (Grand Rapids: Baker, 1977), 2:348. See also "The Jerusalem Sinner Saved, or, Good News for the Vilest of Men," in *The Whole Works of John Bunyan* (London: Blackie and Son, 1862), 1:90. Here Bunyan makes the "bold proclamation" to unbelievers, and says the Son "died for thee."

[50] It is crucial to note Edwards's universal use of the term "redeemed" here, which is like Calamy's above. While some high-Calvinists do say that "Christ died for all" in the sense of purchasing common grace for even the non-elect, they are careful *not* to say that Christ "redeemed" any of the non-elect, since this involves paying their ransom price.

[51] J. Edwards, "On the Freedom of the Will" in *The Works of Jonathan Edwards* (Edinburgh: Banner of Truth, 1979), 1:88. This is not to claim that Edwards saw no sense of particularity in the design or intent of Christ's death, but only that he did not see any limitation in the *extent* of Christ's suffering on behalf of the whole world.

[52] J. Edwards [1743], "Book of Minutes on the Arminian Controversy" Gazeteer Notebook, in *Works of Jonathan Edwards Online*, vol. 37, *Documents on the Trinity, Grace and Faith* (Jonathan Edwards Center at Yale University, 2008), 10–11.

Likewise Edwards wrote,

> Christ's incarnation, his labors and sufferings, his resurrection, etc., were
> for the salvation of such as are not elected, in Scripture language, in the
> same sense as the means of grace are for their salvation; in the same
> sense as the instruction, counsels, warnings and invitations that are given
> them, are for their salvation.[53]

From these quotations of Baxter, Bunyan, and Edwards, one can see they clearly did not hold to limited atonement in the Owenic sense of the term.

The historical evidence on the extent of the atonement can be summarized in four statements. First, nearly all[54] of the earliest reformers, including Calvin,[55] held a form of universal atonement. Second, limited atonement as a doctrinal position of Calvinists developed in the second and third generations of reformers, beginning primarily with Beza. Third, the Synod of Dort debated the issue extensively, and the final language of Dort was deliberately left ambiguous on the subject so as to allow those among the delegates who rejected strict particularism and held a form of universal atonement to sign the final document. Fourth, the Westminster Assembly consisted of a minority of delegates who rejected limited atonement (strict particularism) and affirmed a form of universalism, as did several of the Puritans in the seventeenth and eighteenth centuries, including Jonathan Edwards.

The controversy that occurred within the second and third generations of Reformed theologians did not involve the *rejection* of limited atonement but the *introduction* of limited atonement. In fact, chronologically, after the introduction of limited atonement, Calvinism slowly began to open the door to the rejection of the free gospel offer.[56] When the free offer was finally and explicitly rejected, hyper-Calvinism was born.[57]

---

[53] J. Edwards [1743], *Works of Jonathan Edwards Online*, vol. 27, *"Controversies" Notebook* (Jonathan Edwards Center at Yale University, 2008), part III.

[54] There is still some question about the views of Martin Bucer.

[55] D. Ponter hosts the Web site www.CalvinandCalvinism.com (see the index page), which contains the largest collection of quotations in print from John Calvin's works on the subject of the extent of the atonement. By carefully posting them in context, Ponter has proven beyond a reasonable doubt that John Calvin himself did not hold to limited atonement (strict particularism).

[56] In fact, there were already some extreme delegates to the Synod of Dort from Gelderland and Friesland who rejected indiscriminate gospel offers. See Godfrey, *Tensions*, 210; and Thomas, *Extent of the Atonement*, 149.

[57] See Daniel, "Hyper-Calvinism and John Gill," 514. It is not as though hyper-Calvinists were against preaching to all (contrary to popular opinion). Rather, they were against the idea that God is "offering" Christ to all and that preachers should indiscriminately do the same (Daniel, *Hyper-Calvinism and John*

Why talk about history and quote so many men? Truth cannot be determined by counting noses. I disagree significantly with these men in other areas of their Calvinism, not to mention their views on baptism and ecclesiology; but these disagreements do not negate the truth and significance of what they, as influential historic Calvinists, are admitting and affirming on the subject of the *extent*[58] of the atonement. Much has been written on the extent of the atonement in recent years, and much of it relies on modern secondary sources. There is a great deal of ignorance about the views of the early church, the perspectives of the early Reformers, and the diverse opinions on the subject within the Puritan movement.[59] Generally speaking, modern Calvinists have only three categories: the Calvinist position (or five-point Calvinism), which they equate with strict particularism; Amyraldism, which is often filtered through unreliable secondary sources; and Arminianism. This classification is far too simplistic.[60]

Attention will now focus on the biblical data. Ultimately, the question of the extent of the atonement must be settled by appeal to Scripture. Exegesis must precede systematic theology as well as historical theology.

Exegetical Considerations

Three key sets of texts in the New Testament affirm unlimited atonement: the "all" texts, the "world" texts, and the "many" texts. Other texts state Jesus died for His "church," His "sheep," and His "friends." How are we to reconcile these two sets of texts? The high-Calvinist interprets the universal texts in light of the limited texts. Non-Calvinists and moderate-Calvinists interpret the limited texts as a subset of the universal texts.

Some Calvinists argue that biblical authors such as John or Paul believed in limited atonement because they made statements affirming

---

Gill, 448–49; and I. Murray, *Spurgeon v. Hyper-Calvinism: The Battle for Gospel Preaching* [Carlisle, PA: Banner of Truth Trust, 2000], 89).

[58] Note that the extent of the atonement here is to be distinguished from what Calvinists say about Christ's intent in the atonement and the nature of its application.

[59] Few know about the views of John Howe and Stephen Charnock, for example. They both held to a Calvinistic form of universal redemption.

[60] Regarding the first and second categories, Muller has observed that the Ursinus, Bullinger, Musculus, Davenant, Ussher, and Preston trajectory is distinct from the Saumur model, even though all of them held to a form of "hypothetical universalism" (see R. Muller, review of *English Hypothetical Universalism: John Preston and the Softening of Reformed Theology*, by J. Moore, *Calvin Theological Journal* 43 [2008], 149–50). Further, in his *Post-Reformation Reformed Dogmatics*, 1:76–80, Muller states that the Amyraldian view is compatible with Dort and the Westminster Confession. According to Muller, then, there are *at least three* branches *within* the Calvinistic position, and the current discussions surrounding the extent of the atonement rarely recognize this fact.

Christ died for the Church, even though biblical writers do not say that Christ died *only* for the Church or that He did not die for the non-elect. Calvinists usually exegete the relevant portions of Scripture in that manner. For example, John Owen denied the death of Jesus has any reference to the non-elect. According to Owen, the death of Christ is in absolutely no sense for them and is in no sense an expression of God's love to them.[61] When Owen said the use of the word *kosmos* in John 3:16–17 must designate "they whom he intended to save, and none else, or he faileth of his purpose,"[62] it is clear his theology precedes and determines his exegesis. His argument proceeds in this fashion: since "world" is used elsewhere in senses other than "all humanity," it cannot be used in that sense in John 3:16. He also argued the same for the use of the word "all." Since "all" sometimes means "all of some sorts" or "some of all sorts," it can never mean, according to Owen, that all humanity includes each and every person. The logical fallacy of such an approach is evident.

Owen asserted that "we deny that by a supply of the word *elect* into the text any absurdity or untruth will justly follow. . . . So that the sense is, 'God so loved his elect throughout the world, that he gave his Son with this intention, that by him believers might be saved.' "[63] I submit that this does, indeed, inject both absurdity and untruth! For Owen, "world" in John 3:16–17 cannot mean each and every person because by his preconceived theology only the elect are "loved" in this way (note the circular argument here). Owen read his conclusion into his reasons for the conclusion and preempts any alternative, as Neil Chambers has noted in his thesis on Owen.[64] Owen continued his argument that the use of "world" in John 3:17 is a statement of God's intention and hence must refer only to the elect. The same is true of 3:16. Again, Owen read his conclusion into his reasons to prove his conclusion. If Owen is correct that "world" means "elect," when John 3:16 says "whosoever believes shall not perish," the possibility is left open that some of the elect might perish. For Owen, the atonement is only actually sufficient for those for whom it is efficient.

---

[61] J. Owen, *The Death of Death in the Death of Christ*, in *The Works of John Owen* (ed. W. H. Goold; Edinburgh: Banner of Truth Trust, 1993), 10:219. "The fountain and cause of God's sending Christ is his eternal love to his elect, and to them alone." (Owen, *Death of Death*, 231. See also 324.)

[62] Ibid., 306.

[63] Ibid., 326.

[64] N. Chambers, "A Critical Examination of John Owen's Argument for Limited Atonement in 'The Death of Death in the Death of Christ'" (master's thesis, Reformed Theological Seminary, 1998), 122. This thesis can be obtained at www.Tren.com.

Owen's arguments are not linguistic or exegetical but *a priori* theological arguments. He has committed the fallacy of begging the question.

With respect to the use of *kosmos* in the Gospel of John, Carson pointed out the word characteristically means human beings in rebellion against God.[65] In John's prologue *kosmos* means apostate humanity in rebellion against God. In John 1:29, the sins of the "world" are what must be atoned for.[66] In 3:16, the world is spoken of as being loved and condemned, and then some are saved out of it. The latter two outcomes occur because of either belief or unbelief according to 3:18. John 3:19 is consistent with 3:18.

No linguistic, exegetical, or theological grounds exist for reducing the meaning of "world" to "the elect." In fact, in John 17:6, the elect are defined over against the world. Owen made John 3:16 read, "God so loved those he chose out of the world," which changes the sense of the verse into the opposite of its intended meaning. To make the meaning of "world" here "the elect" is to commit a logical and linguistic mistake of confusing categories.[67]

Calvinists who follow Owen on John 3:16 distort John's purpose and thus sever "one's own participation in the continuation of the task of Jesus to save the world in the mission of the apostles from a conviction of love for the lost per se, a conviction grounded in God's love for them."[68] This distortion has immense repercussions for evangelism and preaching! When Letham says, concerning God's intent in the atonement in John 3:16: "neither the term 'world' nor the passage as a whole is reflecting on the question before us," he is dead wrong.[69] Dabney, a moderate-Calvinist, displays the right view when he said, "There is, perhaps, no Scripture which gives

[65] D. A. Carson, *The Gospel According to John* (Leicester, England: InterVarsity/Grand Rapids: Eerdmans, 1991), 123.

[66] In one instance where Charnock cites this text, he references Amyraut's understanding of it (S. Charnock, "A Discourse of Christ Our Passover," in *The Works of Stephen Charnock* [Carlisle, PA: Banner of Truth, 1985], 4:507).

[67] See the excellent discussion in Chambers' "Critical Examination," 116–25. See also E. Hulse, "John 3:16 and Hyper-Calvinism," *Reformation Today* 135 (September/October 1993): 30: "We note well that John 3:16 does not say, for God so loved *the elect*. The Holy Spirit did not write the text that way. Are we to understand that 'the world' here means both Jews and Gentiles? The word 'world' must be interpreted in the way it is used throughout the Gospel, namely, all people without exception not all people without distinction."

[68] Chambers, "Critical Examination," 153–54. See also Turretin's abortive attempt to make "world" in John 3:16 mean "the elect" (F. Turretin, *Institutes of Elenctic Theology* [Phillipsburg, NJ: P&R, 1992], 1:405–8).

[69] R. Letham, *The Work of Christ: Contours of Christian Theology* (Downer's Grove, IL: InterVarsity, 1993), 241.

so thorough and comprehensive an explanation of the design and results of Christ's sacrifice, as John 3:16–19."[70]

In his comments on John 3:16 in *Indiscriminate Proposals of Mercy*, Dabney said that, according to high-Calvinists, when "God so loved the world that he gave his only-begotten Son," "the world" must mean only "the elect." Dabney finds several problems with this inference. If "the world" in v. 16 means "the elect," then the clear implication is that some of the elect may fail to believe and thus perish.[71] To be consistent, we must carry the same sense of the word "world" throughout the passage. In v. 19, "the world," into which the light has come, receives condemnation, and thus cannot be a reference to the elect but must be taken in the wider sense of humanity. The logical connection between v. 17 and v. 18 shows that "the world" of v. 17 is inclusive of "him that believes" eventually and "him that believes not" of v. 18. If the offer of Christ's sacrifice is in no sense a genuine offer of salvation to that part of the world which "believes not," it is difficult to see how their choosing to reject the offer can become the just ground of their condemnation as is expressly stated in v. 19. Dabney poses this question: "Are gospel-rejectors finally condemned for this, that they were so unfortunately perspicacious as not to be affected by a fictitious and unreal manifestation? [something that was never offered for them in the first place?] It is noticeable that Calvin is too sagacious an expositor to commit himself to this kind of extreme exegesis."[72]

Dabney asks, "How shall we escape from this *dilemma?*" Looking at the high-Calvinist interpretation, "if it were a question of the decree of salvation for the elect only, from which every logical mind is compelled to draw the doctrine of particular redemption, the argument would be impregnable." Yet as Dabney pointed out, this approach would make Jesus contradict his own exposition of his statement. The solution, then, must be in a different direction. The phrase "so loved the world" was not designed to refer to the decree of election but to an offer based on love that stops short of the purpose or decree of God to save. Christ's death on the cross as proclaimed in the gospel is a sincere offer of salvation to all sinners. Dabney correctly noted that those who will not believe (the non-elect) will perish notwithstanding the offer of salvation to them. When the death of Christ becomes the occasion

---

[70] R. Dabney, *Lectures in Systematic Theology* (Carlisle, PA: Banner of Truth, 2002), 535.

[71] R. Dabney also makes this argument in his *Lectures in Systematic Theology*, 525.

[72] R. Dabney, *God's Indiscriminate Proposals of Mercy, as Related to His Power, Wisdom and Sincerity*, in *Discussions of Robert Louis Dabney* (Edinburgh: Banner of Truth, 1967 [1982]), 1:312–13.

(not cause) of deeper condemnation to those who refuse to believe, it is only because these voluntarily reject God's offer of salvation in Christ.[73]

J. C. Ryle concurred and said with respect to John 3:16:

> I am quite familiar with the objections commonly brought against the theory I have just propounded. I find no weight in them, and am not careful to answer them. Those who confine God's love exclusively to the elect appear to me to take a narrow and contracted view of God's character and attributes. They refuse to God that attribute of compassion with which even an earthly father can regard a profligate son, and can offer to him pardon, even though his compassion is despised and his offers refused. I have long come to the conclusion that men may be more systematic in their statements than the Bible, and may be led into grave error by idolatrous veneration of a system.[74]

Furthermore, Ryle remarked as he spoke on the subject of election: "We know not who are God's Elect, and whom he means to call and convert. Our duty is to invite all. To every unconverted soul without exception, we ought to say, 'God loves you, and Christ has died for you.' "[75]

In his commentary on John 3:16, Calvin said:

> And He has used a general term, both to invite indiscriminately all to share in life and to cut off every excuse from unbelievers. Such is also the significance of the term "world" which he had used before. . . . He nevertheless shows He is favourable to the whole world when He calls all *without exception* to the faith of Christ, which is indeed an entry into life.[76]

Christ offered Himself as a sacrifice for the salvation of the "whole world" and therefore invites all "indiscriminately" to share in God's favor. In commenting on John 3:16, Calvin equates "world" with the terms "indiscriminately all" and "all without exception." Note carefully how Calvin contrasts the few who believe with the rest of the world; he does not say "all who believe," as is common among Calvinist writers on this verse, but "all without exception." Some may think that Calvin and others taught that Christ *only* suffered for the sins of the elect because they interpret the "world" in 1 John 2:2 as limited to the church, following Augustine.

---

[73] Ibid., 1:312–13.

[74] J. C. Ryle, *Expository Thoughts on the Gospels* (Grand Rapids: Baker, 1979), 3:157.

[75] J. C. Ryle, *Old Paths* (Edinburgh: Banner of Truth, 1999), 479.

[76] J. Calvin, *The Gospel According to St. John 1–10* (ed. D. W. Torrance and T. F. Torrance; trans. T. H. L. Parker, new edition, in Calvin's New Testament Commentaries; Grand Rapids: Eerdmans/Carlisle: Paternoster, 1995), 74.

However, Jerome Zanchi and Jacob Kimedoncius interpret the passage the same way, and yet Richard Muller acknowledges that these two men held a form of universal redemption, just like Heinrich Bullinger (who took an unlimited reading of 1 John 2:2). While there may be agreement *in principle* among classical Calvinists on universal redemption, there may be *practical* differences in terms of their exegesis of certain specific passages.

The strength of any theological position is only as great as the exegetical basis upon which it is built. Limited atonement (strict particularism) is built on a faulty exegetical foundation. Those who affirm limited atonement usually affirm God's love for all humanity and God's desire to save all humanity (in His revealed will, though not in His secret will). However, they deny that Jesus died for the sins of all humanity. Any teaching that says God does not love all humanity,[77] God has no intent or desire to save all humanity, or Jesus did not die for the sins of all humanity, is contrary to Scripture and should be rejected.[78]

Theological Considerations

Probably the key theological argument to support limited atonement is the double payment argument, famously propounded by Owen,[79] which basically says that justice does not allow the same sin to be punished twice. This argument faces several problems. First, it is not found in Scripture. Second, it confuses a pecuniary (commercial) debt and penal satisfaction for sin. Third, the elect are still under the wrath of God until they believe (Eph 2:4). Fourth, it negates the principle of grace in the application of the atonement—nobody is *owed* the application.

---

[77] For an excellent article on John 3:16 and hyper-Calvinism, see E. Hulse, "John 3:16 and Hyper-Calvinism," 27–30. Hulse's opening sentences are instructive: "By selective use of the Reformed Confessions it is possible to claim to be reformed but at the same time hide the fact that you are a hyper-Calvinist. The hyper-Calvinist denies that God loves all mankind and that the gospel is good news to be declared to all without exception" (27).

[78] Space does not permit an examination of the many texts affirming universal atonement. One key text is 1 John 2:2. In this verse, based on the 23 uses of the word in 1 John, "world" cannot mean "the elect" or "non-Jewish believers," as is usually asserted by Calvinists. Dabney said: "It is indisputable, that the Apostle extends the propitiation of Christ beyond those whom he speaks of as 'we,' in the first verse. . . . It would seem then, that the Apostle's scope is, to console and encourage sinning believers with the thought, that since Christ made expiation for every man, there is no danger that he will not be found a propitiation for them who, having already believed, now sincerely turn to him from recent sins" (Dabney, *Lectures in Systematic Theology*, 535). Those who hold to limited atonement err because they try to make indefinite and universal terms to be definite and group specific. For a balanced treatment of 1 John 2:2 that comes down on the side of universal atonement, see D. Akin, *1, 2, 3 John* (NAC; ed. R. Clendenen; Nashville: B&H, 2001), 84–86.

[79] See his *The Death of Death in the Death of Christ*, 173–74.

Several prominent Calvinists did not employ the Double Payment Argument. Zacharius Ursinus, in his commentary on the Heidelberg Catechism, said:

> Objection. 2. All those ought to be received into favor for whose offences a sufficient satisfaction has been made. Christ has made a sufficient satisfaction for the offences of all men. Therefore all ought to be received into favor; and if this is not done, God is unjust to men.
>
> Answer. The major is true, unless some condition is added to the satisfaction; as, that only those are saved through it, who apply it unto themselves by faith. But this condition is expressly added, where it is said, "God so loved the world that he gave his only begotten Son, that whosoever believeth in him should not perish, but have everlasting life." (John 3:16).[80]

John Davenant, signatory of the Canons of Dort, also wrote criticizing the double payment argument:

> I answer, That this would indeed be most unjust, if we ourselves had paid this price to God, or if our Surety, Jesus Christ, had so offered to God his blood as a satisfactory price, that without any other intervening condition, all men should be immediately absolved through the offering of the oblation made by him; or, finally, if God himself had covenanted with Christ when he died, that he would give faith to every individual, and all those other things which regard the infallible application of this sacrifice which was offered up for the human race. But since God himself of his own accord provided that this price should be paid to himself, it was in his own power to annex conditions, which being performed, this death should be advantageous to any man, not being performed it should not profit any man. Therefore no injustice is done to those persons who are punished by God after the ransom was accepted for the sins of the human race, because they offered nothing to God as a satisfaction for their sins, nor performed that condition, without the performance of which God willed not that this satisfactory price should benefit any individual. Nor, moreover, ought this to be thought an injustice to Christ the Mediator. For he so was willing to die for all, and to pay to the Father the price of redemption for all, that at the same time he willed not that every individual in any way whatsoever, but that all, as soon as they believed in him, should be absolved from the guilt of their sins.

---

[80] Z. Ursinus, *The Commentary of Dr. Zacharias Ursinus on the Heidelberg Catechism*, 107.

We will illustrate all these things by a similitude; Suppose that a number of men were cast into prison by a certain King on account of a great debt, or that they were condemned to suffer death for high treason; but that the King himself procured that his own Son should discharge this debt to the last farthing; or should substitute himself as guilty in the room of those traitors, and should suffer the punishment due to them all, this condition being at the same time promulgated both by the King and his Son, That none should be absolved or liberated except those only who should acknowledge the King's Son for their Lord and serve him: These things being so determined, I enquire, if those who persist in disobedience and rebellion against the King's Son should not be delivered, would any charge of injustice be incurred, because after this ransom had been paid, their own debts should be exacted from many, or after the punishment endured by the Son, these rebels should nevertheless be punished? By no means; because the payment of the just price, and the enduring of the punishment was ordained to procure remission for every one under the condition of obedience, and not otherwise.[81]

Other Calvinists have been critical of the double payment argument, including Edward Polhill, R. L. Dabney, A. A. Hodge, Charles Hodge, W. G. T. Shedd, and Curt Daniel.[82] Though Christ died sufficiently for all people, the promise of deliverance is conditional. One must repent and believe in order to benefit unto salvation. The gospel not only *sincerely promises* life to the unbelieving elect and unbelieving non-elect on the condition of faith, but it also *sincerely threatens* them both with hell if they do not believe, despite the fact that Christ suffered sufficiently for their sins.[83] The double payment argument entails that the non-elect cannot, with any consistency, receive genuine offers of salvation by God through the preaching of the gospel. It also entails that the unbelieving elect (those who will be saved but are yet unsaved) are not receiving sincere threats from God by means of the preaching of the gospel. God would be making counterfeit

---

[81] J. Davenant may have been the first to use this illustration (*A Dissertation on the Death of Christ*, 376–77).

[82] E. Polhill, "The Divine Will: Considered in Its Eternal Decrees," *Works*, 7.4.3, Objection 4, 168–69; R. L. Dabney, *Lectures in Systematic Theology*, 521; A. A. Hodge, *The Atonement* (Philadelphia: Presbyterian Board of Publication, 1867), 35–37; C. Hodge, *Systematic Theology*, 2:557–58; W. G. T. Shedd, *Dogmatic Theology* (Nashville: Thomas Nelson, 1980), 2:443; and C. Daniel, *The History and Theology of Calvinism* (Springfield: Good Books, 2003), 371.

[83] As Lazarus Seaman said, "All in the first Adam were made liable to damnation, so all liable to salvation in the second Adam. . . . It comes only to this: look as every man was *damnabilis* . . . so is every man *salvabilis*." Mitchell and Struthers, *Minutes*, 154.

offers to the non-elect (they cannot be saved anyway according to strict Calvinism), and God would be making counterfeit threats of perishing to the unbelieving elect since there is no longer any legal grounds for their remaining under condemnation. Their "debt" is literally paid,[84] including their unbelief. They now have a *right* to be saved.

Another argument in favor of limited atonement is the triple choice argument of John Owen. This argument was built on the double payment argument. Owen's famous "Treble Choice" argument claims that Christ died for all the sins of all men, or all the sins of some men, or some of the sins of all men. He then argued that if Christ's death for all men's sins were correct, then why are not all men saved? Also, if Christ's death for some of all men's sins were correct, then no man will be saved, for there would remain some sins still on the books. Hence, only that Christ died for all the sins of only the elect can be true.[85] This argument sounds like impeccable logic, but it is flawed on several levels. First, Scripture never says that a man goes to hell because no atonement was provided for him. Rather, some men perish, and their punishment is compounded because they rejected the atonement made for them. Second, some men are said to perish because they did not believe when they heard the gospel. Third, Christ died for all men, but He does not apply salvation to all men. The limitation was not in the provision of His death, but in the application.[86] Fourth, the argument quantifies the imputation of sin to Christ, as if there is a commercial ratio between all the sins of those He represents and the one indivisible and infinitely meritorious divine sacrifice.

Alan Clifford took Owen to task over the triple choice argument with some additional objections. He cited Owen's argument that if one follows the thinking of universal atonement, what is one to do with unbelief? According to Owen, if unbelief is not a sin, how can people be punished for it? If it is a sin, then Christ either underwent punishment for it, or

---

[84] For some criticism of the literal notion of debt regarding the atonement, see R. Wardlaw's *Discourses on the Nature and Extent of the Atonement of Christ* (Glasgow: James Maclehose, 1844), 58–59. Andrew Fuller said: "If the atonement of Christ were considered as the literal payment of a debt—if the measure of his sufferings were according to the number of those for whom he died, and to the degree of their guilt, in such a manner as that if more had been saved, or if those who are saved had been more guilty, his sorrows must have been proportionately increased—it might, for aught I know, be inconsistent with indefinite invitations. But it would be equally inconsistent with the free *forgiveness* of sin, and with sinners being directed to reply for mercy as *supplicants*, rather than as claimants" (*The Gospel Worthy of All Acceptation*, in *Works*, 2:373).

[85] J. Owen, *The Death of Death*, 173–74.

[86] Calvinists also see some limitation in Christ's *purpose* in dying that corresponds to their view of election.

He did not. If He did, then how can unbelief hinder them any more than their other sins for which Christ died? If Christ did not die for the sin of unbelief, then He did not die for all sins. Clifford responds: "For all its apparent cogency, this compelling argument raises some important problems. It is clear that unbelievers are guilty of rejecting nothing if Christ was not given for them; unbelief surely involves the rejection of a definite provision of grace. It also makes nonsense of the means of grace, depriving general exhortations to believe of all significance."[87]

Clifford continues his logical assault on Owen's position by noting that, in Owen's view, the cross not only deals with the guilt of the believer's preconversion unbelief, it is also causally related to the *removal* of that unbelief. But what of the problem of Christians who continue to be plagued with unbelief in their Christian life? For Clifford, Owen's argument applies as much to supposed believers as it does to unbelievers. The consequences are problematic,

> for if partial unbelief in a Christian hinders him from enjoying the fullness of those blessings Christ has died to purchase for him, this is no different in principle from saying that total unbelief in a non-Christian hinders him from "partaking of the fruit" Christ's death makes available for him too. . . . Unlike Owen, the Reformers had little difficulty in establishing the basis of human guilt. While guilt is undoubtedly defined in terms of transgressing the law, a very significant component of it arises from ungrateful neglect of the gospel remedy. But on Owen's account, if the atonement relates only to the sins of the elect, then it is doubtful justice to condemn anyone for rejecting what was never applicable to them.[88]

Clifford went on to point out that Owen's

> acceptance of the "free offer" of the gospel is embarrassed by his strict commercialist position. He does indeed assert that the gospel is to be preached to "every creature" because "the way of salvation which it declares is wide enough for all to walk in." But how can this be if the atonement is really only sufficient for the elect? Calvin and his colleagues had no difficulty in speaking like this, but Owen cannot consistently do so. Not surprisingly, Gill and his fellow hypercalvinists

---

[87] A. Clifford, *Atonement and Justification: English Evangelical Theology 1640–1790: An Evaluation* (Oxford: Clarendon Press, 1990), 111–12.

[88] Ibid.

employed the very kind of commercialism espoused by Owen, but did so to deny the validity of universal offers of grace.[89]

Finally, Chambers offered this salient critique of Owen's position:

> What needs to be seen is that Owen's argument defeats itself by proving too much. If, in Owen's terms, Christ died for all the sins of some people, the elect, then he must also have died for their unbelief, where "died for" is understood to mean having paid the penalty for all their sins at Calvary. If this is the case, then why are the elect not saved at Calvary? If Owen replies that it is because the benefits of Christ's death are not yet applied to them, then I would ask what it means for those benefits not to be applied to them? Surely it means that they are unbelieving, and therefore cannot be spoken of as saved. But they cannot be punished for that unbelief, as its penalty has been paid and God, as Owen assures us, will not exact a second penalty for the one offense. If then, even in their unbelief, there is no debt against them, no penalty to be paid, surely they can be described as saved, and saved at Calvary. That being the case, the gospel is reduced to nothing more than a matter of informing the saved of their saved condition.
>
> These last two conclusions are positions that Owen would deny, for he is committed to the necessity and integrity of the universal gospel call and the indissoluble bond between faith and salvation. There is then a real tension in Owen's position brought about by a number of factors. The first is what might be called polemical reductionism in his consideration of "unbelief" here, for unbelief is not just an offense like any other, it is also a state, which must be dealt with not only by forgiveness but by regeneration. Owen recognizes this in relating the cross to the causal removal of unbelief as a state, but unbelief regarded as a sin and unbelief as a state bear a different relation to the cross. Sin bears a direct relation to the cross, which is the enduring of the penalty for sin; the change of state an indirect relation, dependent upon preaching and regeneration by the Spirit. To acknowledge that reality Owen would have to say that Christ died for all the sin, including the unbelief, of those who believe, and for none of the sins of those who won't believe.[90]

---

[89] Ibid., 112–13. Edmund Calamy also perceived the necessary connection between *offerability* and *salvability*. He said, "It cannot be offered to Judas except he be salvable." See Mitchell and Struthers, *Minutes*, 154.

[90] Chambers, "Critical Examination of John Owen's Argument for Limited Atonement," 235–36. Chambers's thesis is a devastating critique of Owen on the notion of the double payment argument. See especially 241–93. Note the thesis was done at Reformed Theological Seminary. Chambers himself is a Calvinist, and one of the thesis readers who approved it was Ligon Duncan.

John Owen falsely understood redemption to involve literal payment to God so that the atonement itself secures its own application. This model is the controlling one in his book *The Death of Death in the Death of Christ*. He has distorted and thus contradicted Scripture in his effort to defend a strictly limited atonement.

In drawing this section on theological considerations to a close, let us juxtapose comments by D. A. Carson and John Calvin. Carson wrote:

> I argue, then, that both Arminians and Calvinists should rightly affirm
> that Christ died for all, *in* the sense that Christ's death was sufficient
> for all and that Scripture portrays God as inviting, commanding,
> and desiring the salvation of all, *out of love.* . . . Further, all Christians
> ought also to confess that, in a slightly different sense, Christ Jesus, in
> the intent of God, died effectively for the elect alone, *in line with the*
> *way the Bible speaks of God's special selecting love for the elect.* . . . This
> approach, I contend, must surely come as a relief to young preachers
> in the Reformed tradition who hunger to preach the Gospel effectively
> but who do not know how far they can go in saying things such as
> "God loves you" to unbelievers. When I have preached or lectured in
> Reformed circles, I have often been asked the question, "Do you feel
> free to tell unbelievers that God loves them? . . . From what I have
> already said, it is obvious that I have no hesitation in answering this
> question from young Reformed preachers affirmatively: *Of course* I tell
> the unconverted God loves them.[91]

This quote from Carson is telling for many reasons. Notice he states that Christ's death "for all" is "in the sense that Christ's death was *suffi-cient* for all." Here Carson's meaning is dependent upon his usage of the word "sufficient." Upon first blush, one might assume that Carson believes Christ's death satisfied the sins of every human being. In this case, he would be using the word "sufficient" to mean "extrinsic sufficiency," or in the classic sense. That Carson also says "Arminians" should rightly affirm this fact bolsters this possible reading. Arminians would, indeed, affirm it in the sense of an unlimited imputation of sin to Christ. But note Carson says "both Arminians *and* Calvinists should rightly affirm" it. No high-Calvinist would ever affirm "extrinsic sufficiency" because they believe the death of Christ only satisfied the sins of the elect. Thus, by his use of the term "sufficient," Carson may mean "intrinsic sufficiency." All Calvinists

---

[91] D. A. Carson, *The Difficult Doctrine of the Love of God* (Wheaton: Crossway Books, 2000), 77–78.

and non-Calvinists can affirm the statement "Christ's death was sufficient for all," where "sufficient" is understood to mean Christ's infinite dignity and where the value of His death is capable of satisfying the sins of all unbelievers. The problem is that moderate-Calvinists and all non-Calvinists understand the term *sufficient* to mean not only that Christ's death *could have* satisfied the sins of all unbelievers had that been God's intention but that His death in fact *did* satisfy the sins of all humanity. Carson probably rejects, along with all high-Calvinists, this meaning of sufficiency. For them Christ's death was *intended* only for the elect, and that intention also limits the imputation of sin to Christ (or the *extent* of His sufferings as well). Carson's intended meaning here is ambiguous since his statement can have a number of different interpretations,[92] and his ambiguity may be deliberate.

Moreover, do Carson's words "effectively" and "alone" mean that "Christ's death only results in the salvation of the elect"? If so, then no moderate-Calvinist or non-Calvinist would disagree with the statement. Everyone agrees that the atonement applies only to the elect. This reading is potentially bolstered by Carson's argument that "all Christians" (which includes non-Calvinists) should be able to affirm this statement. However, if this interpretation is his meaning, it is something of a tautology. Carson's words could be read as meaning that Jesus died especially for the elect *alone*, where "alone" is explained in the immediately following clause: "*in line with the way the Bible speaks of God's special love for the elect.*" On this interpretation the death of Jesus had a dualistic design: Christ died in one sense for the sins of all people but in a special sense for the elect alone. Here again Carson is correct that all Christians can affirm this claim when the following implicit assumptions in his statements are made explicit. First, by his statement that Jesus "died for the elect alone" in line with "God's special selecting love for the elect," Carson means that the nature of the love God has for the elect differs from that which He has for the non-elect. This difference becomes exhibited in God's "selection" of the elect to be the recipients of Christ's atoning death *in a way that is not true for the non-elect*. That is, God's love for His children must in some way differ from His love for those who are not His children. Second, Christ's death for the non-elect brings them common grace. Assuming one leaves the meaning

---

[92] Carson has read G. Michael Thomas's work on *The Extent of the Atonement*, so he should be familiar with these significant historical differences. Carson, *The Difficult Doctrine*, 88n4. Or see D. A. Carson, "God's Love and God's Wrath," *Bibliotheca Sacra* 156 (October-December 1999): 394.

of "select" ambiguous, all non-Calvinists can affirm these statements *in so far as they go*. For moderate-Calvinists and non-Calvinists, however, his statements do not go far enough since Carson does not specify for whose sins Christ suffered.

The following interpretation of Carson's words is also possible. If he means to say that Christ actually died for the sins of the elect *only* and not for the sins of the non-elect, then logically Christ's death cannot be "sufficient" for the non-elect so that it is able to be applied to them. This limited sin-bearing is the position of all high-Calvinists, and it is the crux of limited atonement (strict particularism).[93] Notice he encourages young Reformed preachers to tell "unbelievers" that God loves them, but he is silent on the subject of telling *unbelievers* that Christ *died for them* in the sense that His death satisfied the penalty for their sins. His theology may prohibit it. If this interpretation is Carson's intended meaning, then his statement that "all Christians" should be able to affirm this interpretation is erroneous. No moderate-Calvinist or non-Calvinist believes that the death of Christ provided *only* common grace benefits for the non-elect.

The second interpretation may be Carson's intended meaning. But if so, he is leaving much too much to be read between the lines. Did Jesus' death on the cross satisfy for the sins of all humanity? Carson's paragraph ultimately does not answer the question in any explicit way, but if he actually sides with high-Calvinism, Carson must answer "no." With respect to the intent and extent of the atonement, high-Calvinists believe the following: God loves all people (but not equally), God desires the salvation of all people, but Jesus only satisfied the sins of the elect and none others. Moderate-Calvinists and all non-Calvinists believe the following: God loves all people, God desires the salvation of all people, and Christ died for all people in the sense that His death satisfied for the sins of all people.[94]

Now listen to John Calvin on John 3:16:

> And indeed our Lord Jesus was *offered to all the world*. For it is not speaking of three or four when it says: "God so loved the world, that He spared not His only Son." But yet we must notice what the Evangelist

---

[93] In Dever's audio interviews with Carson, posted on Dever's Nine Marks Web site, it is clear that Dever (a high-Calvinist) thinks Carson agrees with his limited imputation views. Dever attempts to pit Carson against Bruce Ware, professor at Southern Baptist Theological Seminary in Louisville and a moderate-Calvinist. See http://media.9marks.org/2009/02/25/on-books-with-d-a-carson.

[94] The moderate-Calvinists, however, argue that God's love for all is unequal, His saving desire is unequal, and, therefore, Christ's *intention* in dying for the sins of all was also unequal.

adds in this passage: "That whosoever believes in Him shall not perish but obtain eternal life." Our Lord Jesus *suffered for all*[95] and there is neither great nor small who is not inexcusable today, for we can obtain salvation in Him.[96] Unbelievers who turn away from Him and who deprive themselves of Him by their malice are today *doubly culpable*, for how will they excuse their ingratitude in not receiving the blessing in which they could share by faith.[97]

First, Calvin asserts that Jesus was "offered" to all the world. Non-Calvinists, moderate-Calvinists, and high-Calvinists all agree that God has a "universal saving will"[98] in that He desires the salvation of all people in His revealed will. But this salvation of all people is not all that Calvin affirms. Notice that he also said Jesus "suffered for all." The word "all" here cannot mean the elect only since the quotation of John 3:16 flanks it with the word "whosoever" and the statement that no one is inexcusable ("for we can obtain salvation in Him"), and is followed by the statement that "unbelievers who turn away from Him . . . are doubly culpable" and fail to receive "the blessing in which they could share by faith." Here Calvin clearly equates the "all" with "all unbelievers" and says explicitly "Jesus suffered for all." Because of these clear statements, those who reject Christ are "doubly culpable." Why? They are rejecting the death of Christ on their behalf, which could provide them salvation if they were to believe. Unlike Carson, Calvin has no qualms *explicitly* stating that "Jesus suffered for all." Calvin does not employ the famous double payment argument as do high-Calvinists since Owen, asserting instead that unbelievers are "doubly culpable" for their rejection of this "blessing" made available in Christ "in which they could share by faith." Calvin never used the double payment argument because he did not believe Scripture taught a limitation in the sin-bearing or the extent of Christ's death.

---

[95] "Suffered for all" is an unlimited sin-bearing.

[96] His death is actually *applicable* to all men since He "suffered for all" men.

[97] J. Calvin, *Sermons on Isaiah's Prophecy of the Death and Passion of Christ* (London: James Clark, [1559] 1956), 141 (emphasis added).

[98] This expression is found three times in J. Piper's "Are There Two Wills in God?," in *Still Sovereign* (ed. T. R. Schreiner and B. Ware; Grand Rapids: Baker, 2000), 107, 108, 122; and also in Daniel's *The History and Theology of Calvinism*, 208. B. Ware also uses it affirmatively in "Divine Election to Salvation: Unconditional, Individual, and Infralapsarian," in *Perspectives on Election: Five Views* (ed. C. Brand; Nashville: B&H, 2006), 32.

Logical Considerations

Logically, one argument for a strictly limited atonement goes like this: Christ died "for His sheep," for "His Church," and for "His friends." These categories of people are limited; thus, this argument is proof of limited atonement. Not so fast! Dabney correctly noted that statements such as Christ died for "the church" or "His sheep" do not prove a strictly limited atonement because to argue such invokes the negative inference fallacy: "the proof of a proposition does not disprove its converse."[99] One cannot infer a negative (Christ did *not* die for group A) from a bare positive statement (Christ did die for group B), any more than one can infer that Christ *only* died for Paul because Gal 2:20 says that Christ died for Paul. Additionally, if I frequently repeat that I love my wife, it may be, hypothetically speaking, that I *only* love my wife, but it does not follow with deductive certainty. This is the same kind of logical mistake that Owen makes numerous times in his *The Death of Death in the Death of Christ*, and it is a logical fallacy constantly made by high-Calvinists with regard to the extent of the atonement.[100] Consequently, the fact that many verses speak of Christ dying for His "sheep," His "church" or "His friends" does not prove that He did not die for others not subsumed in these categories.

There is no statement in Scripture that says Jesus died *only* for the sins of the elect. Those who hold to limited atonement commit the negative inference fallacy when they infer from certain restricted statements in Scripture concerning the death of Christ that He died only for the sins of those so mentioned. High-Calvinists fail to address adequately the many verses in the New Testament that affirm universal atonement.

---

[99] Dabney, *Lectures in Systematic Theology*, 521.

[100] Even R. Reymond, a supralapsarian hyper-Calvinist, noted: "It is true, of course, that logically a statement of particularity in itself does not necessarily preclude universality. This may be shown by the principle of subalternation in Aristotelian logic, which states that if all S is P, then it may be inferred that some S is P, but conversely, it cannot be inferred from the fact that some S is P that the remainder of S is not P. A case in point is the 'me' of Galatians 2:20: the fact that Christ died for Paul individually does not mean that Christ died only for Paul and for no one else" (R. Reymond, *A New Systematic Theology* [2nd ed.; Nashville: Thomas Nelson, 1998], 673–74).

Practical Considerations

We are now prepared to turn to issues of a practical nature. Adherence to limited atonement, if not careful, can negatively impact seven areas of practical theology.

1. The Problem of the Diminishing of God's Universal Saving Will

High-Calvinists have trouble defending God's universal saving will from the platform of limited atonement. The basic issue involves the question that if Christ did not die for the non-elect, how can this circumstance be reconciled with passages of Scripture such as John 17:21,23; 1 Tim 2:4; and 2 Pet 3:9,[101] which affirm that God desires the salvation of all people? Moderate-Calvinists and non-Calvinists have no trouble here since they affirm Christ did, indeed, die for the sins of all people, and hence God can make "the well-meant offer" to all. Note carefully the point here is not just *our* making the offer of salvation to all by means of our preaching but that *God Himself* makes the offer to all through us (2 Cor 5:20). How could He do so with integrity if Christ did not die for the sins of all people? Polhill wrote about this question:

> 1. I argue from the will of God. God's will of salvation as the fontal cause thereof, and Christ's death, as the meritorious cause thereof, are of equal latitude. God's will of salvation doth not extend beyond Christ's death, for then he should intend to save some *extra Christum*. Neither doth Christ's death extend beyond God's will of salvation, for then he should die for some whom God would upon no terms save; but these two are exactly co-extensive. Hence it is observable, that when the apostle speaks of Christ's love to the church, he speaks also of the giving himself for it, (Eph. v. 25), and when he saith God will have all men to be saved, (1 Tim. ii. 4), he saith withal, Christ gave himself a ransom for all, (v. 6). Therefore, there cannot be a truer measure of the extent of Christ's death, than God's will of salvation, out of which the same did issue; so far forth as that will of salvation extends to all men, so far forth the death of Christ doth extend to all men. Now then, how far doth God will the salvation of all? Surely thus far, that if they believe they shall be saved. No divine can deny it, especially seeing Christ himself hath laid it down so positively, "This is the will of him that sent me, saith he, that every one which seeth

---

[101] E. Hulse and R. Letham have dealt with the errors of the Owenic interpretation of 2 Pet 3:9 in "John Owen and 2 Peter 3:9," *Reformation Today* 38 (July–Aug., 1977): 37–38.

the Son and believeth on him may have everlasting life," (John vi. 40). Wherefore, if God will the salvation of all men thus far, that if they believe they shall be saved; then Christ died for all men thus far, that if they believe they shall be saved.[102]

Without belief in the universal saving will of God and a universal extent in Christ's sin-bearing, there can be no well-meant offer of the salvation *from God* to the non-elect who hear the gospel call. Central to hyper-Calvinism is its rejection of the doctrine that God desires the salvation of all men[103] and they have accused their high-Calvinist brothers of inconsistency and/or irrationality.[104] The rise of Calvinism in the evangelical

---

[102] E. Polhill, "The Divine Will Considered in Its Eternal Decrees," in *The Works of Edward Polhill*, 163–64.

[103] Both Curt Daniel and Iain Murray associate the denial of God's universal saving desire with hyper-Calvinism since it is *the* key point in the dispute regarding the free offer. C. Daniel, *The History and Theology of Calvinism*, 90; I. Murray, *Spurgeon v. Hyper-Calvinism: The Battle for Gospel Preaching* (Carlisle, PA: Banner of Truth Trust, 2000), 89. Murray summarizes his book as follows: "The book is intended to show the momentous difference between evangelistic Calvinistic belief and that form of Calvinism which denies any desire on the part of God for the salvation of all men" (I. Murray, "John Gill and C. H. Spurgeon," *Banner of Truth* 386 [Nov., 1995], 16). In Murray's correspondence with David Engelsma on the subject of the free offer, he wrote, "The critical issue here, of course, is not the mere use of the term 'offer,' but whether the offer of the gospel is an expression of God's desire that it should be received by sinners." See *Banner of Truth* 307 (December 1995): 24–25. In a review of David Silversides' book which defends *The Free Offer*, Murray says: "To side-line the question of desire will not, we think, blunt the hyper-Calvinist's claim that a free offer, expressive of love to all, attributes two wills to God—fulfilled in the case of the elect and unfulfilled in the case of all others. . . . we do not think that Scripture allows us to make the question of God's desire secondary" ("Book Reviews," *Banner of Truth* 507 [Dec. 2005], 22.

[104] On December 7, 2001 on the Theology List, Phil Johnson said the following to a hyper-Calvinist: "The root of your problem is that you apparently imagine a conflict would exist in the will of God if God, who has not ordained some men to salvation, nonetheless desires all men to repent and seek His mercy. That is, in fact, precisely the false dilemma virtually all hyper-Calvinists make for themselves. They cannot reconcile God's preceptive will with His decretive will, so they end up (usually) denying the sincerity of the preceptive will, or else denying that the pleading and calls to salvation apply to all who hear the gospel." http://groups.yahoo.com/group/Theology_list. Also, in a book addressing various issues related to open theism, Johnson dealt with the question of whether God in any sense "desires" what He does not bring to pass. He says that Scripture "often imputes unfulfilled desires to God" and cites several important verses. He then rightly cautions against taking "expressions of desire and longing from the heart of God" in a "simplistically literal sense," as this would result in compromising God's sovereignty. Therefore, "the yearning God expresses in these verses must to some degree be anthropopathic." Johnson says that, nevertheless, we "must also see that these expressions mean *something*. They reveal an aspect of the divine mind that is utterly impossible to reconcile with the view of those who insist that God's sovereign decrees are equal to His 'desires' *in every meaningful sense*. Is there no sense in which God ever wishes for or prefers anything other than what actually occurs (including the fall of Adam, the damnation of the wicked, and every evil in between)? My own opinion—and I think Dabney would have agreed—is that those who refuse to see any true expression of God's heart whatsoever in His optative exclamations have embraced the spirit of the hyper-Calvinist error." (P. Johnson, "God Without Mood Swings," in *Bound Only Once: The Failure of Open Theism* [ed. D. Wilson; Moscow, ID: Canon Press, 2001], 118). This article can also be accessed here: http://www.spurgeon.org/~phil/articles/impassib.htm. Both of Johnson's quotes (in addition to his references on the will of God in his *Primer on Hyper-Calvinism*) would seem to implicate James White (Alpha & Omega Ministries) as a

world has historically carried on its coattails a rise of hyper-Calvinism as well.[105] It's crucial to note that no Calvinist ever moves from moderate-Calvinism directly to hyper-Calvinism. One must first be committed to limited atonement, and from there one would make the logical leap into the rejection of well-meant gospel offers. Hyper-Calvinism cannot exist without a belief in limited atonement.

2. Problems for Evangelism

Some Calvinists today are engaged in evangelism for the simple reason that *they do not know who the elect are*, in addition to Christ's missionary commands.[106] While we do not know who the unbelieving elect are, this motive for evangelism is insufficient. Evangelism must occur *because God wills all men to be saved* according to His revealed will. We are also to express and display God's *saving* love[107] for humanity in the way we command all men to repent, in our preaching of the gospel, in our compassionate invitations, and in our indiscriminate offerings of Christ to all. Christ's own heart and

---

hyper-Calvinist since White concurs with Reymond's view that God does *not* desire the salvation of the non-elect *in any sense*. Both White and Reymond think affirming the contrary imputes irrationality to God, and Reymond explicitly appeals to John Gill's teaching in this respect. See R. L. Reymond, *A New Systematic Theology*, 692–93. White is not just quibbling over optative expressions, as Johnson seems to think. Both Reymond and White reject the *concept* that God desires the salvation of all men. Whatever the case may be, it is nevertheless clear that White, a Reformed Baptist, is *thoroughly* out of sync with Sam Waldron's strong statements about the will of God and John 5:34 as he expounds the "free offer" teaching in the 1689 London Baptist Confession. See Waldron's *Modern Exposition of the 1689 Baptist Confession of Faith* (Darlington, UK: Evangelical Press, 1989), 121–22. In contrast to White, and as I noted during the John 3:16 Conference, Tom Ascol agrees with Johnson's orthodox Calvinist view that "God desires all people to be saved" in His revealed will. It is, therefore, troubling to think that Ascol (or anyone in the Southern Baptist Founders movement) would ally himself with White, a non-Southern Baptist Calvinist who rejects the well-meant gospel offer, when planning to debate other Southern Baptists on Calvinism. This was my point at the John 3:16 Conference.

[105] Johnson wrote in a 1998 online article: "I wrote and posted this article because I am concerned about some subtle trends that seem to signal a rising tide of hyper-Calvinism, especially within the ranks of young Calvinists and the newly Reformed. I have seen these trends in numerous Reformed theological forums on the Internet. . . . History teaches us that hyper-Calvinism is as much a threat to true Calvinism as Arminianism is. Virtually every revival of true Calvinism since the Puritan era has been hijacked, crippled, or ultimately killed by hyper-Calvinist influences. Modern Calvinists would do well to be on guard against the influence of these deadly trends" (P. Johnson, "A Primer on Hyper-Calvinism," http://www.spurgeon.org/~phil/articles/hypercal.htm online).

[106] This is the thrust of J. I. Packer's points in *Evangelism and the Sovereignty of God* (Downer's Grove, IL: InterVarsity, 1991).

[107] Some Calvinists distinguish between God's universal *saving* love and *redemptive* love since they think the latter pertains to the elect alone, as Christ only died for the elect's sins. Even though some historic Calvinists have thought that Christ redeemed only the elect [hence *redemptive* love] in the death He died, they still admit that God wills to save all humankind out of His love of *benevolence* [as distinguished from a love of *complacence*]. These terms *benevolence* and *complacence* are common in the Calvinist discussion of the love of God, especially among older writers.

ministry, in this respect, are our pattern. We are to point the lost to the sufficiency of Christ to save them.[108] In addition to Christ's express evangelistic commands and God's will that all be saved, Christ's actual sufficiency to save all men should also form a basis for our evangelism. *Knowledge* of God's revealed will should drive our evangelism, not our *ignorance* of His secret will. Our missionary activity should be a way of conforming ourselves to the heart of God's own missionary interests.

In his book *The Gospel and Personal Evangelism*, Mark Dever suggested three motives for evangelism: obedience to Scripture, a love for the lost, and a love for God.[109] I agree completely, but Dever fails to mention two other critical motives: Christ's death for all men, and God's universal saving will. Unless I have missed it, his book never mentions these two as motives for evangelism. Of course, Dever cannot affirm Christ's death for the sins of all men because he holds to limited atonement. His theology prohibits it. I assume he would agree with God's universal saving will, though he nowhere explicitly states it in his book, as far as I can tell.

Owenic Calvinists inadvertently undermine the well-meant gospel offer. Christians must evangelize *because God wills all men to be saved* and has made atonement *for all men*, thus removing the legal barriers that necessitate their condemnation. Arguably a high-Calvinist cannot look a congregation in the eyes or even a single unbelieving sinner in the eye and say, "Christ died for your sins." Furthermore, when high-Calvinists say, "Christ died for sinners," the term "sinners" becomes a code word for "the elect only."[110] To be consistent with their own theology, they have to say the deliberately vague statement "Christ died for sinners." Since Christ did

---

[108] This was the frequent practice of D. Brainard. See "Life and Diary of the Rev. D. Brainard" in *The Works of Jonathan Edwards*, 2:432.

[109] M. Dever, *The Gospel and Personal Evangelism* (Wheaton, IL: Crossway, 2007), 96.

[110] See the "Together for the Gospel" doctrinal statement. Notice the careful use of phrases like "Christ died for sinners" in numerous places rather than something along the lines of "Christ died for the world," or for "all men," etc. The leaders of "Together for the Gospel" deliberately seem to avoid using the obviously broader, or all-encompassing, scriptural language to describe the extent of the atonement, such as 2 Cor 5:14 ("one [Jesus] died for *all*"), 2 Cor 5:19 ("God was in Christ, reconciling the *world* to himself"), and Heb 2:9 ("Jesus tasted death for *every man*"). Although their language is biblical in the connotative sense that those for whom Christ died are "sinners" (as Paul says in Rom 5:8: "While we were yet sinners, Christ died for us," and again in 1 Tim 1:15: "Christ Jesus came into the world to save sinners."), their language is *not* biblical in the denotative sense that no *explicit* form of the words "died for sinners" appears in the NT. The "Together for the Gospel" confessional language with respect to the extent of the atonement seems to be a calculated avoidance of the more frequent and more explicit biblical terms like "all," "world," and "every man." This studied ambiguity seems deliberate and may be driven by their commitment to the doctrine of limited atonement. In "Together for the Gospel," what binds these Baptists and Presbyterians together confessionally is high-Calvinism, or more specifically their belief in limited atonement.

not die for the sins of the non-elect and since they do not know who the elect are, it is simply impossible in a preaching or witnessing situation to say to all directly "Christ died for you."[111] I do not see how this untenable position can do anything but undermine one's evangelistic zeal since the actual "saveability" of the listeners may secretly be in question.

Nathan Finn criticized Jerry Vines for stating, "When a Calvinist is a soul-winner, it is in spite of his theology."[112] Interestingly, Curt Daniel, a moderate-Calvinist, pointed out that John Bunyan, a Calvinist who held to universal atonement, contended that few will be saved through the Particularist Gospel and that those who will, are saved in spite of the distinctive element, not because of it.[113]

3. Problems for Preaching

Anything that operates to undermine the centrality, universality, and necessity of preaching is wrong. Anything that makes preachers hesitant to make the bold proclamation[114] of the gospel to *all people* is wrong. Thinking that Christ only suffered for some will deeply affect preaching. Preachers do not know who the elect are so they must preach to all as if Christ's death is applicable to them even though they know and believe all are not capable of salvation. This stance seems to make preachers operate on the basis of something they know to be untrue and creates a problematic context for preaching in the pulpit.

Rather, because Christ did, in fact, die for the sins of all, God Himself is offering salvation to all, and the preacher can preach the bold proclamation of salvation to all, offering Christ's benefits to every single person (2 Cor 5:18–21). John Bunyan maintained that the gospel is to be preached to all because the purpose for Christ's death extended to all.[115] Curt Daniel

---

[111] I have occasionally heard this said in sermons by high-Calvinists, but when this is done, it is an inconsistency that stands in direct contradiction to their theology. Most high-Calvinists will not use the terminology "Christ died for you" in their sermons. Sometimes theory does not match practice when it comes to preaching. Consider this quote from Spurgeon, a high-Calvinist, in addressing unbelievers: "Come, I beseech you, on Calvary's mount, and see the cross. Behold the Son of God, he who made the heavens and the earth, *dying for your sins.* Look to him, is there not power in him to save? Look at his face so full of pity. Is there not love in his heart to prove him willing to save? Sure sinner, the sight of Christ will help thee to believe" (Charles Spurgeon, "Compel Them to Come In," New Park Street Pulpit, vol. 5, Sermon #227).

[112] N. Finn, "Southern Baptist Calvinism: Setting the Record Straight," 176.

[113] C. Daniel, "Hyper-Calvinism and John Gill," 590.

[114] The "bold proclamation" is telling every man that Christ died for their sins according to the Scriptures.

[115] J. Bunyan, *Reprobation Asserted*, in The Works of John Bunyan, ed. G. Offor (Avon, Great Britain: The Bath Press/Banner of Truth, 1991), 2:348.

pointed out how Calvin warned "that if one limits the 'all' of the atone-ment, then one limits the revealed salvific will of God, which necessarily infringes on the preaching of the gospel and diminishes the 'hope of salva-tion' of those to whom the Gospel is preached."[116]

Writing on limited atonement, Waldron makes this comment: "The free offer of the gospel does not require us to tell men that Christ died for them." He also explains that "this way of preaching is utterly with-out biblical precedent," that "if the free offer of the gospel meant tell-ing unconverted sinners, 'Christ died for you,' then particular redemption would be inconsistent with the free offer," and that "nowhere in the Bible is the gospel proclaimed by telling unconverted sinners that Christ died for them."[117] This last statement is remarkable. Such bold assertions are squarely contradicted in numerous places in the New Testament. For example, consider Paul's statement of the gospel he preached in 1 Cor 15:3 (NKJV): "For I delivered to you first of all that which I also received: that Christ died for our sins." Note that Paul is telling the Corinthians what he preached to them *before they were saved!* He preached to them "Christ died for their sins." Waldron's statement is also contradicted by Acts 3:26 (NKJV): "To you first, God, having raised up His Servant Jesus, sent Him to bless you, in turning away every one of you from your iniqui-ties." Peter is telling his unbelieving audience that God sent Jesus to bless *each* and *every* one of them and to turn *every one of them* from their iniqui-ties. *This message is equivalent to Peter's saying that Christ died for you.* How could Jesus save every one of them (which is what blessing and turning away from iniquity involves) if He did not *actually* die for the sins of all of them? Certainly "each one" of the Jews whom Peter addressed must have included some who were non-elect! As if these verses were not enough, what will Waldron do with Luke 22:20–21? "Likewise He also took the cup after supper, saying, 'This cup is the new covenant in My blood, which is shed for you. But behold, the hand of My betrayer is with Me on the table.'" Here Jesus clearly states His blood was shed for Judas.[118] Arguing that Judas was not at the table at this time offers no remedy since the text clearly states that he was. Calvin himself explicitly says Judas was at the

---

[116] C. Daniel, "Hyper-Calvinism and John Gill," 603.

[117] S. Waldron, "The Biblical Confirmation of Particular Redemption," in *Calvinism: A Southern Bap-tist Dialogue*, 149.

[118] He cannot biblically say that the "you" does not include Judas, given what Mark 14:18 says.

table in numerous places in his own writings.[119] If Jesus shed His blood for Judas, then His death was not restricted to the elect alone, for Judas was not among the elect. The free and well-meant offer of the gospel for all people necessarily presupposes that Christ died for the sins of all men in some sense.[120]

J. C. Ryle said it well:

> I will give place to no one in maintaining that Jesus loves all mankind, came into the world for all, died for all, provided redemption sufficient for all, calls on all, invites all, commands all to repent and believe; and ought to be offered to all—freely, fully, unreservedly, directly, unconditionally—without money and without price. If I did not hold this, I dare not get into a pulpit, and I should not understand how to preach the Gospel.
>
> But while I hold all this, I maintain firmly that Jesus does special work for those who believe, which He does not do for others. He quickens them by His Spirit, calls them by His grace, washes them in His blood—justifies them, sanctifies them, keeps them, leads them, and continually intercedes for them—that they may not fall. If I did not believe all this, I should be a very miserable, unhappy Christian.[121]

These words reflect my sentiments exactly. People are not damned for lack of a sufficient substitutionary sacrifice but for their sins and lack of faith. A man cannot be punished for rejecting what was never meant for him in the first place. Limited atonement negatively affects preaching because it prohibits the preacher from preaching, "Christ died for your sins!" so that the despairing hearers may be assured that God is not only willing but also prepared to save them.

---

[119] See J. Calvin, *Tracts and Treatises on the Doctrine and Worship of the Church*, vol. 2 (trans. H. Beveridge; Grand Rapids: Eerdmans, 1958), 93, 234, 297, 370–71, 378, and also his commentary on Matt 26:21 and John 6:56.

[120] According to De Jong, H. Hoeksema and others in the Protestant Reformed Church see "four indispensable elements" which constitute the idea of offer: (1) an honest and sincere desire on the part of the offerer to give something, (2) that the offerer possesses that which he extends to some person(s), (3) a desire that it be accepted, and (4) that the recipients of the offer are able to fulfill the condition of the offer. Concerning his second element, the possession on God's part must be an extrinsically sufficient remedy for the sins of all who hear the gospel call, and this is one of the key reasons the hyper-Calvinist Hoeksema rejects the view that God is giving well-meant offers to all through the gospel proclamation. See A. De Jong, *The Well-Meant Gospel Offer: The Views of H. Hoeksema and K. Schilder* (Franeker: T. Wever, 1954), 43.

[121] J. C. Ryle, *Expository Thoughts on the Gospel*, 3:186.

4. Problems Concerning the Giving of Altar Calls

At a Michigan pastors' conference in November 2008, a Southern Baptist Convention seminary professor spoke on the subject "The Cross and Evangelistic Confidence." The point of his message emphasized that a pastor need not and, in fact, should not extend an evangelistic altar call. He contended the evangelistic altar call is not biblical and also argued that extending an evangelistic altar call is tantamount to attempting to manipulate the sovereignty of God. Alan Streett has debunked both these claims in a monograph.[122] Streett, who serves as the W. A. Criswell Professor of Preaching at The Criswell College in Dallas, Texas, and is a Southern Baptist, wrote his doctoral dissertation on this subject. He demonstrated conclusively that an altar call is historically substantiated, biblically affirmed, and theologically validated. Incidentally, Streett is a moderate-Calvinist. Streett's volume has an appendix where he directly appeals to his Reformed brothers not to reject the use of the altar call.[123] I might also add that in personal conversation with Dr. Louis Drummond before his home going, Drummond told me that during his research in England for his definitive biography on Charles Spurgeon, he found eyewitness accounts of Spurgeon's occasional use of the altar call after his preaching in the recently unsealed vault containing the archives of the Downgrade Controversy. These accounts, of course, debunk a common myth among Calvinists that Spurgeon never gave an altar call.

Many Calvinists reject the altar call precisely because of their commitment to limited atonement. Although anecdotal in nature, observations confirm that virtually all Calvinists who speak or write against altar calls happen to be high-Calvinists.

5. Problems When Calvinism Is Equated with the Gospel

In spite of Spurgeon's famous quote,[124] Calvinism is not the gospel. As Greg Welty said in speaking "bluntly" (Welty's word) to his fellow Calvinists, such a statement is "both misleading and unhelpful," and if taken at face value, would "draw the circle of fellowship more narrowly than Christ

---

[122] R. A. Streett, *The Effective Invitation* (Grand Rapids: Kregel, 2004).

[123] Ibid., 238–45. See also Streett's chapter on this subject in this volume.

[124] C. H. Spurgeon, *The Autobiography of Charles H. Spurgeon* (Cincinnati: Curts & Jennings, 1898), 1:172.

Himself has drawn it."[125] Calvinism is not the *sine qua non* of the gospel. Some modern Calvinists posit a necessary link between penal substitution and definite atonement so that they tend to equate Calvinism with the gospel message. For them, penal substitution equals limited atonement, and, therefore, limited atonement becomes a necessary component of the gospel. That the Reformers who recaptured the penal substitutionary aspect of Christ's death did not hold to limited atonement is interesting. The argument that the rejection of limited atonement entails the need to deny penal substitution ultimately rests on a confusion between *commercial* debt and *penal* debt, as has already been pointed out. Such thinking may reduce the gospel message to a message about how God wants to gather the elect instead of God's sincere desire to save all who hear the message. When Calvinism is equated with the gospel, some Calvinists become militant so that any attack on their system is equivalent to an attack on the gospel.

6. Problems When Non-Calvinist Churches Interview a Calvinist Potential Pastor or Staff Member

One of the growing problems in the Southern Baptist Convention, which seems to correlate with an increase in the number of young seminary graduates who are Calvinistic in their soteriology, concerns the interview process between churches and pastoral/staff candidates. The vast majority of Southern Baptist churches are not Calvinistic. When these churches interview potential pastors and staff who are Calvinistic, problems surface unless both parties are crystal clear about their beliefs and unless both parties ask and answer questions pointedly and not with vagueness. Most of the evidence for this problem is anecdotal in nature, but I am personally aware of numerous examples. Not a few churches in the Southern Baptist Convention have actually divided over this issue.

---

[125] G. Welty, "Election and Calling: A Biblical Theological Study," in *Calvinism: A Southern Baptist Dialogue*, 243. When John MacArthur stands in the pulpit of First Baptist Church, Woodstock, Georgia, during a conference in 2007 and says, "Jesus was a Calvinist," such an unfortunate statement exacerbates the situation between Calvinists and non-Calvinists. I love and appreciate John MacArthur. I have read most everything he has written, and I have listened to him preach on the radio for 30 years, but such a statement is absurd on a number of levels. To begin with, it is anachronistic since Jesus' life on earth antedated Calvin by some 1,500 years. Second, MacArthur, as a high-Calvinist, implied by his statement that Jesus held to limited atonement, a position which Calvin himself did not hold. Third, imagine the outcry from Calvinists if a prominent non-Calvinist should say, "Jesus was a non-Calvinist" or "Jesus was an Arminian."

Oftentimes a pastor search committee is not theologically astute enough to ask the kinds of questions to determine what a potential pastor believes about Calvinism and particularly the extent of the atonement. Let me illustrate with a hypothetical case. Suppose the candidate is asked the following question: "Do you believe Christ died for the world?" The questioner understands the word "world" to refer to all people without exception. The questioner also intends "died for" to mean "died for the sins of" the world. High-Calvinists believe Christ died for humanity *in the sense that His death brings them common grace* but not that Christ died for *the sins of* the world. No high-Calvinist can say, "Christ died for *the sins of* the world" *unless they understand the word "world" to mean the elect*. But this view is precisely how most high-Calvinists understand the word "world" in passages like John 3:16; they interpret it to mean the world of the elect only and not every person individually. So, in our hypothetical case, when the candidate is asked the question, "Do you believe Christ died for the world," he can answer "yes" to that question *by his definition of "world" and "died for."* The problem here is twofold. First, the committee's question is asked without their awareness of the theological nuances involved in the meaning of "world" and "died for." Although this is regrettable, it is understandable. Second, if the candidate answers "yes" to the question, then he is answering the question *according to his definitions of the words "world" and "died for,"* not according to the intended meaning of the question by the committee. If the candidate answers the question in the affirmative and if he knows the committee means by their question to inquire whether Jesus actually died for the sins of all men, then a breach of integrity has occurred. The candidate has made the decision to capitalize on the ambiguity of the question. It is incumbent on the Calvinist candidate to answer the question *according to the meaning of the questioner* and not according to what *he himself can nuance the words to mean as if in a theological discussion with fellow Calvinists*. If the candidate is called to the church as a pastor or staff member and later begins to preach or teach limited atonement, problems result. Even when church search committees do not ask questions concerning a candidate's views on Calvinism, wisdom would seem to dictate that the candidate should be upfront with the committee about these issues. It is incumbent on *both search committees and candidates* that they be forthright with each other about exactly what each believes. Love for the church and the desire not to divide a church ought to spur committees and candidates, whether Calvinist or not.

7. *Problems When Being Truly Southern Baptist Is Equated with Being a Calvinist*

While this problem does not pertain to the atonement *per se*, it is about Calvinism in general and illustrates a growing problem in the Southern Baptist Convention. When Tom Ascol publishes Tom Nettles's article in the *Founders Journal*, titled "Why Your Next Pastor Should Be a Calvinist," the publication of this article, coupled with the posting of the statement of purpose on the Founders Ministries Web site, makes it obvious that the agenda of the Founders movement in the Southern Baptist Convention is to move the SBC toward high-Calvinism.[126] Read carefully Ascol's own comments about Nettles's article:

> The theme of the latest *Founders Journal* (Winter, 2008) is "the other resurgence." It contains articles by Tom Nettles and Christian George, representing the "old guard" of the reformation efforts within the SBC and the rising generation who is similarly committed to those efforts. Dr. Nettles needs no introduction to most of the readers of this blog. His teaching and writing ministries have been blessed of God to call many back to our biblical and historical roots as Southern Baptists. His book, *By His Grace and For His Glory* (recently revised, updated and republished by Founders Press) has never even been seriously engaged, much less refuted by those who lament the resurgence of the doctrines of grace among Baptists over the last 25 years. It is a classic work. Tom's article in this issue of the *Founders Journal* is entitled, "Why Your Next Pastor Should Be a Calvinist." I highly recommend it.[127]

First, note the phrase "the other resurgence." This phrase is, of course, a reference to the resurgence of Calvinism in the Southern Baptist Convention. Second, Ascol speaks of Nettles's "teaching and writing ministries" being "blessed of God *to call many back to our biblical and historical roots as Southern Baptists*" [emphasis added]. Ascol's reference to our "biblical" roots implies that those who do not affirm Calvinism are "unbiblical." When he speaks of our "historical" roots, Ascol is distorting the historical record of Southern Baptists with respect to Calvinism. He is prejudicing the Charleston tributary over against the Sandy Creek tributary. Richard Land poignantly said concerning Southern

---

[126] T. Nettles, "Why Your Next Pastor Should Be a Calvinist," *Founders Journal* 71 (Winter 2008): 5–15.

[127] T. Ascol, "The Other Resurgence—FJ 71," Founders Weblog, Wednesday, April 2, 2008, http://www.founders.org/blog/archive/2008_04_01_archive.html; accessed Oct 29, 2008.

Baptist history and Calvinism: "Ever since the First Great Awakening, the Separate Baptist Sandy Creek Tradition has been our melody,
with Charleston and other traditions providing harmony."[128] Founders
Ministries has chiefly erred in assigning the melody to the Charleston
tradition in Southern Baptist life. Third, I cannot imagine using such a
title as "Why Your Next Pastor Should Be a Calvinist," much less arguing the topic in print. A church's next pastor should be the man God
leads that church to call, Calvinist or not. Imagine the outcry if some
group of non-Calvinists should publish an article titled, "Why Your Next
Pastor Should Not Be a Calvinist." Of course, Ascol is well within his
rights to direct the Founders Ministries and to publish such an article
in his journal. These rights are not in question. What is in question is
whether such an article constitutes evidence that he has *an agenda
to press* for a resurgence of Calvinism in the Southern Baptist Convention
and whether such an agenda is a problem for the Southern Baptist Convention. In my judgment the evidence clearly indicates both are true.

Consider Nettles's comments in his chapter "A Historical View of the
Doctrinal Importance of Calvinism Among Baptists" in the book *Calvinism: A Southern Baptist Dialogue*. He concluded with a statement that any
effort to seek the repression or elimination of Calvinism within the SBC
would be "a theological tragedy and historical suicide."[129] I certainly agree.
In the next sentence Nettles introduced a lengthy quotation by P. H. Mell
with the following remark: "In fact, one could argue along with P. H. Mell
that exactly the opposite should be the case."[130] What exactly did Mell
say to elicit such a comment from Nettles? The first portion of Nettles's
quotation of Mell reads as follows:

> In conclusion, it becomes a serious and practical question—whether
> we should not make these doctrines [the Doctrines of Grace] the
> basis of all our pulpit ministrations. If this be, indeed, the gospel
> system, sustained by such arguments, and attested by such effects,
> every minister should be imbued with its spirit, and furnished with its
> panoply; it is not necessary, indeed, that we should present its truth,
> always in the form of dogmatic or polemic theology—though even

---

[128] See page 50 of this volume.

[129] T. Nettles, "A Historical View of the Doctrinal Importance of Calvinism Among Baptists," in
Calvinism, 68.

[130] Ibid.

these should not be entirely neglected, if our people are not, as yet, thoroughly indoctrinated.[131]

Nettles continues Mell's quotation that outlines "the fundamental truths" of the "doctrines of grace." Curiously, Mell mentions total depravity and perseverance of the saints, but he says nothing specific concerning unconditional election, limited atonement, and irresistible grace. Mell is clearly advocating that these doctrines of Calvinism should be the "basis of all our pulpit ministrations." He calls the doctrines of grace "the gospel system" and indicates "our people" should be "thoroughly indoctrinated" in them. One could indeed argue, as Nettles said, for Mell's point, but the point is *one should not argue this point.* There are wide chasms between "could" and "would" and "should." I get the distinct impression that Nettles would indeed like to argue this and that he has semantically done so by means of Mell's quotation.

Jeff Noblit concluded "The Rise of Calvinism in the Southern Baptist Convention: Reason for Rejoicing" with these words: "I am convinced that the rise of Spirit-filled, evangelistic Calvinism is an essential agent to the revival and reformation needed in order to build strong true churches and bring God the glory He deserves."[132] Look at that sentence carefully. Noblit is *convinced* that Calvinism is an *essential* agent needed for the revival and reformation of the church in order to build *true* churches. Is Calvinism *essential* to the revival we need? Will our churches only be *true* churches when they are permeated with Calvinistic theology? Such statements and their implications are problematic.

In conclusion, regarding Calvinism and the SBC, attempting to run all Calvinists out of Dodge will not bring us together in the SBC. Attempting to return us as a convention to the so-called "Founders" theology of Calvinism will also not bring us together. If we are to come together, we must do so *as Baptists,* not as Calvinists and non-Calvinists. We must unite around *Baptist distinctives,* which are the only glue that can hold us together: a biblical Baptist theology wedded to a Great Commission Resurgence of evangelism and missions. It is any and every Baptist's right to be persuaded that Calvinism reflects the teaching of Scripture. Being a Calvinist should not be a convention crime. Calvinists have and should always be free to

---

[131] Ibid.; P. H. Mell, *Calvinism: An Essay Read Before the Georgia Baptist Ministers' Institute* (Atlanta: G. C. Conner, 1868; reprint Cape Coral: Christian Foundation, 1988), 19–20.

[132] J. Noblit, "The Rise of Calvinism in the Southern Baptist Convention: Reason for Rejoicing," *Calvinism: A Southern Baptist Dialogue,* 112.

have a place at the SBC table. Any church that feels God's leading to call a Calvinist pastor should do so without hesitation. On the other hand, Calvinism should not be a convention cause either. When Calvinists, individually or as organized groups, seek to make it a cause with the intention of moving the SBC toward Calvinism, then we have and will continue to have a problem. Let us debate the theology of Calvinism and let the chips fall where they may, but let us refrain from attempting to Calvinize or de-Calvinize the SBC. The majority of Baptists have always been, to use Dr. Leo Garrett's term, "Calminians."

Conclusion

I have attempted to demonstrate the following: (1) Historically, neither Calvin nor the first generation of reformers held the doctrine of limited atonement. From the inception of the Reformation until the present, numerous Calvinists have rejected it, and furthermore, it represents a departure from the historic Christian consensus that Jesus suffered for the sins of all humanity. (2) Biblically, the doctrine of limited atonement simply does not reflect the teaching of Scripture. (3) Theologically and logically, limited atonement is flawed and indefensible. (4) Practically, limited atonement creates serious problems for God's universal saving will; it provides an insufficient ground for evangelism by undercutting the well-meant gospel offer; it undermines the bold proclamation of the gospel in preaching; and it contributes to a rejection of valid methods of evangelism such as the use of evangelistic altar calls.

I cannot help but remember the words of the venerable retired distinguished professor of New Testament at Southwestern Baptist Theological Seminary, Dr. Jack McGorman, in his inimitable style and accent: "The doctrine of limited atonement truncates the gospel by sawing off the arms of the cross too close to the stake."[133] Should the Southern Baptist Convention move toward "five-point" Calvinism? Such a move would be, in my opinion, not a helpful one.[134]

---

[133] Spoken to the author in a personal conversation.

[134] We should heed the words of Thomas Lamb, seventeenth-century Baptist and Calvinist, who said: ". . . yet I deny not, but grant with him [John Goodwin], that the denial of Christs [sic] Death for the sins of all, doth detract from God's *Philanthropy*, and deny him to be a lover of men, and doth in very deed destroy the very foundation and ground-work of Christian faith" (Thomas Lamb, *Absolute Freedom from Sin by Christs Death for the World* [London: Printed by H. H. for the authour, and are to be sold by him, 1656], 248).

{ Chapter 5 }

A Biblical and Theological Critique of Irresistible Grace

Steve W. Lemke

The Background of the Issue

The doctrine of irresistible grace was addressed most famously at the Dutch Reformed Synod of Dort, which offered a response to the concerns voiced by the Remonstrants, who were themselves Dutch Reformed Calvinists. This difference of opinion was echoed in Baptist history in the distinction between General Baptists (who generally agreed with the Remonstrants on these points) and Particular Baptists (who generally agreed with the Synod of Dort on these points). While both the Remonstrants and the Dortians agreed that humans are all depraved and totally helpless to save themselves apart from God's grace, they mainly argued whether God's grace is resistible. In Articles III and IV of their "remonstrance" (or statement of concerns), the Remonstrants expressed their conviction that some of their fellow Calvinists had become so extreme in their beliefs that they had departed from scriptural teachings. In particular, while affirming that salvation comes only by God's grace, the Remonstrants were concerned about the teaching that God forces His grace on sinners irresistibly. The Remonstrants affirmed:

That this grace of God is the beginning, continuance, and accomplishment of all good, even to this extent, that the regenerate man himself, without prevenient or assisting, awakening, following and cooperative grace, can neither think, will, nor do good, nor withstand any temptations to evil; so that all good deeds or movements, that can be conceived, must be ascribed to the grace of God in Christ. But respects the mode of the operation of this grace, it is not irresistible; inasmuch as it is written concerning many, that they have resisted the Holy Ghost. Acts 7, and elsewhere in many places.[1]

In other words, the Remonstrants taught that the only way for anyone to be saved is for God's grace to come before, during, and after justification because even the best-intentioned human being can "neither think, will, nor do good" apart from God's grace.[2] They even went so far as to say that all good in "any way that can be conceived must be ascribed to the grace of God in Christ."[3] But the question is, Why is this saving grace of God not appropriated or experienced by all persons? Has God failed in some way? Does God not truly love all persons? Does God not desire the salvation of all persons? No. The Remonstrants refused to blame this failure on God but rightfully assigned this failure to the rebellion and resistance of fallen human beings. God created human beings with the free will either to cooperate with God and receive His grace or to reject finally God's gracious gift. Again, human beings would have no salvation at all apart from the grace of God; but God refuses to actualize that salvation in the life of anyone who continually resists God's grace, refuses to humbly receive it, and finally rejects it.

The Synod of Dort, however, strenuously objected to the Remonstrants' denial of irresistible grace:

Who teach that the grace by which we are converted to God is nothing but a gentle persuasion, or (as others explain it) that the way of God's acting in man's conversion that is most noble and suited to human nature is that which happens by persuasion, and that nothing prevents this grace of moral suasion even by itself from making natural men spiritual; indeed, that God does not produce the assent of the will except in this manner of moral suasion, and that the effectiveness of God's work

---

[1] "The Five Arminian Articles," Articles III and IV, in *The Creeds of Christendom* (ed. P. Schaff; 6th ed.; Grand Rapids: Baker, 1983), 3:547, available online at http://www.apuritansmind.com/Creeds/ArminianArticles.htm; accessed November 1, 2008.

[2] Ibid.

[3] Ibid.

by which it surpasses the work of Satan consists in the fact that God promises eternal benefits while Satan promises temporal ones. . . .

Who teach that God in regenerating man does not bring to bear that power of his omnipotence whereby he may powerfully and unfailingly bend man's will to faith and conversion, but that even when God has accomplished all the works of grace which he uses for man's conversion, man nevertheless can, and in actual fact often does, so resist God and the Spirit in their intent and will to regenerate him, that man completely thwarts his own rebirth; and, indeed, that it remains in his own power whether or not to be reborn.[4]

The Problem of Defining Irresistible Grace

The term "irresistible grace," then, came initially as a view denied by the Remonstrants and defended by the Dortian Calvinists. The Synod of Dort rejected the notion that God's grace was limited to His exerting strong moral persuasion on sinners by the Holy Spirit to lead them to salvation. They also rejected the notion that a person can "resist God and the Spirit in their intent and will to regenerate him."[5] Instead, the Dort statement asserted that God brings to bear the "power of his omnipotence whereby he may powerfully and unfailingly bend man's will to faith and conversion."[6]

In order to understand how Calvinists say that God effects irresistible grace, one must understand the important distinction they draw between what is variously known as the "general" or "outward" call from the "special," "inward," "effectual," or "serious" call. Steele, Thomas, and Quinn virtually equate the "efficacious call" with irresistible grace, based on this distinction between these proposed two different callings from God:

> The gospel invitation extends a call to salvation to every one who hears
> its message. . . . But this outward general call, extended to the elect and
> the non-elect alike, will not bring sinners to Christ. . . . Therefore, the
> *Holy Spirit*, in order to bring God's elect to salvation, extends to them
> a *special inward call* in addition to the outward call contained in the
> gospel message. Through this special call the Holy Spirit performs a

---

[4] "The Canons of the Synod of Dort," Heads III and IV, Rejection of Errors, Articles VII and VIII, in Schaff, 3:570 (in Latin). For an English translation, see L. M. Vance, *The Other Side of Calvinism* (rev. ed.; Pensacola: Vance, 1999), Appendix 4, 621–22, which is also available online at http://www.reformed. org/documents/index.html; accessed November 1, 2008.

[5] Ibid.

[6] Ibid.

work of grace within the sinner which inevitably brings him to faith in Christ. . . .

Although the general outward call of the gospel can be, and often is, rejected, the special inward call of the Spirit never fails to result in the conversion of those to whom it is made. This special call is not made to all sinners but is issued to the elect only! The Spirit is in no way dependent upon their help or cooperation for success in His work of bringing them to Christ. It is for this reason that Calvinists speak of the Spirit's call and of God's grace in saving sinners as being "efficacious," "invincible," or "irresistible." For the grace which the Holy Spirit extends to the elect cannot be thwarted or refused, it never fails to bring them to true faith in Christ![7]

As this statement indicates, some contemporary Calvinists seem to be a little embarrassed by the term "irresistible grace" and have sought to soften it or to replace it with a term like "effectual calling." They also object when others criticize that "irresistible grace" suggests that God forces persons to do things against their wills. Instead, they insist, God merely woos and persuades. Calvinists thus sometimes sound disingenuous in affirming a strong view of irresistible grace while simultaneously softening the language about it to make it more palatable. For example, John Piper and the Bethlehem Baptist Church staff affirm that irresistible grace "means the Holy Spirit can overcome all resistance and make his influence irresistible. . . . The doctrine of irresistible grace means that God is sovereign and can overcome all resistance when he wills."[8] Yet, just a few paragraphs later, they affirm that "irresistible grace never implies that God forces us to believe against our will. . . . On the contrary, irresistible grace is compatible with preaching and witnessing that tries to persuade people to do what is reasonable and what will accord with their own best interests."[9] No attempt is made in the article to reconcile these apparently contradictory assertions.

Likewise, R. C. Sproul argues at great length that John 6:44 ("No one can come to Me unless the Father who sent Me draws him" HCSB) does *not* refer merely to the necessity that God "woo or entice men to Christ,"

---

[7] D. N. Steele, C. C. Thomas, and S. L. Quinn, *The Five Points of Calvinism: Defined, Defended, Documented* (expanded ed.; Philadelphia: Presbyterian and Reformed, 2004), 52–54.

[8] J. Piper and the Bethlehem Baptist Church staff, "What We Believe About the Five Points of Calvinism," http://www.desiringgod.org/ResourceLibrary/Articles/ByDate/ 1985/1487_What_We_ Believe_About_the_Five_Points_of_Calvinism/#Grace, p. 10, or at http://c4.atomicplaypen.com/sites/ BBC/resources/images/1250.pdf; accessed November 1, 2008.

[9] Piper and the Bethlehem Baptist Church staff, "What We Believe About the Five Points of Calvinism," 12.

and humans can "resist this wooing" and "refuse the enticement."[10] In philosophical language, Sproul says, this wooing is a necessary but not sufficient condition for salvation "because the wooing does not, in fact, guarantee that we will come to Christ."[11] Sproul states that such an interpretation is "incorrect" and "does violence to the text of Scripture."[12] Instead, Sproul insists, the term "draw" is "a much more forceful concept than to woo," and means "to compel by irresistible superiority."[13]

However, in discussing irresistible grace, Sproul tells of a student who, hearing a lecture on predestination by John Gerstner, rejected it. When Gerstner asked the student how he defined Calvinism, the student described it as the perspective that "God forces some people to choose Christ and prevents other people from choosing Christ." Gerstner then said, "If that is what a Calvinist is, then you can be sure that I am not a Calvinist either."[14] Sproul likewise chastised a Presbyterian seminary president for rejecting the Calvinist doctrine that "God brings some people, kicking and screaming against their wills, into the kingdom." Sproul describes this Presbyterian theologian's view as "a gross misconception of his own church's theology," as a "caricature," and "as far away from Calvinism as one could possibly get."[15] So which way is it? If God compels persons with "irresistible superiority," in what way is it inaccurate to say that God is forcing people to choose Christ?

The Synod of Dort insisted that such attempts at moral persuasion of unsaved persons was wasted time. That God's grace was resistible and not merely the use of strong moral persuasion was *precisely* what the Synod of Dort rejected and the Remonstrants affirmed. The Remonstrants insisted that the compelling grace of God persuaded the lost to receive Christ as Lord and Savior. The Synod of Dort insisted that this was not going far enough. Note their explicit denial that a person can "resist" God. Note the use in the Synod of Dort language of divine omnipotence, which can "powerfully and unfailingly bend man's will to faith and conversion."[16]

---

[10] R. C. Sproul, *Chosen by God* (Carol Stream, IL: Tyndale House, 1994), 69–70.

[11] Ibid.

[12] Ibid.

[13] Ibid.

[14] Ibid., 122.

[15] Ibid.

[16] "The Canons of the Synod of Dort," Heads III and IV, Rejection of Errors, Articles VII and VIII, in Schaff, 3:570 (in Latin). For an English translation, see L. M. Vance, *The Other Side of Calvinism*, Appendix 4, 621–22, which is also available online at http://www.reformed.org/documents/index.html; accessed November 1, 2008.

Bending the will of a fallible being by an omnipotent Being powerfully and unfailingly is not merely sweet persuasion. It is forcing one to change one's mind against one's will.

Calvinists often describe their position as *monergism* as opposed to *synergism*. In monergism, God works entirely alone, apart from any human role. In synergism, on the other hand, humans cooperate with God in some way in actualizing their own conversion. None of us non-Pelagians would affirm for a minute that we can achieve salvation apart from God. The question is whether humans have any role at all in accepting or receiving their own salvation. On the one hand, the Calvinists say, "No! Your salvation is monergistic, provided only by the grace of God." When a critic says this response means that God imposes irresistible grace against a person's will or that humans do not have a choice in the matter, the Calvinists protest that they are being misunderstood and caricatured.

When challenged that irresistible grace goes against someone's will, most Calvinists reply that it is not against a person's will at all. God changes their will through regeneration invincibly, such that the person is irresistibly drawn to Christ. Calvinists call this willing, which is externally driven, *compatibilist volition*, as opposed to the more common view, *libertarian freedom*. In libertarian freedom a person does not have absolute freedom (a frequent Calvinist stereotype), but the person chooses between at least two alternatives. In every case a person could have, at least hypothetically, chosen something else. But in compatibilism, people always choose their greatest desire. They have no alternative choice but to will to do what they want to do. So when God changes their will through irresistible grace or enabling grace, they really have no choice. They will what God has programmed them to will. So the Calvinist system advocates both monergism (God is the only actor) and compatibilism (they go along with what God wants them to do after He changes their will through preconversion regeneration).

The problem is that Calvinists cannot have their cake and eat it, too. They cannot insist that an omnipotent God overwhelms and bends human will powerfully and unfailingly, and then transform this doctrine into something other than it is by softening it with more palatable language such as "effectual calling" and "compatibilism." The effectual calling means precisely the same thing as irresistible grace. Effectual calling just sounds nicer. At the end of the day, people have no choice but to do what God has programmed them to do. Nonetheless, Calvinists often attempt to sidestep criticism by asserting that the doctrine has been misunderstood, even when non-Calvinists have quoted or paraphrased what Calvinists themselves have said in describing their own doctrine.

For example, at the "Building Bridges" conference, Nathan Finn chastised Southwestern Baptist Theological Seminary professor Roy Fish for the following description of irresistible grace, which Finn described as a "stereotype" and a "misunderstanding" of the doctrine:

> The "I" in the TULIP is what is called irresistible grace. That means that people who are going to be saved have no other option. They really don't have a choice. The grace of God cannot be resisted. They cannot resist this special saving grace.[17]

A line-by-line study of Fish's description reveals that Calvinists define irresistible grace in virtually the same words:

> Roy Fish: (Irresistible grace) "means that people who are going to be saved have no other option. They really don't have a choice."

> The Synod of Dort: "And this is the regeneration, the new creation, the raising from the dead, and the making alive so clearly proclaimed in the Scriptures, which God *works in us without our help*. But this certainly does not happen only by outward teaching, by moral persuasion, or by such a way of working that, after God has done his work, it remains in man's power whether or not to be reborn or converted. Rather, it is an entirely supernatural work. . . . As a result, all those in whose hearts God works in this marvelous way are *certainly, unfailingly*, and effectively reborn and do actually believe. . . ."[18]

> James White: "The doctrine of 'irresistible grace' . . . is simply the belief that when God chooses to move in the lives of His elect and bring them from spiritual death to spiritual life, *no power in heaven or on earth can stop Him from so doing*. . . . It is simply the confession that when God chooses to raise His people to spiritual life, He does so without the fulfillment of any conditions on the part of the sinner. Just as Christ had the power and authority to raise Lazarus to life *without obtaining his 'permission' to do so*, He is able to raise His elect to spiritual life with just as certain a result."[19]

---

[17] Nathan Finn, "Southern Baptist Calvinism: Setting the Record Straight," in *Calvinism: A Southern Baptist Dialogue* (ed. E. R. Clendenen and B. J. Waggoner; Nashville: B&H Academic, 2008), 171–92, esp. 184; citing "The C-Word," a sermon preached at Cottage Hill Baptist Church in Mobile, AL, on August 11, 1997, posted online at http://www.sbccalvinist.com/cword.htm; accessed October 31, 2008.

[18] "The Canons of the Synod of Dort," Heads III and IV, Articles 10 and 12, in Schaff, 3:589–90.

[19] J. White, "Irresistible Grace: God Saves Without Fail," in *Debating Calvinism: Five Points, Two Views*, by Dave Hunt and James White (Sisters, OR: Multnomah, 2004), 197 (italics mine).

David Steele, Curtis Thomas, and S. Lance Quinn: "The Holy Spirit extends a special inward call that *inevitably* brings them to salvation. . . . [T]he internal call (which is made only to the elect) *cannot be rejected*. It always results in conversion. By means of this special call the Spirit *irresistibly* draws sinners to Christ. He is not limited in His work of applying salvation by man's will, nor is He dependent upon man's cooperation for success. . . . God's grace, therefore, is invincible; it never fails to result in the salvation of those to whom it is extended."[20]

Roy Fish: "The grace of God cannot be resisted. They cannot resist this special saving grace."

The Synod of Dort: The Synod rejects that . . . "God in regenerating man does not bring to bear that power of his omnipotence whereby he may powerfully and unfailingly *bend man's will* to faith and conversion. . . ." (The Synod *rejects that someone*) "*can, and in actual fact often does, so resist God* and the Spirit in their intent and will to regenerate him."[21]

John Piper: Irresistible grace "means the Holy Spirit can *overcome all resistance* and make his influence *irresistible*. . . . The doctrine of irresistible grace means that God is sovereign and can *overcome all resistance* he wills. . . . When God undertakes to fulfill his sovereign purpose, *no one can successfully resist him*. . . . When a person hears a preacher call for repentance he can resist that call. But if God gives him repentance he cannot resist because the gift is *the removal of resistance*. . . . So if God gives repentance it is the same as *taking away the resistance. This is why we call this work of God 'irresistible grace.'*"[22]

Was Fish reflecting the statements of some Calvinists in his definition? Distinguishing Fish's from Finn's is so difficult that one must ask, What exactly is it in Fish's description that Finn objects to so strenuously? Fish has echoed Calvinist descriptions of irresistible grace, and yet Finn takes him to task for doing so. No matter how modern-day Calvinists may attempt to gloss over the hardness of irresistible grace and project it in a softer, gentler light, the doctrine remains what it is. When pressed by their own words, Calvinists sometimes seem to play word games or equivocate their words in order to make their beliefs more palatable. However,

---

[20] Steele, Thomas, and Quinn, *Five Points of Calvinism*, 7 (italics mine).

[21] "The Canons of the Synod of Dort," Heads III and IV, Rejection of Errors, Articles VII and VIII, in Schaff, 3:570 (in Latin); for an English translation, see Vance, *The Other Side of Calvinism*, Appendix 4, 621–22 (italics mine).

[22] Piper and the Bethlehem Baptist Church staff, "What We Believe About the Five Points of Calvinism," 10, 12 (italics mine).

this study will examine irresistible grace as it is described and defined in standard Calvinist doctrinal teachings.

The Bible and Irresistible Grace

What does the Bible say about irresistible grace? The easy answer is that the Bible does not specifically address irresistible grace. The phrase "irresistible grace" does not appear anywhere in Scripture. Of course, this absence alone does not mean that irresistible grace might not be a reality. Other doctrines such as the Trinity are described in Scripture but not with the theological name that we now give them. So what does the Bible say about grace being irresistible?

Key Texts Affirming Resistible Grace

Some Scripture texts appear to deny irresistible grace or to affirm resistible grace explicitly. Proverbs 1 challenges the notion of irresistible grace. The wisdom of God personified speaks to those whom "I have called" (Prov 1:24 NASB), to whom "I will pour out my spirit on you" (Prov 1:23b), and to whom wisdom has made "my words known to you" (Prov 1:23c). Nevertheless, no one regarded God's truth, for the hearers refused God's message and disdained Wisdom's counsel (Prov 1:22–26).

Some might claim that this message merely exemplifies the resistible outward call. The problem becomes complicated because these are God's elect people, the Jews, with whom God had entered into covenant: "I called and you refused" (Prov 1:24a NASB). God makes them the offer: "I will pour out my spirit on you" (Prov 1:23b), but they would not "turn" and instead "refused" to accept the message (Prov 1:24). The grace that was so graciously offered was ungraciously refused. The proffered grace was conditional on their response. Acceptance of God's Word would have brought blessing, but their rejection of it now brings calamity upon themselves.

In the prophets and the Psalms, God responds to the Israelites' refusal to repent and their rejection of the Word of God:

> "When Israel was a child, I loved him, and out of Egypt I called My son.
> As they called them, so they went from them; they sacrificed to the
> Baals, and burned incense to carved images. I taught Ephraim to walk,
> taking them by their arms; but they did not know that I healed them. I
> drew them with gentle cords, with bands of love, and I was to them as

those who take the yoke from their neck. I stooped and fed them. He shall not return to the land of Egypt; but the Assyrian shall be his king, because they refused to repent. And the sword shall slash in his cities, devour his districts, and consume them, because of their own counsels. My people are bent on backsliding from Me. Though they call to the Most High, none at all exalt Him. How can I give you up, Ephraim? How can I hand you over, Israel? How can I make you like Admah? How can I set you like Zeboiim? My heart churns within Me; My sympathy is stirred. I will not execute the fierceness of My anger; I will not again destroy Ephraim. For I am God, and not man, the Holy One in your midst; and I will not come with terror" (Hos 11:1–9 NKJV).

They did not keep the covenant of God; they refused to walk in His law (Ps 78:10 NKJV).

"But My people would not heed My voice, and Israel would have none of Me. So I gave them over to their own stubborn heart, to walk in their own counsels. Oh, that My people would listen to Me, that Israel would walk in My ways!" (Ps 81:11–13 NKJV).

"They have turned their backs to Me and not their faces. Though I taught them time and time again, they do not listen and receive discipline" (Jer 32:33 HCSB).

In the New Testament the most direct reference to the resistibility of grace is in Stephen's sermon in Acts 7:2–53, just before his martyrdom in Acts 7:54–60. In confronting the Jews who had rejected Jesus as Messiah, Stephen said, "You men who are stiff-necked and uncircumcised in heart and ears are always resisting the Holy Spirit; you are doing just as your fathers did" (Acts 7:51 NASB). The Remonstrants referenced this specific Scripture, and most scholars who reject the notion of irresistible grace cite it. Stephen is not speaking to believers but to Jews who have rejected Christ. He not only accuses them of "resisting the Holy Spirit" but many of their Jewish ancestors for resisting God as well. The word translated as "resist" (*antipiptō* in Greek) means not "to fall down and worship," but to "oppose," "strive against," or "resist."[23] Clearly this Scripture teaches that the influence of the Holy Spirit is resistible. A similar account in Luke 7:30 describes the Pharisees' response to the preaching of John the

---

[23] W. E. Vine, *An Expository Dictionary of New Testament Words* (Old Tappan, NJ: Revell, 1966), 286; J. H. Thayer, *A Greek-English Lexicon of the New Testament* (Nashville: Broadman, 1977), 51; F. W. Danker, ed., *A Greek-English Lexicon of the New Testament and Other Early Christian Literature* (Chicago: University of Chicago Press, 2000), 90.

Baptist: "But the Pharisees and lawyers rejected the counsel of God against themselves, being not baptized of him" (Luke 7:30 KJV).

Another example of resistance occurs in Paul's salvation experience in Acts 26. As Saul was going down the Damascus road to persecute Christians, a blinding light hit him, and a voice out of heaven said, "Saul, Saul, why are you persecuting Me? It is hard for you to kick against the goads" (Acts 26:14 HSCB). Obviously, Saul had resisted the conviction of the Holy Spirit in events such as the stoning of Stephen, but now God broke through Saul's resistance in a dramatic way. Even so, some time lapsed before Ananias arrived and Paul received the Holy Spirit (Acts 9:17).

What do Calvinists say about these texts? First of all, Calvinists do not deny that persons can resist the Holy Spirit in some situations. Unbelievers can resist the mere "outward call" of the gospel, and believers can resist the Holy Spirit as well. As John Piper has said, "What is irresistible is when the Spirit is issuing the effectual call."[24] However, these explanations do not appear to help in this instance. The Jews, after all, were God's chosen people, and the entirety of the Jewish people were covered under the covenant, not just individual Jews. Calvinist covenantal theology sees the entire nation of Israel as being God's chosen people. The elect, after all, are supposed to receive the effectual call. Calvinists often quote, "Jacob I have loved, but Esau I have hated" (Rom 9:13 HCSB), as their strongest evidence for election.[25] But these divinely elected people have not only rejected Jesus as Messiah but resisted the Holy Spirit through many generations in history. Therefore, it would seem that God's grace is resistible, even among the elect who are eligible to receive the effectual call.

Resistible Grace in the Ministry and Teachings of Jesus

Throughout His teaching ministry, Jesus taught and ministered in ways that seem to be inconsistent with the notion of irresistible grace. In each of these occasions, Jesus appears to advocate the idea that God's grace is resistible. For example, hear again Jesus' lament over Jerusalem: "Jerusalem, Jerusalem! The city who kills the prophets and stones those who are

---

[24] J. Piper and the Bethlehem Baptist Church staff, "What We Believe About the Five Points of Calvinism."

[25] Israel's election to service as a chosen people and individual election to salvation for Christians is interwoven in Romans 9–11. Calvinists often do not give adequate attention to the former.

sent to her! How often I wanted to gather your children together, as a hen gathers her chicks under her wings, *yet you were not willing!*" (Matt 23:37 HCSB, cf. Luke 13:34). What was Jesus lamenting? He was lamenting that despite God's gracious love for Jerusalem and desire to gather them to eternal security under His protection, and the many prophets and messengers He sent them with His message, they rejected the message that was sent them and they "were not willing" to respond to God. In fact, the Greek sets the contrast off even more sharply than the English does because forms of the same Greek verb *thelō* (to will) are used twice in this verse: "I willed . . . but you were not willing."[26] Schrenk describes this statement as expressing "the frustration of His gracious purpose to save by the refusal of men."[27] Note also that His lament concerns the entire city of Jerusalem, not just a small number of elect within Jerusalem. Indeed, Jesus is concerned about not only the persons living in Jerusalem at that particular time but for many generations of Jerusalemites.

Again, one might suggest that the prophets were merely the vehicles for proclaiming the general call, and thus these Jerusalemites never received the efficacious call, but this argument will not do. First of all, these are God's chosen people. As the elect, they should have received the efficacious call, but, in fact, they were still unwilling to respond. Some Calvinists might make this argument: the election of Israel included individuals within Israel, not all of Israel as a people. That only a remnant of physical Israel, not all of it, will be saved has the strongest backing, but the proposal that God sent the efficacious call to just a portion of Israel nevertheless does not match up well with this text or numerous other texts. Even so, the greater issue is that if Jesus believed in irresistible grace, with both the outward and inward calls, His apparent lament over Jerusalem would have been just a disingenuous act, a cynical show because He knew that God had not and would not give these lost persons the necessary conditions for their salvation. His lament would have been over God's hardness of heart, but that lament is not what the Scripture says. Scripture attributes the people's not coming to God to their own unwillingness, that is, the hardness of their own hearts.

What is generalized in Jesus' lament over Jerusalem is personalized in the incident with the rich young ruler (Luke 18:18–23). The ruler asked,

---

[26] G. Schrenk, s.v. "*thelō, thelēma, thelēsis,*" in *Theological Dictionary of the New Testament* (ed. G. Kittel; Grand Rapids: Eerdmans, 1965), 3:48–49.

[27] Ibid.

"What must I do to inherit eternal life?" (Luke 18:18 HCSB). If Jesus were a Calvinist, one might have expected Him to answer, "Nothing!" and admonish the young ruler for the impertinence of his question, particularly the idea that he could do anything to inherit eternal life. Instead, Jesus tells him what he could do: he could go and sell all his possessions and give them to the poor. Of course, this instruction was not just about the young ruler's money; it was about his heart. He loved his money and the privileges it gave him, and he just could not live without it. In other words, Jesus would not grant him eternal life unless he was willing to make a total commitment of his life to God, but the young ruler was unwilling. Jesus let him walk away and face the solemn consequences of his decision. Noting the rich young ruler's unwillingness, Jesus then comments about how hard it is for a rich person to enter into heaven—indeed, as hard as a camel going through the eye of a needle (Luke 13:24–28). This instruction provoked the disciples to point out that they had sacrificed much to follow Him so that He promised them a significant reward for their efforts (Luke 18:28–30).

Of course, if Jesus were a Calvinist, He never would have suggested that it was harder for rich persons to be saved by God's irresistible grace than poor persons. Their wills would be changed immediately and invincibly upon hearing God's effectual call. It would be no harder for a rich person to be saved by God's monergistic and irresistible calling than it would be for any other sinner. But the real Jesus was suggesting that their salvation was tied in some measure to their response and commitment to His calling.

The same idea of resistible grace arises frequently in the parables of Jesus' teaching ministry. In the parable of the two sons (Matt 21:28–32), Jesus describes their differing responses. One son initially refuses to do the work he was told to do, saying "I don't want to," but later "changed his mind" and did it (Matt 21:29 HCSB). Meanwhile, the other son says he will do the work, but later he does not do the work (Matt 21:29). One ought not to stretch a parable into an allegory, so what was the main point of this parable? The point was that tax collectors and prostitutes were going to enter into the kingdom of heaven before the chief priests and elders who resisted His teaching (Matt 21:31). Note that the distinction between the two was not that one was a son and one was not, for they both were sons from whom the father desired obedience. The distinction is the response of each son—resistance from one, repentance and obedience from the other.

A similar teaching follows in the parable of the vineyard (Matt 21:33–44). Using the familiar Old Testament symbol of a vineyard to represent Israel, Jesus told of the owner of the vineyard going away and leaving it in the hands of the tenants. He sends back a series of messengers and finally his own son to instruct the tenants about running the vineyard, but they reject each messenger and kill his son in the hope of seizing the vineyard for themselves. The owner then returns and exacts a solemn punishment on the rebellious tenants. Jesus then speaks of the cornerstone, the rock that was rejected by the builders but became the chief cornerstone, obviously speaking of Himself (Matt 21:42–44). Jesus then told the Pharisees that the kingdom of God would be taken from them and "given to a nation producing its fruit" (Matt 21:43 HCSB). Again, the key differential was whether persons were willing to be responsive to the Word of God.

The parable of the Sower (or of the Soils) in Matt 13:1–23; Mark 4:1–20; and Luke 8:1–15 highlights the issue of personal responsiveness to the Word of God. The nonvariable element is the seed, which represents the Word of God. The variable factor is the receptiveness of the soil on which the sower sows the seed. The seed on the path, on the rocky ground, and among the thorns never becomes rooted enough in the soil to flourish. The seed on the path is snatched away by the evil one. The rocky ground represents the person who "hears the word" and "receives it with joy" (Matt 13:20 HSCB) but does not flourish because "he has no root in himself" (Matt 13:21 HSCB). The seed that falls among thorns represents the person who also hears the Word of God, but the message becomes garbled by worldly interests. Only the seed that falls on good, receptive ground flourishes. Again, the variable is not the proclamation of the Word but the *response* of the individual.

The All-Inclusive Invitations in Scripture

One of the most frequently repeated themes throughout many genres of Scripture is the broad invitation of God to "all" people. This invitation parallels in many ways Dr. David Allen's discussion on the issue of a limited atonement. The main intuition that differs between Calvinists and others in this regard is why some come to salvation and many do not. The Calvinists essentially blame God for those who do not come. While they would insist, of course, that the sinners who rejected the message of salvation were

merely receiving their just deserts, there is really more to it than that. Calvinists say that God elected some to glory for His own reasons from before
the world began, and He gave them irresistible grace through His Spirit so
they inevitably would be saved. Obviously, those whom He did not choose
did not receive the irresistible effectual call but merely the resistible outer
ineffectual call. The alternative perspective is that God does extend the
general call to all persons and unleashes the Holy Spirit to persuade and
convict them of their need for repentance and faith. The Holy Spirit, however, does not impose His will irresistibly. So at the end of the day, response
to the grace of God determines whether the call is effectual.

The key issue, then, is whether salvation is genuinely open to all persons or merely just to a few who receive irresistible grace. What does the
Scripture say concerning this issue? First of all, Scripture clearly teaches
that God desires the salvation of all people. The Bible teaches that:

> "He Himself is the propitiation for our sins; and not for ours only, but
> also for those of the whole world" (1 John 2:2 NASB).

> "It is not the will of your Father who is in heaven that one of these little
> ones perish" (Matt 18:14 NASB).

> God "is not willing that any should perish, but that all should come to
> repentance" (2 Pet 3:9 KJV).

> God "wants everyone to be saved and to come to a knowledge of the
> truth" (1 Tim 2:4 HSCB).

The Greek word *pas*, meaning "all" or "everyone," which is found in 1 Tim
2:4 and in 2 Pet 3:9, in all the standard Greek dictionaries means "*all*"![28]

Those who would like to translate the word *pas* as something other
than a synonym for "all" should ponder the theological cost of such a move
merely because it disagrees with their theological system. For example,
Paul uses the same term in 2 Tim 3:16, when he declares that "*all* Scripture is given by inspiration of God" (2 Tim 3:16 KJV). He does not mean
that God inspires merely some selected portions of Scripture but that
God inspires all Scripture. Likewise, the Greek word *pas* ("all"), used in
the prologue to John, makes the enormous claim about creation that "*all*
things were made by him; and without him was not any thing made that

---

[28] B. Reicke, s.v. "*pas*" in *Theological Dictionary of the New Testament* (ed. G. Kittel and G. Friedrich;
trans. G. W. Bromiley; Grand Rapids: Eerdmans, 1977), 5:886–96; Thayer, "*pas*," *A Greek-English Lexicon*,
491–93; Danker, "pas," *A Greek-English Lexicon*, 782–84. Danker notes that *pas* pertains "to totality"
with a "focus on its individual components" (p. 782).

was made" (John 1:3 KJV). Jesus was not involved in merely creating a few trees and hills here and there, but all things were created by Him. We see the word again in Ephesians when Paul looks toward the eschaton and claims that in the fullness of time will be gathered "*all* things in Christ, both which are in heaven, and which are on earth" (Eph 1:10 KJV). Thus, an accurate doctrine of the creation of the world, the inspiration of Scripture, and the consummation of the world hinge on an accurate rendering of the Greek word *pas* as "all." So does the doctrine of salvation—that God desires the salvation of all people and has made an atonement through Christ that is sufficient for all people.

This same all-inclusive Greek word *pas* (translated as "everyone," "all," or "whosoever") is used repeatedly in the New Testament to offer an invitation to all people who would respond to God's gracious initiative with faith and obedience (italics in the following Scripture passages are mine):

> "Therefore *whoever* (*pas, hostis*) hears these sayings of Mine, and does them, I will liken him to a wise man who built his house on the rock" (Matt 7:24 NKJV; see Luke 6:47).

> "*Whosoever* (*pas hostis*) therefore shall confess me before men, him will I confess also before my Father which is in heaven. But *whosoever* (*hostis an*) shall deny me before men, him will I also deny before my Father which is in heaven" (Matt 10:32–33 KJV; see Luke 12:8).

> "Come to Me, *all* (*pantes*) who are weary and heavy-laden, and I will give you rest" (Matt 11:28 NASB; see Luke 7:37).

> John the Baptist "came as a witness, to testify about the light, so that *all* (*pantes*) might believe through him" (John 1:7 HCSB).

> Jesus is the true Light "who gives light to *everyone*" (*panta*) (John 1:9 HCSB).

> "*Whoever* (*pas*) believes in Him should not perish but have eternal life. For God so loved the world that He gave His only begotten Son, that *whoever* (*pas*) believes in Him should not perish but have everlasting life" (John 3:15–16 NKJV).

> "*Everyone* (*pas*) who drinks of this water will thirst again; but whoever (*hos an*) drinks of the water that I will give him shall never thirst; but the water that I will give him will become in him a well of water springing up to eternal life" (John 4:13–14 NASB).

"For this is the will of My Father, that *everyone* (*pas*) who beholds the Son and believes in Him will have eternal life, and I Myself will raise him up on the last day" (John 6:40 NASB).

"*Everyone* (*pas*) who lives and believes in Me will never die. Do you believe this?" (John 11:26 NASB).

"I have come as Light into the world, so that *everyone* (*pas*) who believes in Me will not remain in darkness" (John 12:46 NASB).

"And it shall be that *everyone* (*pas, hos an*) who calls on the name of the Lord will be saved" (Acts 2:21 NASB).

"Of Him [Jesus] all (*pantes*) the prophets bear witness that through His name *everyone* (*panta*) who believes in Him receives forgiveness of sins" (Acts 10:43 NASB).

"As it is written: 'Behold, I lay in Zion a stumbling stone and rock of offense, and *whoever* (*pas*) believes on Him will not be put to shame'" (Rom 9:33 NKJV).

"For the Scripture says, '*Whoever* (*pas*) believes in Him will not be disappointed'" (Rom 10:11 NASB).

"*Whoever* (*pas*) denies the Son does not have the Father; the one who confesses the Son has the Father also" (1 John 2:23 NASB).

"*Whoever* (*pas*) believes that Jesus is the Christ is born of God, and whoever loves the Father loves the child born of Him" (1 John 5:1 NASB).

Many more of these broad invitations are found throughout Scripture. In addition, the New Testament often uses a form of *hostis*, which when combined with *an* or *ean* is an indefinite relative pronoun best translated as "anyone," "whosoever," or "everyone" and refers to the group as a whole, with a focus on each individual member of the group.[29]

An All-Inclusive Invitation in the Prophets

In the famous prophecy of Joel, this prophet comments on whom God delivers:

---

[29] Thayer, "hostis," *A Greek-English Lexicon*, 33–34, 454–57; Danker, "hostis, "*A Greek-English Lexicon*, 56–57, 725–27, 729–30. Danker notes that *hostis* means "whoever, everyone, who, in a generalizing sense," and when combined with *an* "the indefiniteness of the expression is heightened" (p. 729).

And it shall come to pass, that *whosoever* shall call on the name of the LORD shall be delivered: for in mount Zion and in Jerusalem shall be deliverance, as the LORD hath said, and in the remnant whom the LORD shall call (Joel 2:32 KJV).

Note that the "whosoever" (translated "everyone" in NASB and HCSB) is seen as consonant with "the remnant whom the Lord shall call." These are not two distinct groups but are one and the same.

All-Inclusive Invitations Offered by Jesus

Jesus offered this all-inclusive invitation in the Sermon on the Mount and throughout His teaching ministry. One might note that Jesus does not say "whoso-elect" in these invitations; the invitation is always addressed to "whosoever":[30]

"And blessed is he, *whosoever* (*hos ean*) shall not be offended in me" (Matt 11:6 KJV; see Luke 7:23).

"For *whosoever* (*hostis an*) shall do the will of my Father which is in heaven, the same is my brother, and sister, and mother" (Matt 12:50 KJV; c.f. Mark 3:35).

"If *any* man (*tis*) will come after me, let him deny himself, and take up his cross, and follow me. For *whosoever* (*hos an*) will save his life shall lose it: and *whosoever* will lose his life for my sake shall find it" (Matt 16:24–25 KJV; c.f. Mark 8:34–35; Luke 9:23–24).

"I am the living bread that came down out of heaven; if *anyone* (*ean tis*) eats of this bread, he will live forever; and the bread also which I will give for the life of the world is My flesh" (John 6:51 NASB).

"If *anyone* (*ean tis*) is willing to do His will, he will know of the teaching, whether it is of God or whether I speak from Myself" (John 7:17 NASB).

Now on the last day, the great day of the feast, Jesus stood and cried out, saying, "If *anyone* (*ean tis*) is thirsty, let him come to Me and drink" (John 7:37 NASB).

"Truly, truly, I say to you, if *anyone* (*ean tis*) keeps My word he will never see death" (John 8:51 NASB).

---

[30] See also Mark 8:38/Luke 9:26; Mark 9:37/Luke 9:48; Mark 10:15; and Luke 14:27.

All-Inclusive Invitations in the Proclamation and Epistles of the Early Church

> "And it shall be that *everyone* (*pas, hos an*) who calls on the name of the Lord will be saved" (Acts 2:21 NASB).

> "Of Him [Jesus] all (*pantes*) the prophets bear witness that through His name *everyone* (*panta*) who believes in Him receives forgiveness of sins" (Acts 10:43 NASB).

> "For *everyone* (*pas hos an*) who calls on the name of the Lord will be saved" (Rom 10:13 HCSB).

> "*Whoever* (*hos an*) confesses that Jesus is the Son of God, God abides in him, and he in God" (1 John 4:15 NASB).

All-Inclusive Invitations in John's Revelation

> "Behold, I stand at the door and knock; if *anyone* (*ean tis*) hears My voice and opens the door, I will come in to him and will dine with him, and he with Me" (Rev 3:20 NASB).

> "And the Spirit and the bride say, Come. And let him that heareth say, Come. And let him that is athirst come. And *whosoever will*, let him take the water of life freely" (Rev 22:17 KJV).

Overlooking or reinterpreting some of these verses could make them fit within a theological system. But when such a vast array of Scriptures from the various genres of Scripture offers the same all-inclusive invitation over and over again, a point comes when the question must be asked if one's theological system is doing justice to the biblical text. Is Scripture being shaped to make it agree with one's theological system, or is one's theological system being shaped according to Scripture?

Descriptions of How to Be Saved

Another line of evidence in Scripture supports the idea that grace is resistible. Whenever anyone in the New Testament asks a direct question about how to be saved, the answer never refers to election. The answer always calls for an action on the part of the person to receive the salvation that God has provided for and offers to each person. What should we say in the face of such a crowd of witnesses? It would clearly appear the gospel is offered to all those who would respond, not merely to a few select persons who receive effectual grace irresistibly. Several times in the New Testament, formulas from more of a theological perspective are expressed about how to be saved. Several times in the New Testament, salvation formulas are expressed in a variety of wordings. Again, these formulas focus on the desired response of the sinners, not the question of whether they are elect.

The Teachings of Jesus. Jesus directly tied salvation to faith in Him realized through the proclamation of the gospel: "And as Moses lifted up the serpent in the wilderness, even so must the Son of Man be lifted up, that whoever believes in Him should not perish but have eternal life. For God so loved the world that He gave His only begotten Son, that whoever believes in Him should not perish but have everlasting life" (John 3:14–16 NKJV). Therefore, Jesus commissioned His disciples to "go into all the world and preach the gospel to the whole creation. Whoever believes and is baptized will be saved, but whoever does not believe will be condemned" (Mark 16:15–16 HCSB).

The Invitation at Pentecost. At the end of the sermon at Pentecost, some of the hearers "were pierced to the heart" and said to Peter and the apostles, "Brethren, what shall we do?" (Acts 2:37 NASB). Peter's answer was not, "Are you elect or not?" His answer was, "Repent, and let each of you be baptized in the name of Jesus Christ for the forgiveness of your sins; and you will receive the gift of the Holy Spirit" (Acts 2:38 NASB). Even after this, "with many other words he [Peter] solemnly testified and kept on exhorting them, saying, 'Be saved from this perverse generation!'" (Acts 2:40 NASB). Of course, had Peter known that grace was irresistible, he wouldn't have wasted his time with such a solemn exhortation for fear that those who were hearing only the general call would be confused into being saved.

The Appeal to the Philippian Jailer. Similarly, when the Philippian jailer saw the miraculous intervention of God in releasing Paul and Silas from his jail, he fell at their feet and asked the salvation question in the most direct way possible: "Sirs, what must I do to be saved?" (Acts 16:30 NASB). Peter did not respond by talking about election. Instead, he answered, "Believe in the Lord Jesus, and you will be saved, you and your household" (Acts 16:31 NASB).

The Appeal to the Ethiopian Eunuch. After Philip had witnessed to the Ethiopian eunuch from the Old Testament prophesies, the eunuch exclaimed, "'Look! Water! What prevents me from being baptized?' And

Philip said, 'If you believe with all your heart, you may.' And he answered and said, 'I believe that Jesus Christ is the Son of God' " (Acts 8:36–37 NASB). And so he was baptized. Note that his being baptized was conditional upon "if" he believed.

The Teaching of Paul. "If you confess with your mouth, 'Jesus is Lord,' and believe in your heart that God raised Him from the dead, you will be saved. With the heart one believes, resulting in righteousness, and with the mouth one confesses, resulting in salvation" (Rom 10:9–10 HCSB).

To summarize, the Scriptures contain significant evidence against irresistible grace. The Bible specifically teaches that the Holy Spirit can be resisted. It repeatedly calls upon all people to respond to God's gracious invitation. The descriptions of how to be saved seem to focus on human response to God's initiative. The texts do not seem to support irresistible grace, but they call upon persons to respond to the grace of God in specific ways. This is not to say, of course, that Calvinists cannot reach different interpretations of these texts, based upon their theological presuppositions. It means that the plain sense reading of these texts tends to support the belief that God's grace, by His own intent and design, is resistible.

A Theological Assessment of Irresistible Grace

What about irresistible grace from a theological perspective? How does irresistible grace fit in with persons from a Baptist heritage? What does the Baptist Faith and Message say about irresistible grace and the other so-called "doctrines of grace"?

The Baptist Faith and Message 2000 and Irresistible Grace

The Bible is our ultimate standard for faith and practice. However, as a Southern Baptist, The Baptist Faith and Message 2000,[31] the confessional affirmation of the United States of America's largest Protestant denomination, provides valuable insight about doctrinal issues. What does the

---

[31] In this section I write with reference to The Baptist Faith and Message 2000, available online at the Baptist Center for Theology and Ministry at http://baptistcenter.com/bfm2000.html. Commentary on the confession can be found in C. S. Kelley Jr., R. Land, and R. A. Mohler Jr., *The Baptist Faith and Message 2000* (Nashville: Lifeway, 2007); and D. Blount and J. Wooddell, *The Baptist Faith and Message 2000: Critical Issues in America's Largest Protestant Denomination* (New York: Rowman and Littlefield, 2007).

BF&M 2000 say about irresistible grace? The term "irresistible grace" does not appear in the BF&M 2000. Furthermore, the BF&M 2000 does not explicitly endorse total depravity, unconditional election, limited atonement, or irresistible grace, although Calvinists and non-Calvinists alike can point to language in the confession that could support each position. In my understanding, irresistible grace is not supported in the definitions of "salvation," "regeneration," and "justification" in Article IV of the BF&M 2000. Salvation "is offered freely to all who *accept* Jesus Christ as Lord and Saviour." Regeneration "is a change of heart wrought by the Holy Spirit through conviction of sin, to which the sinner *responds* in repentance toward God and faith in the Lord Jesus Christ." Justification "is God's gracious and full acquittal upon principles of His righteousness of *all sinners who repent and believe* in Christ." The BF&M 2000 explicitly states, *"There is no salvation apart from personal faith in Jesus Christ as Lord."* Likewise, the kingdom of God in Article IX is defined as "the realm of salvation *into which men enter by trustful, childlike commitment to Jesus Christ."*

In addition, the BF&M 2000 holds a high view of human freedom and moral accountability. Article V affirms that God's election is *"consistent with the free agency of man."* Article III also affirms that we were endowed at creation with "freedom of choice," and nowhere in the confession is the removal of this free choice affirmed. Article III twice affirms the creation of all humans in the image of God and also affirms the "sacredness of all human personality." Article III affirms the age of accountability, that although after Adam humans are all born with a sinful nature into a sinful environment, not until humans "are capable of moral action" do they "become transgressors" and come "under condemnation,"[32] thus underscoring human freedom and individual moral accountability. All of these descriptions suggest a human responsiveness to God's grace, rather than the notion of grace being irresistibly imposed on someone's will.

Of course, the Baptist Faith and Message often equally affirms that God's grace initiates and brings about salvation. Baptists believe in justification by grace through faith. The BF&M 2000 teaches that "only the grace of God can bring man into His holy fellowship and enable man to fulfill the creative purpose of God."[33] It describes regeneration or the new birth as "a work of God's grace whereby believers become new creatures

---

[32] Baptist Faith and Message 2000, Article III, "Man."
[33] Ibid., Article III, "Man."

in Christ Jesus. It is a change of heart wrought by the Holy Spirit through conviction of sin, to which the sinner responds in repentance toward God and faith in the Lord Jesus Christ."[34] The BF&M 2000 describes election as "the gracious purpose of God, according to which He regenerates, justifies, sanctifies, and glorifies sinners," and "is the glorious display of God's sovereign goodness."[35] The Holy Spirit, according to the BF&M 2000, "convicts men of sin, of righteousness, and of judgment. He calls men to the Saviour, and effects regeneration. At the moment of regeneration He baptizes every believer into the Body of Christ."[36]

The BF&M 2000 does not attempt to relieve the tension between God's sovereignty and human free will into a neat theological system; it leaves this dynamic tension as we find it in the pages of Scripture. It affirms both a high view of the sovereignty of God and a high view of human free will and moral accountability. It affirms both the necessity (because of human fallenness) for God's initiative in salvation through His grace, and the necessity that persons must respond to God's gracious gift of salvation and receive it into their lives.

Seven Theological Concerns About Irresistible Grace

From my perspective, irresistible grace does not square well with a number of doctrines. I will raise a number of questions about the viability of a doctrine of irresistible grace from a Southern Baptist Christian theological perspective. These concerns are addressed primarily to some who go to extremes in Calvinism and do not apply to all Calvinists. If these concerns or criticisms do not pertain to you, then God bless you! It would greatly help if you would be specific and deliberate in distinguishing yourself from these more extreme forms of Calvinism. My primary concern is the trajectory that seems to be emerging in moving from moderate Calvinism to more militant forms of Calvinism. My concern is less where young Calvinists may be now than where they or their followers may be a decade from now. Where are the limits? In the pages that follow, I will raise seven specific theological concerns about the notion of irresistible grace.

---

[34] Ibid., Article IV, "Salvation."
[35] Ibid., Article V, "God's Purpose of Grace."
[36] Ibid., Article Ic, "God the Holy Spirit."

1. Irresistible Grace Can Lead to the Denial of the Necessity for Conversion

Some Calvinists understand the effectual call to be grounded in double predestination; therefore, conversion is unnecessary, and infant baptism is affirmed. Because they understand the covenant of God includes children through their parents, personal conversion is not necessary. In fact, this brand of Calvinists bristles at the notion that children from Christian families should be seen as needing to be converted at all. David Engelsma states, "Speaking for myself, to the brash, presumptuous question sometimes put to me by those of a revivalist, rather than covenantal, mentality, 'When were you converted?' I have answered in all seriousness, 'When was I not converted?' "[37] He further declares, "As a Reformed minister and parent, I have no interest whatever in conversion as the basis for viewing baptized children as God's dear children, loved of him from eternity, redeemed by Jesus, and promised the Holy Spirit, the author of faith. None!"[38] So from Engelsma's perspective, children of believers are automatically saved under their parents' covenant and thus have no need for personal conversion. However, children of unbelievers who die in infancy are reprobate and go to hell.[39]

Engelsma's position, although perhaps embarrassing and unpopular among some contemporary Calvinists, is consistent with the teachings of John Calvin himself, as well as affirmations in the Synod of Dort and the Westminster Confession. According to Article 17 in Section I of the Synod of Dort, titled "The Salvation of the Infants of Believers," the Synod of Dort affirmed, "Since we must make judgments about God's will from his Word, which testifies that the children of *believers* are holy, not by nature but by virtue of the gracious covenant in which they together with their parents are included, godly parents ought not to doubt the election *and salvation* of their children whom God calls out of this life in infancy."[40] Likewise, section III of chapter X of the Westminster Confession, titled "Of Effectual Calling," affirms: "Elect infants, dying in infancy, are regenerated, and saved by Christ, through the Spirit, who works when, and where,

---

[37] D. J. Engelsma, *The Covenant of God and the Children of Believers: Sovereign Grace in the Covenant* (Grandville, MI: Reformed Free Publishing Association, 2005), 13–16.

[38] Ibid., 82.

[39] Ibid., 70–78.

[40] "The Canons of the Synod of Dort," Head I, Article 17, in Schaff, 3:585.

and how He pleases: so also are all other elect persons who are incapable of being outwardly called by the ministry of the Word."[41]

In the perspective of Calvinists such as Engelsma, conversion is an unnecessary add-on because children of believers are covered under the covenant of their parents. The obverse of this doctrine, the eternal damnation of the children of unbelievers, obviously brings with it challenging implications for pastoral ministry. Contemporary outspoken Calvinists such as R. C. Sproul Jr. also affirm that the eternal destiny of infants has nothing to do with their personal decision to accept or reject Christ after the age of accountability. They are already guilty of original sin unless they have been baptized as infants. Therefore, only believers' children who have experienced infant baptism can be saved. Sproul Jr. chided Billy Graham for his words in comforting the victims of the Oklahoma City bombing (which included many victims from a children's day care center). Graham said, "Someday there will be a glorious reunion with those who have died and gone to heaven before us, and that includes all those innocent children that are lost. They're not lost from God because any child that young is automatically in heaven and in God's arms."[42] Sproul Jr. insisted that since we are born guilty of original sin, and infants have no opportunity for justification by faith, they have no real hope of salvation. He accused Graham of advocating "a new gospel—justification by youth alone."[43] Sproul's article was infamous not only in quickly setting the record for the number of letters to the editor but also in setting the record for producing not a single letter affirming Sproul's position.

Baptists have always believed that since infants are not yet capable of actual sin until the age of accountability and since their sinful nature is saved through the atonement, they go to heaven. Humans are not held accountable for their sins until they are morally accountable, and at that point their eternal destiny is decided by their response to God's initiative of grace, not the spiritual heritage of their parents.

Hopefully, few Calvinistic Baptists are tempted to practice nonconversionist Calvinism in the manner of Engelsma. When Baptists go out of their way to organize fellowship with such Presbyterians rather than fellow Baptists, or when they push to allow people christened as infants

---

[41] "The Westminster Confession of Faith," chapter X, Article III, in Schaff, 3:625.

[42] R. C. Sproul Jr., "Comfort Ye My People—Justification by Youth Alone: When Does Comfort Become Confusion?" *World* 10, no. 7 (May 6, 1995): 26.

[43] Ibid.

into the membership of their own church without believer's baptism,[44] or when they speak of public invitations as sinful or as a rejection of the sovereignty of God, seeing much difference between them is difficult.

2. Irresistible Grace Reverses the Biblical Order of Salvation

All major forms of Calvinism (both David Engelsma's nonconversionist "Old Light Calvinism" and the more popular conversionist/New Light Calvinist perspective) affirm an *ordo salutis*, an order of salvation, which is the foundation upon which the Calvinist theological system is built. One of the key elements of this order of salvation is that regeneration precedes conversion. Fundamental to belief in irresistible grace is the presupposition that all persons are spiritually dead as a result of Adam's sin, so humans are incapable of responding in any way to the gospel apart from the prior act of being regenerated by the Spirit of God. Calvinists and Arminians agree that only God can raise people to new life; humans cannot save or regenerate themselves. As Calvinist writer James White has acknowledged, "Neither side in the debate will deny that God is the one who raises men to spiritual life."[45] So what is the difference? In irresistible grace persons are totally unable to respond at all to God's grace until the Holy Spirit has totally regenerated them, whereas in the opposing per-

---

[44] For example, John Piper, pastor of Bethlehem Baptist Church in Minneapolis (a Baptist General Conference church), presented the church's elders a paper called "Twelve Theses on Baptism and Its Relationship to Church Membership, Church Leadership, and Wider Affiliations and Partnerships of Bethlehem Baptist Church" in January 2002. In this paper Piper proposed the following amendment concerning the requirement for baptism for membership in the church: "Therefore, where the belief in the Biblical validity of infant baptism does not involve baptismal regeneration or the guarantee of saving grace, this belief is not viewed by the elders of Bethlehem Baptist Church as a weighty or central enough departure from Biblical teaching to exclude a person from membership, if he meets all other relevant qualifications and is persuaded from Bible study and a clear conscience that his baptism is valid. In such a case we would not require baptism by immersion as a believer for membership but would teach and pray toward a change of mind that would lead such members eventually to such a baptism" (John Piper, "Twelve Theses on Baptism and Its Relationship to Church Membership, Church Leadership, and Wider Affiliations and Partnerships of Bethlehem Baptist Church," in *Baptism and Church Membership at Bethlehem Baptist Church: Eight Recommendations for Constitutional Revision* [by J. Piper, A. Chediak, and T. Steller, available online at http://desiringgod.org/media/pdf/baptism_and_membership.pdf], 14). The doctrinal confession of the Baptist General Conference of which Bethlehem Baptist Church is a part affirms: "We believe that Christian baptism is the immersion of a believer in water into the name of the triune God." (See "The Ordinances," art. 9 of *An Affirmation of Our Faith*, available at the Baptist General Conference Web site at http://www.bgcworld.org/intro/affirm.htm.) Piper's proposed statement did not find general agreement among the church's elders. After the issue was discussed for several years, an amended policy was approved eventually by the elders in August 2005 but later was withdrawn in the face of public outcry.

[45] White, *Debating Calvinism*, 197–98.

spective humans can respond to the gracious initiative of God with the help of the Holy Spirit.

Calvinists base much of their teachings on Eph 2:1, that those who are lost are "dead in trespasses and sins." However, they tend to equate spiritual deadness with physical deadness and do not qualify this spiritual deadness in the light of other descriptions of lostness even in the same chapter. Ephesians 2 also speaks of the lost as "foreigners" and "aliens" (Eph 2:12, 19). Foreigners do not enjoy citizenship and are far from God, but foreigners are still alive. Ephesians 2:1 is further qualified by 1 Cor 1:18 ("the message of the cross is foolishness to those who are perishing" NASB), 2 Cor 2:15 ("For to God we are the fragrance of Christ among those who are being saved and among those who are perishing" HCSB), and 2 Cor 4:3 ("And even if our gospel is veiled, it is veiled to those who are perishing" NASB). The concept of spiritual deadness is present in all three passages, but the deadness is not yet complete. The lost are perishing but not yet dead. Opportunity remains for a response that can result in a different destiny.

But Calvinists take spiritual deadness as not only the primary metaphor but the literal basis on which they build the rest of their theology superstructure. For example, in a sermon on Ephesians 2, John MacArthur said that "spiritual death is an inability to respond to stimulus." A sinner "has no capacity to respond to God. . . . Spiritually dead people are like zombies—they don't know they're dead and they're still going through the motions of living."[46] Therefore, Calvinists reason, people must be regenerated (spiritually reborn, born again) before they can be alive enough spiritually to respond to God. As John Piper and the staff at Bethlehem Baptist Church affirm, "We do not think that faith precedes and causes new birth. Faith is the evidence that God has begotten us anew."[47]

Clearly, being saved before believing in Christ is getting "the cart before the horse." This question can be divided into three questions about which comes first: Regeneration or salvation? Receiving the Holy Spirit or salvation? Salvation or repentance and faith? Many key texts make these issues clear.

---

[46] J. MacArthur, "Coming Alive in Christ," a sermon available online at http://www.biblebb.com/files/MAC/sg1908.htm; accessed October 10, 2008.

[47] J. Piper and the Bethlehem Baptist Church staff, "What We Believe About the Five Points of Calvinism," available at http://www.desiringgod.org/ResourceLibrary/Articles/ByDate/ 1985/1487_What _We_Believe_About_the_Five_Points_of_Calvinism/#Grace, p. 12, or at http://c4.atomicplaypen.com/sites/BBC/resources/images/1250.pdf; accessed November 1, 2008.

First, in regard to regeneration preceding faith, R. C. Sproul affirms that "a cardinal point of Reformed theology is the maxim: Regeneration precedes faith. . . . We do not believe in order to be born again; we are born again in order to believe."[48] What does the Bible say? Does regeneration (spiritual life, being born again, new birth) come first or does faith?

> Jesus told Nicodemus that the Son of Man must be lifted up like Moses lifted up the serpent in the wilderness, "*so that* everyone who believes in Him *will have* eternal life. For God loved the world in this way: He gave His only Son, so that everyone who believes in Him will not perish but have eternal life" (John 3:15–16 HCSB). Note that proclamation of the gospel comes first, is followed by belief, and then is followed by eternal life.

> "He who believes in the Son has eternal life; but he who does not obey the Son will not see life, but the wrath of God abides on him" (John 3:36 NASB).

> "Truly, truly, I say to you, he who hears My word, and believes Him who sent Me, has eternal life, and does not come into judgment, but has passed out of death into life" (John 5:24 NASB)

> In dealing with the Pharisees, Jesus said, "And you are unwilling to come to Me, *that* you may have life" (John 5:40 NASB).

> "I am the living bread that came down out of heaven; if anyone eats of this bread, he *will live* forever" (John 6:51 NASB).

> So Jesus said to them, "Truly, truly, I say to you, unless you eat the flesh of the Son of Man and drink His blood, you have no life in yourselves. He who eats My flesh and drinks My blood has eternal life, and I will raise him up on the last day. . . . As the living Father sent Me, and I live because of the Father, so he who eats Me, he also *shall live* because of Me" (John 6:53–54,57 NASB).

> "Jesus said to her, 'I am the resurrection and the life; *he who believes in Me shall live* even if he dies'" (John 11:25 NASB). If Jesus thought that regeneration preceded conversion, He would have said that he who is spiritually alive will believe; but what Jesus said is that he who believes will live.

---

[48] Sproul, *Chosen by God*, 72–73.

"But these have been written that you may believe that Jesus is the Christ, the Son of God; and that believing you may have life in His name" (John 20:31 NASB). Again, note that it does not say that by having life humans might believe that Jesus is the Christ, but it says believe in order that you might have life.

"Whoever believes that Jesus is the Christ is born of God; and whoever loves the Father loves the child born of Him" (1 John 5:1 NASB).

In each of these cases, faith and salvation clearly precede the new life in Christ.

The second related issue is, When does the Spirit come into a believer's life? Does the Holy Spirit come into deadened lives before or after conversion? What do the Scriptures say about the order of believing and receiving the Spirit?

"He who believes in Me, as the Scripture said, 'From his innermost being shall flow rivers of living water.' But this He spoke of the Spirit, whom those who believed in Him were to receive; for the Spirit was not yet given, because Jesus was not yet glorified" (John 7:38–39 NASB).

"Peter said to them, 'Repent, and let each of you be baptized in the name of Jesus Christ for the forgiveness of your sins; and you shall receive the gift of the Holy Spirit'" (Acts 2:38 NASB).

"Because you are sons, God has sent forth the Spirit of His Son into our hearts, crying, 'Abba! Father'" (Gal 4:6 NASB).

"The purpose was that the blessing of Abraham would come to the Gentiles in Christ Jesus, so that we could receive the promise of the Spirit through faith" (Gal 3:13 HCSB). Were the Calvinist perspective correct, we would expect this verse to read, "That we might receive faith through the work of the Spirit."

In Him, you also, after listening to the message of truth, the gospel of your salvation—having also believed, you were sealed in Him with the Holy Spirit of promise, who is given as a pledge of our inheritance, with a view to the redemption of God's own possession, to the praise of His glory" (Eph 1:13–14 NASB).

These texts show that the Spirit and spiritual life do not come into a person's life fully until after their conversion. Instead, the Holy Spirit convicts and convinces the sinner through enabling or "prevenient" grace, leading and enabling the person to respond in faith, resulting in regeneration, justification, and salvation.[49]

Charles Spurgeon, an evangelistic Calvinist who took issue with more extreme Calvinists, said in a sermon defending Dwight L. Moody's preaching, "We are all ready to set our seal to the clearest statement that men are saved by faith in Jesus Christ, and saved the moment they believe. We all hold and teach that there is such a thing as conversion, and that when men are converted they become other men than they were before, and a new life begins which will culminate in eternal glory."[50] Spurgeon, at least, seemed to teach that conversion preceded "the new life."

A third related issue is, Which comes first, repentance and faith or regeneration? The Calvinist theologian Loraine Boettner dares to say, "A man is not saved because he believes in Christ; he believes in Christ because he is saved."[51] Again, what does the Bible say?

> Then He said to them, "Go into all the world and preach the gospel to the whole creation. Whoever believes and is baptized will be saved, but whoever does not believe will be condemned" (Mark 16:15–16 HCSB).

> But as many as received him, to them gave he power to become the sons of GOD, even to them that believe on his name (John 1:12 KJV).

> But these have been written that you may believe that Jesus is the Christ, the Son of God; and that believing you may have life in His name (John 20:31 NASB).

> "Through him everyone who believes is justified from everything you could not be justified from by the law of Moses" (Acts 13:39 NIV).

> "Believe in the Lord Jesus, and you shall be saved, you and your household" (Acts 16:31 NASB).

> Crispus, the leader of the synagogue, believed in the Lord with all his household, and many of the Corinthians when they heard were believing and being baptized (Acts 18:8 NASB).

---

[49] I am using the term *enabling grace* to be synonymous with prevenient grace. The issue is *not* whether unaided humans would naturally seek God without His grace. The issue is whether the Holy Spirit regenerates persons before they respond in faith to God. In both approaches, it is the Holy Spirit who, through gospel preaching and other means, convicts and convinces sinners to repent of their sins and to trust Christ.

[50] Charles Spurgeon, "Mssrs. Moody and Sankey Defended; or, A Vindication of the Doctrine of Justification by Faith," *The Metropolitan Tabernacle Pulpit*, vol. 21 (1875): 337.

[51] Loraine Boettner, *The Reformed Doctrine of Predestination* (Philadelphia: Presbyterian and Reformed, 1991), 101.

For I am not ashamed of the gospel, for it is the power of God for salvation to everyone who believes, to the Jew first and also to the Greek (Rom 1:16 NASB).

If you confess with your mouth, "Jesus is Lord," and believe in your heart that God raised Him from the dead, you will be saved. With the heart one believes, resulting in righteousness, and with the mouth one confesses, resulting in salvation (Rom 10:9–10 HCSB).

God was well-pleased through the foolishness of the message preached to save those who believe (1 Cor 1:21 NASB).

And without faith it is impossible to please Him, for he who comes to God must believe that He is, and that He is a rewarder of those who seek Him (Heb 11:6 NASB).

In all these Scriptures, repentance and faith clearly precede regeneration. In addition to these biblical statements, it is difficult to imagine how regeneration preceding faith would function realistically. Some, such as John Piper, suggest that "regeneration and faith are so closely connected that in experience we cannot distinguish them."[52] How would regeneration preceding faith play out in real life? Why did the person attend church in the first place? A lost man, according to Calvinists, will not seek God, so he must first be regenerated before he seeks God. But this regeneration would not happen immediately. If he was regenerated on Wednesday and his regenerated will resolved to go to church the following Sunday, then it would be several days before he heard the gospel so he could believe. Perhaps he stumbled into a Unitarian Universalist church on the first Sunday, and it took several Sundays before he heard an authentic gospel message. In other cases he may live in an area where the gospel is not readily accessible to him. Perhaps he will struggle for years about this decision, like C. S. Lewis, who famously struggled for years before coming to Christ. As Lewis described it, he "came into Christianity kicking and screaming" as "the most dejected and reluctant convert in all England."[53] What if Lewis had been killed in an accident before he came to faith? Is it possible to be among the elect but not saved? Evidently so, for the Westminster Confession asserts that not only are the children of the elect saved without

---

[52] Piper and the Bethlehem Baptist Church staff, "What We Believe About the Five Points of Calvinism," 14.

[53] C. S. Lewis, *Surprised by Joy: The Shape of My Early Life* (Orlando: Harcourt Brace, 1955), 28–29, 229.

hearing the gospel but also "other elect persons who are incapable of being outwardly called by the ministry of the Word."[54]

On the other hand, if Piper is right and the two events occur virtually simultaneously, how did it happen that this totally depraved, lost man was seeking Christ? Since he was spiritually dead with a depraved will, his own will could not have impelled him to go to church on Sunday or for many Sundays. Theoretically, this idea sounds good, but it does not make any sense in real life. Instead, we affirm the scriptural order that repentance and faith precede conversion/regeneration/justification, and the new life in the Spirit.

3. Irresistible Grace Could Weaken the Significance of Preaching the Word of God, Evangelism, and Missions

With their strong emphasis on election and regeneration worked directly by the Holy Spirit preceding and without the preaching of the gospel, Calvinism may inadvertently discount the preaching of the Word of God. This challenge may come as a surprise since many Calvinists expound the Word of God well, and Calvinist confessions clearly call for the proclamation of the gospel in the "general call." But if the primary means of salvation is either as children through infant baptism under the covenant of their parents, or through the Holy Spirit directly regenerating people apart from and prior to the preaching of the gospel, why is preaching that important?

In the same light it also seems that the doctrine of irresistible grace could have a stultifying effect on evangelism and missions.[55] Is proclamation of the gospel an unnecessary add-on after people have already been saved? If, as Calvinist theologian Loraine Boettner has said, "A man is not saved because he believes in Christ; he believes in Christ because he is saved,"[56] then why would preaching and evangelism be essential for the furtherance of the gospel? The New Testament seems to put a higher value on the preaching and hearing of the Word of God than this sort of Calvinism allows. From the biblical perspective, preaching the gospel is the primary delivery system for salvation:

---

[54] "The Westminster Confession of Faith," chapter X, Article III, in Schaff, 3:625.

[55] For interesting statistical data, see Steve Lemke, "The Future of the Southern Baptist Convention as Evangelicals," a paper presented at the Maintaining Baptist Distinctives Conference at Mid-America Baptist Theological Seminary in April 2005, available online at http://www.nobts.edu/Faculty/ItoR/LemkeSW/Personal/SBCfuture.pdf.

[56] Boettner, 101.

For after that in the wisdom of God the world by wisdom knew not God, it pleased God by the foolishness of preaching to save them that believe (1 Cor 1:21 KJV).

And on the Sabbath day we went outside the gate to a riverside, where we were supposing that there would be a place of prayer; and we sat down and began speaking to the women who had assembled. And a certain woman named Lydia, from the city of Thyatira, a seller of purple fabrics, a worshiper of God, was listening; and the Lord opened her heart to respond to the things spoken by Paul. And when she and her household had been baptized (Acts 16:13–15 NASB).

For this reason we also constantly thank God that when you received the word of God which you heard from us, you accepted it not as the word of men, but for what it really is, the word of God, which also performs its work in you who believe. For you, brethren, . . . also endured the same sufferings at the hands of your own countrymen, even as they did from the Jews, who both killed the Lord Jesus and the prophets, and drove us out. They are not pleasing to God, but hostile to all men, hindering us from speaking to the Gentiles so that they may be saved (1 Thess 2:1–16 NASB).

For "whoever calls on the name of the LORD shall be saved." How then shall they call on Him in whom they have not believed? And how shall they believe in Him of whom they have not heard? And how shall they hear without a preacher? And how shall they preach unless they are sent? . . . So then faith comes by hearing, and hearing by the word of God (Rom 10:13–15, 17 NKJV).

However, speaking on this passage of Scripture, John Calvin insisted that gospel preaching was not the only way people could be saved:

But they do not consider, that when the apostle makes hearing the source of faith, he only describes the ordinary economy and dispensation of the Lord, which he generally observes in the calling of his people; but does not prescribe a perpetual rule for him, precluding his employment of any other method; which he has certainly employed in the calling of many, to whom he has given the true knowledge of himself in an internal manner, by the illumination of his Spirit, without the intervention of any preaching.[57]

---

[57] J. Calvin, *Institutes of the Christian Religion* (ed. John T. McNeill; Philadelphia: Westminster John Knox, 1980), 2:622.

When John Frame answered the question, What doctrines must be believed to be saved?, he was being consistent within his Calvinistic heritage. Frame responded, "None. I hold the Reformed view that children in infancy, even before birth, can be regenerated and saved, presumably before they have any conscious doctrinal beliefs."[58] To cite another example, Calvinist theologian Terrance Tiessen proposes that (a) persons can be saved outside of and apart from the church, (b) that genuine revelatory experiences can be had in other world religions that lead to saving faith, (c) that one can be saved without becoming a Christian, (d) that one can be saved without a conscious commitment to Jesus Christ, (e) that since other revelatory and salvific means are available, the missionary mandate is important but not essential to the fulfillment of God's kingdom, (f) that a child or mentally incompetent person can and must be saved in the same way as a competent adult, and (g) that all the unsaved upon their death will have one last opportunity to accept Christ without any knowledge of Christ.[59]

This approach is defective because it heightens the idea that conscious personal acceptance of the gospel is not essential, and thus it diminishes the role of the preaching of the gospel. Since the New Testament holds preaching in exceptional regard, we ought to take pause when a theological system lessens this value.

Directly connected with the issue of the proclamation of the gospel is a cluster of issues within Calvinism: (a) whether or not the gospel should be preached "promiscuously" to all people, (b) whether the "well-meant offer" or "free offer" of the gospel should be made to all persons, and (c) should public invitations be offered? These questions flow directly from the font of the Synod of Dort:

> Moreover, the promise of the gospel is that whosoever believes in Christ crucified shall not perish, but have eternal life. This promise, together with the command to repent and believe, ought to be declared and published to all nations, and to all persons promiscuously and without distinction, to whom God out of His good pleasure sends the gospel.[60]

---

[58] John Frame, interview by Marco Gonzalez, posted December 2, 2005 available online at http://www.reformationtheology.com/2005/12/an_interview_with_john_frame_b_1.php; accessed October 23, 2008.

[59] T. Tiessen, *Who Can Be Saved? Reassessing Salvation in Christ and in World Religions* (Downers Grove: InterVarsity, 2004). For a critique of this book, see S. Lemke, "Teaching Them to Observe the Doctrine of Salvation: Tiessen's Accessibilism vs. Jesus' Exclusivism" (paper presented at the Evangelical Theological Society, in San Diego, CA, on November 14, 2007 available online at http://www.nobts.edu/Faculty/Itor/LemkeSW/Personal/Tiessen%20salvation%20ETS%20 paperfinal.pdf).

[60] "The Canons of the Synod of Dort," head II, article V, in Schaff, 3:586.

Challenging the phrase about preaching the gospel "to all persons promiscuously" is tempting since in modern English doing something promiscuously suggests the idea of doing something inappropriate or violating the rules. But the root idea of the word is to preach "without differentiation," in this case between the elect and the non-elect.

The question of whether the "well-meant offer" of the gospel should, indeed, be offered is a controversial point among Calvinists. David Engelsma has defined "the well-meant offer" as

> the conception, or doctrine, of the preaching of the blessed gospel in Calvinistic circles that holds that God sends the gospel to all who hear out of an attitude of grace to them all and with a desire to save them all. The 'well-meant offer' insists, at the very least, on these two notions: God is gracious in the preaching to all hearers; and God has a will, or sincere desire, for the salvation of every man who hears the gospel.[61]

The Protestant Reformed Churches of which Engelsma is a part, while affirming that the gospel is to be preached to everyone and denying that it should be preached only to the elect, "deny that the preaching of the gospel is grace to all who hear it."[62] In answer to the question, Is Jesus Christ gracious in the gospel to all who hear the preaching?, "the answer of the PRC is an unqualified, emphatic 'no!' Neither is there a gracious operation of the Spirit of Christ upon the heart of the reprobate who hears the preaching, nor is there a gracious attitude in the Father of Jesus Christ toward the reprobate who comes under the preaching."[63] The PRC is aghast at their fellow Calvinists who make the well-meant offer; indeed, Engelsma alleges that "the entire, massive weight of the Canons [of Dort] comes down on the side of the denial of the offer and against 'the well-meant offer,'" that making the offer is evidence of "the apostasy of Reformed churches from the great creedal doctrines of sovereign, particular grace," thus leading to the consequence that "the Canons of Dordt are in error."[64] To Engelsma, "the doctrine of the 'well-meant offer' will

---

[61] D. Engelsma, "Is Denial of the 'Well-Meant Offer' Hyper-Calvinism?," available online at http://www.prca.org/pamphlets/pamphlet_35.html; accessed October 23, 2008.

[62] Although the Protestant Reformed Churches are often labeled as hyper-Calvinists, Engelsma strenuously objects to that caricature and rejects that description because the PRC still advocates preaching the gospel to all persons, not just the elect. He describes hyper-Calvinists as "an aberration, if not a heresy" for refusing to preach to anyone but the elect (Engelsma, "Is Denial of the 'Well-Meant Offer' Hyper-Calvinism?," *op. cit.*). From my experience, no one wants to be labeled a hyper-Calvinist since the term lacks consistent definition and thus is not a useful term.

[63] Engelsma, "Is Denial of the 'Well-Meant Offer' Hyper-Calvinism?", *op.cit.*

[64] Ibid.

drive out the doctrine of predestination,"[65] and amounts to an affirmation of Arminianism:

> We charge, in dead earnest, that the offer is the Arminian view of gospel-preaching. . . . This doctrine of preaching was fundamental to the entire Arminian theology. . . . On the Arminian view of preaching, there cannot be a decree of predestination in God excluding any from salvation. And if there is no decree of predestination, as confessed by Reformed orthodoxy, neither is there any of the other of "the five points of Calvinism." The PRC see the "well-meant offer" of professing Calvinists as identical with the Arminian doctrine of preaching in at least two basic respects: grace for all in the gospel of Christ and a divine will for the salvation of all. It is incontrovertible that the offer teaches— does not imply, but teaches—that God's grace in the preaching is resistible, *and resisted*, and that God's will for the salvation of sinners is frustrated. Many towards whom grace is directed in the preaching successfully refuse it; and many whom God desires to save perish.[66]

If the concession were made that the well-meant offer is truly a gracious offer, Engelsma argues, Calvinists should acknowledge that "the Arminians were right," and should "renounce Dordt."[67] As he says, "Let us call a world-wide Reformed synod, preferably at Dordt, in order to rescind the condemnation of Arminianism and in order to make humble confession of our fathers' sins against Arminius, Episcopius, and the others!"[68]

Without engaging in this internecine discussion within Calvinism, I will suggest three observations: (1) If these Calvinist doctrines lead Calvinists to extensive debates on these issues, something must be wrong with their doctrines; (2) the heated rhetoric some Calvinists use against evangelistic invitations does nothing but heighten these concerns;[69] and

---

[65] Ibid.

[66] Ibid.

[67] Ibid.

[68] Ibid.

[69] For a discussion on this issue, see J. Elliff, K. Keathley, and M. Coppenger, "Walking the Aisle," in *Heartland* (Summer 1999): 1, 4–9. Three articles in this issue discuss the public invitation: J. Elliff, "Closing with Christ," 1, 6–7; K. Keathley, "Rescuing the Perishing," 1, 4–6; and M. Coppenger, "Kairos and the Altar Call," 8–9. Elliff argues that altar calls are unbiblical, Keathley argues that invitations are biblical and appropriate, and Coppenger allows for some limited use of altar calls. See also K. Keathley, "Rescue the Perishing: A Defense of Giving Invitations," *Journal for Baptist Theology and Ministry* 1, no. 1 (Spring 2003): 4–16, available online from the Baptist Center for Theology and Ministry of New Orleans Baptist Theological Seminary at http://baptistcenter.com/Journal%20Articles/Spr%20 2003/02% 20Rescuing%20the%20Perishing%20- %20Spr%202003.pdf.

(3) if some Calvinist views are taken seriously, it could lead to diminishing a vital approach to preaching, evangelism, and missions.

4. Irresistible Grace Creates Questions About the Character of God, Particularly Regarding the Problem of Evil

In several ways the notion of irresistible grace creates questions about the character of God. First, the two callings (the outward and inward, effectual and ineffectual, serious and not serious callings) correspond to two apparently contradictory wills within God (the revealed and secret wills of God). The revealed will of God issues for the Great Commission that the gospel should be preached to all nations, but the secret will is that only a small group of elect will be saved. The revealed will commands the general, outward call to be proclaimed, but the secret will knows that only a few will receive the effectual, serious calling from the Holy Spirit. The God of hard Calvinism is either disingenuous, cynically making a pseudo-offer of salvation to persons whom He has not given the means to accept, or there is a deep inner conflict within the will of God. If He has extended a general call to all persons to be saved, but has given the effectual call irresistibly to just a few, the general call seems rather misleading. This conflict between the wills of God portrays Him as having a divided mind. In response to this challenge, Calvinists appeal to mystery. Is that a successful move?

The Remonstrants, against whom the Synod of Dort was directed, raised the concern that the hard Calvinist perspective advocated by the Synod of Dort portrayed God as riddled by inner conflict. The Remonstrants later affirmed in a response written after the Synod of Dort:

8. Whomsoever God calls, he calls them seriously, that is, with a sincere and not with a dissembled intention and will of saving them. Neither do we subscribe to the opinion of those persons who assert that God outwardly calls certain men whom he does not will to call inwardly, that is, whom he is unwilling to be truly converted, even prior to their rejection of the grace of calling.

9. There is not in God a secret will of that kind which is so opposed to his will revealed in his word, that according to this same secret will he does not will the conversion and salvation of the greatest part of those whom, by the word of his Gospel, and by his revealed will, he seriously calls and invites to faith and salvation.

10. Neither on this point do we admit of a holy dissimulation, as it is the manner of some men to speak, or of a twofold person in the Deity.[70]

Some Calvinists attempt to downplay this criticism by advocating the "well-meant offer" or "free offer" of the gospel to the lost. As the Synod of Dort affirms in doctrine 2, article 5:

Moreover, the promise of the gospel is that whosoever believes in Christ crucified shall not perish, but have eternal life. This promise, together with the command to repent and believe, ought to be declared and published to all nations, and to all persons promiscuously and without distinction, to whom God out of His good pleasure sends the gospel.

However, not only do Arminians find this contradictory—so do strong Calvinists! David Engelsma finds little to differentiate the "free offer" Calvinists from Arminians. Engelsma will not permit the appeal by those advocating the promiscuous offer of the gospel to retreat to mystery as an explanation for the apparent conflict within God's will:

Indeed, we ask the defender of the offer, "On this view why are some saved by the gospel, and others not?" The answer cannot be God's grace and God's will, for His grace and His will to save are the same both to those who are saved and to those who perish. The answer must be the will of the sinner—free will. . . .

A customary response by Reformed defenders of the offer to this attack on the offer has been the appeal to "mystery" and "paradox." How the offer harmonizes with predestination is a "sacred mystery," unknown and unknowable. . . . Presbyterian and Reformed churches that defend the offer necessarily hold that God is, at one and the same time, gracious to all men and gracious only to some men; and that God, at one and the same time, wills that a certain man be saved and wills that that man be damned. Predestination has them teaching the one thing; and the offer has them teaching the other thing. This, they admit, is seeming contradiction—a "paradox." This does not embarrass them, for Reformed, biblical truth (so they argue) is paradoxical, illogical, and "mysterious."

---

[70] "The Opinions of the Remonstrants," Responses to article III of the Synod of Dort, comments 8–10, in Vance, *The Other Side of Calvinism*, appendix 3, 604; or available online at http://www.apuritansmind.com/Creeds/ArminianOpinions.htm.

The contention of those who deny the offer is that the God of
the Reformed doctrine of predestination cannot be gracious in the
gospel to all, and that the God Who has willed the salvation of some
and the damnation of others cannot will to save all by the gospel.
Particular grace in the gospel is in accord with the particular grace
of predestination. The definite will of God for men's salvation in the
gospel is in accord with His definite will in predestination (and, for
that matter, with His definite will in the limited atonement of our
Savior). The truth of the Reformed faith is consistent, harmonious,
and logical. . . . We charge that the offer involves a Calvinist in sheer
contradiction. That God is gracious only to some in predestination,
but gracious to all in the gospel, and that God wills only some to be
saved in predestination but wills all to be saved by the gospel, is flat,
irreconcilable contradiction. It is not paradox, but contradiction. I speak
reverently: God Himself cannot reconcile these teachings. . . .

There is no relief for the sheer contradiction in which the offer involves
a Calvinist in the doctrine of "common grace," as though the grace of
predestination were a different kind of grace from that revealed in the
gospel. For the offer exactly teaches that the grace of God for *all is grace
shown in the preaching of the gospel.* This grace is not some non-saving
favor directed towards a prosperous earthly life, but saving grace, the
grace of God in His dear Son, a grace that desires eternal salvation for
all who hear the gospel. The offer proposes universal saving grace—
precisely that which is denied by predestination.

Nor is there any relief from this absolute, intolerable contradiction
in a distinction between God's hidden will and God's revealed will.
This is attempted as some kind of explanation and mitigation of the
contradiction: The desire to save all (of the offer) is God's revealed
will; the will to save only some (of predestination) is His hidden will.
But this effort to relieve the tension of the contradiction in which the
offer involves Calvinists gets us nowhere. . . . The distinction leaves us
right where we were before the distinction was invented: God has two,
diametrically opposite, conflicting wills.[71]

Obviously, portraying God as having a divided mind and will is not
the way we want to go. It seems disingenuous for God to offer a definitive,
serious calling to some but not at all offer a serious calling to others.

---

[71] Engelsma, "Is Denial of the 'Well-Meant Offer' Hyper-Calvinism?", *op.cit.*

The second concern deals with the problem of evil. If God is in total control of everything that happens, and He is the only one who can monergistically regenerate humans, then God has much to answer for in the problem of evil. This concern is heightened by high Calvinist views on divine sovereignty. John Calvin taught that "not one drop of rain falls without God's sure command,"[72] and that "God by His secret bridle so holds and governs (persons) that they cannot move even one of their fingers without accomplishing the work of God much more than their own."[73] Wayne Grudem claims that God "exercises an extensive, ongoing, sovereign control over all aspects of His creation."[74] If God then is responsible for everything that happens, then He is responsible for evil. Most Calvinists reject this notion, but you cannot have absolute sovereignty without paying the price of God being the creator of evil things.

Some Calvinists, however, in the name of exalting God's sovereignty, accuse God of causing all things, including sin. R. C. Sproul Jr., for example, says, "Every Bible-believing Christian must conclude at least that God in some sense desired that man would fall into sin. . . . I am not accusing God of sinning; I am suggesting that he created sin."[75] Sproul Jr. describes God as "the Culprit" that caused Eve to sin in the garden.[76] Sproul Jr.'s argument is that God changed Eve's inclination to cause her to sin and thus created sin so that His mercy and wrath may be gloriously displayed. His views appear to be at variance with the Westminster Confession, which

---

[72] J. Calvin, *Institutes of the Christian Religion* (LCC 20, 21; London: SCM Press, 1960), I.16.4–5. Calvin also asserts God's meticulous providence in matters such as which mothers have milk and others do not (*Institutes*, I.16.3).

[73] J. Calvin, *A Defence of the Secret Providence of God, by Which He Executes His Eternal Decrees* (trans. Henry Cole; London: Sovereign Grace Union, 1927), 238.

[74] W. Grudem, *Systematic Theology* (Grand Rapids: Zondervan, 1994), 355. For example, John Piper has unambiguously attributed causal origin of disasters such as aircraft crashes to God alone. For example, regarding a well-publicized airline crash, Piper states that "the crash of flight 1549 was designed by God." According to Piper, God precisely guided the geese into both engines of the plane, but also assisted the captain's hands in the amazing landing of the flight in the Hudson River. Piper opines that the reason God did this was to provide a parable for the upcoming inauguration of President Obama. See John Piper, "The President, the Passengers, and the Patience of God," January 21, 2009, at http://www.desiringgod.org/ResourceLibrary/TasteAndSee/ByDate/2009/3520_The_President_the_ Passengers_and_the_Patience_of_God/; accessed 12/31/09. Piper apparently did not provide an explanation of God's purpose (nor does any sensible explanation come to mind) for crashing a Continental Airlines flight into a house in Clarence Center (near Buffalo), New York, the next month (2/13/09), killing all 49 persons on board and one in the house that was hit. For details, see http://www.cnn.com/2009/US/02/13/plane.crash.new.york/; accessed 12/31/09.

[75] R. C. Sproul Jr., *Almighty in Authority: Understanding the Sovereignty of God* (Grand Rapids: Baker, 1999), 53–54.

[76] Ibid., 51.

affirmed that God is not "the author of sin."[77] Scripture also denies that God is the author of evil:

> Let no one say when he is tempted, "I am being tempted by God";
> for God cannot be tempted by evil, and He Himself does not tempt
> anyone. . . . Do not be deceived, my beloved brethren. Every good thing
> bestowed and every perfect gift is from above, coming down from the
> Father of lights, with whom there is no variation or shifting shadow (Jas
> 1:13, 16–17 NASB).

The biblical image of God is based on God as love (1 John 4:7–8) and God as holy (1 Pet 1:16). A God who says He loves all people and desires to save all people but intentionally saves just a few is not the God of the New Testament. Imagine a fireman who goes into a burning orphanage to save some young children because they are unable to escape by themselves and can be saved only if he rescues them. Only he can save them because he has an asbestos suit. He comes back in a few minutes bringing out 3 of the 30 children, but rather than going back in to save more children, the fireman goes over to the news media and talks about how praiseworthy he is for saving the three children. Indeed, saving the three children was a good, heroic deed. But the pressing question on everyone's mind is, What about the other 27 children? Since he has the means to rescue the children and, indeed, is the only one who can save the children since they cannot save themselves, do we view the fireman as morally praiseworthy? I suggest that we would not. In fact, probably he would be charged with depraved indifference. He had the means to help them, but he would not. If we do not find that praiseworthy in a human, why would we find it praiseworthy in God?

In the final analysis two possible answers explain why there is so much evil in the world and why so many people do not become Christians and will receive eternal torment in hell. The Calvinist answer is that God willed it to be that way. Since God ordains and causes all things, He is responsible for all the suffering and pain in our world. Since God is the only One who can save and because He is all-loving, all-powerful, and all-knowing, He could save everybody. But He does not even save the majority of people. Most people go to hell for all eternity. Why? Some deep mysterious secret will in the character of God is the reason given. That approach, I believe, is not the most honoring approach to God.

---

[77] Westminster Confession, Art. 3, par 1.

But what if we take human responsibility more seriously? Then most of the suffering in the world is our own doing. Those who reject Christ are only getting the just deserts of their own choices. God's honor is vindicated. He is holy, loving, and righteous. He does love all people and desires the salvation of all people. He does save all those who come to faith through grace unto salvation. This approach gives God the greatest glory and honor—the approach that the Bible teaches.[78]

5. Irresistible Grace Does Not Have an Adequate Account of Human Freedom

The Calvinist account of willing, developed largely by Jonathan Edwards,[79] often goes by the name of compatibilism, which assumes that we always act according to our greatest desire. When God changes our wills through irresistible grace, with the Holy Spirit regenerating our spiritual life, then we genuinely desire to trust Christ. We did not have the ability to choose or do anything else. Compatibilism, in any standard definition, affirms the compatibility of freewill and determinism.[80] The discussion about compatibilism has been muddled sometimes when some theologians define compatibilism as something that it is not—that is, the compatibility of human freewill with divine sovereignty or God's will.[81] Compatibilism is

---

[78] For more on this concern about Calvinism and the problem of evil, see "Evil and God's Sovereignty," by Bruce A. Little, in chapter 11 of this book.

[79] Edwards, *Freedom of the Will* (New York: Cosimo, 2007). For more contemporary advocates of compatibilism, see P. Helm, *The Providence of God* (Downers Grove: InterVarsity, 1994); P. Helm, "Classical Calvinist Doctrine of God," in *Perspectives on the Doctrine of God: 4 Views* (ed. B. Ware; Nashville: Broadman and Holman), 5–75; J. Feinberg, *No One Like Him: The Doctrine of God*, Foundations of Evangelical Theology (Wheaton: Crossway, 2001), chap. 14, 677–776; and "God Ordains All Things," in *Predestination and Free Will: Four Views of Divine Sovereignty*, ed. D. and R. Basinger (Downers Grove: InterVarsity, 1986), 17–60.

[80] E. Craig, ed., *Routledge Encyclopedia of Philosophy*, s.v. "Free Will," by G. Strawson (New York: Routledge, 1998), 3:743–53; *Concise Routledge Encyclopedia of Philosophy*, s.v. "Free Will," by G. Strawson (New York: Routledge, 2000), 293–95; S. Blackburn, *The Oxford Dictionary of Philosophy*, s.v. "Free Will" (Oxford: Oxford University Press, 1994), 147; R. Audi, ed., *The Cambridge Dictionary of Philosophy*, s.v. "Free Will," by T. Kapitan (Cambridge: Cambridge University Press, 1999), 326–28; D. Borchart, *Encyclopedia of Philosophy*, s.v. "Determinism and Freedom," by T. Honderich, 3:24–29; T. Mautner, *A Dictionary of Philosophy*, s.v. "Compatibilism" (Cambridge: Blackwell, 1996), 76; *Stanford Encyclopedia of Philosophy*, online at http://plato.stanford.edu/entries, s.v. "Compatibilism," by M. McKenna, and "Arguments for Incompatibilism," by K. Vihvlin; accessed 10/27/09.

[81] For examples of this confusion, see D. A. Carson, *How Long, O Lord? Reflections on Suffering and Evil* (Grand Rapids: Baker, 1990), 200–204; B. Ware, *God's Greater Glory: The Exalted God of Scripture and the Christian Faith* (Wheaton: Crossway, 2004), 73–85, and in "A Modified Calvinist Doctrine of God" in *Perspectives on the Doctrine of God*, 98–99. Paul Helm points out Ware's inconsistent use of these terms in *Perspectives*, 44. An example of a compatibilist who avoids these confusions is John Feinberg in *No One Like Him*, 635–39.

not the compatibility of human freewill and the sovereignty of God. An open theist, an Arminian, and even a Pelagian would affirm the compatibility of human freedom and God's sovereignty. Nor is compatibilism the compatibility of human freedom with God's will. Again, an open theist, an Arminian, and even a Pelagian would affirm the compatibility of human freedom and some sense of God's will. The compatibility of God's sovereignty and/or God's will with human freedom is noncontroversial. The issue is whether or not Christianity is compatible with hard determinism, or whether God exercises His sovereignty in a way that allows for meaningful human freedom.

Strictly speaking, compatibilist "freedom" is really not freedom at all; it is voluntary but not free—that is, just being willing to do something does not mean that a person is free. If someone is pointing a gun at you, you might be willing to hand over your wallet to him, but that does not mean that you do so freely. You give him the wallet because you are under compulsion and have no real choice. To truly be free, there must be a choice between at least two alternatives (even if the only alternatives are "yes" or "no").

Instead of compatibilist willing, I advocate soft libertarian freedom.[82] In soft libertarianism, limited choices are available in almost every aspect of life. Absolute freedom, of course, is just a myth. Time does not permit a more thorough discussion of this issue, but soft libertarian freedom has at least the following advantages over compatibilist willing:[83]

(a) Soft libertarianism squares with our experience of decision making in real life. Almost universally, we think that when we make decisions, we are genuinely deciding something between real alternatives, not just doing what we most desire all the time.

(b) We do not always do what we desire the most, as compatibilism claims. We often do what we do not want to do, as Paul expresses in Rom 7:15–16.

---

[82] For more details, see S. Lemke, "Agent Causation, or How to Be a Soft Libertarian," available online at http://www.nobts.edu/Faculty/ItoR/LemkeSW/Personal/Agent-Causation- Or-How-to-Be-A-Soft-Libertarian-Dr.-Lemke.pdf; S. Lemke, "Agent Causation and Moral Accountability: A Proposal of the Criteria for Moral Responsibility," available online at http://www.nobts.edu/resources/pdf/ETS%20 Agent%20Causation%20and%20Moral%20Accountability.pdf; cf. A. Mele, "Soft Libertarianism and the Flickers of Freedom," in Moral Responsibility and Alternative Possibilities: Essays on the Importance of Alternative Possibilities (ed. D. Widerker and M. McKenna (Burlington: Ashgate, 2003), 251–64; and A. Mele, Free Will and Luck (New York: Oxford University Press, 2006).

[83] For more on this concern, see "Lemke, "Agent Causation, or How to Be a Soft Libertarian"; Lemke, "Agent Causation and Moral Accountability"; and "Reflections on Determinism and Human Freedom," by Jeremy Evans, in chapter 10 of this book.

(c) Compatibilist willing is not really freedom. You have to have a choice to have freedom. Acts under compulsion are not really free. The human analogies that come to mind about God changing our will in irresistible grace, whereby others change our minds irresistibly and invincibly, are unpleasant phenomena such as hypnotism or brainwashing. Obviously, these are not pleasant phenomena, and are not appropriate when applied to God.

(d) In libertarian freedom, we are morally accountable for our choices. In compatibilism, it is difficult to hold us morally accountable because we really had no choice.

(e) Only libertarian freedom offers the real choice required to accept, receive, or respond actively to the gracious offer of God through the Holy Spirit.

6. Irresistible Grace Has an Inadequate View of Time and Eternity

The entire superstructure of Calvinism is built upon the *ordo salutis*, the order of salvation, which begins with God's decrees. God predestines those whom He has chosen and then effectually calls them when their time on earth comes along. The others receive the general call but not sufficient grace to be saved.

Romans 8:29–30 provides the pattern for the order of salvation:

> For those He foreknew He also predestined to be conformed to the image of His Son, so that He would be the firstborn among many brothers. And those He predestined, He also called; and those He called, He also justified; and those He justified, He also glorified (Rom 8:29–30 HCSB).

Note that the pattern begins with God's exhaustive foreknowledge of all things, including who is going to respond to His gracious initiative in faith. My position follows the order of Rom 8:28–30—God foreknows those who will respond in faith, and on the basis of that foreknowledge He predestines, calls, justifies, and glorifies them. However, some say that basing election on comprehensive divine foreknowledge (including foreseen faith responses of individuals) does not make sense. They point out that it does not fit neatly into the categories of human logic. How could God foreknow all things before the foundation of the world and yet allow us genuine libertarian free will? How could God be sure of something before we do it? If He knows for sure what we are going to do and choose before we do it, do we really have a choice? How could God foreknow that we are going to change our minds? Once God knows what we are going to do, does it not become fixed and determined so that we have no real free choice—we can choose nothing else?

How do we respond to these concerns? The fundamental problem is that these objections apply limitations to God's omniscience and foreknowledge. God is by definition outside of time and space, and so these things are like child's play to Him. Perhaps the critics are right—it really is impossible from a human perspective. Who could traverse outside of time? Who could do what seems so impossible to human logic?

Who could do such a thing? It would have to be Someone whose ways and thoughts are above human ways and thoughts as the heaven is above the earth, Someone who is eternal and transcends time, the great I AM who is from everlasting to everlasting, Someone who was, is, and is to come, and Someone who is Creator of the heavens and the earth, who set the foundations of the universe in place and established the laws of nature. It would have to be Someone who created all the laws of logic and is Himself Truth, and Someone who is the same yesterday, today, and forever. It would have to be Someone who could become incarnate among us and live as fully God yet fully man, Someone who could turn water into wine, heal lepers, make the lame to walk, make the blind to see, and make the dead to live, Someone who could win the victory over death and the grave by being resurrected to life, and Someone who is going to come again for us and lead us into eternity. Is anything too hard for God (Jer 32:27; Matt 19:26; Luke 1:37)?

From a human perspective for God to foreknow our responses before we make them is impossible. But what is impossible for man is possible with God, who transcends space and time.

7. Irresistible Grace Does Not Maximize God's Sovereignty and Glory

Clearly, Calvinism is associated with a high view of the sovereignty of God. This reputation is well deserved. In particular, Calvinists were among those who pointed out the errors of the low-sovereignty approach of the openness of God. We join Calvinists such as Bruce Ware in opposing the diminished sovereignty view of Open Theism, especially because of its denial of exhaustive divine sovereignty.[84] Several excellently written

---

[84] Ware's devastating critique is in B. Ware, *God's Lesser Glory: The Diminished God of Open Theism* (Wheaton: Crossway, 2000).

books affirming a high view of divine sovereignty have been published recently by Calvinist scholars.[85] Likewise, we affirm the strong emphasis on glorifying God that John Piper has articulated so well, that glorifying God should be our primary vocation.[86] These are hardly doctrines that are unique to Calvinism. Acknowledging the sovereignty of God and praising the glory of God are simply basic Christian beliefs, sort of like being for mom and apple pie. Not much controversy there. So we are glad to share these affirmations with Calvinists.

Since we all agree that God is sovereign and worthy of glory, two related questions arise: How does God express His sovereignty, and what gives God maximal glory? The contention here is that, *contra* Calvinists, irresistible grace does not accord God maximal sovereignty and glory, while resistible grace does.

First, how is God's sovereignty exhibited? Calvinists understand that God exhibits His sovereignty by essentially micromanaging creation through meticulous providence—that is, He rules in such a way that nothing happens without His control and specific direction. God made decrees before the foundation of the world, which scripted everything that is going to happen, so that now we are just playing out the puppet show that God has decreed. John Frame defines "God's decretive will" as His "highly mysterious" purpose that "governs whatever comes to pass."[87] Therefore, Calvinists such as John Feinberg defend the deterministic dictum that "God ordains all things."[88] Feinberg follows Richard Taylor's definition of determinism "that for everything that happens there are conditions such that, given them, nothing else could happen," and thus "for every decision a person makes, there are causal conditions playing upon his or her will so as to decline it decisively or sufficiently in one direction or the other. Consequently, the agent could not have done otherwise, given the prevailing causal influences."[89] Paul

---

[85] See B. Ware, *God's Greater Glory: The Exalted God of Scripture and the Christian Faith*; and T. Schreiner and B. Ware, eds., *Still Sovereign: Perspectives on Election, Foreknowledge, and Grace* (Grand Rapids: Baker, 2000). The title of the latter book seems a bit misleading in that it suggests multiple perspectives, but, in fact, the book is written entirely from a Calvinistic perspective.

[86] J. Piper, *God's Passion for His Glory: Living the Vision of Jonathan Edwards* (Wheaton: Crossway, 1998).

[87] J. Frame, *Apologetics to the Glory of God: An Introduction* (Phillipsburg: P & R Publishing, 1994), 175.

[88] J. Feinberg, "God Ordains All Things," in *Predestination and Freewill: Four Views on Divine Sovereignty and Human Freedom*, by J. S. Feinberg, D. Basinger, R. Basinger, and C. Pinnock (Downers Grove: InterVarsity, 1986), 17–60.

[89] Ibid., 21, citing the definition in R. Taylor, "Determinism," in *The Encyclopedia of Philosophy* (ed. P. Edwards; New York: Macmillan, 1967): 2:359.

Helm explains that "God controls all persons and events equally" because "God could hardly exercise care over them without having control over it."[90] However, although persons do not have the ability to choose from among various alternatives, we are willing to do what is done: "He [God] exercises his control, as far as men and women are concerned, not apart from what they want to do, or (generally speaking) by compelling them to do what they do not want to do, but through their wills."[91]

Doing what humans will or desire, as opposed to what they choose, is what Calvinists call compatibilist freedom. In the compatibilist approach, humans always do what they desire the greatest. So in regard to salvation, when God changes humans' wills through the effectual calling and regeneration, they voluntarily choose to follow Christ. But they do this only after God has irresistibly and invincibly changed their wills. Apart from this total control, Calvinists argue, God would not be sovereign. Calvinists often invoke mocking and scornful language to characterize the belief that salvation is synergistic, depending to some extent on human response. They see the genuine free choice of humans as an insult to God's sovereignty, making God a lesser God who does not ordain or decree everything that happens. In particular, like most evangelicals, they have opposed the view of open theism that God cannot foreknow the future with 100 percent accuracy, especially the free choices of human beings.

Again, Baptists reject the lesser God of open theism. In the Baptist Faith and Message 2000, the following statement was added in article II to deny expressly the belief of open theism that God does not have exhaustive foreknowledge: "God is all powerful and all knowing; and His perfect knowledge extends to all things, past, present, and future, including the future decisions of His free creatures."[92] We are all in agreement that human choices are never outside of God's knowledge, and nothing is ever beyond God's ability to control.

On the face of it, the Calvinist argument seems to make sense from a human perspective. God is God and He can do anything He wants. Of course, He can! Nothing can limit God. God's kingdom is going to come, and His will is going to be done, whether anybody on earth likes it or not. So there is no question that God has the *right* to reign in this way, and the *ability* to reign in this way. From a human perspective, we tend to equate

---

[90] P. Helm, *The Providence of God* (Contours of Christian Theology series; ed. G. Bray; Downers Grove: InterVarsity, 1994), 20–21.

[91] Ibid., 22.

[92] Baptist Faith and Message 2000, Article II, "God."

sovereignty with power and control. If, for example, you were a tyrannical despot in a late medieval European city, you might well think that being sovereign means to have total control, to banish, exile, torture, and kill those who disagree with you. But is this the way of Christ?

Does this notion of sovereignty as total control bring glory to God? No. Suppose a couple desires to have a baby. They have at least two options. Option one is that they can go down to Wal-Mart and purchase a doll. That plastic doll, for every time they pull its string, will say, "Daddy, I love you!" Now that is total control. They can have that doll say, "I love you" anytime they want. They just pull its string; the doll has no decision but to react the way it has been programmed to react. Option two, however, is to have a real baby. Now, they know from the beginning that the baby is going to be more trouble. Babies do not come home from the hospital housebroken. They cry all night. They break their toes, and they break your hearts. But when that child of his or her own volition says, "Daddy, I love you," it really means something. The parents are more glorified with a real child than with a doll that could not have praised them had they not pulled its string. So, then, which gives God the greater glory—a view that the only persons who can praise God are those whose wills He changes without their permission, or the view that persons respond to the gracious invitation of God and the conviction of the Holy Spirit to praise God truly of their own volition?

So the question is not, Is God powerful enough to reign in any way He wants? Of course, He is. God is omnipotent and can do anything He wants. As the Scripture says, "For who can resist His will?" (Rom 9:19 HCSB). But the question is, What is God's will? How has God chosen to reign in the hearts of persons? If God is truly sovereign, He is free to choose what He sovereignly chooses. So how has He chosen to reign?

We know that natural, sinful humanity does not seek God (Rom 3:11). However, God has sovereignly chosen to allow human choices to have eternal significance, to receive, to assent, or to respond to His gracious initiatives. Nothing could possibly force God to do that. It is His own sovereign choice. He obviously could force irresistible grace on us, but He does not. That is not the way He tends to work. He could have written all of Scripture with His own fingers, as He did with the Ten Commandments, but He did not. He worked through human authors to write down His inerrant Word. He could have sent angels as His messengers so that the message was accurate. But He chose to work through prophets and preachers, through the "foolishness of preaching," as earthen vessels communicate an infinitely valuable message. He could have saved us by irresistible grace, but I do not believe that He does. He requires us to respond.

The three parables in Luke 15 are instructive about human response. The lost sheep and the lost coin must be sought out and rescued by the owner. But in the parable of the Prodigal Son, the one parable dealing with a human being who is lost, the account differs. The prodigal son wanders into the far country out of his own lust and arrogance. Not until he has "wasted his substance with riotous living" and is "in want" does he come "to himself" (Luke 15:13–14,17 KJV). The waiting father eagerly hopes for the son's return but does not go and find him and compel him to come home.

Jesus talked about receiving the grace of God. In Mark 10:15 (see Luke 9:48; 18:17), He said that unless you receive the kingdom of God like a little child, you will never enter it. The Greek word is *dechomai*, which means "to receive," "to take up," "to take by the hand."[93] Likewise, in John 1:12, "As many as received him, to them gave he power to become the sons of God, even to them that believe on his name" (KJV). Here the Greek word is *paralambanō*, meaning "to take to oneself," "to join an associate to oneself," "to accept or acknowledge one to be such as he professes to be," "not to reject," or "to receive something transmitted."[94] In John 3:11 we see the negative, "You do not accept Our testimony" (John 3:11 HCSB), again using *lambanō*, "to receive."[95]

Throughout Scripture we have one imperative command after another—hundreds of imperatives. Each of these imperatives calls upon us to respond. Why do you think God put so many imperatives in His Word if He did not require a response from us?

"Choose you this day whom ye will serve" (Josh 24:15 KJV).

"Seek the LORD and His strength; seek His face continually" (1 Chron 16:11 NASB).

"Seek the LORD" (Zeph 2:3 HCSB).

"Come to Me, all who are weary and heavy-laden, and I will give you rest" (Matt 11:28 NASB; c.f. Luke 7:37).

---

[93] Thayer, 130, ref. 1209.
[94] Ibid., 484, ref. 3880.
[95] Ibid., 870–971, ref. 2983.

"Repent, and let each of you be baptized in the name of Jesus Christ for the forgiveness of your sins; and you will receive the gift of the Holy Spirit" (Acts 2:38 NASB).

"Believe in the Lord Jesus, and you will be saved, you and your household" (Acts 16:31 NASB).

Why does God offer so many conditional promises if He does not intend to receive them?

"If my people, who are called by my name, will humble themselves and pray and seek my face and turn from their wicked ways, then will I hear from heaven and will forgive their sin and will heal their land" (2 Chron 7:14 NIV).

"If you seek Him, He will be found of you" (2 Chron 15:2 HCSB).

"If any man will come after me, let him deny himself, and take up his cross, and follow me. For whosoever will save his life shall lose it: and whosoever will lose his life for my sake shall find it" (Matt 16:24–25 KJV; c.f. Mark 8:34–35; Luke 9:23–24).

"If you confess with your mouth, 'Jesus is Lord,' and believe in your heart that God raised Him from the dead, you will be saved. With the heart one believes, resulting in righteousness, and with the mouth one confesses, resulting in salvation" (Rom 10:9–10 HCSB).

"Behold, I stand at the door and knock; if anyone hears My voice and opens the door, I will come in to him, and will dine with him, and he with Me" (Rev 3:20 NASB).

"And the Spirit and the bride say, 'Come.' And let him that heareth say, 'Come.' And let him that is athirst come. And whosoever will, let him take the water of life freely" (Rev 22:17 KJV).

Why does God give us promises if they are not meant for us to claim?

You, LORD, have not forsaken those who seek You (Ps 9:10 NKJV).

They who seek the LORD shall not be in want of any good thing (Ps 34:10 NASB).

"Men and brethren, children of the stock of Abraham, and whosoever among you feareth God, to you is the word of this salvation sent" (Acts 13:26 KJV).

Granted, in and of themselves, people's choices accomplish nothing. Perhaps the best model is the story of Naaman in 2 Kings 5. Naaman, the commander of the Aramite army, had leprosy. He asked for help. The prophet Elisha told him to go wash in the Jordan River seven times. Naaman initially rejected that notion, complaining about having to bathe in the dirty Jordan River. Finally, after his servants prevailed upon him, he did it, and his leprosy was cleansed. What was it that cleansed Naaman's leprosy? Was it his dunking himself in the Jordan River seven times? Of course not! He could have dunked himself in the river a thousand times and nothing would have happened. On the other hand, what happened when he did not go bathe? Nothing! God allowed him to suffer the results of his own rebellion. But when Naaman responded obediently to God's direction through the prophet, Naaman was healed.

So it is with our salvation. Humans do not do anything to earn or deserve salvation. Humans are too sinful in nature to seek God independently or take the initiative in their own salvation. Humans can come to salvation only as they are urged to by the conviction of the Holy Spirit, and they are drawn to Christ as He is lifted up in proclamation. Cooperation contributes absolutely nothing to human salvation. God's grace provides the necessary and sufficient conditions for salvation. However, God in His freedom has sovereignly decided that He will give the gift of salvation to those who believe, who trust Jesus Christ as Savior and Lord. So salvation truly is monergistic—only God provides for human salvation, and He alone. Before He does so, He requires humans to respond. If humans do not respond, then He does not save. If humans do respond, He surrounds them with overpowering grace impelling them forward until they come to the point of repentance and faith.

Almost everyone in the evangelical tradition, including Baptists, affirms that salvation is not by works. Everyone affirms Eph 2:8–9 (NKJV): "For by grace you have been saved through faith, and that not of yourselves; it is the gift of God, not of works, lest anyone should boast." If salvation is by grace alone through faith alone, what alternatives are there to affirming irresistible grace? The most common alternative to irresistible grace is usually called *prevenient* or *assisting* grace. In *assisting grace*, God through the Holy Spirit convicts, convinces, and impels the unsaved toward repentance and faith. God can exert powerful influences through the Holy Spirit to incline unbelievers toward faith and obedience without literally forcing them to do so or changing their wills. Humans cannot save themselves. They are like drowning men in the middle of a vast ocean. There is no way they could even approach swimming to shore. "Salvation" must come from without, from beyond themselves. Perhaps a rescue ship might come alongside and throw life buoys out to us, and the rescuers yell for us to grab the life buoy so they could pull us out of the water. Perhaps we would be so weakened that we could not even do that, and a rescue helicopter would have to lower a line with a rescuer to pick us up out of the water. In these situations we do not and cannot save ourselves. We can do no "good works." The only thing humans would have to do is assent to be rescued, or at least not resist being rescued. Giving one's assent to be saved is not "good work." Unfortunately, in the world of salvation, all too many refuse to accept Jesus' gracious offer of salvation. Most do not even recognize that they are drowning and rejecting all efforts to warn them. Some foolishly think they can save themselves, but they cannot. In the end, because of their rejection of the persistent witness of the Holy Spirit and the salvation proffered through Christ, God reluctantly allows them to drown eternally in their own sins (Matt 12:32; Mark 3:29; Luke 12:10; Rom 1:21–32, 5:6–21).

Billy Graham puts it so well:

> There is also volitional resolution. The will is necessarily involved in conversion. People can pass through mental conflicts and emotional crises without being converted. Not until they exercise the prerogative of a free moral agent and will to be converted are they actually converted. This act of will is an act of acceptance and commitment. They willingly accept God's mercy and receive God's Son and then commit themselves to do God's will. In every true conversion the will of man comes into line with the will of God. Almost the last word of the Bible is this invitation: "And whosoever will, let him take of the water of life freely" (Rev 22:17). It is up to you. You must will to be saved. It is God's will, but it must become your will, too.[96]

Not surprisingly, God does not think the way we do. As God says in His Word, "For as the heavens are higher than the earth, so are my ways higher than your ways, and my thoughts than your thoughts" (Isa 55:9 KJV). Hear again God's statement in Hosea 11:

---

[96] B. Graham, *The World Aflame* (Minneapolis: Billy Graham Evangelistic Association, 1967), 134.

> How can I give you up, Ephraim? How can I hand you over, Israel?
> How can I make you like Admah? How can I set you like Zeboiim? My
> heart churns within Me; My sympathy is stirred. I will not execute the
> fierceness of My anger; I will not again destroy Ephraim. For I am God,
> and not man, the Holy One in your midst; and I will not come with
> terror (Hos 11:8–9 NKJV).

If you or I had omnipotent power and were faced with a stubborn and
rebellious people, perhaps we would just torch them in our anger. We
might feel not only that we were exercising greater sovereignty and authority, but in so doing we might deem ourselves more glorious. But God said,
"I am God, and not man, the Holy One in your midst." Evidently, God's
ways are truly not like our ways. Jesus taught us that God sees greatness in
a different light—doing things God's way involves not total control or the
arbitrary use of power, but a servant spirit:

> But Jesus called them to Himself and said, "You know that the rulers
> of the Gentiles lord it over them, and those who are great exercise
> authority over them. Yet it shall not be so among you; but whoever
> desires to become great among you, let him be your servant. And
> whoever desires to be first among you, let him be your slave—just as
> the Son of Man did not come to be served, but to serve, and to give His
> life a ransom for many" (Matt. 20:25–28 NKJV; c.f. Mark 10:42–45;
> Luke 22:25–28).

In Luke's account Jesus mentions that these Gentile authorities were
called "benefactors" (Luke 22:25), persons who dispensed gracious acts
on which subjects they chose. But Jesus said it should not be so for God's
people, and He grounded that on nothing other than Himself—"just as the
Son of Man did not come to be served, but to serve."

Although God truly has the right and ability to do whatever He
wants whenever He wants, God does not normally choose to express
His sovereignty in that way. God evidently sees servanthood and allowing the free choices of His creatures as more glorious than the arbitrary
exertion of power and authority. The plan that some of Jesus' disciples
had to glorify Christ was for Him to overthrow the Romans, seize the
throne of Israel, and exercise control as king, but God had a better plan.
He sent Jesus to the shameful cross. It is hard for humans to understand
sovereignty and glory in this way, but we are truly to have the mind of
Christ Jesus,

who, being in the form of God, did not consider it robbery to be equal with God, but made Himself of no reputation, taking the form of a bondservant, and coming in the likeness of men. And being found in appearance as a man, He humbled Himself and became obedient to the point of death, even the death of the cross. Therefore God also has highly exalted Him and given Him the name which is above every name, that at the name of Jesus every knee should bow, of those in heaven, and of those on earth, and of those under the earth, and that every tongue should confess that Jesus Christ is Lord, to the glory of God the Father (Phil 2:6–11 NKJV).

We have it from God's own Word—that is the way He wants to exercise sovereignty, and that is what He finds to be glorious. We should understand sovereignty and glory from God's perspective, not from a human perspective. We believe God deserves more than the lesser glory and sovereignty of open theism and even more than the greater glory and sovereignty offered by Calvinism. Let us recognize God's maximal sovereignty and give Him the maximal glory that He deserves!

Conclusion

This essay has raised significant biblical and theological issues that challenge the viability of the doctrine of irresistible grace. I believe that the cumulative case that has been raised against irresistible grace is compelling. Certainly, high-Calvinists have their own explanations for some of these concerns. I encourage each believer, like the Bereans encountered by Paul (Acts 17:10–11), to search what the Scriptures say concerning these issues, under the guidance of the Holy Spirit who leads us into all truth (John 16:13).

{ Chapter 6 }

Perseverance and Assurance of the Saints

KENNETH D. KEATHLEY

At a symposium honoring Dale Moody, I. Howard Marshall recited the old saw that Arminians know they are saved but are afraid they cannot keep it, while Calvinists know they cannot lose their salvation but are afraid they do not have it.[1] Aside from being witty, this highlights the two components of the question about assurance. First, is it possible to know absolutely or even confidently that one is saved, and second, is it possible for those who currently believe they are saved to have assurance that they will remain in a state of grace until the day of redemption? It is more than just a little ironic that though they travel different routes, many Arminians and Calvinists arrive basically at the same answer—assurance is based on evidence of sanctification.[2] Michael Eaton points to the nineteenth-century preacher Asahel Nettleton as a good example of

---

[1] See I. H. Marshall, *Kept by the Power of God: A Study of Perseverance and Falling Away*, 3rd ed. (London: Paternoster, 1995), 267.

[2] Both Marshall and D. A. Carson make this observation. See D. A. Carson, "Reflections on Christian Assurance," *Westminster Theological Journal* 54 (1992), 21. Carson states, "Thus at their worst, the two approaches meet in strange and sad ways."

this odd state of affairs when he quotes Nettleton: "The most that I have ventured to say respecting myself is, that I think it possible I may get to heaven."[3] Words perhaps expected from an Arminian, but Nettleton was a Calvinist.

Paul gives the two aspects of assurance of salvation when he states, "For I know whom I have believed, and am persuaded that he is able to keep that which I have committed unto him against that day" (2 Tim 1:12 KJV). The apostle affirms that (1) a person can know with certainty he is presently saved ("For I know whom I have believed"), and that (2) he can know with certainty he will remain saved ("and am persuaded that he is able to keep that which I have committed unto him against that day").[4] This chapter argues that the basis of assurance is the same as the basis for salvation itself: Jesus Christ—who He is, what He has done, and what He has promised. In other words, assurance is found in our justification in Christ rather than in our sanctification.

The doctrine of *forensic justification* is crucial for assurance of salvation. "Forensic" means that justification is the legal act where God *declares* a sinner righteous through Jesus Christ. This is in contrast to *sanctification*, which is the lifelong work of grace whereby God *makes* a sinner righteous. This distinction between justification and sanctification liberated Martin Luther from the bondage of attempting to merit salvation. Luther tells of meditating on Rom 1:17 ("For in it God's righteousness is revealed from faith to faith, just as it is written: The righteous will live by faith") and coming to the realization that God's righteousness was a gift given to sinners rather than a standard that sinners must meet.

> There I began to understand that the righteousness of God is that by which the righteous lives by a gift of God, namely by faith. And this is the meaning: the righteousness of God is revealed by the gospel, namely, the passive righteousness with which merciful God justifies us by faith. . . . Here I felt that I was altogether born again and had entered paradise itself through open gates. There a totally other face of the entire Scripture showed itself to me.[5]

---

[3] Cited by M. Eaton, *No Condemnation: A New Theology of Assurance* (Downers Grove: InterVarsity, 1995), 3.

[4] For a defense of this view of *tēn parathēkē mou*, lit. "my deposit," in 2 Tim 1:12 see W. D. Mounce, *Pastoral Epistles*, Word Biblical Commentary (Nashville: Thomas Nelson, 2000), 487–88; G. W. Knight III, *The Pastoral Epistles*, New International Greek Testament Commentary (Grand Rapids: Eerdmans, 1992), 378–80.

[5] M. Luther, "Preface to Latin Writings," in *Luther's Works*, vol. 34 (Philadelphia: Muhlenberg, [1545] 1960), 337.

Like Luther, I argue that a person finds assurance when he trusts the justi-fying work of Christ alone. I also contend that the gift of faith remains (i.e., perseveres), and it inevitably manifests itself in the life of a believer. How-ever, the level of manifestation varies from saint to saint. Abraham and Lot were both justified (2 Pet 2:7–8), but they evidenced it very differently.

Recently, Reformed scholars Thomas Schreiner and Ardel Caneday presented an updated version of the position set forth earlier by Louis Berkhof and G. C. Berkouwer. They attempted to reconcile the biblical passages that affirm unconditional election with passages that warn of divine judgment (particularly the five warning passages in the book of Hebrews) by positing that, in Schreiner's words, "adhering to the warn-ings is the means by which salvation is obtained on the final day."[6] The believer's salvation is not merely manifested by perseverance, but rather, eschatologically speaking, a believer actually is saved by perseverance (i.e., in the faith). However, Schreiner and Caneday deny that the elect will apostatize, claiming that the warning passages are a "crucial" means by which God has chosen to preserve the elect.

Schreiner and Caneday call their position the "means-of-salvation" view. Though they affirm salvation by grace through faith alone, at times they use language that seems to meld Arminian and Calvinist soteriology.[7] For example, on the one hand they define perseverance as a persistent and abiding faith, but on the other hand they speak of obtaining final salvation through persevering obedience. Most who hold to eternal security also affirm that saving faith produces the evidence of a godly life. Schreiner and Caneday go beyond that. Based especially on 1 Tim 2:15 and 4:16, they state, "Persevering in godly behavior and sound teaching are neces-sary to obtain salvation," and believers "must practice godly behavior to receive it [i.e., final salvation]."[8] One cannot help but appreciate their attempts to take the warning passages seriously. For this reason at least,

---

[6] T. R. Schreiner, "Perseverance and Assurance: A Survey and a Proposal," *The Southern Baptist Jour-nal of Theology* 2:1 (1998): 53. See T. R. Schreiner and A. B. Caneday, *The Race Set Before Us: A Biblical Theology of Perseverance and Assurance* (Downers Grove: InterVarsity, 2001); G. C. Berkouwer, *Faith and Perseverance* (Grand Rapids: Eerdmans, 1958), 88–124; L. Berkhof, *Systematic Theology*, rev. ed. (Grand Rapids: Eerdmans, 1996), 548. John Piper takes a similar position in *Future Grace* (Sisters, OR: Multnomah, 1995), 231–59.

[7] John Mark Hicks claims that since both Arminians and Calvinists affirm that perseverance is neces-sary to obtain final salvation, then—despite appearances—both positions concerning the conditions to salvation are essentially the same. He concludes that a truce, or at least the calling of a draw, is in order. See J. M. Hicks, "Election and Security: An Impossible Impasse?" (paper presented at the annual meeting of the Evangelical Theological Society, Colorado Springs, CO, November 14–16, 2001), 12–17.

[8] Schreiner and Caneday, *The Race Set Before Us*, 51.

I must confess some sympathies for their position. However, some critics, such as Roy Zuck, charge that their view "comes dangerously close to salvation by works, and it fails to give absolute unqualified assurance of salvation for any believer."[9] His charge is not entirely baseless, and some of Schreiner and Caneday's arguments are less than clear, although they affirm that "because God is the one who enables those who persevere," their view "cannot be labeled works-righteousness."[10]

First, we will briefly survey the answers that have been proposed to our two questions regarding assurance of salvation and eternal security. Second, additional attention will be given to the means-of-salvation position of Schreiner and Caneday, which is sure to be the topic of continuing discussion in evangelical circles. Third, I will argue that, though Schreiner and Caneday have made a positive contribution to the discussion about assurance, a variation of the evidence-of-genuineness position best explains the tension between the biblical texts that assure and those that admonish.

Component 1: Present Certainty
How do we know we are genuinely saved?

Three schools of thought have provided three different answers to the question of how an individual believer knows if he or she is genuinely saved. The first view, held by the Roman Catholic Church, regards the claim of assurance of salvation to be a demonstration of spiritual arrogance. Roman Catholic soteriology does not separate sanctification from justification and therefore does not present assurance as something currently available. The second view is that of the Reformers. Flying the banner of *sola fide*, they trumpeted a certainty to salvation that made saving faith and assurance virtual synonyms. The post-Reformation Calvinists and Puritans held to a third view which saw assurance as a grace given subsequent to conversion and discerned by careful self-examination. The second and third answers still predominate in evangelicalism today.

The Roman Catholic View: Assurance Is Not Possible

If salvation is a lifetime process that may or may not be successfully completed, then assurance of salvation is not possible. Following Augustine,

---

[9] R. B. Zuck, "Review of *The Race Set Before Us*," *Bibliotheca Sacra* 160 (April-June 2003): 241–42.
[10] Schreiner and Caneday, *The Race Set Before Us*, 16–17.

official Catholic doctrine views justification as a process that occurs within the individual Christian over the course of his lifetime and perhaps even continues after death. No one can know for sure how far along he is on the journey of faith or if he will continue the difficult task of walking in the Way. Seen from this light, the Reformed doctrine of justification by faith alone seems to present a truncated soteriology. The Council of Trent condemned all who claim to have assurance of salvation, declaring, "If any one saith, that a man, who is born again and justified, is bound of faith to believe that he is assuredly in the number of the predestinate; let him be anathema."[11] The Tridentine Council reasoned that since only the elect will persevere, and since only God knows who is and who is not elect, then special revelation would be required for someone to have assurance of salvation.[12] Calvin responded by declaring that the Word of God was all the special revelation the elect needed to have assurance.[13]

The Reformers: Assurance Is the Essence of Faith

So how do we know if we are saved? The answer of the Reformation was that this knowledge is a part of salvation itself. Calvin defined faith as "a firm and certain knowledge of God's benevolence toward us, founded upon the truth of the freely given promise in Christ, both revealed to our minds and sealed upon our hearts through the Holy Spirit."[14] The nature of conversion and regeneration ensures that the believer will know when he has believed. Anyone can know whether he has believed in Jesus Christ, and all who believe in Him are saved. Therefore, assurance is of the essence of saving faith.[15]

Having certain knowledge at the time of conversion does not exclude the possibility that a believer may have doubts after his salvation, nor does it mean that only those with absolute certainty are saved. Luther stated:

---

[11] "Canons Concerning Justification," canon 15 (DS 1565) in *The Teaching of the Catholic Church*, ed. K. Rahner (Cork: Mercer, 1966), 400.

[12] Ibid., canon 16 (DS 1566). For a Catholic discussion of the Council's view on assurance see A. Dulles, *The Assurance of Things Hoped For* (New York: Oxford University Press, 1994), 48–50.

[13] J. Calvin, "Acts of the Council of Trent with the Antidote," in *Selected Works of John Calvin*, vol. 3 (Grand Rapids: Baker, 1983), 155. Calvin asks, "What else, good Sirs, is a certain knowledge of our predestination than that testimony of adoption which Scripture makes common to all the godly?"

[14] J. Calvin, *Institutes of the Christian Religion* (Philadelphia: Westminster, 1960), 551.

[15] Heb 11:1, "Now faith is being sure of what we hope for and certain of what we do not see" (NIV). Both Zane Hodges and Thomas Schreiner hold that assurance is the essence of saving faith. When we get to the "once-saved-always-saved" section it will become evident that Hodges and Schreiner generally disagree more than they agree.

Even if I am feeble in faith, I still have the same treasure and the same
Christ that others have. There is no difference; through faith in him
(not works) we are all perfect. It is just as if two people have a hundred
gulden—one may carry his in a paper bag, the other store and bar his
in an iron chest; but they both have the treasure whole and complete.
So with Christ. It is the self-same Christ we possess whether you or
I believe in him with a strong or weak faith. And in him we have all,
whether we hold it with a strong or weak faith.[16]

Both Luther and Calvin realized that many genuine believers have
subsequent doubts. Nevertheless, this view does contend that when a person is saved, he knows it, and this core conviction, though buffeted, will
never die.

However, certain doctrines advocated by the Reformers for the purpose of establishing assurance often produced the opposite effect. The
doctrines of the absolute decree of election and reprobation made within
the hidden will of God, limited atonement, and temporary faith created
a tension in later Calvinist theology and made assurance of salvation difficult to obtain. This difficulty manifests itself particularly in the theology
and practice of the Puritans.

The Puritans: Assurance Is Logically Deduced

A number of significant Puritans struggled terribly with assurance of salvation. It is intensely debated whether these struggles were the result of
their departure from the teachings of Calvin or if they simply took Calvin's
theology to its logical conclusion. R. T. Kendall and Charles Bell argue that
Calvin held to a doctrine of unlimited atonement and to a Christocentric
doctrine of assurance. Their thesis is that later Calvinism, beginning with
Theodore Beza, departed from Calvin by adhering to a doctrine of limited
atonement and to a doctrine of assurance that begins with the absolute
decree of the hidden God as its starting point.[17] Others have responded
that the confusion begins with Calvin himself and that his followers' works

---

[16] Cited by R. Olmsted, "Staking All on Faith's Object: The Art of Christian Assurance According to
Martin Luther and Karl Barth," *Pro Ecclesia* 10/2 (2001): 138.

[17] R. T. Kendall, *Calvin and English Calvinism to 1649* (New York: Oxford University Press, 1979);
and C. Bell, *Calvin and Scottish Theology: The Doctrine of Assurance* (Edinburgh: The Handsel Press,
1985).

simply highlighted his confusion.[18] Either way, it is a historical fact that much of the Puritans' life was defined by their search for assurance. This concern about assurance would mystify the average Evangelical today.

Post-Reformation Calvinists stressed the doctrines of double predestination and limited atonement to emphasize that the believer's salvation is completely by grace and is as secure as the nature and character of God Himself. But the doctrine of limited atonement implies that the anxious inquirer cannot presume that Christ died for him; Christ died for an individual if and only if that person is one of the elect. How does one know if he is elected? The electing decree is part of the hidden will of God, so the only way a person knows that he is elect is if he truly believes in Jesus Christ for salvation. But how does one know whether his faith is genuine or if he is deceived? A genuine faith manifests itself by persevering in doing good works. In the final analysis the basis of assurance in post-Reformation theology is sanctification, not justification.

The doctrine of temporary faith, a notion first formulated by Calvin but later developed by Beza and William Perkins, further intensified the problem of assurance in Calvinist and Puritan theology. According to them, God gives to the reprobate, whom He never intended to save in the first place, a "taste" of His grace. Based on passages such as Matt 7:21–23; Heb 6:4–6, and the parable of the Sower, Beza and Perkins attribute this false, temporary faith to an ineffectual work of the Holy Spirit. Perkins propounds a system in which the reprobate might experience five degrees of ineffectual calling that to him is indistinguishable from a genuine conversion experience. Those who profess to be believers are encouraged to examine themselves lest they are found to possess only this temporary faith.[19] Beza declared that the reason God gives temporary faith to the

---

[18] Zachman and Thomas argue that the trouble begins with the inconsistencies of Calvin's formulation of the doctrine of assurance and that the later Calvinists are closer to Calvin than Kendall or Bell want to admit. Thorson concludes that "Calvin is not just complex, but inconsistent." See R. Zachman, *The Assurance of Faith: Conscience in the Theology of Martin Luther and John Calvin* (Minneapolis: Fortress, 1993); G. M. Thomas, *The Extent of the Atonement: A Dilemma for Reformed Theology from Calvin to the Consensus (1536–1675)* (Carlisle: Paternoster, 1997); and S. Thorson, "Tensions in Calvin's View of Faith: Unexamined Assumptions in R. T. Kendall's *Calvin and English Calvinism to 1649*," *Journal of the Evangelical Theological Society* 37.3 (1994): 423. Beeke and Hawkes defend the Puritan approach to assurance, calling it a thoroughly Trinitarian model and "especially elegant." See J. Beeke, *The Quest for Full Assurance: The Legacy of Calvin and His Successors* (Edinburgh: Banner of Truth, 1999); and R. M. Hawkes, "The Logic of Assurance in English Puritan Theology," *Westminster Theological Journal* 52 (1990): 260.

[19] See R. A. Muller, "Perkins' *A Golden Chaine:* Predestinarian System or Schematized *Ordo Salutis?*" *Sixteenth Century Journal* 60/1 (1978): 75. Perkins devised an elaborate chart that expounds a supralapsarian view of salvation. Under the heading of "A Calling Not Effectual," Perkins lists five evidences

reprobate is so that "their fall might be more grievous."[20] In Olmsted's opinion, Beza's teaching "comes perilously close to ascribing the matter to divine sadism."[21]

History shows that these doctrines produced a crippling anxiety in the later Calvinists and Puritans that drove them to an introspection which an objective observer might describe as pathological. John Bunyan's *Pilgrim's Progress* has blessed multitudes of Christians, but his spiritual autobiography, *Grace Abounding to the Chief of Sinners*, is disturbing. He recounts how, in his seemingly endless search for assurance of salvation, he was haunted by the question, "How can I tell if I am elected?"[22]

Kendall and Bell document the pastorally damaging results of the Puritan approach to assurance. Even those who disagree with Kendall's thesis concede that his "devastating critique" of the miserable travails produced by Puritan theology and practice is more or less "on the mark."[23] Kendall recounts the life and work of William Perkins (1558–1602), who is often called the father of Puritanism. Perkins wrote extensively and almost exclusively on the subject of assurance, having devoted 2,500 pages to the topic. Unfortunately, the preaching and teaching of Perkins on assurance often had the opposite effect, creating more doubts than were resolved. Ironically, Perkins, like so many other Puritans of his day, died without a clear assurance of his own salvation.[24] In a similar fashion Bell chronicles the struggle for assurance among the Scottish Calvinists. He says:

> It is well known, for example, that for generations many in the Scottish
> Highlands have refused to receive the communion elements because
> of the want of personal assurance of their salvation. Although believing
> that Jesus Christ is the Savior and the Son of God, self-examination
> fails to yield sufficient evidence of their election to salvation. Fearing

---

of the ineffectual work of the Holy Spirit: (1) an enlightening of the mind, (2) a penitence accompanied by a desire to be saved, (3) a temporary faith, (4) a taste of justification and sanctification that is accompanied by the heartfelt sweetness of God's mercy, and (5) a zeal for the things of religion. See also Kendall, *Calvin and English Calvinism*, 67–76. Kendall quotes Perkins as saying that the quest for assurance ultimately requires a "descending into our own hearts" (75), which is a type of introspection that Calvin warned against.

[20] Cited in Kendall, *Calvin and English Calvinism*, 36.

[21] Olmsted, "Staking All on Faith's Object," 140–41.

[22] J. Bunyan, *Grace Abounding to the Chief of Sinners* (Chicago: Moody, 1959), 26.

[23] G. Harper, "Calvin and English Calvinism to 1649: A Review Article," *Calvin Theological Journal* 20 (November 1985): 257.

[24] Kendall cites Thomas Fuller, the nineteenth-century historian, who reports that Perkins died "in the conflict of a troubled conscience." See Kendall, *Calvin and English Calvinism*, 75.

that apart from such assurance they may eat and drink in an unworthy manner, and thereby incur the judgment of God, they abstain from receiving the Lord's Supper.[25]

The later Calvinists and Puritans employed two syllogisms, the practical syllogism and the mystical syllogism, in their attempt to ascertain assurance by way of logical deduction. They used the practical syllogism (*syllogismus practicus*) to determine whether they had believed and the mystical syllogism (*syllogismus mysticus*) to search for evidence of true faith.[26] The practical syllogism is as follows:

> *Major premise*:   If effectual grace is manifested in me by good works, then I am elect.
>
> *Minor premise*
> *(practical)*:   I manifest good works.
>
> *Conclusion*:   Therefore, I am one of the elect.

But how does one know the minor premise of the practical syllogism is true for him? The Puritans attempted to answer this question by an introspective self-examination using the mystical syllogism. The mystical syllogism is as follows:

> *Major premise*:   If I experience the inward confirmation of the Spirit, then I am elect.
>
> *Minor premise*
> *(mystical)*:   I experience the confirmation of the Spirit.
>
> *Conclusion*:   Therefore, I am one of the elect.

Beza concludes, "Therefore, that I am elect, is first perceived from sanctification begun in me, that is, by my hating of sin and my loving of righteousness."[27] The post-Reformation Calvinist and the Puritan believed that the basis of assurance is sanctification.

Of the three answers given to the question, How does one know that he is genuinely saved? only the second option, Assurance is the essence of saving faith, provides certainty of salvation. Assurance of salvation must be based on Jesus Christ and His work for us—nothing more and nothing less.

---

[25] Bell, *Calvin and Scottish Theology: The Doctrine of Assurance*, 7.

[26] Beeke, *The Quest for Full Assurance*, 132–39.

[27] T. Beza, *A Little Book of Christian Questions and Responses* (Allison Park, PA: Pickwick Publications, 1986), 96–97.

Component 2: Eventual Certainty
How secure is one's salvation?

Even if a believer knows he is saved, the question of perseverance is still unanswered. This brings us to the second aspect of assurance—how secure is one's salvation? Arminians have traditionally answered that apostasy is possible for the believer while Calvinists have affirmed the perseverance of the saints. Some scholars have offered mediating positions arguing that while the Scriptures warn against the danger of apostasy, the possibility of apostasy does not exist for the genuine believer. Thomas Schreiner and Ardel Caneday's means-of-salvation position is one such midway proposal, and we will give additional attention to it.

Apostasy Is Possible	Apostasy Is Not Possible	Apostasy Is Threatened but Not Possible
Non-elect Believers Fall—Augustine	*Implicit Universalism*—Barth	*Irreconcilable Tension*—Carson
Nonpersevering Believers Fall—Moody	*Once Saved, Always Saved*—Grace Evangelical Society	*Means of Salvation*—Schreiner and Caneday
	Evidence of Genuineness—Demarest	*Middle Knowledge*—Craig

Augustinian and Arminian View: Apostasy Is Possible

Two positions accept the possibility that a believer may lose his salvation. Augustine believed that non-elect believers will fall from grace, while traditional Arminians argue that all believers are at risk of apostasy.

Non-elect believers fall. According to Augustine (354–430), only elect believers persevere, and only God knows which believers are the elect.[28] God has not elected every believer whom He regenerates. A believer can lose his salvation and be placed back under the wrath of God by committing mortal sins. Augustine gives an example of two pious men, both "justified men" and both "renewed by . . . regeneration." Yet one perseveres and the other does not because God has chosen only one. God regenerates

---

[28] B. Demarest, *The Cross and Salvation* (Wheaton: Crossway, 1997), 437–38.

more than He elects. Why would God do this? Augustine answers, "I do not know."[29]

However, God grants repentance and perseverance to His elect. Since election is part of the hidden will of God, all believers must strive to endure until the end. On a practical level the Augustinian perspective operates much like the Arminian one.

Nonpersevering believers fall. Arminians interpret the assurance passages in the light of the warning passages and understand salvation to be a present condition that a believer enjoys but could lose. Two recent proponents of this position, Dale Moody and I. Howard Marshall, argue that the Scriptures are filled with explicit warnings to believers that they must persevere if they are to be saved.[30] Moody claims that because of preconceived theological positions, the full impact of these verses has been muted. He laments, "Yet cheap preaching and compromise with sin have made such texts forbidden for serious study."[31] He argues, "Eternal life is the life of those who continue to follow Jesus. No one can retain eternal life who turns away from Jesus."[32]

Schreiner points out that Moody solves the tension between the assurance passages and the warning passages by denying there is a tension.[33] Moody asserts that Calvinists have put so much emphasis on the assurance passages that they have bleached out the full force of the warning passages. However, he appears to have committed the same error in reverse when he ignores the unconditional nature of the promises of preservation and makes them subordinate to the warning passages.

Calvinist and Free Grace View: Apostasy Is Not Possible

Three positions argue apostasy is not possible, and the believer's eventual salvation is guaranteed. The first position is the implicit universalism of Karl Barth based upon his view of election, while the Grace Evangelical Society advocates the second view—the once-saved-always-saved position—as a

---

[29] Augustine, *A Treatise on the Gift of Perseverance*, 21, in *Nicene and Post-Nicene Fathers*, vol. 5, ed. Philip Schaff. Available online at http://www.ccel.org/ccel/schaff/npnf105.xxi.iii.xxiii.html.

[30] I. H. Marshall, *Kept by the Power of God*; and D. Moody, *The Word of Truth: A Summary of Christian Doctrine Based on Biblical Revelation* (Grand Rapids: Eerdmans, 1981).

[31] Moody, *The Word of Truth*, 350.

[32] Ibid., 356. Moody defends his position by claiming that it is also the position of A. T. Robertson, the famed New Testament scholar at Southern Seminary.

[33] Schreiner, "Perseverance and Assurance," 33.

major plank of their doctrinal platform. Wayne Grudem argues for a third view, the evidence-of-genuineness position, which argues that saving faith manifests itself by perseverance.

Implicit Universalism. In a famous discussion in his *Church Dogmatics*, Karl Barth demonstrated that the Reformer's formulation for assurance stands upon an unstable platform. Beginning the search for certainty with the electing decree that is hidden in the secret will of God dooms the enterprise from the start. He argued that the Reformers erred when they attempted to develop a doctrine of assurance with a Christological beginning and an anthropological ending.[34]

Barth resolved the question of assurance by using his idiosyncratic view of election. According to Barth, Jesus Christ is both the electing God and the elected Man. God relates to the elect only through Christ, but Christ is also the rejected Man of the reprobate. Therefore, God relates to all—both elect and rejected—through Christ with the end result that God rejects the rejectedness of the reprobate. Barth solves concerns about assurance by placing all mankind in Christ.[35]

Barth never conceded that his position implied universalism. J. I. Packer observes that this was "a conclusion that Barth himself seems to have avoided only by will power."[36] However, his approach seems to conclude that a reprobate is someone who is elect but does not yet know it.

Once Saved, Always Saved. The once-saved-always-saved position rejects the traditional Reformed doctrine of the perseverance of the saints in favor of the doctrine of eternal security. Proponents of the view include Zane Hodges, Charles Stanley, Joseph Dillow, and R. T. Kendall.[37] Advocates of the once-saved-always-saved position, while not accepting Barth's view on election, agree with him that any attempt to arrive at assurance of salvation that involves looking at the believer's life for evidence or support will not succeed.

According to this view, assurance of salvation comes only by trusting the promises of the Word of God. The believer should manifest the fruit

---

[34] K. Barth, *Church Dogmatics* II/2 (Edinburgh: T&T Clark), 333–40.

[35] Ibid., 344–54. Randall Zachman and G. Michael Thomas currently advocate Barth's position. See Zachman, *The Assurance of Faith*, viii, 244–48; and Thomas, *The Extent of the Atonement*, 252–53.

[36] J. I. Packer, "Good Pagans and God's Kingdom," *Christianity Today* 30/1 (January 17, 1986): 22–25.

[37] See Z. Hodges, *Absolutely Free!* (Grand Rapids: Zondervan, 1989); C. Stanley, *Eternal Security: Can You Be Sure?* (Nashville: Thomas Nelson, 1990); J. Dillow, *The Reign of the Servant Kings* (Haysville, NC: Schoettle, 1992), 187, 194; R. T. Kendall, *Once Saved, Always Saved* (Chicago: Moody, 1983), 49–53.

of salvation, but there is no guarantee that he will. At best, works provide a secondary, confirmatory function.[38]

Critics argue that this position has three weaknesses. First, it either ignores or explains away what seems to be the clear meaning of the warning passages directed to the saints. Second, it tends toward laxity in Christian commitment, and third, it gives false comfort to those who walk in disobedience to the commands of Scripture and who in fact really may not be saved.[39]

The advocates of the once-saved-always-saved position argue that the Bible provides plenty of motivation for Christian service without threatening the believer with eternal damnation.[40] First, the believer is moved to service by a sense of gratitude for his salvation. Second, the believer who fails to follow the Lord faithfully experiences the chastening hand of God, even to the point of death, if necessary. Third, in addition to divine chastening in this life, the disobedient believer experiences the loss of rewards at the judgment seat of Christ. The carnal believer enjoys the preservation of God even if he does not persevere in the faith.[41]

Evidence of Genuineness. The evidence-of-genuineness position, traditionally understood as the doctrine of the perseverance of the saints, agrees with the once-saved-always-saved view that the believer's salvation is eternally secure. They also agree that good works are not necessary to procure salvation. However, unlike those who advocate the doctrine of eternal security, the advocates of the evidence-of-genuineness position contend that the fruits of salvation will necessarily and eventually manifest themselves in the life of a believer.[42]

The evidence-of-genuineness proponents base their doctrine of perseverance on God's promises in Scripture that He will complete His work of salvation in the individual believer.[43] Even though a believer may fail miserably and sin terribly, he cannot remain in that condition. A

---

[38] See the doctrinal statement of the Grace Evangelical Society at http://www.faithalone.org/. Stanley explains that "in all probability, a Christian who has expressed faith in Christ and experienced forgiveness of sin will always believe that forgiveness is found through Christ. But even if he does not, the fact remains that he is forgiven!" (*Eternal Security*, 79). He likens salvation to a tattoo that a person may come to regret but cannot get rid of (p. 80). Also see pp. 74, 93–94.

[39] Moody, *The Word of Truth*, 361–65.

[40] See the section entitled "Motivation" of the Grace Evangelical Society at http://www.faithalone.org/.

[41] Stanley, *Eternal Security*, 92–100.

[42] Demarest, *The Cross and Salvation*, 439–44.

[43] Philippians 1:6, "I am sure of this, that He who started a good work in you will carry it on to completion until the day of Christ Jesus" (HCSB).

Christian may fall totally, but his fall will not be final. The true believer will persevere.

The warning passages serve as litmus tests, according to the evidence-of-genuineness position.[44] Those who are not genuinely converted will eventually show their true colors. Therefore, the judgments threatened in those passages are not directed toward believers but are intended for false disciples, who for one reason or another are masquerading as real Christians.

Schreiner and Caneday agree with the advocates of the evidence-of-genuineness position that true believers will persevere, but they believe that the evidence-of-genuineness advocates have misinterpreted the warning passages in the New Testament. Schreiner and Caneday argue the warning passages are orientated toward the future, while the evidence-of-genuineness position turns the warnings into tests of past or present behavior.[45]

Mediating Views: Apostasy Is Threatened, but Is Not Possible

Some scholars understand the warning passages to be admonishing believers about the danger of eternal judgment, although a believer cannot apostatize. Three positions attempt to reconcile these two seemingly contrary concepts. The first view, the irreconcilable tension position, argues that the two types of passages are irresolvable and that a compatibilistic approach must be taken. Second, the means-of-salvation position argues that the warnings serve as an essential means by which the believer is preserved; and third, William Lane Craig argues that the means-of-salvation view is a middle knowledge approach.

Irreconcilable Tension. Certain scholars have given up any attempt to reconcile the assurance passages with the warning passages and have ascribed the whole matter to mystery. In his book *Assurance and Warning,* Gerald Borchert concludes that the two types of passages are in irreconcilable tension and must be held in a "delicate balance."[46]

---

[44] See W. Grudem, "Perseverance of the Saints: A Case Study from the Warning Passages in Hebrews," in *Still Sovereign: Contemporary Perspectives on Election, Foreknowledge, and Grace,* ed. T. R. Schreiner and B. A. Ware (Grand Rapids: Baker, 2000), 133–82.

[45] Schreiner and Caneday, *The Race Set Before Us,* 29–35.

[46] G. L. Borchert, *Assurance and Warning* (Nashville: Broadman, 1987), 194.

D. A. Carson takes a similar tack when he argues for taking a compatibilist approach to the issue at hand. He defines compatibilism as,

> the view that the following two statements are, despite superficial evidence to the contrary, mutually compatible: (1) God is absolutely sovereign, but his sovereignty does not in any way mitigate human responsibility; (2) human beings are responsible creatures (i.e., they choose, decide, obey, disobey, believe, rebel, and so forth), but their responsibility never serves to make God absolutely contingent.[47]

Since we do not know how God operates in time, how God operates through secondary agents, or how God is both sovereign and personal at the same time, then we are not going to know how the two types of passages interface. In the end we are left with a theological antinomy. Carson concludes, "So we will, I think, always have some mystery."[48]

Neither Schreiner nor Hodges is impressed with Carson's appeal to compatibilistic mystery. Schreiner cautions against appealing to mystery too quickly; otherwise we may be simply avoiding the hard labor and hard choices of doing theological work. He suspects that Borchert and Carson are using "tension" and "mystery" as code words for "contradiction."[49] Likewise Hodges argues that an assurance based on a mystery is not much of an assurance at all. He says, "If 'assurance' were indeed a mystery, then it would be a deeply disquieting mystery to those who need assurance the most. Does Dr. Carson know beyond question that he himself is regenerate? If so, let him tell us *how* he knows. The compatibilist cannot have a mystery and a confident answer, too!"[50]

Means of Salvation. In their book *The Race Set Before Us,* Thomas Schreiner and Ardel Caneday present a position they label the means-of-salvation view. They agree with the advocates of the evidence-of-genuineness position that a believer cannot apostatize. However, they argue that the warning passages, such as those found in the book of Hebrews, threaten believers with eternal damnation in hell if they fail to persevere. They reject the way proponents of the once-saved-always-saved position interpret 1 Cor 9:23–27 to mean that Paul was concerned about losing his qualifications for the ministry when he spoke of keeping his body in

---

[47] Carson, "Reflections on Christian Assurance," 22.

[48] Ibid., 26.

[49] Schreiner, "Perseverance and Assurance," 52.

[50] Z. Hodges, "The New Puritanism Part 1: Carson on Christian Assurance," http://www.faithalone.org/journal/1993i/Hodges.htm; accessed 24 January 2002.

subjection so that he would not be cast away. Rather, they agree with Gordon Fee that Paul was warning the Corinthian Christians that without remaining faithful to the end even he would not go to heaven. "Fear to become *adokimos* ["disqualified, reprobate"] motivates Paul to be diligent and deliberate in perseverance."[51]

The means-of-salvation position contends that the New Testament is always referring to the gift of salvation when it speaks of the believer's reward.[52] Passages that exhort the elect to pursue crowns of life, glory, and righteousness are making reference to salvation itself, not to any subsequent reward that the believer may earn in addition to salvation. This is one of the central themes of their book.

> We have insisted throughout this book that the New Testament directs its admonitions and warnings to believers. We have also argued that these warnings do not merely threaten believers with losing rewards but that eternal life itself is at stake. Biblical writers frequently warn believers that if they turn away from Jesus Christ they will experience eternal judgment. If believers apostatize their destiny is the lake of fire, the second death, hell. These warnings cannot be waved aside and relegated to those who are not genuine Christians. They are directed to believers and must be heeded for us to be saved on the last day. We will win the prize of eternal life only if we run the race to the end. If we quit during the middle of the race, we will not receive eternal life.[53]

They also argue that obtaining eternal life requires not only continuing faith but also great effort. They conclude from 2 Pet 1:5–11 ("Make every effort to supplement your faith with goodness, . . . knowledge, . . . self-control, . . . endurance, . . . godliness, . . . brotherly affection, and . . . love. . . . [M]ake every effort to confirm your calling and election. . . . For in this way, entry into the eternal kingdom of our Lord and Savior Jesus Christ will be richly supplied to you," HCSB) that

> Virtuous living is not encouraged simply because it makes life on earth more fulfilling, nor is the idea that living a godly life will lead to greater rewards in heaven. These virtues are imperative to escape the fate of the

---

[51] Schreiner and Caneday, *The Race Set Before Us*, 179. Cf. G. Fee, *The First Epistle to the Corinthians*, New International Commentary on the New Testament (Grand Rapids: Eerdmans, 1987), 431–41. According to Fee, Paul understands that "he and they [the Corinthians] must persevere in the gospel to share in its promises" (432) and that Christians must "exercise self-control lest they fail to obtain the eschatological prize" (440)

[52] Schreiner and Caneday, *The Race Set Before Us*, 89–95.

[53] Ibid., 268.

false teachers. That is, righteous living is necessary to obtain entrance into the kingdom of Jesus Christ.[54]

But Schreiner and Caneday argue that though the threats of damnation addressed to the saints are genuine, the possibility of apostasy is not. They affirm from passages such as 1 John 2:19 that "persevering in Christ is the mark of authenticity" because believers "have the promise of God that he will supply the necessary power" to persevere. "Thus, we can be certain that every believer will most certainly finish the race and obtain the prize."[55] This is because God uses means—including the warning passages—to fulfill His promise to save all who have trusted Jesus Christ as Savior. They claim that warning someone about certain behavioral consequences does not imply anything about the likelihood of their engaging in that behavior. "[C]onditional warnings in themselves do not function to indicate anything about possible failure or fulfillment. Instead, the conditional warnings appeal to our minds to conceive or imagine the invariable consequences that come to all who pursue a course of apostasy from Christ."[56] In assessing the warnings, they make a distinction between that which is conceivable and that which may or is likely to happen. They liken the warnings to road signs, which "caution against conceivable consequences, not probable consequences."[57] They further explain, "The truthfulness of a warning or admonition does not depend on whether or not the thing supposed may come to pass. . . . Rather, they function by supposing a particular course of action that has an invariable and inviolable consequence."[58]

The way Schreiner and Caneday see it, rather than causing consternation in the elect, the threats of damnation produce encouragement and confidence.

> The admonitions and warnings of the Scriptures threaten believers with eternal judgment for apostasy, but these warnings do not violate assurance and confidence regarding final salvation. . . . The warnings do

---

[54] Schreiner and Caneday, *The Race Set Before Us*, 290. They also explain, "Peter summons the church to godly living so that they will enter the eternal kingdom," and they agree with Richard Bauckham that "the ethical fruits of Christian faith are objectively necessary for the attainment of final salvation" (p. 291).

[55] Ibid., 245.

[56] Ibid., 199.

[57] Ibid., 208.

[58] Ibid., 209.

not rob us of assurance. They are signposts along the marathon runner's pathway that help us maintain our confidence.[59]

The tension between threats of judgment and signposts of confidence may be resolved, according to Schreiner and Caneday, by recognizing the "already but not yet" aspect of the gospel of the kingdom. They argue that the advocates of the other positions have overlooked this fundamental interpretative principle that is often referred to as inaugurated eschatology.[60] With the resurrection of Christ, the end of the age has begun, so all the blessings of the kingdom of God and its salvation on behalf of the elect are an accomplished fact. However, our Lord has not returned, so the full enjoyment of our salvation is not yet accomplished. This sets up a tension in the world, in the church, and in the hearts of individual believers that is expressed in the biblical record.

Schreiner and Caneday argue that the once-saved-always-saved position is particularly guilty of an overrealized eschatology that collapses the "not yet" into the "already." They contend that those like Hodges and Stanley have emphasized the conversion event to the point of making salvation a completely past event. The opposite would be a theology in which salvation is only a future possibility. The means-of-salvation view teaches that saving faith is not just a one-time event but also a lifetime journey. All the components and aspects of salvation have an "already–not yet" orientation—even justification. They agree that justification is primarily forensic,[61] but they also understand that "righteousness should be included in the already-but-not-yet tension that informs New Testament soteriology. Believers are righteous now, yet they still await the gift of righteousness that will be theirs on the day of redemption."[62]

---

[59] Ibid., 269.

[60] Ibid., 46–86. "Both the present and future dimensions of salvation should be viewed as two aspects of an indivisible whole" (p. 47). On this influential hermeneutical approach see G. E. Ladd, *The Presence of the Future* (Grand Rapids: Eerdmans, 1974), 139.

[61] By "forensic" is meant that righteousness/justification terms use a legal or courtroom metaphor describing the believer as one declared right before the divine judge. Schreiner's views on the forensic nature of justification have evolved. Most recently, he stated, "[R]ighteousness and justification in Paul should be understood as forensic only." See T. R. Schreiner, *New Testament Theology* (Grand Rapids: Baker, 2008), 355. He further explains, "God's declaration about sinners is an end-time verdict that has been announced before the end has arrived. The verdict is effective in the sense that every verdict announced by God constitutes reality." Also, "By virtue of union with Christ believers already enjoy justification in this present evil age" (p. 361).

[62] Schreiner and Caneday, *The Race Set Before Us*, 77–79. They derive the future dimension of justification from passages such as Gal 5:5 and Rom 2:13; 3:20.

As a way to understand the basis of assurance, Schreiner and Caneday present a three-legged stool.[63] The first leg is the promises of God, the second leg is the evidence of a changed life, and the third leg is the inward witness of the Holy Spirit. They admit that the analogy is an imperfect one, since the promises of God are primary for assurance,[64] but they deny that there can be a discontinuity between the first leg and the other two. They warn, "Even though the promises of God are primary in establishing our assurance, it would be a serious mistake to expel the necessity of believing obedience to confirm assurance." In fact, "a transformed life is evidence of and necessary for salvation."[65]

Schreiner and Caneday strongly affirm that a Christian can know he is saved based on God's promises, although various New Testament warning passages threaten him with final condemnation if he does not persevere in godly faith and life. Their attempt to explain the latter in terms of only "conceivable" rather than possible or probable consequences, however, seems to leave the two propositions in conflict. They affirm that the believer experiences forensic justification, full adoption, and divine regeneration as present realities. How then is it conceivable that a believer so positioned in Christ is in any danger of damnation? This objection does not arise merely from an overrealized eschatology, as they contend. In spite of their efforts to avoid it, they seem to sacrifice some of the "already" component of the "already–not yet" tension.

Second, in their discussion of 1 Cor 9:27, Schreiner and Caneday say that Paul's "fear to become *adokimos*," that is, a castaway, motivated him to persevere. They say his fear was not of losing his salvation (although their wording sounds like it was), nor was it a fear of losing rewards.[66] What is the alternative except a fear that he might not be a genuine believer? If so, what kind of confidence is that? Their position seems to be unclear at this point. Dale Moody scoffs at the means-of-salvation view as Arminianism that has lost its nerve. In his opinion it ultimately "reduces the warnings to bluffing."[67]

---

[63] Ibid., 276–305.

[64] They declare, "Our primary focus must be on the promises of God in Christ and his objective work on our behalf." Further, "The fundamental leg is the promises of God." Ibid., 283.

[65] Ibid., 283–84. They explain from 1 John that righteous living, love for fellow believers, and right belief about Christ "are necessary conditions to belong to the people of God, but they are not sufficient conditions" (p. 287). They also declare, "Assurance does not rest only on God's promises; it also is confirmed by the way we live" (p. 289).

[66] Ibid., 179.

[67] Moody, *The Word of Truth*, 361.

Third, what can we say about those who do not persevere? Many who at one time professed faith in Christ later renounce their faith. Our authors acknowledge that the failure of such people to persevere indicates they were never truly saved.[68] So what the warning passages describe happens to false professors but not to the elect, and the means-of-salvation position seems to collapse into the standard evidence-of-genuineness view held by most Calvinist evangelicals.[69]

Fourth, as the first section of this chapter demonstrated, the Puritans employed an approach similar to the means-of-salvation position and found it to be pastorally disastrous. Schreiner and Caneday acknowledge the experience of the Puritans and warn against it, but they give little reason to believe the same problems would not reoccur if the means-of-salvation view were to become widespread again.[70] The subtitle to their book is *A Biblical Theology of Perseverance and Assurance*, but the work seems to be long on perseverance and short on assurance. In discussing the function of the fruit of the Spirit in Christian assurance, they repeatedly say that the role is only to "confirm" the believer's assurance derived from God's promises.[71] And yet the nature of the means-of-salvation view seems to do just the opposite.

Fifth, at times it appears that the means-of-salvation proposal comes dangerously close to a works-salvation position, in spite of their declarations to the contrary.[72] Graciously enabled works are still works. Most evangelicals agree that true saving faith works, but it is still faith alone and not faith plus godliness that is the means of salvation. Yet Schreiner and Caneday state, "Perseverance is a necessary means that God has appointed for attaining final salvation."[73]

Calvin addressed this approach in his response to the Council of Trent when he stated:

---

[68] See Schreiner and Caneday, *The Race Set Before Us*, 214–44.

[69] This is, in fact, the position that Schreiner and Caneday take about those who lapse. See Schreiner and Caneday, *The Race Set Before Us*, 243. They acknowledge that "New Testament writers are also concerned about those who claim to believe and yet do not match their confession of faith with believing obedience" (p. 283). Such people "might presume upon God's grace" and "use the promises of Scripture to console their consciences" (p. 292). So it sounds like the warning passages apply more to false professors than to true believers.

[70] Ibid., 277–78.

[71] Ibid., 283–99.

[72] Ibid., 86. But see Zuck, "Review of *The Race Set Before Us*," 142. In his argument salvation begins with faith but is completed by works, A. P. Stanley cites Schreiner and Caneday for support. See *Did Jesus Teach Salvation by Works?* (Eugene, OR: Pickwick, 2006), 244.

[73] Ibid., 152.

Here there is no dispute between us as to the necessity of exhorting believers to good works, and even stimulating them by holding forth a reward. What then? First, I differ from them in this, that they make eternal life the reward; for if God rewards works with eternal life, they will immediately make out that faith itself is a reward which is paid, whereas Scripture uniformly proclaims that it is the inheritance which falls to us by no other right than that of free adoption.[74]

Even though they are careful to insist that the works done by the believer are actually accomplished by the grace of God, their position is difficult to reconcile with the Reformation principle of *sola fide*. Perhaps Schreiner and Caneday could address this concern by giving a clear definition of what they mean when they use the word "perseverance." Do they understand it to be an undying faith (that produces good works) or a continuing in godly behavior?[75]

Middle Knowledge. Does the means-of-salvation view inadvertently abandon the traditional Reformed understanding of divine sovereignty and instead hold a Molinist position? William Lane Craig believes that it does. He argues that the means-of-salvation position implicitly employs middle knowledge. Craig asks that if the believer's will is so overwhelmed by God's grace, then why does God give the warnings at all? And if the warnings themselves bring about perseverance, does this mean that the believer is capable of apostasy, even if he does not apostatize? Hypothetically, at least, the elect can fall away, but God, using middle knowledge, has chosen to actualize a world in which scriptural warnings will operate as means to keep His children from apostasy. This is a novel understanding of perseverance, but it appears to be the view argued by those who hold to the means-of-salvation position.[76] Craig states:

> The classical defender of perseverance must, it seems, if he is to
> distinguish his view from Molinism, hold to the intrinsic efficacy
> of God's grace and, hence, the causal impossibility of the believer's

---

[74] Calvin, "Acts of the Council of Trent with the Antidote," 144–45.

[75] After I wrote this chapter, Dr. Schreiner was kind enough to send me a draft of his upcoming book *Run to Win the Prize* (InterVarsity). In it he clarifies his position and provides a helpful response to many concerns expressed by me and others. Most helpful is his description of perseverance, which he defines as "persevering in faith"—a definition with which I agree wholeheartedly. However, I remain unconvinced that the warning passages of the New Testament threaten believers with damnation.

[76] W. L. Craig, "'Lest Anyone Should Fall': A Middle Knowledge Perspective on Perseverance and Apostolic Warnings," *Philosophy of Religion* 29 (1991): 65–74.

apostasy. But in that case, the warnings of Scripture against the danger of apostasy seem to become otiose and unreal.[77]

Craig concludes that the means-of-salvation view is, in fact, a Molinist perspective and represents an abandonment of the classic Reformed doctrine of perseverance.

Schreiner and Caneday's response to Craig's article seems to indicate they miss the point to his argument. In an appendix to their book, *The Race Set Before Us*, they contend that Craig misunderstands the difference between his view of how God's grace works in the human will and the view of Reformed theology.[78] Since Craig assumes a "false disjunction" between God's grace that overwhelms the believer's will and the warnings themselves, he thinks the efficacy of the warnings reside merely in themselves. Schreiner and Caneday claim Craig wrongly attributes his own view to the proponents of the means-of-salvation position, and "thus his whole argument against the Reformed view takes a trajectory that misses its mark."[79]

However, Craig does fully realize the difference between the Reformed view and the Molinist view of God's use of means. That is exactly his point. If God is using the warnings as the means to ensure perseverance, then either the saints would fall without the warnings (which is contrary to how Reformed theology understands how God's grace works in the believer) or the saints would persevere even without the warnings (which would make the warnings superfluous). Either way, the means-of-salvation position seems to depart from standard Reformed soteriology.

A Modest Proposal: A Variation of the Evidence-of-Genuineness Position

The model for assurance offered over the next few pages is close to the once-saved-always-saved view. However, it differs in that it simultaneously affirms both God's preservation of the redeemed and their persistent, persevering faith, so it is more accurately described as a variant of the evidence-of-genuineness view. This position has four points: (1) the only basis for assurance is the objective work of Christ; (2) assurance is

---

[77] Ibid., 72.
[78] Schreiner and Caneday, *The Race Set Before Us*, 332–37.
[79] Ibid., 337.

the essence of saving faith; (3) saving faith perseveres; and (4) God offers rewards available to the believer subsequent to salvation.

The Four Tenets of a Modified Evidence-of-Genuineness View	
1. *The only basis for assurance is the objective work of Christ.*	Christ is the foundation of assurance; good works merely support and confirm.
2. *Assurance is the essence of saving faith.*	A certain knowledge of salvation is simultaneous with being saved. Subsequent doubts may come, but a core conviction remains.
3. *Saving faith perseveres or remains until the day when it gives way to sight.*	Perseverance is a faith that cannot be annihilated. Perseverance is more a promise than a requirement.
4. *Rewards subsequent to salvation are for the believer to win or lose.*	Believers will be judged and rewarded according to their service.

First, *the only basis for assurance is the objective work of Christ.* Any doctrine of assurance that includes introspection as a component will produce anxiety in the hearts of the people it is intended to encourage. Barth is right when he points out that no system that has a Christological beginning and an anthropological ending can provide genuine and sustained assurance.

This is why Schreiner and Caneday's analogy of a three-legged stool for assurance fails. They admit the analogy is imperfect because they view the leg of God's promises as preeminent over the other legs of sanctification and the inward testimony of the Spirit. Nevertheless, a stool that has one leg that is longer, stronger, and sturdier than the others is an inherently unstable platform. To change metaphors, when it comes to providing assurance, Christ is the soloist, and evidences are just members of the back-up choir.

A close corollary to the premise that Christ is the only basis for assurance is the necessity to reaffirm the doctrine of *sola fide.* Perseverance cannot be understood in terms of good works and great effort without having the result of dismantling the Reformation. The doctrine of perseverance must be formulated so that it does not create the impression that the Scriptures contradict themselves about grace and works.[80]

Second, *assurance is the essence of saving faith.* The nature of conversion and regeneration guarantees that certain knowledge of salvation is simultaneous with being saved. Subsequent doubts and fears may come, but a core conviction about one's relationship with God will remain.

Good works and the evidences of God's grace do not provide assurance. They provide warrant to assurance but not assurance itself. Perhaps a good analogy is how a Christian knows the love of God. He experiences the love of God every day in a myriad of ways. However, all those countless blessings merely affirm what the Christian already knows—God loves him. Even during those times when the good favor of God seems to be circumstantially absent and the Christian's confidence is tested, he still knows that God loves him the same way he has always known this—by the promises of God. So it is with the assurance of salvation. Good works play the mere supporting role of confirmation.

Third, *saving faith perseveres or remains until the day when it gives way to sight.* Perseverance should be understood as a faith that cannot be annihilated and therefore persists. This persistent faith eventually and inevitably exhibits itself in the believer's life in such a way as to bring glory to God. The point of Hebrews 11 is that saving faith manifests itself by the journey of discipleship. One may stumble and falter but never leave the trail. Perseverance should be viewed more as a promise than a requirement.

I cannot agree with Schreiner and Caneday when they contend that the evidence-of-genuineness position makes the mistake of turning the forward-looking warning passages into retrospective tests. Rather, the warning passages that look forward (such as those found in the book of Hebrews) are pointing out the obvious: genuine belief will not turn back. Warnings about future behavior can be tests of genuineness without being retrospective.

Some passages teach that past behavior can be an indicator of genuineness. The genuinely saved person hungers and thirsts for righteousness, even when he is struggling with temptation or even if he stumbles into sin. In fact, I am not as concerned about the destiny of those who struggle as I am about those who do not care enough to struggle. Indifference is more of a red flag than weakness.

---

[80] Romans 11:6, "And if by grace, then it is no longer of works; otherwise grace is no longer grace. But if it is of works, it is no longer grace; otherwise work is no longer work" (NKJV).

The absence of a desire for the things of God clearly indicates a serious spiritual problem, and a continued indifference can possibly mean that the person professing faith has never been genuinely converted. God is infinitely more dedicated to our salvation than we are, and He will not fail to finish that which He has begun. If a believer engages in willful disobedience or deliberate indifference, our heavenly Father promises him decisive and appropriate action. The indwelling of the Holy Spirit ensures that no peaceful backslider exists.

Fourth, *there are rewards that are subsequent to salvation for the believer to win or lose.* One of the great weaknesses of the Schreiner and Caneday proposal is the necessity to deny that there are any subsequent rewards available for the believer and that all promises of reward must be references to salvation itself. Their position is difficult to reconcile with many biblical passages. For example, 1 Cor 3:12–15 speaks of one Christian's work remaining while another Christian's work burns. The believer whose work remains receives a reward while the other believer suffers loss. Schreiner and Caneday admit the passage teaches "some will be saved that have done shoddy work."[81] This admission undermines the major plank of their position—that persevering in good works is a necessary means by which our salvation is completed. A better understanding of the role of works in believers' lives is to hold that we will be judged and rewarded according to our service.

In the end assurance comes from depending on Christ alone. I agree with Calvin's retort to the Catholic controversialist Albert Pighius, "If Pighius asks how I know I am elect, I answer that Christ is more than a thousand testimonies to me."[82]

---

[81] Schreiner and Caneday, *The Race Set Before Us,* 51.

[82] J. Calvin, *Concerning the Eternal Predestination of God* (Louisville: Westminster John Knox, 1997), 321.

{ Part Two }

Chapter 7

Was Calvin a "Calvinist"? John Calvin on the Extent of the Atonement

KEVIN KENNEDY

Was Calvin a Calvinist? That question is like asking whether Augustine was an Augustinian or whether Luther was a Lutheran. If anyone could be regarded as a Lutheran, then certainly Martin Luther qualifies. By the same token, the Bishop of Hippo certainly meets the criteria for being an Augustinian. However, if one were to ask whether Lutheranism and Augustinianism accurately represent the teachings of the theologians for whom these theological traditions are named, many theologians and church historians would say that they do not. In the same way, some theologians and historians have said the system of doctrine popularly referred to as Calvinism does not necessarily reflect the thinking of John Calvin himself. The possibility exists that the thinking of Calvin differs significantly from that of the later theological school frequently bearing his name.

The theological tradition known as Reformed theology, often popularly referred to simply as "Calvinism," can actually claim many significant theologians as sources, not the least of whom include Ulrich Zwingli, Martin Bucer, Heinrich Bullinger, and Theodore Beza. Referring to Reformed theology simply as "Calvinism," therefore, would itself be both inaccurate and misleading, for the term *Calvinism* obscures the fact that Reformed theology owes its existence to many significant churchmen and theologians. Furthermore, the term *Calvinism* is frequently used as a sort of shorthand to describe the Reformed theological consensus articulated at the conclusion of the Synod of Dort in the Netherlands (1618–1619), a full 55 years after John Calvin's death in 1564. The familiar "Five Points" of Calvinism—Total depravity, Unconditional predestination, Limited atonement, Irresistible grace, and Perseverance of the saints (a.k.a. TULIP)—are a popular summary of the Reformed consensus arrived at during the Synod of Dort. Frequently, people are referring to this consensus, and these five points, when they speak of "Calvinism." Therefore, since these points were articulated over half a century after Calvin's death, and since they represent a consensus among many Reformed theologians, the question would naturally arise whether the five points of "Calvinism" accurately represent the thought of Calvin himself.

In fact, some of Calvin's own countrymen teaching at the Protestant Academy of Saumur, in France, raised the question as to whether the Synod of Dort accurately reflected Calvin's thought, shortly after that synod met. This group of French Calvinists, the most famous of whom was Moise Amyraut, began to raise questions about the theological consensus of Dort. In his *Treatise on Predestination*, Amyraut presented a view of unconditional predestination based upon a universal atonement demonstrating God's universal benevolence toward all mankind—a position he claimed was not only more true to Scripture but also more true to the teachings of Calvin.[1] Amyraut claimed that the view of the atonement expressed in the Canons of the Synod of Dort, which most people understood to teach that Christ died only for the elect, was actually a departure from Calvin's teaching.

That Calvin did not hold a view of limited atonement (or particular atonement as it is often called) is a claim that has persisted over the

---

[1] For a brief discussion of Moise Amyraut and Amyraldism, see "Amyraldism" in *The New Dictionary of Theology* (ed. S. B. Ferguson, D. F. Wright, and J. I. Packer; Downer's Grove, IL: 1988), 16–18. For a more extensive analysis of Amyraut and the French Calvinists, see B. G. Armstrong, *Calvinism and the Amyrault Heresy: Protestant Scholasticism and Humanism in Seventeenth-Century France* (Madison: Univ. of Wisconsin Press, 1969). Armstrong concluded that Amyraut "recaptured some of the genius of Calvin's teaching which had been lost by the logically constructed theologies of the orthodox" (265).

intervening years. Many, including the present writer, have argued Calvin taught that Christ died for the sins of the entire world.[2] Despite frequent claims that Calvin taught universal atonement and not limited atonement, many "Calvinists" have come to Calvin's defense, as it were, in an attempt to set the record straight, once and for all, that the theologian for whom their theological system is named certainly agreed with that system.

Two such theologians to come to Calvin's defense on this issue are Paul Helm and Roger Nicole. Following the 1979 publication of R.T. Kendall's book, *Calvin and English Calvinism to 1649*, both Nicole and Helm defended Calvin against Kendall's bold claim that Calvin taught that Christ died indiscriminately for the sins of the entire world.[3] Helm published an article and a monograph in which he took Kendall to task for claiming that Calvin taught universal atonement.[4] Nicole wrote a lengthy article in which he discussed the various passages from Calvin's writings that have been offered in support of the claim that Calvin taught that Christ died for all of humanity.[5] Still others joined the discussion as people on both sides of the question often cited the same or similar passages from Calvin's writings in support of the claim that Calvin taught either a limited atonement or a universal atonement.[6] The current writer even joined the discussion as a late arrival when he wrote his Ph.D. dissertation on the question of Calvin's view on the extent of the atonement.[7]

---

[2] K. D. Kennedy, *Union with Christ and the Extent of the Atonement in Calvin* (Bern: Peter Lang, 2002). See also R. T. Kendall, *Calvin and English Calvinism to 1649* (Oxford: Oxford Univ. Press, 1979); J. B. Torrance, "The Incarnation and Limited Atonement," *Evangelical Quarterly* 55 (April 1983): 83–94; M. Charles Bell, "Calvin and the Extent of the Atonement," *Evangelical Quarterly* 55 (April 1983): 115–23.

[3] Kendall, *Calvin and English Calvinism*, 13.

[4] P. Helm wrote a review article of Kendall's book, titled "Calvin, English Calvinism and the Logic of Doctrinal Development," *Scottish Journal of Theology* 34 (1981): 179–85. Helm later expanded this into a short monograph titled *Calvin and the Calvinists* (Edinburgh: The Banner of Truth, 1982).

[5] R. Nicole, "John Calvin's View of the Extent of the Atonement," *Westminster Theological Journal* 47, no. 2 (Fall 1985): 197–225. This article has recently been reprinted in *Standing Forth: Collected Writings of Roger Nicole* (Fearne, Scotland: Christian Focus Publishers, 2002). Nicole specifically notes Kendall's book as the catalyst to the then current discussion over the question of Calvin's view on the extent of the atonement.

[6] J. B. Torrance, "The Incarnation and 'Limited Atonement,'" *Evangelical Quarterly* 55 (April 1983): 83–94; T. Lane, "The Quest for the Historical Calvin," *Evangelical Quarterly* 55 (April 1983): 95–113; M. C. Bell, "Calvin and the Extent of the Atonement," *Evangelical Quarterly* 55 (April 1983): 115–23. Bell also wrote a review article on Helm's book (*SJT* 36, no. 4 [1983]: 535–40) in which he states that, among his other shortcomings, Helm clearly misrepresented Calvin at several places in his attempt to argue that Calvin held to limited atonement.

[7] K. D. Kennedy, "Union with Christ as Key to John Calvin's Understanding of the Extent of the Atonement" (Ph.D. diss., The Southern Baptist Theological Seminary, 1999), later revised and published as *Union with Christ and the Extent of the Atonement in Calvin* (Bern: Peter Lang, 2002).

That Calvin never addressed the question of the extent of the atone-ment as a separate doctrinal point makes this debate especially fascinat-ing. Also, since those on either side of the issue frequently quoted the same passages from Calvin's writings in order to make their cases, the var-ious debaters often would appeal to other elements of Calvin's theology, or to the overall logic of his theology, in order to try to make their case. Those who were adamant that Calvin taught a limited atonement often argued that this position was the only one that fit the logic of the rest of his theology. Their arguments frequently reduced to something like the following: since Calvin taught that Christ died as our substitute and since Calvin taught that not all would be saved, Calvin must have held that Christ died only for the elect. In other words, a limited atonement was a necessary logical inference based on other elements of Calvin's theology.

Both Paul Helm and Roger Nicole employed this way of arguing. Both Helm and Nicole also stressed that since Calvin held a substitutionary view of the atonement, he could not possibly hold the view of universal atonement.[8] They argued that since Calvin taught that Christ actually secured salvation on the cross, then only the following are possible: (1) if Christ died for all of humanity, then all of humanity must be saved, owing to the fact that Christ's death actually saves all those for whom it was intended; or (2) if not all of humanity is to be saved, then Christ must not have died for all of humanity. Therefore, since Calvin held to a sub-stitutionary atonement and further held that not all would be saved, then Calvin must have held the view of a limited atonement. Helm and Nicole argue by inference from Calvin's substitutionary understanding of the atonement that Calvin necessarily must have held a doctrine of limited atonement. Although Helm admits that Calvin never presents limited atonement as an explicit doctrine, he states that "Calvin, not being a uni-versalist, could be said to *be committed to* definite atonement, even though he does not *commit himself to* definite atonement."[9] Roger Nicole makes a far more interesting remark. When addressing what he claims is a nec-essary link between limited atonement and the concept of substitution, Nicole remarks that "it is difficult to imagine that Calvin failed to per-ceive the necessary link between substitution and definite [i.e. limited] atonement, or that, having perceived it, he carried on without regard to

---

[8] Helm, *Calvin and the Calvinists,* 43–44; and Nicole, "John Calvin's View," 218.
[9] Helm, *Calvin and the Calvinists,* 18, emphasis in original.

this matter!"[10] Nicole rightly assumes that Calvin was a careful thinker. However, Nicole's statement begs the question in that it is based on a supposed necessary corollary of the issue under debate. The question is whether Calvin held the view of a definite atonement. If Calvin did *not* hold the view of a definite atonement, then Calvin probably would not have affirmed the supposed necessary corollary of that doctrine Nicole offers as evidence that Calvin held the view of a definite atonement.

Despite Nicole's improper argument at this point, he does draw attention to an important point: whatever Calvin's understanding of the extent of the atonement, certain other elements within his theology should coalesce with his view on the extent of the atonement. For instance, if Calvin did profess limited atonement, one would not expect to find him intentionally universalizing scriptural passages that theologians from the later Reformed tradition claim are, from a simple reading of the text, clearly teaching that Christ died only for the elect. Furthermore, if Calvin truly believed that Christ died only for the elect, then one would not expect to find Calvin claiming that unbelievers who reject the gospel are rejecting an actual provision that Christ made for them on the cross. Nor would one expect Calvin, were he a proponent of limited atonement, to fail to refute bold claims that Christ died for all of humanity when he was engaged in polemical arguments with Roman Catholics and others. However, the truth is, Calvin does all of this and more.

While the debate over Calvin's view on the extent of the atonement cannot be resolved in a paper of this length, an initial investigation can show that those who claim that Calvin held the view of universal atonement are well within their rights to make that claim. Also, in a relatively short work such as this, we must pose a question that can be reasonably answered in the space allotted. Roger Nicole's claim that Calvin's view on the question of the extent of the atonement should "square" with the rest of his theology suggests that question: Are there elements in Calvin's writings that one should *not* expect to find there if Calvin were a proponent of limited atonement? While the short answer to this question is yes, it will take some investigation in order to show that this conclusion is a reasonable one. Therefore, the remainder of this chapter will be devoted to setting before the reader some of the elements in Calvin's writings that are incongruous with a limited atonement. However, the reader should remember that this argument is not meant to be an exhaustive investigation of Calvin's vast

---

[10] Nicole, "John Calvin's View," 224.

theological production, nor can an argument of this sort be conclusive. This chapter is simply offered as an attempt to show how it is not unreasonable to claim that Calvin held to a universal atonement.[11]

Universal Language in Calvin

Even though Calvin nowhere deals explicitly with the issue of the extent of the atonement as he does other doctrines such as predestination or the number and nature of the sacraments, Calvin does make many statements that bear on the question of his view on the extent of the atonement. What is rather conspicuous, and perhaps somewhat troubling to those who claim that Calvin held to particular redemption, is the extent to which Calvin employs universal language to describe the atonement. Furthermore, Calvin uses universal language in many different contexts such as in his *Institutes of the Christian Religion*, in his commentaries and sermons, as well as in several of his polemical writings. Were Calvin a proponent of limited atonement, one would not expect to see so many passages in which he employs universal language to describe the death of Christ. A sample of these passages will demonstrate how freely Calvin used universal language to describe the atonement.

Unqualified Universal Statements in Calvin

When reading Calvin, one is struck with the sheer number of unqualified universal statements that he makes regarding the atonement. Many of these simply assert that Christ died for the redemption of humanity or the salvation of the whole human race. The following are a few examples:

> They had already been warned so many times that the hour was approaching in which our Lord Jesus would have to suffer for the redemption of the whole world (*en laquello nostre Seigneur Iesus devoit souffrir pour la redemprion du genre humain*).[12]

---

[11] For a more thorough analysis of the question of Calvin's view on the extent of the atonement, see Kennedy, *Union with Christ*. For an analysis from the limited atonement perspective, see: G. M. Thomas, *The Extent of the Atonement: A Dilemma for Reformed Theology from Calvin to the Consensus, 1536–1675* (Carlisle: Paternoster, 1998).

[12] Calvin, *The Deity of Christ and Other Sermons* (trans. Leroy Nixon; Grand Rapids: Wm. B. Eerdmans, 1950), 55; *Ioannis Calvini Opera quae Supersunt Omnia* (ed. W. Baum, E. Cunitz, and E. Reuss; *Corpus Reformatorum*; Brunswick: C. A. Schwetschke and Son, 1863–1900), 46:836. All Latin references to Calvin's New Testament commentaries are from *Ioannis Calvini in Novum Testamentum Commentarii* (ed. A. Tholuck; Amsterdam: Berolini, 1833–1834), hereafter NTC. All references to the Latin

God commends to us the salvation of all men without exception, even as Christ suffered for the sins of the whole world. (*nam omnium salus sine exceptione nobis a Deo commendatur, quemadmodum pro peccatis totius mundi passus est Christus*).[13]

When he says "the sins of the world," he extends this kindness indiscriminately to the whole human race (*Et quum dicit mundi peccatum, hanc gratiam ad totum genus humanum promiscue extendit*) that the Jews might not think that the Redeemer has been sent to them alone. . . . Now it is for us to embrace the blessing offered to all, that each may make up his own mind that there is nothing to hinder him from finding reconciliation in Christ if only, led by faith, he come to him.[14]

For it is very important for us to know that Pilate did not condemn Christ before he himself had acquitted him three or four times, so that we may learn from it that it was not on his own account that he was condemned but for our sins. We may also learn how voluntarily he underwent death, when he refused to use the judge's favorable disposition to him. It was this obedience that made his death a sacrifice of sweet savour for expiating all sins.[15]

He must be the redeemer of the world (*Redempteur du monde*). He must be condemned, indeed, not for having preached the Gospel, but for us he must be oppressed, as it were, to the lowest depths and sustain our cause, since he was there, as it were, in the person of all cursed ones and of all transgressors (*d'autant qu'il estoit la comme en la personne de tous maundits et de tous transgresseurs*), and of those who had deserved eternal death (*et de ceux qui avoyent merité la mort eternelle*). Since, then, Jesus Christ has this office, and he bears the burdens of all those who had offended God mortally, that is why he keeps silent (*D'autant donc que Iesus Christ ha vest office-lá, et qu'il porte les fardeaux de tous ceux qui avoyent offensé Dieu mortelle, ent, voyla porquoy is se taist*).[16]

---

edition of the *Institutes* are from Calvin, *Ioannis Calvini Opera Selecta* (ed. P. Barth and G. Niesel; 2d ed.; Munich: Chr. Kaiser, 1926–1936), hereafter OS. All other Latin and French references are from *Ioannis Calvini Opera quae Supersunt Omnia*, hereafter CO.

[13] Calvin, *Comm.* Gal 5:12, NTC 6:68.
[14] Calvin, *Comm.* John 1:29, NTC 3:21.
[15] Calvin, *Comm.* John 19:12, NTC 3:343.
[16] Calvin, *The Deity of Christ and Other Sermons*, 95, CO 46:870.

All of the above excerpts state in one way or another that Christ died for the sins of the whole world. In none of these cases does Calvin qualify the universal language that he employs.[17]

In other instances Calvin presents Christ as providing expiation for or bearing the sins and guilt of the whole world.

> [Paul] says that this redemption was procured by *the blood of Christ*, for by the sacrifice of his death all the sins of the world have been expiated (*nam sacrificio mortis eius expiata sunt omnia mundi peccata*).[18]

> On him was laid the guilt of the whole world.[19]

> God is satisfied and appeased, for he bore all the wickedness and all the iniquities of the world.[20]

> The death and passion of our Lord Jesus would not have served anything, to wipe away the iniquities of the world, except insofar as he obeyed.[21]

> Christ interceded as his [man's] advocate, took upon himself and suffered the punishment that, from God's righteous judgement, threatened all sinners (*poenam in se recepisse ac luisse quae ex iusto Dei iudicio peccatoribus omnibus imminebat*); that he purged with his blood those evils which had rendered sinners hateful to God; that by this expiation he made satisfaction and sacrifice to God the Father.[22]

In a few instances Calvin presents Christ as appearing before the judgment seat of God in the place of all sinners.

> But though our Lord Jesus by nature held death in horror and indeed it was a terrible thing to him to be found before the judgement-seat of God in the name of all poor sinners (for he was there, as it were, having

---

[17] There are some who argue that in some of these passages Calvin also uses more particular language such as Christ's being "oppressed for *us*." It is argued that this more specific language, referring to Christians, indicates the true extent of whom Calvin was speaking. This objection will be dealt with below.

[18] Calvin, *Comm.* Col 1:14, NTC 6:225.

[19] Calvin, *Comm.* Isa 53:12, vol. 4, 131. All references to Calvin's Old Testament commentaries are from the Calvin Translation Society series (Edinburgh: T & T Clark, 1845–1854) unless otherwise noted.

[20] Calvin, *Sermons on Isaiah's Prophecy of the Death and Passion of Christ*, 70, CO 35:637.

[21] Calvin, *The Deity of Christ and Other Sermons*, 155, CO 46:919.

[22] Calvin, *Institutio Christianae religionis* [1559] 2.16.2, under title of *Institutes of the Christian Religion* (ed. J. T. McNeill; trans. F. L. Battles; LCC 20–21; Philadelphia: Westminster, 1960), 505, OS 3:483.

to sustain all our burdens), nevertheless he did not fail to humble himself to such condemnation for our sakes.[23]

Let us note well, then, that the Son of God was not content merely to offer his flesh and blood and to subject them to death, but he willed in full measure to appear before the judgement seat of God his Father in the name and in the person of all sinners (*au nom et en la personne de tous pecheurs*), being then ready to be condemned, inasmuch as He bore our burden.[24]

At this point introducing an objection sometimes raised by particularist interpreters of Calvin would be appropriate. Some particularists have appealed to the fact that Calvin often includes exclusive phrases in otherwise universal statements, such as the phrase "our burden" at the end of the passage immediately above. They argue that Calvin's use of this more exclusive phrase constitutes a qualification of the previous universal phrase(s), thus indicating that the entire sentence or passage was meant to refer only to the elect.[25] Yet it may be argued that a particular reference to what Christ has done for "us" need not be understood as necessarily excluding the non-elect. Furthermore, several of the passages cited above make clear that Calvin carefully points out that it was for *us* and not for *Himself* that Christ died. Two examples will illustrate this theme. Notice Calvin's concern that we understand that Christ died for *others* and not for *Himself.*

For it is very important for us to know that Pilate did not condemn Christ before he himself had acquitted him three or four times, *so that we may learn from it that it was not on his own account that he was condemned but for our sins.* We may also learn how voluntarily he underwent death, when he refused to use the judge's favorable disposition to him. It was this obedience that made his death a sacrifice of sweet savor for expiating all sins.[26]

He must be the redeemer of the world. *He must be condemned, indeed, not for having preached the Gospel, but for us he must be oppressed,* as it were, to the lowest depths and sustain our cause, since he was there, as it were, in the person of all cursed ones and of all transgressors, and

---

[23] Calvin, *The Deity of Christ and Other Sermons*, 155–56, CO 46:919. (*Mais en tant que nostre Seigneur Iesus da nature avoit la mort en horreur, et mesmes que ce luy estoit une chose espovanrable de se trouver devant le siege iudicial de Dieu au nom de tous povres pecheurs.*)

[24] Calvin, *The Deity of Christ and Other Sermons*, 155–56, CO 46:52.

[25] Nicole makes this point in relation to the two quotations above in his article, "John Calvin's View," 197–225. See also Helm, *Calvin and the Calvinists*, 43–44.

[26] Calvin, *Comm.* John 19:12, NTC 3:343, emphasis added.

of those who had deserved eternal death. Since, then, Jesus Christ has this office, and he bears the burdens of all those who had offended God mortally, that is why he keeps silent.[27]

Notice how, in both of these passages, Calvin underscores the fact that Christ was not condemned to death for anything *He* had done, but rather He was condemned for *our* sins. Calvin employs "exclusive" language here not to teach that Christ died only for *us* Christians, the elect, but to make clear that *Christ* is not to be included among the number of those who needed redemption.

In this last quotation Calvin makes no distinction between *all* of those who were cursed, those deserving eternal death, and those whose burdens Christ bore. While the elect were at one time cursed and deserving of eternal death, nothing here indicates that Calvin has only the elect in mind. Calvin specifically mentions that "he bears the burdens of all those who had offended God mortally." Surely the elect were not the only ones "who had offended God mortally." Should not the non-elect be included in this number as well? In this passage Calvin can only reasonably be understood to have been writing about what Christ had done for the whole human race. Furthermore, considering how Calvin elsewhere uses universal language so freely to describe the death of Christ, there is no good reason to understand passages such as the two above as indicating a conscious decision on Calvin's part to limit the death of Christ to the elect alone—that is, unless one is predisposed to qualify all such language oneself. The previous unqualified statements demonstrate that Calvin was not so predisposed.

These passages provide just a sampling of the many places where Calvin uses universal language to describe the atonement.[28] Passages like these have led many to claim that Calvin did not hold to particular redemption. However, the evidence that Calvin might have held the view of universal atonement is not limited to these simple, straightforward universal state-

---

[27] Calvin, *The Deity of Christ and Other Sermons*, 95, CO 46:870, emphasis added.

[28] Other well-known passages include: Calvin, *Sermons on Isaiah*, 70, CO 35:637; *Comm*, John 1:5, NTC 3:4; *Comm*. John 1:11, NTC 3:8; *Comm*. Rom 5:18, NTC 5:78; *Institutes*, 3.1.1., OS 4:1; *The Deity of Christ and Other Sermons*, 242, CO 48:622. Some have also drawn attention to Calvin's statement in his last will and testament as proving that he held to universal atonement (see C. Daniel, "Hyper-Calvinism and John Gill" [Ph.D. diss., University of Edinburgh, 1983], 789). The statement in question reads as follows: "I further testify and declare that as a suppliant I humbly implore of him to grant me to be so washed and purified by the blood of that sovereign Redeemer, shed for the sins of the human race, that I may be permitted to stand before his tribunal in the image of the Redeemer himself," *Letters of John Calvin* (ed. J. Bonnet, trans. D. Constable; Philadelphia: Presbyterian Board of Publication, 1858), 4:365–69. Roger Nicole also includes an extensive list of passages where Calvin is said to have employed universal language to describe the atonement, "John Calvin's View," 198, note, 7.

ments. In fact, there are far stronger reasons to make this claim. The next section will examine Calvin's interpretation of a class of biblical texts that proponents of limited atonement claim are, from a simple reading of the text, clearly teaching that Christ died only for the elect. Were Calvin a proponent of limited atonement, one would expect him to interpret these texts in a way similar to the interpretations other proponents of limited atonement give. Instead, we find Calvin universalizing texts that the later tradition claims are clearly teaching limited atonement—something we should certainly *not* expect from Calvin, were he truly a proponent of limited atonement.

Calvin's Universalizing of the "Many" Passages

When proponents of limited atonement argue for their position, they frequently begin with an appeal to Scripture passages that speak of Christ dying for "many," "*his* sheep," or "*his* Church." John Owen's argument in *The Death of Death in the Death of Christ* begins this way. The first chapter of this work asks for whom Christ died. He appeals to Matt 20:28 ("the Son of Man did not come to be served, but to serve, and to give his life a ransom for *many*" NIV, emphasis added) and other similar passages as setting forth the normative scriptural teaching on the question of the extent of the atonement. Owen argues that these passages are properly to be understood as teaching that Christ died *only* for *many* people and not for *all* people.[29] He assumes that Christ and the biblical writers consciously used the word "many" with the intention of excluding some. Otherwise, Christ and the biblical writers would have used the word *all*. Even contemporary particularists frequently use this argument.[30]

Looking at how Calvin handled this passage and similar ones reveals a striking dissimilarity between his interpretation and the interpretations of later "Calvinists" such as Owen. Passages such as Matt 20:28 provided

---

[29] J. Owen, *The Death of Death in the Death of Christ* (Edinburgh: Johnstone & Hunter, 1852; repr., Edinburgh: Banner of Truth Trust, 1967). Owen begins with the assumption that these are the normative passages for interpreting all passages that speak of those for whom Christ died. Not until book 4 of this work does he address those passages speaking of Christ's dying for the whole world. Having already arrived at the conclusion that the "many" passages provide the norm for understanding the extent of the atonement, he is left to attempt to explain away all the passages that speak of Christ dying for the whole world.

[30] This argument from Owen is one of the most common arguments employed in defense of particular redemption. J. I. Packer affirms it in the introduction to the Banner of Truth Trust's edition of *The Death of Death*. See also J. Murray, *Redemption Accomplished and Applied* (Grand Rapids: Eerdmans, 1955), 62–63.

Calvin with a perfect opportunity to affirm particular redemption if he had so desired. Instead of interpreting the word "many" as indicating that some were excluded from the atonement, Calvin universalizes the word "many" by interpreting it to mean "all." The following passage illustrates how Calvin interprets Christ's use of the word "many" as it occurs in Matt 20:28:

> "Many" is used, not for a definite number, but for a large number (*Multos ponit non definite pro certo numero, sed pro pluribus*), in that he sets Himself over against all others. And this is the meaning also in Rom. 5:15, where Paul is not talking of a part of mankind but of the whole human race (*ubi Paulus non de aliqua hominum parte agit, sed totum humanum genus complectitur*).[31]

Instead of taking the opportunity presented by this text to limit the atonement to the elect alone, Calvin universalizes it.[32] Furthermore, as was noted previously, Calvin frequently wants to underscore that Christ died for *others* and not for *Himself*. The phrase "he sets himself over against all others" seems to indicate that Calvin had this interest here as well. This practice of universalizing the word "many" occurs frequently in Calvin's writings. When commenting on Isa 53:12 ("he bore the sins of many"), Calvin writes:

> He alone bore the punishment of many, because on him was laid the guilt of the whole world. It is evident from the fifth chapter of the Epistle to the Romans, that "many" sometimes denotes "all" (*multos enim pro omnibus interdum accipi*).[33]

Calvin interprets Mark 14:24 ("This is my blood of the new testament, which is shed for many" KJV) in the same manner:

---

[31] Calvin, *Comm.* Matt 20:28, NTC 2:181. In his commentary on Rom 5:15, Calvin asks us to observe "that a larger number (*plures*) are not here contrasted with many (*multis*), for he speaks not of the number of men: but as the sin of Adam has destroyed many, he draws this conclusion,—that the righteousness of Christ will be no less efficacious to save many," NTC 5:76. He specifically states that "many" is not to be understood as being contrasted with a larger number, such as "all."

[32] Limited atonement, or particular redemption, is frequently termed "definite" atonement, particularly in deference to those who might take offense at the idea that there may have been "limits" to the death of Christ. Some Calvinists (e.g., Nicole) thus employ the phrase "definite atonement" to clarify that Christ came to die for certain people only, not that there was any limit as to how many people for whom Christ *could* have died. Calvin's use of the word "definite" here seems to indicate that he rejected the idea that there were any for whom Christ did not die.

[33] Calvin, *Comm.* Isa 53:12, CO 37:266.

The word "many" does not mean a part of the world only, but the whole human race: he contrasts "many" with "one," as if to say that he would not be the Redeemer of one man, but would meet death to deliver many of their cursed guilt. No doubt that in speaking to a few Christ wished to make His teaching available to a larger number. . . . So when we come to the holy table not only should the general idea come to our mind that the world is redeemed by the blood of Christ, but also each should reckon to himself that his own sins are covered.[34]

Calvin's exegesis of Heb 9:28 ("Christ was once offered to bear the sins of many" KJV) follows the same line of interpretation:

"To bear the sins" means to free those who have sinned from their guilt by his satisfaction. He says many meaning all (*Multos dicit pro Omnibus*), as in Rom. 5:15. It is of course certain that not all enjoy the fruit of Christ's death (*non omnes ex Christi morte fructum percipere*), but this happens because their unbelief hinders them. The question is not dealt with here because the apostle is not discussing how few or how many benefit from the death of Christ, but meant simply that he died for others, not for himself. He therefore contrasts the many to the one (*Itaque multos uni opponit*).[35]

Once again Calvin universalizes the word "many" to include all sinners, not just the elect. Note also in this passage that Calvin seems to understand that, despite the fact that Christ has died for all, unbelief hinders people from enjoying the fruit of Christ's death.

Notice also the contrast that Calvin makes in the two previous passages. Calvin understands the biblical writers as contrasting the "many" with the "one," Jesus Christ. As mentioned previously, Calvin wants his readers to understand the teaching of Jesus: it was not for *Himself* that He died but for *others*. Had the text said that Christ died for "all," then presumably that number would have included Christ Himself. Therefore, Calvin explains that the the word "many" in these biblical passages functions to exclude *Christ* from among those who were in need of an atoning sacrifice. It does not *function* to exclude the *non-elect*.

In contrast to Calvin's handling of these and similar passages, particularists usually claim Jesus and the biblical writers deliberately chose the word *many* instead of the word *all*. A typical particularist interpretation

---

[34] Calvin, *Comm.* Mark 14:24, NTC 2:311.
[35] Calvin, *Comm.* Heb 9:27, NTC 7:93–94.

of these passages would be that Christ and the biblical writers intend to teach that Christ died only for "many" sinners as opposed to "all" sinners.[36] Contrary to this reading, Calvin interprets the presence of the word *many* as indicating that Christ died for *others* and not for *Himself.* Jesus and the biblical writers are not distinguishing between the *many* people and *all* people; rather, they are contrasting the *many* people from the *one* Jesus Christ. One last passage in which Calvin universalizes the word *many* comes from a sermon on Isa 53:12 ("he bore the sin of many" NIV).

> That, then is how our Lord Jesus bore the sins and iniquities of many. But in fact, the word "many" is often as good as equivalent to "all." And indeed our Lord Jesus was offered to all the world. For it is not speaking of three or four when it says: "God so loved the world, that he spared not his only Son." But yet we must notice what the Evangelist adds in this passage: "That whosoever believes in him shall not perish but obtain eternal life." Our Lord Jesus suffered for all and there is neither great nor small who is inexcusable today, for we can obtain salvation in him. Unbelievers who turn away from him and who deprive themselves of him by their malice are today doubly culpable, for how will they excuse their ingratitude in not receiving the blessing in which they could share by faith?[37]

The five passages above seem to demonstrate a conscious and deliberate universalizing of the atonement by Calvin. Contrary to the practice of most particularists, Calvin did not take the opportunity presented by these verses to interpret the word *many* in such a way as to limit the atonement only to the elect. Were Calvin a proponent of limited atonement, one would certainly not expect Calvin consciously and deliberately to universalize texts that later proponents of limited atonement claim are, from a simple reading of the text, explicitly teaching limited atonement. That this practice of universalizing the word *many* occurs so frequently and in different contexts (in his commentaries as well as his sermons) goes far toward demonstrating not just a predisposition toward a belief in a universal atonement but an explicit teaching on the matter.

---

[36] See Owen, *The Death of Death*, book 1, chapter 1, and Murray, *Redemption Accomplished and Applied*, 59–61.

[37] Calvin, *Sermons on Isaiah*, 141, CO 35:679.

The Culpability of Unbelievers and the Gospel Offer

The last passage above introduces yet another element in Calvin's under-standing of the atonement that one would not expect, were Calvin a proponent of limited atonement—that unbelievers will be held doubly culpable for rejecting the one who died for them. As the preceding pas-sage has already shown, Calvin presents Christ as having suffered for all. At the end of the passage, he points to the unbelievers' rejection of this same Christ as increasing their culpability. The last sentence of the passage in question reads as follows: "Unbelievers who turn away from Him and who deprive themselves of Him by their malice are today doubly culpable, for how will they excuse their ingratitude in not receiving the blessing in which they could share by faith?"[38] Here Calvin points to the unbeliev-ers' rejection of the Christ who died for them as yet another reason for their condemnation. Calvin had previously stated that Christ suffered for all and that there is no one who is "inexcusable today, for we can obtain salvation in Him." In this passage Calvin seems to assume that Christ has indeed died for those who reject Him. Otherwise, how could their rejec-tion of Christ increase their culpability and demonstrate their ingratitude if Christ has not actually made provision for them?

Calvin's understanding of the content of the gospel offer should be noted at this point, in that he understands that the Christ who is offered in the gospel has died for the one to whom He is offered, even when He is offered to those who reject Him. This understanding of the gospel offer differs significantly from that usually held by particularists. One of the perennial problems of the doctrine of limited atonement is that, if Christ has not actually died for the sins of all of humanity, then we can never assume that Christ has died for the person to whom we are now presenting the gospel. In order to get around this problem, proponents of particular redemption may say that Jesus Christ died for *sinners* in general and not necessarily for *you*, or for *this particular sinner.* The content of the gospel that unbelievers are rejecting is *not* that Christ died for *them* but, rather, simply that Christ died for *sinners.* The same concept holds true when the believer trusts in the gospel. That the prospective con-vert believe that Christ died for *him* is not required. That he believe that Christ died for *sinners* or that Christ is truly Savior of all those who believe

---

[38] Calvin, *Sermons on Isaiah,* 141, CO 35:679. See also *Comm.* Gal 1:3–5, NTC 6:3–4; Gal. 1:16, NTC 6:11.

is only required.[39] Yet Calvin's writings make fairly clear that the offer of salvation is based on Christ's dying for all those to whom salvation is offered, even those who reject the gospel. That saving faith consists of the belief that Christ has died for "me" personally is found throughout Calvin's writings. One such instance is in his commentary on Gal 2:20 ("I have been crucified with Christ; it is no longer I who live, but Christ lives in me; and the life I now live in the flesh I live by faith in the Son of God, who loved me and gave Himself for me," NKJV). He comments on this verse: "*For me* is very emphatic. It is not enough to regard Christ as having died for the salvation of the world; each man must claim the effect and possession of this grace for himself."[40] Calvin seems clear in his statement that claiming that Christ died for the world, or for *sinners*, is not enough. In a sermon on the same passage, Calvin's words are much more to the point: "Whereas it is said that the Son of God was crucified, we must not only think that the same was done for the redemption of the world: but also every one of us must on his own behalf join himself to our Lord Jesus Christ, and conclude, it is for me that he hath suffered."[41] Notice that in order to be joined with Christ, it is necessary to believe that "it is for me that he hath suffered." Merely believing that Christ suffered for "sinners" is not sufficient.

That Calvin grounds the universal offer of the gospel in a universal atonement can be seen throughout his writings. His commentary on Rom 5:18 ("Then as one man's trespass led to condemnation for all men, so one man's act of righteousness leads to acquittal and life for all men," RSV) displays a clear example. Calvin interprets this verse as follows: "Paul makes grace common to all men, not because it in fact extends to all, but because it is offered to all. Although Christ suffered for the sins of the world, and is offered by the goodness of God without distinction to all, yet not all receive him."[42] The final clause in Rom 5:18 might seem to indicate that *salvation* will actually come to all men. However, since Calvin was well aware of the biblical teaching that not all of human-

---

[39] See Owen, *The Death of Death*, 199–204, 292–98. See also J. I. Packer's introduction to this same volume, pp. 15–18; John Murray, *Redemption Accomplished and Applied*, 109.

[40] Calvin, *Comm.* Gal 2:20, NTC 6:28. (*Neque parum energiae habet* pro me: *quia non satis fuerit Christus pro mundi salute mortuum reputare, nisi sibi quisque effectum ac possessionem huius gratiae privatim vindicet.*)

[41] Calvin, *Sermons on Galatians*, 106, CO 50:453.

[42] Calvin, *Comm.* Rom 5:18, NTC 5:78. (*Communem omnium gratiam facit, quia omnibus expositae est, non quod ad omnes extendatur re ipsa: nam passus est Christus pro peccatis totius mundi, atque omnibus indifferenter Dei benignitate offetur, non tamen omnes apprehendunt.*)

ity will be saved, he explains that the universal language of this verse points to God's gracious *offer* of the gospel to all men, not to a universal salvation. Calvin clearly recognizes a universal intent in Paul's statement but interprets the passage to mean that Christ is *offered* to all the world. What is striking is that, contrary to the practices of many proponents of limited atonement, Calvin goes out of his way at this point to state that Christ suffered for the sins of the whole world. Furthermore, he seems to ground the universal offer of the gospel in a universal atonement, something which the later tradition claims is unnecessary. Proponents of limited atonement want to claim that all that is necessary for the gospel offer to be a legitimate offer to all humanity is for there to exist a command from God to offer the gospel to the world. Calvin, however, seems to connect the legitimacy of the universal offer of the gospel to the fact that Christ has died for the sins of the whole world. This idea is certainly *not* what one would expect from Calvin were he a proponent of limited atonement. Finally, Calvin explains the limited extent of *salvation*, not by recourse to a limited extent of the *atonement* but rather by recourse to the limited extent of *faith*. Calvin's commentary on Gal 5:12 also indicates that he understood the universal preaching of the gospel as grounded in a universal atonement. He writes: "God commends to us the salvation of all men without exception, even as Christ suffered for the sins of the whole world."[43]

In the passages cited here, Calvin seems to assume that something makes the universal offer of salvation to the world a legitimate offer of salvation—that Christ has, indeed, died for the sins of the whole world. Without this grounding, the universal offer of salvation might be a disingenuous offer. However, Calvin repeatedly ties the legitimacy of the universal offer of salvation to Christ's suffering for the sins of the entire world—something that we would certainly *not* expect to find, were Calvin a proponent of limited atonement. A universal atonement also explains how Calvin can claim that unbelievers are "doubly culpable" for rejecting the gospel because they are rejecting an actual provision God has graciously made for them in Christ.[44]

---

[43] Calvin, *Comm.* Gal 5:12, NTC 6:68 (*nam omnium salus sine exceptione nobis a Deo commendatur, quemadmodum pro peccatis totius mundi passus est Christus*).

[44] Calvin, *Sermons on Isaiah*, 141, CO 35:679. See also *Comm.* Gal 1:3–5, NTC 6:3–4; Gal 1:16, NTC 6:11.

Universal Atonement in Calvin's Polemical Writings

Were Calvin a proponent of limited atonement, one would expect that in his disagreements with other theologians he would have taken the opportunity to argue for this position when combating the beliefs of those who affirmed a universal atonement.[45] Upon examination however, this proves not to be the case. For example, it has been widely recognized that in Calvin's refutation of the decrees from the Council of Trent, he did not disagree with the statement on universal atonement.[46] Indeed, he specifically mentions the decree dealing with the extent of the atonement and states that he does not disagree with it.[47] Calvin quotes the decree as follows: "Him God set forth to be a propitiation through faith in his blood for our sins, and not only for ours, but also for the sins of the whole world. . . . But though he died for all, all do not receive the benefit of his death, but only those to whom the merit of his passion is communicated."[48] The wording in this statement is explicitly universal with regard to the atonement; yet, Calvin indicates no disagreement with it. Had Calvin held to particular redemption, it is difficult to believe that he would not have taken the opportunity to dispute the Roman Church on this point.

One particularly significant passage in Calvin's polemical writings goes far to demonstrate that not only does Calvin not hold to particular redemption, neither does he hold to a certain theological presupposition that lies at the heart of the limited atonement position. In the second half of his treatise *Concerning the Eternal Predestination of God*, Calvin defends his doctrine of predestination against Georgius, a Sicilian monk who had

---

[45] Paul Helm argues that the lack of extensive debate on this issue until the rise of Arminianism before the Synod of Dort may account for Calvin's near silence on the question of the extent of the atonement (*Calvin and the Calvinists*, 18). Helm is arguing from the assumption that limited atonement was the predominant view long before Dort and thus the reason Calvin had no occasion to enter into debate on the issue. While this might explain why Calvin never argued this point with other Reformed theologians, it does not explain why Calvin does not raise the issue in his polemics with the Roman Catholic Church. Furthermore, Robert Letham in his Aberdeen University Ph.D. dissertation argued that universal atonement was the original Reformation view and that particularism began to predominate about the time of Beza ("Saving Faith and Assurance in Reformed Theology: Zwingli to the Synod of Dort" [2 vols.; Ph.D. diss., Aberdeen University, 1979]). While I differ with Letham's contention that Calvin (and Bullinger) introduced particularism, the early Reformed theologians were not universally particularist as Helm seems to assume.

[46] Kendall mentions this in his brief argument at the outset of *Calvin and English Calvinism*, 12. See also Daniel, "Hyper-Calvinism and John Gill," 790.

[47] Calvin, *Tracts and Treatises on the Doctrine and Worship of the Church* (trans. H. Beveridge; Edinburgh: Calvin Translation Society, 1849; repr. Grand Rapids: Eerdmans, 1958), 3:109. Calvin's words are "the third and fourth heads I do not touch" (*tertium et quartum capita non attingo*), CO 7:443.

[48] Calvin, *Tracts and* Treatises, 93, CO 7:436.

spoken out against Calvin's teaching on predestination. The passage in question is rather lengthy but is worth reading in its entirety:

> Georgius thinks he argues very acutely when he says: Christ is the propitiation for the sins of the whole world; and hence those who wish to exclude the reprobate from participation in Christ must place them outside the world (*Ergo extra mundum reprobus constituant oportet qui a Christi participatione arcere eos volunt*). For this, the common solution does not avail, that Christ suffered sufficiently for all, but efficaciously only for the elect. By this great absurdity, this monk has sought applause in his own fraternity, but it has no weight with me. Wherever the faithful are dispersed throughout the world, John extends to them the expiation wrought by Christ's death. But this does not alter the fact that the reprobate are mixed up with the elect in the world. It is incontestable that Christ came for the expiation of the sins of the whole world (*Controversia etiam caret, Christum expiandis totius mundi peccatis venisse*). But the solution lies close at hand, that whosoever believes in him should not perish but should have eternal life (Jn 3.15). For the question is not how great the power of Christ is or what efficacy it has in itself, but to whom he gives himself to be enjoyed. If possession lies in faith and faith emanates from the Spirit of adoption, it follows that only he is reckoned in the number of God's children who will be a partaker (*particeps*) of Christ.[49]

In this passage Calvin is countering Georgius's argument that, since Christ is said to have died for the whole world, Calvin must place the reprobate outside of the world for the death of Christ not to apply to them. My use here of the word "apply" is carefully chosen. Calvin's polemic with Georgius clearly indicates that he understood Georgius to hold to universal salvation, that the benefits of the death of Christ will actually be "applied"

---

[49] Calvin, *Concerning the Eternal Predestination of God* (trans. J. K. S. Reid; London: James Clark & Co., 1961), 149, CO 8:336. Whether Calvin or Georgius mentions Lombard's formula that the death of Christ was "sufficient for all but efficient only for the elect" is unclear (see Daniel, "Hyper-Calvinism and John Gill," 807). If it is Calvin, then he clearly does not think that this formula is of any help in this circumstance. Yet, in his commentary on 1 John 2:2, Calvin admits the truth of the formula but indicates that it has no bearing in that context. If this is an instance of Calvin alluding to this formula, there is no reason to think he rejects it, considering his affirmation of the formula in his commentary on 1 John 2:2. Even if Calvin's quotation of Georgius ends after the recitation of this formula, thus making the allusion to the formula Georgius's rather than Calvin's, Calvin elsewhere affirmed the truth of the formula. Calvin may be inconsistent in this instance. Also, the "absurdity" to which Calvin referred may be Georgius's conclusion that all would be joined to Christ, which was certainly Calvin's primary critique of Georgius. Calvin's primary complaint concerned Georgius's failure to see the necessity of faith and participation in Christ for the atonement to be applied to the believer.

to all those for whom Christ died.[50] Calvin, then, is not just arguing against someone who holds the view of a universal atonement, but with someone who claims that Christ's death for the sins of the whole world will actually result in the salvation of the whole world.

Georgius's position seems to be based on two assumptions. First, he understood that Christ had died for the sins of the whole world. Second, he believed that all those for whom Christ died will actually reap the benefits of that death—eternal life. Georgius's argument, in essence, is that there can be no reprobate since salvation will actually be "applied" to all those for whom Christ died. Since Christ is said to have died for the whole world, then Christ must have died for the so-called reprobate as well. Otherwise, the reprobate must be placed somewhere outside the world.

Calvin does not counter Georgius's argument by denying Georgius's first premise—that Christ died for the sins of the whole world. Rather, Calvin counters the argument by attacking Georgius's second premise— that all those for whom Christ died will ultimately be saved. In fact, Calvin states explicitly that it is "incontestable that Christ came for the expiation of the sins of the whole world."[51] Were Calvin a proponent of limited atonement, he certainly would have corrected Georgius's belief that Christ died for the sins of the whole world. Instead, he agrees with this part of Georgius's argument but rejects the assumption that everyone for whom Christ died will be saved. Calvin argues that not all those for whom Christ died will ultimately be saved, for not all believe and are made partakers of Christ.

This passage strikes at the heart of one of the central assumptions of the limited atonement position—that the atonement, because of its nature, absolutely and without exception brings eternal life to everyone for whom that atonement was made. This is the central point from which Georgius is arguing and the point that Calvin is rejecting. Had Calvin been a proponent of limited atonement, his answer to Georgius would have been simple. He could have easily argued that the reprobate are lost, not because they were "outside" the world when atonement was made but because Christ simply did not atone for their sins when He died on the cross. But Calvin does not argue in this way. He affirms, with Georgius, that Christ died for the sins of the whole world. However, he disagrees with Georgius's second premise that the atoning death of Christ actually

---

[50] See, Calvin, *Concerning the Eternal Predestination of God*, 151–52, CO 8:337.
[51] Calvin, *Concerning the Eternal Predestination of God*, 149, CO 8:336.

saves all of those for whom atonement was made. By rejecting their second premise Calvin is also rejecting the later Reformed tradition's insistence that the atonement saves all those for whom atonement was made. [52]

Conclusion

This discussion of universal atonement in Calvin's writings, though by no means exhaustive, should be sufficient for the reader to understand why so many scholars since Calvin's time have claimed that he did not hold to limited atonement. Nevertheless, this discussion is sufficient to demonstrate that, were Calvin a proponent of limited atonement, there is a great deal of problematic material in his writings that is not commensurate with that position. This argument also shows that those who dare to claim that Calvin held to a universal atonement are not making such claims without good reasons.

This discussion has not raised all of the possible objections that particularists have raised surrounding the claim that Calvin taught a universal atonement. For example, while it is true that Calvin does frequently interpret the word *many* as being virtually equivalent to *all* when it appears in certain verses of Scripture, Calvin also frequently interprets the word *all* as meaning something less than "all the people in the world." Particularists have appealed to this feature of Calvin's interpretation of Scripture as evidence that he did not differ significantly from the interpretive practices of the later Reformed tradition.[53] Many particularist interpreters of Calvin also appeal to Calvin's commentary on 1 John 2:2 as evidence that Calvin explicitly affirmed limited atonement. Calvin's comments on this passage do, indeed, appear to affirm limited atonement. However, his comments also demonstrate that his greatest fear in regard to this text was not that someone might interpret this verse as teaching that Christ died for all of humanity but rather that some *had* interpreted this verse to teach that the whole world, including Satan and his demons, will actually inherit eternal life with God. This simple fact introduces a certain ambiguity in Calvin's meaning in his commentary on 1 John 2:2.[54] Also, we must remember

---

[52] Both Paul Helm and Roger Nicole claim that Calvin affirmed that all those for whom Christ died will actually be saved, despite any evidence to support their claims. For a more detailed discussion of this issue, see my *Union with Christ and the Extent of the Atonement in Calvin*, 40–41.

[53] Nicole, "John Calvin's View," 211–12, 217. See also, Kennedy, *Union with Christ*, 42–53.

[54] The ambiguity arises from Calvin's statement that "John's purpose was only to make this blessing common to the whole Church." The question is whether the antecedent to the word "this" is "atonement"

the passage from *Concerning the Eternal Predestination of God* that was addressed above in which Calvin argues against Georgius. In that treatise, published one year *after* his commentary on 1 John, Calvin states, "It is incontestable that Christ came for the expiation of the sins of the whole world."[55] So, even if one does not grant any ambiguity in Calvin's commentary on 1 John 2:2, there is certainly ambiguity within Calvin's writings in general regarding his interpretation of 1 John 2:2. Suffice it to say that those on both sides of the question of Calvin's understanding of the extent of the atonement are well aware of the various "problem" texts that Calvin presents his readers. While the debate over Calvin's view on the extent of the atonement will likely continue, hopefully this short discussion demonstrates sufficient reasons to question whether Calvin was in complete agreement with the later tradition that often bears his name.

---

or "salvation." Since the *danger* Calvin clearly perceives in this passage is that some *have already* taken this verse to mean that the entire world, including Satan and all his demons, will actually be saved, then it is possible that Calvin's claim is that John is limiting the extent of actual *salvation* to the church and not the extent of the atonement *per se*. For a full discussion of this issue, see Kennedy, *Union with Christ*, 49–53. See also, Daniel, "Hyper-Calvinism and John Gill," 803–4.

[55] Calvin, *Concerning the Eternal Predestination of God*, 149, CO 8:336.

Chapter 8

The Potential Impact of Calvinist Tendencies upon Local Baptist Churches

Malcolm B. Yarnell III

I n recent years the subject of Calvinism has risen drastically in impor-tance within Baptist conversations, around both the dinner table and the seminar table, and often around the table of the Lord's Supper. Although an element of Calvinism has always been functioning within Baptist circles, there has been a rise of late, by most accounts, in Cal-vinism's influence on local churches. This influence is evident among Baptists generally and among Southern Baptists in particular. There are both active proponents and opponents of Calvinism's influence, in both the academic and ecclesial realms. However, evaluating the promoters and detractors of Calvinism among Baptists is not the concern of this essay.[1] Also, significant stories regarding the influence of Calvinism on local Baptist churches have appeared in the religious news in recent years.

---

[1] E. R. Clendenen and B. J. Waggoner, eds., *Calvinism: A Southern Baptist Dialogue* (Nashville: B&H Academic, 2008).

Detailing those recent events is not the intent of this essay. That task is left to the journalist.[2]

Relying on biblical theology and historical theology, this essay intends to outline a potential range of theological changes that Calvinism may introduce into the reader's local Baptist church, especially with regard to church polity and practice. This sketch of possible theological changes will be accomplished by discussing certain ecclesiological tendencies that Calvinism evinces. The theological orientation of this essay intends to help non-Calvinists develop the ability to understand their Calvinist counterparts in conversation. A theological orientation to the ecclesiological principles of Calvinism may aid readers in envisioning for themselves the potential impact that Calvinism can have upon their local churches. That impact may vary according to local events, but the active principles will prove somewhat consistent.

Even further qualification is needed at this point. First, because the author has summarized the Baptist view of church polity and practice elsewhere, the New Testament foundation of Baptist views will not be defended but assumed here.[3] Second, because the author addresses the development of the Baptist heritage and identity elsewhere, the historical ebb and flow of Baptist Calvinism, though certainly an important and integral part of the Baptist tradition, will not be considered here.[4] Finally, while the development of Calvinism within the evangelical tradition as a whole is itself an important and broad conversation, the broader context may be touched upon but will not be thoroughly delineated here.

Again, our purpose, alongside the soteriological discussions handled ably by the other contributors to this book, is simply to inform local Baptist church leaders of the potential impact that Calvinism could have upon their churches. The use of the subjunctive in that last sentence is intentional and noteworthy. Calvinism as a movement does not demonstrate monolithic agreement, although there are certainly broadly common characteristics and tendencies within the movement. Moreover, some advocates of Calvinism, whether by temperamental, experiential, or contextual restraints, are subtle in their enthusiasm for the Reformed faith and

---

[2] Although written with a pro-Calvinist agenda, one may consult C. Hansen, *Young, Restless, Reformed: A Journalist's Journey with the New Calvinists* (Wheaton, IL: Crossway, 2008).

[3] M. B. Yarnell III, "Article VI: The Church," in *Baptist Faith and Message 2000: Critical Issues in America's Largest Protestant Denomination* (ed. D. K. Blount and J. D. Wooddell; New York: Rowman & Littlefield, 2007), 55–70.

[4] For a summary review of Baptist Calvinism, see M. B. Yarnell III, "Calvinism: Cause for Rejoicing, Cause for Concern," in *Calvinism*, ed. Clendenen and Waggoner, 73–95.

practice when compared to other Calvinists. Both the success stories and failure stories that Calvinists and non-Calvinists repeat need to be received with some reserve. Every movement has its embarrassing enthusiasts, and the opponents of every movement have their enthusiasts, too. Movements should not be judged primarily by their enthusiastic fringes, as terrible as those fringes may be, but by their original and overall influence.

In light of the desire to understand Calvinism according to its original and overall influence, studying the importance of the Swiss Reformed movement is fundamental to developing a working theological outline of the broader movement known as Calvinism or Reformed. As a result of his importance, this essay will focus particularly upon the theology explicated by John Calvin, drawing upon both earlier and later historical developments to illuminate the typical polity and practices of Calvinism. The shades of nuance between Calvin and the later Dortian Calvinists—important when considering the doctrine of salvation—are of minimal significance when it comes to the doctrine of the church. Of greater significance for Baptists are the apparently insurmountable differences between Calvinist ecclesiology and Baptist ecclesiology.

Calvinism's Ecclesiological Tendencies

Calvinism displays certain tendencies that exercise a great impact upon its doctrine of the church, and therefore upon the local church's polity and practice. These ecclesiological tendencies may be summarized as the ancient church, Augustinian innovations, aristocratic elitism, and antinomian tendencies. From the Baptist perspective, many of these tendencies pose a direct challenge to the New Testament standard of the church that Baptists believe is essential for the churches of Jesus Christ to practice today if they wish to be faithful to the Lord. After explaining the origin and import of these tendencies, a summary Baptist response will be provided.

The Ancient Church

The first thing to note about Calvinist ecclesiology is that, in spite of its methodological claim for *sola scriptura*, Calvinism typically moves beyond the Bible in order to create its theological standards. This movement can be seen in Calvinism's penchant for doctrines such as the five points of the

Synod of Dort or a periodically reckless speculation regarding the ordering of the divine decrees. Calvinism also holds to a theological standard for the church that moves far beyond Scripture. John Calvin developed this extrabiblical ecclesiological standard, which he called "the ancient church," furthering the Reformed theology of an earlier reformer in Zurich.[5] Ulrich Zwingli, who formulated Reformed ecclesiology in its earliest years, was dangerously haphazard in his treatment of Scripture. At first, Zwingli sought to return to the New Testament as the standard for the church's theology and practice.[6] Unfortunately, when it came to implementation, Zwingli compromised those earlier convictions for the sake of maintaining his political position, as we shall see.

Politically, Zwingli was beholden to the Zurich city council for the progress of his reformation of the church. In an October 1523 disputation, he explicitly submitted the reformation of the church to the state. "My lords," the Reformed leader said, "will decide whatever regulations are to be adopted in the future in regard to the Mass."[7] Zwingli's students could not quite believe that their leader had just effectively abrogated the Lord's will for His churches. They understood that God had revealed His will for the churches through His Son as recorded in the Bible inspired by the Holy Spirit. Simon Stumpf responded, "Master Ulrich, you do not have the right to place the decision on this matter in the hands of my lords, for the decision has already been made: the Spirit of God decides."[8]

After this event the students of Zwingli noticed that he began to withdraw in major ways from his commitment to institute a New Testament form of the church. For instance, although Zwingli initially agreed with his students that baptism was reserved for believers only, he was not willing to move faster than the conservative city council. The city council was unwilling to change what was considered a universal form of oath-taking to the magistrate's oversight of every citizen—infant baptism. After the first Anabaptists reinstituted believers-only baptism in January 1525, Zwingli strained for a theological response. Rather than referring to the Lord's orderly commands in Scripture, as verified in the apostolic practice of conversion prior to baptism, Zwingli invented a new type of covenant theology. Specifically, he tied the New Testament "sacrament" of baptism

---

[5] For a more detailed discussion of Zwingli's ecclesiology, see W. P. Stephens, *The Theology of Huldrych Zwingli* (New York: Oxford University Press, 1986), 260–70.

[6] W. R. Estep, *The Anabaptist Story* (rev. ed.; Grand Rapids: Eerdmans, 1975), 10.

[7] Ibid., 12.

[8] Ibid.

with the Old Testament practice of circumcision, thereby conflating the Old and New Covenants.[9]

The exegetical twists and turns that Zwingli performed in his May 1525 response to the Anabaptists were necessarily serpentine as he strove to preserve the state church practice of infant baptism. Driven by the political need of the moment, Zwingli extended the church into the Old Testament, misinterpreted Col 2:10–12 by replacing spiritual circumcision with physical circumcision, based Christian baptism in the practice of John the Baptist rather than in the Great Commission of Jesus Christ, and denied that His church should be composed only of verifiable Christians. Subsequently, Reformed theologians have largely followed Zwingli's lead in their theologies of covenant and baptism. Reformed covenantal theology is thus founded upon what even a prominent Calvinist theologian could only helplessly describe as "thinness in exegesis" matched by "a general thinness in the whole theology of baptism."[10]

Zwingli's haphazard treatment of the New Testament doctrine of the church and its practices was amplified in the systematic ruminations of John Calvin. Although Calvin, unlike his predecessor, carefully worked toward some limited distance between the civil and the ecclesiastical orders, he never separated the two but maintained the Constantinian synthesis of church and state. In order to justify this synthesis and its concomitant practice of infant baptism, Calvin repeated many of the failed arguments and twisted hermeneutics of Zwingli. Moreover, he developed the concept of "the ancient church" as a way of providing a substitute standard for the church. As is well known, Calvin and his followers emphasize the "reformation" of the church as a continuing need. However, the goal of that reformation is not necessarily that of the New Testament church. Rather, the goal of Calvin's reformation was a hazy concept known as "the ancient church."

The ancient church appears in Calvin's initial presentation of the doctrine of the church, known as the *Draft Ecclesiastical Ordinances*, prepared for the Genevan city council in 1541.[11] This work is important for understanding the polity of Calvinism, for it is here that the offices and the sacraments of the Reformed churches are first outlined

---

[9] Zwingli, "Of Baptism," in *Zwingli and Bullinger: Selected Translations with Introductions and Notes* (ed. G.W. Bromiley; LCC; Philadelphia: Westminster Press, 1953), 138.

[10] G. W. Bromiley, "Introduction," in ibid., 126.

[11] J. Calvin, *Draft Ecclesiastical Ordinances*, in *John Calvin: Selections from His Writings* (ed. J. Dillenberger; [n.p.]: American Academy of Religion, 1975), 229–65.

systematically. It is notable that the *Ecclesiastical Ordinances* do not rely upon the exegesis of Scripture but spring from Calvin's own ruminations, ruminations formed in the crucible of his experiences as a canon lawyer and his desire to join with the Swiss reformers. Although the Old Testament, the New Testament, and the Word of God are mentioned and roughly undergird his thought, they are not submitted to careful exegesis. In other words, in Calvin's initial ecclesiological system, Scripture is mentioned but not examined. Of more consequence than Scripture's close definition of the church was Calvin's own ill-defined standard of the ancient church.

Calvin furthered this conception of the ancient church in his *Institutes of the Christian Religion,* a periodically revised treatise that reached its final Latin form in 1559. Incredibly, in spite of years of working with the biblical text as a preacher, Calvin never substantially revised his ecclesiology in a more biblical direction. As with the *Ecclesiastical Ordinances,* the ancient church in the *Institutes* served as the rough standard for the contemporary church. The ancient church included (1) the Old Testament patriarchs, whom he believed were regenerated before the appearance of the Savior,[12] (2) the New Testament churches, and (3) the post-New Testament churches into the early Middle Ages.[13] The ancient church was corrupted by the Roman see progressively through the Middle Ages. Thus, not all ecclesiological developments away from the New Testament were inappropriate, although the Roman ones were.[14]

Perhaps most importantly, from the Baptist perspective, the lordship of Christ exercises little importance in Calvin's ecclesiology. Indeed, his ancient church was not based upon the Lord—"Christ here instituted nothing new"—for Christ Himself was a participant in and subject to the ancient church's forms.[15] Although Calvin claims Christ's headship is "the condition of unity" for the church, this theological assertion has no concrete importance. Instead of the standard for His churches established by Jesus, Calvin believed the New Testament did not provide a set form for the church, except in vague terms. The ancient church, according to Calvin, "tried with a sincere effort to preserve God's institution and

---

[12] J. Calvin, *Institutes of the Christian Religion* (trans. F. L. Battles; ed. J. T. McNeill; LCC; 2 vols.; Philadelphia: Westminster Press, 1960) [hereinafter, *Institutes*], 4.16.10–16, 24.

[13] Calvin, *Institutes,* 4.4.1, 10–15.

[14] Calvin, *Institutes,* 4.5.

[15] Calvin, *Institutes,* 4.11.4.

did not wander far from it."[16] In other words, Calvin was not necessarily concerned with a Christological and biblical definition of the church but appealed to what he realized was a flawed doctrine—the ancient church did "wander."

Standing in stark opposition to the Calvinist standard of "the ancient church" is the Baptist standard of "the New Testament church." The Baptists and their sixteenth-century theological kin, the Anabaptists, have not pursued a reformation of their churches according to a partially biblical form of the church. Rather, Baptists have explicitly elevated the standard of the New Testament. Baptists have pursued a thorough reformation, or restitution, of the church as established by the Lord Jesus Christ and modeled in the teaching and practice of the apostles. As Robert A. Baker has argued in his excellent study of the Baptists, we have pursued the "pattern and authority" established in the New Testament.[17] The Southern Baptist Convention, in agreement, defines the church, not according to the Reformed ancient church that confuses the Old and New Testaments and elevates human tradition above Christ's will. The Baptist Faith and Message defines the church from the beginning as "New Testament" and proceeds only on that basis.[18]

Augustinian Innovations

Perhaps the greatest dependence that Calvin demonstrated upon another theologian was his deference to Augustine of Hippo. This early medieval theologian developed the theology that both later Roman Catholics and Protestants followed. It is a common axiom among Christian historians that Protestants typically followed Augustine's soteriology while Roman Catholics followed Augustine's ecclesiology. This is not, however, entirely the case. With regard to the doctrine of the church, Lutherans and Calvinists have retained many of Augustine's theological innovations. The Protestant acceptance of Augustine's ecclesiology is especially notable in the two cases: Augustine's doctrine of the invisible worldwide church and his intolerance toward religious dissent.

---

[16] Calvin, *Institutes*, 4.4.1.

[17] R. A. Baker, *The Baptist March in History* (Nashville: Convention Press, 1958), 1.

[18] All citations of The Baptist Faith and Message derive from *The Baptist Faith and Message: A Statement Adopted by the Southern Baptist Convention, June 14, 2000* (Nashville: LifeWay, 2000) and refer to the Article. The Baptist Faith and Message, Art. VI.

The Invisible Worldwide Church

First, Augustine's doctrine of the church is characterized by a diffuseness reminiscent of his appropriation of Platonic categories of thought. The visible church, for Augustine, is not primarily local and gathered, as defined by the New Testament but universal and inseparable from the world. The Lord's expectation of holiness within His church, moreover, is rendered as an eschatological hope rather than embraced as a contemporary goal. The downplaying of the visible church as a local congregation of born-again believers and the elevation of the universal church as a worldwide congregation, which is visible only in fits and starts, is characteristic of Augustinian and Protestant ecclesiology. Recognizing the problem with his advocacy of a visible and impure church in comparison with the scriptural ideal of a visibly regenerate church (2 Cor 6:11–7:1), Augustine invented the concept of the invisible church composed of only the elect.[19] Unfortunately for Augustine, there is no biblical foundation for the idea of an invisible worldwide gathering of Christians.

John Calvin and the Calvinists have largely adopted these Augustinian innovations in defining the church, without major criticism. The Calvinist adoption of this aspect of Augustinian ecclesiology has created an irresolvable tension within Calvinist ecclesiology, for while affirming the secretive nature of the invisible church, Calvinists also fervently desire to have a visible presence and impact upon their local culture. Evincing this tension, the Reformed confessions typically advocate the invisible church as a major category even as they try to make their churches relevant in their cultures.[20] This extrabiblical innovation allows Calvinists to alternate between definitions of the church based on the particular conversation in which they are engaged. When speaking of ideals, the invisible worldwide church, sometimes termed the universal church, is the primary subject. When speaking of practice, the visible local church is typically in mind. This elastic definition of the church is the source of some confusion in contemporary conversations between Calvinist Baptists and non-Calvinist Baptists.

---

[19] M. B. Yarnell III, "The Development of Religious Liberty: A Survey of Its Progress and Challenges in Christian History," *The Journal for Baptist Theology and Ministry* 6 (2009): 128.

[20] The Second Helvetic Confession, for instance, while maintaining the Constantinian church-culture synthesis, believes the church can be so invisible that at times it "appears extinct." *Reformed Confessions of the Sixteenth Century* (ed. A. C. Cochrane; Louisville: Westminster John Knox Press, 2003), 266–67.

In opposition to the Anabaptist and Baptist ideal of regenerate church membership, for Calvin, as for Augustine, the visible church is definitely *not* intended to be a pure institution. It must rather remain a mixed church with both elect and non-elect secretly ensconced therein.[21] This resort to the mixed church does not mean that Calvinists reject the practice of discipline, for they most certainly advocate such. However, separatism or schism is to be avoided at all costs, even if it means the demise of the regenerate church. Alas, moreover, for Calvin and many Calvinists, the visible local church is often confused with the diffuse Augustinian rendition of the universal church as a worldwide present reality! The local churches are subsumed under the universal church as a present though invisible gathering.[22]

From a Baptist perspective, these Calvinist positions cause difficulties. The Augustinian definition of the universal church contradicts the eschatological definition of the universal church taught by the apostle John (see Rev 19:1–10) and affirmed at the end of Article VI of The Baptist Faith and Message. According to the founder of Southwestern Baptist Theological Seminary, the universal church will not gather until the end of time when Christ is in its midst bodily. Moreover, "all teaching in the direction that there now exists a general assembly which is invisible, without ordinances, and which is entered by faith alone, will likely tend to discredit the particular assembly, which does now really exist and which is the pillar and ground of truth."[23]

Religious Intolerance

Second, Calvin's doctrine of the church depends not only on Augustine's innovation of the invisible church but also upon the earlier theologian's religious intolerance. Augustine misinterpreted the parable of the Wheat and the Tares in Matt 13:24–30 so that he equated the field with the church rather than with the world.[24] This interpretation is disastrous for two reasons. First, it explicitly contradicts the interpretation that Jesus Christ Himself gave to His parable (Matt 13:38). Second, when coupled

---

[21] Calvin, *Institutes*, 4.1.2.

[22] Calvin, *Institutes*, 4.1.9.

[23] B. H. Carroll, *Baptists and Their Doctrines: Sermons on Distinctive Baptist Principles* (New York: Fleming H. Revell, 1913), 42–43.

[24] Yarnell, "The Development of Religious Liberty," 128–29.

with Augustine's diffuse understanding of the universal church, it also enables the persecution of religious dissenters.

On the one hand, Augustine criticized the Donatists for uphold-ing the ideal of the regenerate church, claiming that they were trying to bring schism to the worldwide church. On the other hand, Augustine also encouraged the persecution of the Donatists claiming they were disrupting not only the church but also the state, which were now mixed together in the Constantinian synthesis. The state must enforce unity upon the church as a service to Christ and even to aid in the salvation of the schismatics themselves. Augustine equivocated with regard to persecution, sometimes arguing for and sometimes against religious persecution. Later medieval churchmen radicalized his views, creating a persecuting state that sup-pressed all religious dissent in the name of the universal church.[25]

Calvin adopted the Augustinian arguments for religious persecution, including the misinterpretation of Matthew 13. He repeatedly used such arguments in his emotional rebuttals of the Anabaptists.[26] These earlier free churchmen, in his mind, were "perverted," "malicious," and possessed by "insane pride."[27] In spite of his intolerance toward the Anabaptists, Calvin, like Augustine, also periodically pleaded for religious tolerance.[28] The hypocrisy of Calvin's extreme intolerance, demonstrated in particular toward Michael Servetus, was not lost on the Christian humanist Sebas-tian Castellio. Castellio took Calvin to task for the latter's role in the pros-ecution and execution of Servetus. Servetus was burned at the stake for two matters: his denial of the Trinity and his denial of infant baptism.[29] Servetus did err with regard to the Trinity. The religious intolerance of John Calvin, which has been subsequently defended or downplayed by Calvinists, is also a gross error.

Over against such intolerant attitudes and actions, there stands the clear witness of the baptizing tradition. Religious intolerance is entirely unacceptable for Christians, and religious liberty is a God-given right that all human beings possess. Tolerance has been the consistent witness of the baptizing tradition from the first religious liberty text, written by the Ana-baptist Balthasar Hubmaier in 1524, who was himself tortured by Ulrich

---

[25] Ibid.

[26] Calvin, *Institutes*, 4.1.13, 4.1.16, 4.1.19, 4.12.11–13, and so forth.

[27] Calvin, *Institutes*, 4.1.13, 4.20.7; Calvin, *Brief Instruction Arming All the Good Faithful Against the Errors of the Common Sect of the Anabaptists*, in *Treatises Against the Anabaptists and Against the Libertines* (trans. B. W. Farley; Grand Rapids: Baker Academic, 1982).

[28] Calvin, *Institutes*, 4.12.9.

[29] Yarnell, "The Development of Religious Liberty," 131–32.

Zwingli, until today.[30] The doctrinal rigidity, demonstrated most horribly in the repeated persecution and slaying of the Anabaptists by the Reformed is indicative of two irreconcilable outlooks regarding what it means to be a faithful Christian. The Reformed murder, through public drowning, of Felix Manz in 1527 under Zwingli, and the Reformed murder, through public burning, of Michael Servetus in Geneva under Calvin, manifest a fundamentally flawed outlook toward both God and man.

The Southern Baptist position, on the other hand, is clear: "A free church in a free state is the Christian ideal, and this implies the right of free and unhindered access to God on the part of all men, and the right to form and propagate opinions in the sphere of religion without interference by the civil power."[31] The question is not whether Calvinists today agree with such horrible acts, for they certainly do not. The question today is whether hastiness in judgment is still evident within certain strains of Calvinism.[32]

Aristocratic Elitism

The impact of Calvin and Calvinism on the development of modern democracy has been a subject of much discussion. Some have denied outright that Calvin was a source of modern democracy; others have argued that Calvinism was an unconscious source of democracy.[33] The cultural conversation regarding Calvin's attitude toward forms of civil government is interesting but only tangentially related to Calvin's attitudes about the proper governance of the church. What is relatively clear is that Calvin defended an attenuated form of democracy within the churches even as he advanced an aristocratic elitism among ministers, doctors, and elders. Calvin preferred aristocracy, or more accurately representative aristocracy, to any other form of governance. This preference has created a tendency toward aristocratic polities within Calvinist churches, polities that more

---

[30] T. White, "The Defense of Religious Liberty by the Anabaptists and the English Baptists," in *First Freedom: The Baptist Perspective on Religious Liberty* (eds. T. White, J. G. Duesing, and M. B. Yarnell III; Nashville: B&H Academic, 2007), 52.

[31] Baptist Faith and Message, Art. XVII.

[32] While a conservative evangelical Calvinist like Mark Driscoll accuses his church members of "sinning through questioning" his leadership, others who see themselves as heirs of Calvin's ecclesiology are "changing it, and adapting it." J. D. Douglass, "Calvin and the Church Today: Ecclesiology as Received, Changed, and Adapted," *Theology Today* 66 (2009): 136.

[33] R. M. Kingdon and R. D. Linder, eds., *Calvin and Calvinism: Sources of Democracy?*, Problems in European Civilization (Lexington, MA: D.G. Heath and Company, 1970).

often than not result in extrabiblical organizations that place themselves between Christ and the local churches.

During the sixteenth and seventeenth centuries, the three classical forms of governance—monarchy (rule by one), aristocracy (rule by few), and democracy (rule by all)—were the subjects of extensive discussion for theologians. Many evangelical theologians, especially among the English, concluded that some form of "mixed polity," or facets of all three governmental forms, might be best.[34] Calvin himself concluded that aristocracy, perhaps tempered with some surface democracy, was best: "For if the three forms of government which the philosophers discuss be considered in themselves, I will not deny that aristocracy, or a system compounded of aristocracy and democracy, far excels all the others."[35]

On the one side of aristocracy, monarchy was distasteful to Calvin, partially because of having to flee Paris after the famous placard incident and partially because of the errors propagated by the Roman hierarchy.[36] If Calvinism helped foster modern democracy, it was primarily through cobelligerency with democrats and republicans against the monarchies. However, on the other side of aristocracy, democracy also presented problems for Calvin. Calvin's writings decry the anarchy and disruption to which the "heedless multitude" can lead.[37] Such heedlessness deserved special condemnation when he turned his thoughts toward that sixteenth-century baptizing group which he derisively termed "Anabaptists." Rather than pure democracy, that was characteristic of the "mad ravings" of those who practice believers-only baptism,[38] Calvin advocated the aristocratic model of the ancient church. This aristocratic model is located somewhere between Roman hierarchicalism on the right and Anabaptist congregationalism on the left.

Although Calvin disliked the term "hierarchy," he was not against a streamlined order in the church.[39] Most importantly, a church constitution must be orderly, possess dignity, and encourage moderation.[40] Dignity,

---

[34] Cf. S. Brachlow, *The Communion of the Saints: Radical Puritan and Separatist Ecclesiology* (New York: Oxford University Press, 1988), *passim*.

[35] Calvin, *Institutes*, 4.20.8.

[36] A placard denouncing the Mass was nailed to the king's bedchamber, setting off a round of persecution of evangelicals, resulting in Calvin's exit from Paris. B. Cottret, *Calvin: A Biography* (trans. M. W. McDonald; Grand Rapids: Eerdmans, 2000), 82–88.

[37] See Calvin, *Institutes*, 4.4.12.

[38] Calvin, *Institutes*, 4.16.1.

[39] Calvin, *Institutes*, 4.4.4.

[40] Calvin, *Institutes*, 4.10.28.

order, and moderation were the measures by which Calvinists judged polity; and aristocracy, the rule of the fittest, accorded best with such virtues. Coming to the interpretation of Matt 18:15–20—a critical passage wherein Christ explicitly gave "to the church" the authority over the communion of members—Calvin proved innovative. Because Calvin considered aristocracy the superior form of governance, he advocated the creation of church courts: "Now these admonitions and corrections cannot be made without investigation of the cause; accordingly, some court of judgment and order of procedure are needed. . . . [W]e must give the church some jurisdiction."[41]

By appealing to the need for some sort of "jurisdiction" while maintaining a fluid definition of "church," Calvin created an opening for the introduction of intervening mechanisms above the local churches. Calvin proceeded to argue that this jurisdiction is best exercised by a number of men rather than one: "there is more authority in the assembly than in one man." Calvin's preference for aristocracy, when combined with his legal training, entailed the creation of various church courts above the churches. Citing the writings of Cyprian, Calvin advocated that a "senate of presbyters" be empowered with final governance of the local church.[42] This senate of presbyters is composed of two orders: pastors and teachers on the one hand, and lay elders on the other hand.[43] In many Reformed communions, today, above the local aristocracy of the presbytery stand the regional aristocracy of the synod and the national aristocracy of the general assembly.

The first order of ministers, typically called pastors, is composed of those who are responsible for the preaching of the Word and the administration of the sacraments. Calvin held a high view of pastors, whom he called "the very mouth of God" and "the chief sinew" of the church, endowing them also with the authority for enforcing "fraternal correction."[44] The second order, of doctors, defined as a separate office in the *Draft Ecclesiastical Ordinances* but folded into the office of pastors in the *Institutes*, encourages the Reformed to elevate scholars to the level of pastors. (What academic theologian does not desire that honor!) The next order, of lay ruling

---

[41] Calvin, *Institutes*, 4.11.1.

[42] Calvin, *Institutes*, 4.11.6.

[43] Ibid.

[44] D. Fergusson, "The Reformed Churches," in *The Christian Church: An Introduction to the Major Traditions* (ed. P. Avis; London: SPCK, 2002), 25; J. T. McNeill, *The History and Character of Calvinism* (New York: Oxford University Press, 1954), 161.

elders, depends on a highly speculative interpretation of 1 Tim 5:17.[45] The final order, of deacons, is relegated the task of tending to the poor and the sick, according to the form of the ancient church.[46]

Historically, this principle of aristocracy has impacted not only the structures within the church but often encouraged the creation of structures above the local church, as mentioned above. Although some Calvinists have tended toward congregational independence, they have typically held to a more exalted view of the ministry than was typical among Baptists.[47] Alternatively, on the other side of congregational Calvinism is the historical phenomenon of Reformed episcopacy, wherein bishops hold an exalted place in church polity. Reformed episcopacy has manifested itself among the English Puritans and the Hungarian Reformed.[48] These two extremes—congregationalism and episcopacy—demonstrate the elastic nature of Calvinist ecclesiology, an elasticity encouraged by Calvin's ill-defined "ancient church."

Most often, however, Calvinists have opted for neither congregationalism nor episcopacy. Following Calvin's preference for aristocratic elitism, they have adopted some form of Presbyterianism. The principles of Presbyterianism have been defined as "the parity of the clergy," "the right of the people to a substantive part in the government of the Church," and "the unity of the Church in such sense, that a small part is subject to a larger, and a larger to the whole."[49] The historical result of these principles has been the creation of bodies above the local churches practicing governance in the name of "the church." The confusion of biblical and extra-biblical definitions of the church is thus evident here too.

According to Calvin, the people of the churches do have a role, and a necessary role at that. He even faults the Roman Catholics for doing away with popular consent in the election of ministers. However, the pastors and the elders primarily handle the election of ministers and decisions regarding the admission or discipline of church members. They act on behalf of the church and then bring the decision to the church for its expected ratification. For instance, with regard to discipline, Calvin says:

---

[45] Calvin, *Institutes*, 4.3.8.

[46] Ibid. See Calvin, *Draft Ecclesiastical Ordinances*, 235–37.

[47] Brachlow, *The Communion of Saints*, 157–202.

[48] J. H. Leith, *Introduction to the Reformed Tradition: A Way of Being the Christian Community* (rev. ed.; Atlanta: John Knox Press, 1981), 164–67.

[49] Ibid., 156.

Paul's course of action for excommunicating a man is the lawful one, provided the elders do not do it by themselves alone, but with the knowledge and approval of the church; in this way the multitude of the people does not decide the action but observes as witness and guardian so that nothing may be done according to the whim of a few.[50]

As a result of aristocratic elitism among Calvinists, "Sometimes this right [of the people in critical decisions] was little more than approval of a decision that had already been made."[51]

It must be concluded that this tendency toward aristocratic elitism within Calvinism is incompatible with the teachings of the New Testament, as defined, for instance, in repeated confessions of Southern Baptists. According to the 2000 revision of The Baptist Faith and Message, both the aristocratic tendency and the related Calvinist use of synods and assemblies above the church are inappropriate. In contradistinction to the extralocal governance of the churches in Presbyterianism, Article VI states, "A New Testament church of the Lord Jesus Christ is an autonomous local congregation of baptized believers." In contradistinction to the aristocratic nature of Calvinism, Article VI states, "Each congregation operates under the Lordship of Christ through democratic processes." Of course, Baptists also affirm the leadership of pastors, but there is simply no room for Calvinism's aristocratic elitism among Baptists, who hold dearly to the biblical doctrine of the priesthood of all believers.

Antinomian Tendencies

One of the tendencies that has characterized Protestant Christianity through its history, at times with greater ferocity than at other times, is that of antinomianism. "Antinomianism" derives from the Greek words for "against" (*anti*) and "law" (*nomos*). It refers to the idea that it is not necessary for Christians to obey the law of God. It has typically been advocated by second-generation reformers and eschewed by first-generation reformers. For instance, in Lutheranism, Johann Agricola argued against Martin Luther that the law was not even necessary to prepare people for the reception of the gospel. Luther subsequently modified his emphatic denunciations of the law by writing that Christian discipline also required obedience to the teachings of

---

[50] Calvin, *Institutes*, 4.12.7.
[51] Leith, *Introduction to the Reformed Tradition*, 164.

Christ.[52] Later, antinomianism was present among those eighteenth-century Particular Baptists who emphasized Calvinism as the standard of orthodoxy. Hyper-Calvinistic Baptists were still around to receive rebukes from Charles Haddon Spurgeon in the nineteenth century.[53]

A form of antinomianism, the setting aside of God's law, is evident in the ecclesiology of Calvinism. This form of antinomianism arose in Calvin's own work. While accusing the Anabaptists of "immoderate severity" for desiring a regenerate church membership, Calvin himself tended toward ecclesiological antinomianism. Calvin's personal accusations against the Anabaptists covered over his lack of concern to uphold the Word of God when it came to the doctrine of the church. He believed "that many details of polity cannot be established from Scripture,"[54] and thus considered the Anabaptist insistence that Scripture provided the form for the church to be a form of legalism. Calvin did not arrive at his ecclesial antinomianism without struggle and, perhaps, against his own self-knowledge. Nevertheless, by degrees, he arrived at the point where he was willing to downplay the ethics of the church in the name of preserving the gospel.

A review of Calvin's polemic against the Anabaptists, conducted at the same time he constructed his doctrine of the church, manifests this struggle. First, Calvin emphasized that the church is visible where the Word is preached and the sacraments are administered, but noticeably absent in this discussion of the "marks" of the church is church discipline.[55] Although he saw church discipline as the sinews of the church, he did not consider it necessary for the church.[56] Second, he set himself firmly against the idea of separation, schism, or sectarianism. Here, he demonstrated a subtle form of ecumenism related to his Augustinianism, an ecumenism which many of his followers have found attractive.[57]

Third, Calvin made a distinction between "necessary" doctrines and "nonessential matters." A lengthy quote may be illuminating at this point:

---

[52] R. D. Linder, "Antinomianism," in *Evangelical Dictionary of Theology* (ed. W. A. Elwell; Grand Rapids: Baker Book House, 1984), 58.

[53] Timothy George argues that Gill was not a Hyper-Calvinist, but his followers could tend in that direction. T. George, "John Gill," in *Theologians of the Baptist Tradition* (ed. T. George and D. S. Dockery; Nashville: B&H, 2001), 27. I. H. Murray, *Spurgeon v. Hyper-Calvinism: The Battle for Gospel Preaching* (Carlisle, PA: Banner of Truth Trust, 1995).

[54] Leith, *Introduction to the Reformed Tradition*, 158.

[55] Calvin, *Institutes*, 4.1.9.

[56] Calvin, *Institutes*, 4.12.1.

[57] Calvin, *Institutes*, 4.1.10; David Fergusson, "The Reformed Churches," in *The Christian Church: An Introduction to the Major Traditions* (ed. P. Avis; London: SPCK, 2002), 32.

What is more, some fault may creep into the administration of either doctrine or sacraments, but this ought not to estrange us from communion with the church. For not all the articles of true doctrine are of the same sort. Some are so necessary to know that they should be certain and unquestioned by all men as the proper principles of religion. Such are: God is one; Christ is God and the Son of God; our salvation rests in God's mercy; and the like. Among the churches there are other articles of doctrine disputed which still do not break the unity of the faith.[58]

Immediately following his rough delineation of essential versus non-essential doctrines, Calvin began his assault on the Anabaptists for separating themselves from those who live wicked lives. He referred to them as in the same class with "the Cathari of old" and "the Donatists, who approached them in foolishness."[59] Against the Anabaptist ideal of the regenerate church, Calvin argued, "The church is mingled of good men and bad."[60] Finally, Calvin introduced the doctrine of "forbearance" as a foil to the doctrine of the regenerate church.[61] As a result, Calvin concluded that in the church the Anabaptists must accept "fellowship with wicked persons." He agreed with them that the wicked should ideally not be present in the church, but one must still not separate from them.[62] Calvin was upset with the Anabaptists not only regarding their regenerate church practices but also their denial of infant baptism.

John Calvin never could perceive that infant baptism was an extra-biblical innovation, even as he argued against the extrabiblical innovations introduced by the Roman Catholics. This failure on the part of Calvin and the Calvinists to perceive their own retention of unbiblical practices has been the *cause célèbre* for the separation that has been maintained between Baptists and other free churches, on the one side, and the bulk of the Reformed churches, on the other side. As H. E. Dana stated it, the Protestants—inclusive of the Lutheran, Reformed, and Congregational denominations—have made genuine advances in comparison with the Roman Catholics because they affirm the authority of Scripture: "They now accept the Scriptures as the direct and infallible guide in faith and practice. Where Protestants have erred has been in failing consistently to

---

[58] Calvin, *Institutes*, 4.1.12.
[59] Ibid., 4.1.13.
[60] Ibid.
[61] Ibid., 4.1.14.
[62] Ibid., 4.1.15.

apply this principle. They have retained and advocated practices for which they have no really scriptural grounds."[63] Calvin and the ecclesiological Calvinists are guilty of antinomianism—dismissing the law of Christ as necessary to obey—even though they themselves may not perceive such.

The separation of essential from nonessential doctrines has been part and parcel of Calvinism's ecclesiological antinomianism. Often theological doctrines are defined as essential while ethical and ecclesiological doctrines are defined as nonessential. As John H. Leith stated it, "The Reformed tradition is distinguished not simply by its insistence that polity is important but also by its radical subordination of polity to the gospel." He continued later, "The Calvinist insistence on the prevenience of God's grace and upon the church as the company of the elect undercuts even the significance of the sacraments and, much more, the necessity of any structures of polity."[64] When such attitudes are introduced into the Baptist context, hyper-Calvinism has historically not been far behind.

These subtle antinomian impulses explain why Calvinists are willing to innovate with regard to the church, while Baptists have often argued that God delivered a certain pattern for the church. It also explains why many Calvinists are more open to ecumenism in the name of unity in the essentials while dismissive of polity than are many Baptists.[65] Baptists have often been suspicious of ecumenical schemes for fear that they will supplant the will of the Lord for His churches.[66] Calvinism's antinomian tendencies may also explain why some Calvinists adopt open communion while many Baptists favor either closed Communion or even strict Communion.[67] Many a Calvinist perceives church polity as nonessential to the faith while many Baptists perceive church polity as essential.

The Baptist tendency away from antinomianism is exemplified in the definition of church polity as a fundamental of the faith. According to J. B. Gambrell, three-time president of the Southern Baptist Convention, the Baptist fundamentals include:

---

[63] H. E. Dana, "The Influence of Baptists upon the Modern Conceptions of the Church," *Southwestern Journal of Theology* 51 (2008): 61.

[64] Leith, *Introduction to the Reformed Tradition*, 147.

[65] Ibid., 147–48; Fergusson, *The Reformed Traditions*, 34–42.

[66] *Baptist Relations with Other Christians* (ed. J. L. Garrett; Valley Forge, PA: Judson Press, 1974).

[67] The churches of the Southern Baptist Convention, for instance, officially advocate the closed communion position. The Baptist Faith and Message, Art. VII. For a paradigm of communion, see E. Caner, "Fencing the Table: The Lord's Supper, Its Participants, and Its Relationship to Church Discipline," in *Restoring Integrity in Baptist Churches* (ed. T. White, J. G. Duesing, and M. B. Yarnell III; Grand Rapids: Kregel, 2008), 163–78.

The deity and lordship of Jesus Christ; salvation through the
atonement made on the cross by Christ's death; a personal faith in
Jesus, essential to personal salvation; regeneration by the Spirit of
God; a converted church membership; obedience to the command of
Jesus in baptism, hence immersion of a believer, and this a condition
of church membership; baptism and the Lord's Supper as symbols
not sacraments; each local church independent and self-governing,
on the principle of a pure democracy; no orders in the ministry; the
inalienable right of every soul to worship God or not to worship God,
according to his own volition, or, in brief, the freedom of the soul in
religion; separation of church and state, in the Kingdom of Christ; the
Scriptures the supreme law.[68]

The Baptist Faith and Message affirms Gambrell's understanding of the
essentials as inclusive of church polity and practices. In the preface of
that document, Southern Baptists said, "We are not embarrassed to state
before the world that these are doctrines we hold precious and as essential
to the Baptist tradition of faith and practice."[69] In this regard, Calvinism is
incompatible with the Baptist outlook.

Conclusion

These four tendencies characterize Calvinist ecclesiology: the ancient
church, Augustinian innovations, aristocratic preferences, and ecclesiological antinomianism. As the local Baptist church encounters Calvinism, it
will most likely experience portions or the entirety of these tendencies.
It is the contention of this author that the Calvinist tendencies and their
potential impact have their countervailing tendencies among those who
are confessional and practicing Baptists. The extent of the impact will vary,
dependent on the fervency of the advocate and the acquiescence of the
church. From my own observation of the contemporary anecdotal evidence, the potential changes may include the following, many of which
are a direct result of the four tendencies described above.

Those influences exercised by Calvinism's ancient church concept and
acceptance of the Augustinian innovations may include an increase in conversations about the universal invisible church; an increase in ecumenical

---

[68] J. B. Gambrell, "The Union Movement and Baptist Fundamentals," *Southwestern Journal of Theology* 51 (2008): 46–47.

[69] Baptist Faith and Message, Preface.

relationships, including close cooperation with ministers and churches espousing Reformed polity, as opposed to singular commitment to the local churches; and an increase in conversations about cultural relevancy and cultural transformation alongside a decrease in emphasis upon religious liberty. Those influences exercised by the aristocratic preferences of Calvinism may involve adoption of the multiple elders model as opposed to a single pastor model; and, going one step further, the diminishing of congregational governance in favor of elder rule. Those influences exercised by the antinomian impulses of Calvinism may include admission of members on the basis of infant baptism and/or baptism by sprinkling or pouring, and the opening of Communion to those who have not submitted to baptism according to the Lord's command and the apostles' witness. Finally, related to all four tendencies is a potential increase in conversations about speculative doctrine alongside a decrease in evangelistic practices, such as the decline of invitations at the end of the worship service.

In spite of the challenges to Baptist identity that a zealous strain of Calvinism may present, some Baptists are convinced that they can remain Baptist while also being truly Calvinist. But, although such Baptists—and some capable and virtuous ones at that—have tried to combine Reformed soteriology with Baptist ecclesiology, the combination may ultimately prove unstable. As Richard Muller has argued, from the Reformed perspective, the two belief systems are incompatible. For Muller, being Calvinist is not only about the five points of the Synod of Dort. Being Reformed, which is the same as being Calvinist, entails accepting that tradition's whole way of being Christian. Calvinism includes, among other things, the deemphasizing of personal decisions for Christ, infant baptism, and a healthy working relationship between church and state.[70] Muller, a highly respected Calvinist theologian, may be correct. In the end, it is impossible to be at once both truly Reformed and truly Baptist, especially when the local church is considered.

---

[70] R. A. Muller, "How Many Points?" *Calvin Theological Journal* 28 (1993): 425–33.

{ Chapter 9 }

The Public Invitation and Calvinism

R. Alan Streett

Most Calvinists oppose the use of a public invitation or altar call at the end of sermons.[1] They think such practices tend to be confusing at best, spiritually dangerous at worst, and certainly a hindrance to true evangelism.[2] Strict five-point Calvinists criticize the invitation on three grounds. First, they believe it has no biblical support. Second, they believe its origin can be traced back only a few hundred years. Third, they think it is incompatible with their understanding of total depravity, unconditional election, limited atonement, and irresistible grace. When young preachers or even veteran pulpiteers read Calvinistic tractates railing against the invitation, they might wonder whether they should likewise abandon the practice of calling sinners publicly to confess their faith in Christ. I

---

[1] E. Hulse, *The Great Invitation* (Hertfordshire, England: Evangelical Press, 1986) stands as an example of the strict Calvinist who opposes the public invitation. He disparagingly labels the public invitation an "evangelical sacrament" (103) and devotes the entirety of chapter seven to his claim (104–9). L. S. Chafer, *True Evangelism* (Grand Rapids: Kregel, 2002) is an example of a four-point Calvinist who holds the same position.

[2] Chafer, *True Evangelism*, 17–18.

personally understand this confusion, having gone through a similar period of questioning during my formative years as an itinerate evangelist.

This chapter will include a little of my struggle over the public invitation. Then I will respond to the Calvinistic critics by showing that the invitation has a strong biblical foundation, has been used throughout church history, and should be given by preachers of various theological persuasions. Since John 3:16 states clearly and emphatically that "whoever believes" in Christ might "have everlasting life," it would seem incumbent upon all preachers to invite people to receive that life.

A Personal Story

As a vocational evangelist during the 1970s and 1980s, I conducted evangelistic meetings in churches throughout the Middle Atlantic States. I preached gospel-centered sermons on the great doctrines of the Bible (justification, redemption, forgiveness, reconciliation, judgment, propitiation, regeneration), and then, like Spurgeon, I made a "beeline to the cross." At the conclusion of my messages, I invited listeners to repent of their sins, place faith in the crucified and risen Lord Jesus Christ alone for salvation, and so indicate by coming forward to the altar where they would receive counsel and clarification. Over the years many have responded.

During this period I was introduced to books and articles by Reformed theologians who maligned evangelistic invitations, contending that such appeals lacked biblical support. As a result, I began to question the validity of asking sinners to respond publicly to the gospel.

Since I was an itinerant evangelist, the issue was paramount. I needed to know if an invitation was a legitimate means of calling people to Christ. These lingering doubts had an immediate and noticeable impact on my preaching. While the content of my sermons remained constant, I found myself dreading to give an invitation at the sermon's end for fear of adding works to faith.

In order to resolve these issues to my own satisfaction, I conducted my own investigation into the matter. At the time I was working part-time on my doctorate, so I chose as my dissertation topic, "The Public Invitation: Its Nature, Biblical Validity, and Practicability." With no idea where the journey might lead, I approached the subject with as much objectivity as possible. I only desired to discover the truth, report it, and then act accordingly. After three years of intense study, I concluded that the gospel invitation has scriptural support and, therefore, can be given without contradicting New Testament principles or the conscience of the preacher.

The book *The Effective Invitation*[3] is a popularization of my Ph.D. dissertation. It has become a standard textbook for evangelism and homiletic courses in evangelical Bible colleges and seminaries. After its publication, Errol Hulse wrote a Calvinist response, basing much of his criticism on misinterpretation of what I wrote rather than on substantive issues.[4]

In the remainder of this chapter, I will present a biblical and historical foundation for the public invitation and then answer the theological concerns of the critics. In doing so, I hope to help pastors who may be struggling with this issue to settle the matter once and for all. Second, I hope to show that giving a public invitation and holding to Calvinism are not necessarily incompatible.

Biblical Basis for the Invitation

Calvinist critics contend that the invitation is a modern contrivance, dating back only to nineteenth-century evangelist Charles Finney. In reality, examples abound in the Scriptures from Genesis to Revelation. This section will examine only a sampling of the public invitations found in the Old and New Testaments.

Old Testament Examples

The initial example goes back to the book of beginnings. When the first humans sinned and hid from God, He called them out into the open (Gen 3:8). Forgiveness and redemption were available to them only as they obediently responded to the appeal; thus, coming out into the open was essential to their salvation. To remain hidden means to remain lost. The sinner must answer God's invitation.

A few chapters later God invites Noah's family into the ark where they will escape the wrath to come (Gen 7:1). Had they only "believed in their

---

[3] R. Alan Streett, *The Effective Invitation* (Grand Rapids: Kregel, 1995).

[4] See footnote 1 for complete bibliographical data of Hulse's *The Great Invitation*. Hulse also critically examined R.T. Kendall, *Stand Up and Be Counted* (Grand Rapids: Zondervan, 1984). At the time of Hulse's publication, Kendall served as pastor of Westminster Chapel in London, England, having succeeded Martyn Lloyd-Jones, a thoroughgoing Calvinist who refused to issue a public invitation. When Kendall started calling for public commitments of faith, he became a favorite target of Calvinistic criticism.

heart" but not taken the action required of them, they would have perished in the deluge. They obeyed the Lord's command (vv 6–7) and found safety.

When God summoned Abram physically to leave his family and homeland and proceed by faith to a land unknown, he answered the divine directive (Gen 12:1–4). Upon the basis of Abram's response, God formed a people for Himself.

After the exodus, God led the children of Israel into the Sinai and instructed Moses to declare on His behalf, "You have seen what I did to the Egyptians, and how I bore you on eagles' wings and brought you to Myself. Now therefore, if you indeed obey My voice and keep My covenant, then you shall be . . . to Me a kingdom of priests and a holy nation" (Exod 19:4–6).[5] Moses obediently gathered to one place the elders and the people and conveyed to "them all these words which the LORD commanded him" (v. 7). In an act of public unanimity, the people replied, "All that the LORD has spoken we will do" (v 8). On the basis of their public profession, God instructed Moses to consecrate them as His peculiar people, and a nation was born in a day.

Later when Moses descended the mountain with the law in hand, he was shocked to discover that the people had fallen into licentiousness and faithless idolatry. In righteous indignation reminiscent of Jesus cleaning out the temple, Moses broke the idol, cleansed the camp, and challenged them with the words, "Whoever is on the LORD's side, let him come to me!" (Exod 32:26). His call for a public reply is answered readily: "And all the sons of Levi gathered themselves together unto him" (v. 26).

Then, Joshua, Israel's second great leader, gathered the nation together in a public venue to rehearse for them God's deliverance in times past and to invite them to abandon idolatry and serve Yahweh (Josh 24:14). His conclusion rang loud and clear: "Choose for yourselves this day whom you will serve" (v. 15a). Their choices were between the gods of Egypt or the Amorites or Yahweh. He then announced, "But as for me and my house, we will serve the LORD!" (v. 15b). Joshua forced the people to make a public choice, and they answered, "We will serve the LORD" (v. 21). In response Joshua placed a stone next to the sanctuary of the Lord to remind the people of their commitment (vv. 25–27).

Likewise, the prophet Elijah confronted his generation on Mount Carmel with a similar challenge: "How long will you falter between two

---

[5] Unless otherwise noted, all Scripture passages in this chapter are from the New King James Version.

opinions? If the LORD is God, follow Him; but if Baal, then follow him" (1 Kgs 18:21). When they took no action, Elijah called on God to send fire down from heaven as evidence of His mighty power (vv. 38–39). "Now when all the people saw it, they fell on their faces; and they said, 'The LORD, He is God! The LORD, He is God'" (v. 39).

In the eighteenth year of Josiah's reign as king over Judah, the high priest Hilkiah discovered the lost scroll of the Law (2 Kgs 22:3–10). For years the nation had lived in sin, ignorant of God's Word. Upon hearing the words of the Law, Josiah rent his clothes, showing the depth of his repentance (v. 11). He then called a nationwide convocation to address his people. All gathered before him, including prophets, priests, and people, and he had the Law read aloud (23:1–2).

> Then the king stood by a pillar and made a covenant before the LORD, to follow the LORD, and keep His commandments and His testimonies and His statutes, with all his heart, and all his soul, to perform the words of the covenant that were written in this book. And all the people took their stand for the covenant (2 Kgs 23:3).

Josiah's call and the nation's public affirmation brought revival to Judah and restored true worship of God (vv. 4–23).

New Testament Examples

Jesus called people to follow Him publicly. He promised, "Whosoever confesses Me before men, him will I also confess before My Father in heaven" (Matt 10:32). Conversely, He warned, "But whoever denies Me before men, him I will also deny before My Father who is in heaven" (v. 33). Jesus offered little hope of salvation to those who wished to remain anonymous.

One of His favorite words of exhortation was "Come." To some He said, "Come, follow me" (Matt 19:21). To others he called out, "Come and see" (John 1:39). To the masses He cried, "Come to Me, all you who labor and are heavy laden, and I will give you rest" (Matt 11:28). On another occasion he commanded, "Come, take up the cross and follow Me" (Mark 10:21). All sinners were exhorted to "come like little children" (Matt 19:14). In the Revelation both the Spirit and the bride say, "Come," and partake of "the water of life freely" (Rev 22:17). Both God and the evangelist issued this dual call.

Many responded to Jesus' call. To Zaccheus, perched high in a tree, He said, "Make haste and come down" (Luke 19:5). In full view of friends and foe alike who knew him as a despicable but wealthy tax collector, he answered the appeal (vv. 8–9). Had he remained in a tree, Zaccheus would have missed his opportunity to be saved.

When Jesus said, "Who touched Me?" a woman with an issue of blood responded openly. The record shows that "fearing and trembling . . . [she] came and fell down before Him. . . . And He said to her, 'Daughter, your faith has made you well. Go in peace' " (Mark 5:33–34). Had she remained hidden among the crowd, she might have been healed but not saved. Similarly, the leper returned after his healing, "fell down on his face," and thanked Jesus publicly (Luke 17:16). After inquiring into the whereabouts of the other nine lepers, Jesus pronounced, "Your faith has made you well" (v. 19). Again, an outward action was tied to salvation.

The Importance of Making a Public Profession of Faith

The apostle Paul reminds us "that if you confess with your mouth the Lord Jesus Christ and believe in your heart that God has raised Him from the dead, you will be saved. For with the heart one believes to righteousness, and with the mouth confession is made to salvation" (Rom 10:9–10). However one cuts it, this text links public confession to salvation. One must *both* believe and confess the facts of the gospel in order to be saved (v. 9). Just as the heart believes "*to* righteousness," so the mouth confesses "*to* salvation" (v. 10).

Since confession is important to salvation, we must ask, "In what way did the early believers outwardly confess their allegiance to Christ?" James H. Jauncey believes that the apostolic church considered baptism to be the initial act of public confession.[6] Faris D. Whitesell agrees:

> Baptism stood for about the same thing in apostolic days as coming forward and making an open declaration of faith does today. Baptism was the public line of demarcation between the old life and the new in New Testament times, and most certainly called for public confession and personal identification with the Christian group.[7]

---

[6] James H. Jauncey, *Psychology for Successful Evangelism* (Chicago: Moody Press, 1972), 17.
[7] Ibid., 397

Most likely, sinners demonstrated their repentance and faith through baptism. It is no surprise then to find John the Baptist—the first to announce the imminent arrival of God's kingdom—calling upon a wayward Jewish nation to respond publicly by repenting and submitting to baptism (Matt 3:1; Mark 1:4; Luke 3:3). Those who heeded his instructions "were baptized by him in the Jordan, confessing their sins" (Matt 3:6). This public act of contrition was a required step to receive forgiveness of sins and prepare for entrance into the kingdom of God.

When Jesus began His ministry, He too invited His hearers to respond in a public way through repentance and baptism (Mark 1:15; John 3:26; 4:1). By taking the required action, the respondents signified their desire to follow Him, just as those today are expected to respond in similar fashion.

That the resurrected Jesus included baptism in the Great Commission proves its strategic role in the evangelistic task (Matt 28:18–20). "Baptizing them" marks the initial step in making a disciple. When Jesus directs His apostles to baptize, He is, by implication, charging them to extend a public invitation.

Is it any wonder that after the Lord's ascension, the first preachers of the gospel took seriously Jesus' command to baptize? Speaking from the portico of the temple, Peter concluded his famous Pentecost sermon with these words of exhortation:

> "Repent, and let every one of you be *baptized* in the name of Jesus
> Christ for the remission of sins; and you shall receive the gift of
> the Holy Spirit." . . . Then those who gladly received his word were
> baptized; and that day about three thousand souls were added to them
> (Acts 2:38,41, emphasis added).

Some who reject baptism as part of the gospel call often query, "Where could such a baptism have taken place? After all, the Jordan River is miles away, and the local pools could not accommodate the large numbers." This quandary was answered when the southern wall of the temple mount was excavated in the early 1970s.[8] Numerous ritual pools were unearthed, located in front of the steps leading up to the temple. Since pilgrims had to be cleansed ritually before entering the temple on Pentecost, these pools served that purpose and likely served as the baptismal pools for the 3,000.

---

[8] Bill Grasham, "Archeology and Christian Baptism," *ResQ* 43 (2001). Located at: http://www.acu. edu/sponsored/restoration_quarterly/archives/2000s/vol_43_no_2_ contents/grasham. html.

One can only imagine the impact that this baptism had on the Jewish multitudes making their way to the temple.

On many occasions vast numbers responded to the preaching of Jesus and the apostles. On Pentecost 3,000 stepped forward (Acts 2:41). Another 5,000 were added later to their ranks (Acts 4:4). That it was possible to number the converts indicates that they were identifiable in some way. Baptism was the most likely means of distinguishing between the lost and the saved.

As one walks through the pages of the book of Acts, he finds Philip "preaching Christ" and the "kingdom of God" in Samaria (Acts 8:5, 12) and people responding in faith and baptism (v. 13). After his successful crusade in Samaria, the Spirit directs Philip to Gaza where he meets and expounds the gospel to an Ethiopian eunuch (Acts 8:26–35):

> Now as they went down the road, they came to some water. And the eunuch said, "See, here is water. What hinders me from being baptized?" Then Philip said, "If you believe with all your heart, you may." And he answered and said, "I believe that Jesus Christ is the Son of God." So he commanded the chariot to stand still. And both Philip and the eunuch went down into the water, and he baptized him (vv. 8:36–38).

Likewise, after preaching the gospel in Caesarea to the Gentile household of Cornelius, a Roman centurion, the apostle Peter extended to them an invitation to be baptized (Acts 10:44–47). They obliged and were the first Gentile converts to Christ.

After Saul of Tarsus's experience with Christ on the Damascus road, he is guided to Ananias, a Jewish believer, who calls upon his repentant kinsman to be baptized: "Brother Saul, . . . the God of our fathers has chosen you. . . . [to] be His witness to all men. . . . And now why are you waiting? Arise and be baptized, and wash away your sins, calling upon the name of the Lord" (Acts 22:13–16). Luke records that Saul obeyed the command and submitted to believer's baptism (Acts 9:18).

Propelled into the ministry, the apostle Paul eventually journeys to Philippi where he meets Lydia, a seller of fine fabrics, "whose heart the Lord opened, that she attended unto the things which were spoken of Paul. And [then] she was *baptized*, and her household" (Acts 16:14–15 KJV). While in Philippi, Paul and his companion Silas are arrested and are able to show the local jailer the way to salvation:

Then they spoke the word of the Lord to him and to all that were in his house. And he took them the same hour of the night and washed their stripes. And immediately he and all his family were baptized. Now when he had brought them into his house, he set food before them; and he rejoiced, having believed in God with all his household (Acts 16:32–34).

In Corinth, Paul "reasoned in the synagogue every Sabbath, and persuaded both Jews and Greeks" (Acts 18:4). One of his many converts, "Crispus, the ruler of the synagogue, believed on the Lord with all his household. And many of the Corinthians, hearing, believed and were baptized" (Acts 18:8).

The call to public baptism was an important part of the preaching mission of the early church. Those who responded in obedience demonstrated their faith by identifying with the crucified and risen Lord through baptism (Rom 6:4–5; Col 2:12). It is impossible to separate the proclamation and the invitation to be baptized. What happened when water was not available? The Scriptures are silent. Possibly an interim appeal was given until water became available.

Why Baptize Today?

The mandate to evangelize and baptize extends "until the end of the age." A clarion call must be sounded to restore baptism to its New Testament place of prominence. When water is available, the pastor or evangelist should conclude his gospel message with an appeal for persons to repent and demonstrate it publicly by presenting themselves immediately for baptism. When conditions do not make such an appeal possible, the preacher should give the invitation for sinners to repent and publicly display their commitment in some other way. The new convert should then be told about the importance of baptism, and arrangements should be made for him to be baptized at a future date.

The Invitation Throughout History

Adversaries of the public invitation claim it is a relatively recent homiletic invention.[9] While this assertion has no basis in historical fact, it is

---

[9] According to J. F. Thornbury, *God Sent Revival* (Grand Rapids: Evangelical Press, 1977), Finney first called people in 1831 to come forward and kneel at the anxious bench. This use of "means" or

correct to say that the invitation fell into disuse soon after the apostolic period and did not make a full comeback until modern times. So few examples of invitations can be found in historical records prior to the 1600s because Roman Catholicism dominated the Western world for more than a millennium. A salvation based on the sacraments meant there was no reason to call people publicly to profess faith in Christ. Only with the advent of the Protestant Reformation did the invitation reclaim its rightful place in evangelistic preaching, but only after a struggle. During the first 100 years of the Reformation, Scripture translation into the vernacular tongue and its distribution to the masses were the main vehicles of evangelism.

Roman Catholics Who Were Exceptions to the Rule

Even during the Middle Ages, however, a few Catholic preachers broke with tradition and called upon converts publicly to profess their faith in Christ. According to Lloyd M. Perry, the Crusade-era evangelist Bernard of Clairvaux (1093–1153) issued public invitations on a regular basis. He noted, "The basic appeal of Bernard of Clairvaux was for people to repent of their sins. Often he would call for a show of hands from those who wished to be restored to fellowship with God or the church."[10] Peter of Bruys (?-c.1131) was another evangelist who strongly spoke out against infant baptism, the veneration of the crucifix, and many other unscriptural practices of the established church. He was a forerunner of the Anabaptist movement and preached the gospel, calling men to repent, believe, and be baptized.[11] Arnold of Brescia (1100–1155) also took a strong stand against Roman Catholic sacramentalism and for the pure gospel, calling his hearers to submit to believer's baptism. He was eventually hanged, his body burned, and his ashes emptied into the Tiber River.

"new measures" caused a stir among "Old Light" Calvinistic pastors and evangelists. Finney's staunchest opponents were evangelist Asahel Nettleton and New England pastor Lyman Beecher. After a summit conference to discuss the matter, Beecher chose to side with Finney and declared that the new measures were not incompatible with Calvinistic theology.

[10] L. M. Perry and J. R. Strubhar, *Evangelistic Preaching* (Chicago: Moody Press, 1979), 44.

[11] Streett, *Effective Invitation*, 85.

Anabaptists: Filling the Gap

In the transition from Roman Catholicism to Protestantism, the Anabaptists asked for a public response to the gospel. Opposing the church of Rome on the issues of infant baptism, establishment of the priesthood, and the veneration of Mary, they called sinners to repent of their sins, place their faith in Christ, and present themselves for rebaptism. They immediately faced strong opposition, and as a result, many were martyred. But they also found themselves the target of Protestant ire as well.

Balthasar Hubmaier (1481–1528), the most prominent German Anabaptist of his day, was burned at the stake. His wife was drowned in the Danube River, symbolic of the aversion the established church had to believer's baptism. Prior to his death, Hubmaier had won thousands of converts to Christ.[12]

Conrad Grebel (c. 1498–1526), the father of the Swiss Anabaptist movement, preached the gospel and called upon his hearers to be rebaptized as a profession of their faith. Grebel performed the first adult baptism of the Reformation. The Reformed state church under Zwingli moved into action against him. On March 7, 1526, the Zürich council had passed an edict that made adult rebaptism punishable by drowning. Charged with an illegal act, Grebel was arrested and imprisoned. He managed to escape but died a short time later.[13]

Felix Manz (c. 1498–1527), the best scholar of the movement, became the first casualty of the edict, suffering martyrdom in Zürich by drowning. George Blaurock (c. 1491–1529), a former Roman Catholic priest, was the founder of the Swiss Brethren movement in Zurich and the foremost Anabaptist evangelist of his day. He was condemned and burned at the stake after rebaptizing one thousand new converts in four and one-half years of ministry.[14]

The Reformation

Although leading lights of the Reformation condemned the practice of public rebaptism, they required church members to profess publicly their faith in Christ and declare assurance of salvation before being allowed to

---

[12] Alan Streett, *Effective Invitation*, 87.
[13] Ibid.
[14] Ibid.

take communion.[15] Without an accompanying public profession of faith, a member's salvation was considered spurious. Such a practice likely started with John Calvin, who called on believers to make a public pledge that they had assurance of salvation before partaking of the bread and wine.[16] The 1662 Synod reaffirmed that a public confession of faith "before the church" was necessary to gain admission to the Communion table.[17]

The First Great Awakening

According to McLendon, in the early 1740s, Congregationalist pastor Eleazar Wheelock, a strict Calvinist and founder of Dartmouth College, sensing a move of the Spirit at the conclusion of his evening sermon, "called to the distressed to gather in the seats below so he could more conveniently converse with them."[18] This call predated Finney's revival ministry scene by 90 years.

George Whitefield and Jonathan Edwards, both strong Calvinists during the height of the Great Awakening, exhorted sinners at the close of their sermons to meet with them privately for spiritual counsel.[19] These after-meetings were held in parsonages, barns, or some other conveniently located building. Through use of delayed-response invitations, throngs came to Christ.

Between the first and second Great Awakenings, the Separatist Baptists on this side of the Atlantic[20] and the Methodists on the other side[21] were also calling for the anxious and those under spiritual distress to come forward to find rest for their souls.

The Second Great Awakening

The "camp meetings" of the 1790s on the western frontier of America were the catalyst that sparked the Second Great Awakening. Fervent preaching

---

[15] E. S. Morgan, *Visible Saints: The History of the Puritan Idea* (New York: University Press, 1963), 99–105.

[16] J. Calvin, *Institutes of Christian Religion* (1559), I:IV:8 (trans. Ford Lewis Battles; Philadelphia: Westminster Press, 1960), II:1022–23.

[17] "Result of the Synod of 1662," *The Creeds and Platforms of Congregationalism* (ed. W. Walker; New York: United Church Press, [1893] 1960), 328.

[18] H. B. McLendon, "The Mourner's Bench" (Th.D. diss., Southern Baptist Theological Seminary, 1902), 16.

[19] H. G. Olive, "The Development of the Evangelistic Invitation" (Th.M. thesis, Southern Baptist Theological Seminary, 1958), 15. Also see Streett, *Effective Invitation*, 89.

[20] M. Coppenger, "Kairos and the Altar Call," *Heartland* (Summer 1999): 1.

[21] McLendon, "The Mourner's Bench," 16.

and public invitations characterized these mass gatherings. Organizers erected altars in front of the speaker's platform where convicted sinners could kneel and find comfort for their souls.[22] The Awakening on the East Coast, led by Yale President Timothy Dwight, combined Calvinism and revivalism and employed the after-meeting model of the invitation.

By the time Finney had stepped onto the scene, the public invitation had been practiced in one form or another for over a century. Among Finney's contemporaries and staunchest Calvinistic opponents were "Old Light" Congregationalists, who, like Calvin two centuries before, ironically called for church members publicly to profess faith in Christ and declare assurance of salvation before taking Communion.[23] These same opponents pointed to Asahel Nettleton (1783–1844), the first American-born evangelist and a Finney contemporary, as the ideal evangelist who preached sinners into the kingdom without issuing an invitation. Historical records tell a different story. Nettleton actually gave a delayed-response invitation at the conclusion of his evangelistic sermons, exhorting listeners to attend an "inquirer's meeting" after the service where they would receive special instruction regarding their soul's salvation. He used the inquiry room "for those who felt they were ready for such an adventure."[24] C. E. Autrey explains: "The inquiry room gave him a chance to separate those under conviction from the rest of the congregation in order to instruct them properly. In the inquiry room individuals could speak with others without the excitement and pressure of the crowd."[25]

Nettleton likely borrowed his methods from Whitefield and Edwards, two of his heroes. One wonders how coming forward to an anxious bench qualitatively differs from attending an inquirer's meeting since both ask sinners to move physically from their seats in the auditorium to another location where they will receive instruction.

Two Calvinist Representatives of the Modern Era

Antagonists allege that Charles H. Spurgeon, a five-point Calvinist and arguably the most powerful preacher of the late nineteenth century, resisted all use of the public invitation. Again, the critics offer no evidence

---

[22] McLendon, "The Mourner's Bench," 10.

[23] Morgan, *Visible Saints*, 99–105.

[24] B. Tyler, *Memoirs of the Life and Character of Reverend Asahel Nettleton* (Boston: n.p., 1856), 100. Also see Thornbury, *God Sent Revival*, 113–14.

[25] C. E. Autrey, *Basic Evangelism* (Grand Rapids: Zondervan, 1959), 131.

for their claims. Spurgeon always preached for a verdict and supported others who did the same.[26] According to Eric Hayden, a former pastor of the Metropolitan Tabernacle, since the architecture of the building did not lend itself to hundreds coming forward, Spurgeon did the next best thing. He "would often request enquirers to go below to one of the basement lecture halls to be counseled by his elders."[27] On other occasions he invited seekers to meet with him, usually in the vestry on Tuesday at 3:00 PM, to discuss their soul's salvation.[28] He regularly used lay exhorters to watch out for people who came under conviction during a sermon, a practice John Wesley popularized a century before.[29] These exhorters were given freedom to deal with the troubled souls. Spurgeon's magazine, *The Sword and the Trowel*, often reported on the evangelistic exploits of his ministerial students and other ordained evangelists who spread the gospel throughout London. One entry tells how "a score came into the inquiry room nightly; and on Monday evening about fifty stood up to acknowledge having received Christ during the meeting."[30]

John MacArthur Jr., well-known Bible expositor and strict Calvinist, was reared in the home of a Southern Baptist pastor. Following in his father's footsteps, he attended seminary, entered the ministry, and was called by Grace Community Church (CA) to be its pastor. Under his tutelage, the congregation grew from 450 people to more than 5,000. In an interview MacArthur explained his invitational method: "We see hundreds saved and baptized every year. We never have a service without an invitation, and we never have an invitation without people coming into our prayer rooms."[31] He went on to say:

I personally believe that all preaching must be persuasive preaching. When someone comes to hear me speak, I am trying to urge him to make a decision. In other words, the whole goal of my preaching is to pin the guy to the wall. He is going to have to say, "I will" or "I won't do that." At the close of every service I say something like, "If you want

---

[26] Bob Ross, president of Pilgrim Press, probably knows more than anyone else about Spurgeon. He devotes an entire page on his Web site exploring Spurgeon's attitude toward the public invitation. See http://www.pp.com/invite1.htm.

[27] E. W. Hayden, *Searchlight on Spurgeon* (Pasadena: Pilgrim, 1973), 7–8. Also see B. Ross, *The Pictorial Biography of Spurgeon* (Pasadena, TX: Pilgrim, 1981), 98; L. Drummond, *Spurgeon* (Grand Rapids: Kregel, 2000), 308–9; and Kendall, *Stand Up*, 56.

[28] Drummond, *Spurgeon*, 307–8.

[29] Streett, *Effective Invitation*, 91–92.

[30] Kendall, *Stand Up*, 56.

[31] "An Interview with John MacArthur, Jr.," *Fundamentalist Journal* (November 1984): 48.

to know Jesus Christ . . . and embrace Jesus Christ, then I want you to come to the prayer room."[32]

Answering the Critics: Theological Considerations

One of last century's most vocal opponents of the public invitation was the late Martyn Lloyd-Jones, successor to G. Campbell Morgan as senior pastor at Westminster Chapel in London, England.[33] In his book *Preaching and Preachers*, he says he will give 10 reasons for opposing the public invitation.[34] As Lloyd-Jones was a leading spokesman for Reformed thought, his arguments against the public invitation can be considered representative of the movement as a whole.

Examining and answering each objection in turn can put to rest the charge that the public invitation is based on defective theology. First, Lloyd-Jones claims that the public invitation is wrongheaded because it puts direct pressure on the human will.[35] Believing three parts—intellect, emotions, and will—comprise the inner man, he insists that the will should never be approached directly but only indirectly by first going through the intellect and the emotions.[36] His concern is that the invitation is an effort in coercion.

Dr. Lloyd-Jones's concern about directly approaching the will does not speak convincingly against the public invitation but only against what is perceived to be the abuse of the invitation. Of course, appeals should never seek to coerce or manipulate people but rather aim at persuading them by use of Scripture.

Second, Lloyd-Jones postulates that many people come forward because of the personality of the evangelist, or for psychological influences, rather than valid spiritual reasons.[37] This argument is difficult to prove or disprove since it is next to impossible to judge accurately an inquirer's motives. However, like his first argument, this objection only addresses invitational abuses, not the legitimate use of an invitation.

---

[32] Ibid.

[33] E. Fife, "D. Martyn Lloyd-Jones: Twentieth-Century Puritan," *Eternity* (November 1981): 29–30.

[34] In fact, he only lists nine reasons. See M. Lloyd-Jones, *Preaching and Preachers* (Grand Rapids: Zondervan, 1971), 271.

[35] Ibid.

[36] Ibid.

[37] Ibid., 272.

Third, Lloyd-Jones objects that public invitations are often tacked onto sermons; thus, they divide proclamation into two distinct parts.[38] Lloyd-Jones's problem, however, is with the use of Scripture. Peter not only preached the gospel on the day of Pentecost but called for listeners to repent and present themselves publicly for believer's baptism. The invitation to repent included a call for public action.

Fourth, he is concerned that the public invitation implies that sinners have an inherent power to come to Christ, which they do not. He argues against "self-conversion," noting that those dead in trespasses and sins are unable to respond to the invitation (1 Cor 2:14; Eph 2:1).[39]

Lloyd-Jones fails to mention that God uses the preached Word to "grant" repentance and faith (Acts 5:30–31; 11:18; Rom 10:17). That which is normally impossible becomes possible through the supernatural power of God. As Leighton Ford reminds us:

> If anyone feels that he cannot give an invitation for a sinner to come to Christ, because of man's inablility, let him remember that Jesus invited a man whose hand was paralyzed to do what he could not do! ". . . Stretch out your hand . . ." Jesus commanded (Matthew 12:13), and the man obeyed the command and did what he would not do! Let him remember also that Jesus told a dead man to do something he could not do—to live! ". . . Lazarus, come forth," He commanded (John 11:43), and Lazarus obeyed the voice of Jesus and did what he could not do.[40]

During the invitation time, God speaks through the evangelist, calling the spiritually dead to life (2 Cor 5:20). God, not man, resurrects the soul.

Fifth, Lloyd-Jones argues that most evangelists attempt to manipulate the Holy Spirit via the invitation.[41] Exactly what Lloyd-Jones means is unclear since he does not elaborate. Possibly he is saying that evangelists often succeed in getting people down the aisle when the Holy Spirit is not moving. No respectable gospel preacher attempts to manipulate his listeners or coerce the Holy Spirit to act against His will. As an ambassador of the King, he simply delivers the King's ultimatum and awaits the reply.

Sixth, Dr. Lloyd-Jones states that many people come forward for selfish reasons, that is, to gain acceptance by family, to escape judgment, and

---

[38] Ibid., 273.
[39] Ibid., 274.
[40] Leighton Ford, *The Christian Persuader* (New York: Harper and Row, 1966), 120.
[41] Lloyd-Jones, *Preaching and Preachers*, 274–75.

so on.[42] Again, assessing a person's motive for answering the gospel call is impossible, but by giving precise instructions during his invitation, the preacher can be assured that his audience clearly understands what he is asking them to do and why. Another preventive step is to make sure those who come forward are thoroughly counseled to ascertain why they responded. The gospel can then be explained again, and the seeker challenged to repent and believe in Christ.

Seventh, Lloyd-Jones believes public invitations cause people to think walking forward saves them.[43] Since people can embrace erroneous beliefs, the evangelist must explain prior to the invitation that coming forward saves no one. He needs to explain further that coming forward is the outward expression of repentance and faith.

The eighth criticism is that the public invitation supplants the work of the Holy Spirit.[44] Earlier Lloyd-Jones said the evangelist tries to *manipulate* the Spirit; now he argues that the evangelist attempts, by the public invitation, to *do* the Spirit's work.

In reality the preacher and the Spirit work hand in hand in evangelism, and at times distinguishing where one starts and the other ends is difficult. They are united in a single mission. Together they exhort, convince, persuade, and call people to Christ. The apostle Paul said to Timothy, "The Lord *stood with me* . . . that all the Gentiles might hear" (2 Tim 4:17, emphasis added). To the Colossians he wrote: "We preach, warning every man and teaching every man in all wisdom, that we may present every man perfect in Christ Jesus. To this end, I also labor, striving according to *His working which works in me* mightily" (Col 1:28–29, emphasis added).

John the apostle closes his book with this exhortation: "The Spirit *and* the bride say, 'Come!'" (Rev 22:17). Clearly, the evangelist views his preaching the gospel and issuing the invitation as working in unison with the Spirit. As C. E. Autrey logically deduces, "The evangelist is not pushing the Holy Spirit aside when he pleads in the invitation any more than when he prepares and delivers the body of the sermon."[45]

Finally, Martyn Lloyd-Jones objects that the public invitation calls sinners to "decide" for Christ.[46] Here he argues that no one decides for God since their wills are in bondage.

[42] Ibid., 275.
[43] Ibid., 276.
[44] Ibid., 277.
[45] Autrey, *Basic Evangelism*, 128.
[46] Lloyd-Jones, *Preaching and Preachers*, 278.

But God holds listeners responsible for responding to the gospel. The evangelist urgently declares, "God . . . now commands all men everywhere to repent" (Acts 17:30). He then calls for sinners to obey that command and be saved. The responsibility for salvation lies with the hearers, not God. They must choose! Stephen Olford made this observation:

> There is nothing more thrilling in all the world than to issue the call of
> the gospel and to see men and women believe. [The] . . . redemptive
> invitation of God demands a verdict. Man can never confront the gospel
> of the Lord Jesus Christ and remain indifferent, apathetic or aloof. He
> has to decide. With the revelation and invitation of the gospel man has
> to give an answer. If he believes he is saved; if he rejects he is lost.[47]

Ironically, although Lloyd-Jones criticized others for giving an invitation, he issued an appeal himself. At the end of each sermon, he called upon his listeners to repent and believe the gospel. While not inviting them forward, he did exhort them to meet with him in private after the church service or in his office the next morning, when he would personally lead them to Christ. Such incongruence is remarkable. As Billy Graham once commented:

> We have noticed that some who are against public evangelistic
> invitations go to almost any length using the appeal in personal
> evangelism. If it is right to ask a single sinner to repent and receive the
> Lord Jesus Christ, why is it not right to ask a whole audience to do the
> same?[48]

A Modest Proposal for Calvinists

Examining the concept of "the call" offers a possible solution for Calvinists who oppose the invitation. Calvinists believe in two "calls." The first is the "general" call, also known as the "universal" or "outer" call. The second is designated the "specific" or the "inner" call, also known as the "effectual" call. The general call can be identified with the public invitation. It is a summons for all sinners to repent and believe in the Lord Jesus Christ. This exhortation, aimed at the entire audience, seeks an immediate response. On behalf of God, the preacher demands a response (Acts 17:31). The general call can be and often is resisted (Acts 7:51; Luke 18:18–24).

---

[47] S. F. Olford, *The Christian Message for Contemporary Man* (Waco: Word, 1972), 54.

[48] B. Graham, *Biblical Invitations* (Minneapolis: Billy Graham Evangelistic Association, n.d.), 18–19.

Whereas the outer call is the work of the evangelist, the inner call is the work of the Spirit (John 6:37,44,65). He opens hearts and makes sinners ready and willing to respond (Acts 16:14). This understanding of the two kinds of call should be an encouragement to the gospel herald. Jesus speaks of the "many" who "are called" [via the general call], "but few" that "are chosen" [via the effectual call] (Matt 20:16).

Once one distinguishes between the two calls, he must also recognize that not all who respond to the outward call will be regenerated. The parable of the four soils is proof of that (Mark 4:1–20), but some indeed will be instantly born again. Thomas Watson wrote, "The outward call brings men to a *profession* of Christ, the inward to a *possession* of Christ."[49] The evangelist preaches the gospel and calls people to repent, believe, and demonstrate their desire to do so in a public manner, preferably through baptism. Since he cannot see the hearts of those who respond outwardly, he must accept their profession of faith at face value. On the day of Pentecost, those heeding Peter's admonition took a public stand for Christ and were welcomed immediately into the church. We should do likewise.

Only time will reveal the genuineness of one's commitment to Christ. In due course, those who show no evidence of conversion and remain in their sin can be dealt with according to the principles of church discipline (Matt 18:15–18).

Conclusion

While a public profession of faith is not a guarantee of salvation, it always accompanies salvation (Rom 10:9–10). That is why we give an invitation.

We do not practice calling people to follow Christ publicly for pragmatic reasons but because we honestly desire to follow the pattern found in the Gospels and the Acts of the Apostles. Therefore, let us not shy away from giving an invitation because of its critics or its many abuses. Let us strive instead to emulate Christ and the apostles by inviting people to follow in the Master's footsteps.

If Calvinist preachers, as well as others from different theological persuasions, would start calling their hearers to a public profession of faith, I believe the Holy Spirit would draw many more people to Christ under their ministry. Do we actually believe we can improve on the New Testament method of calling people to Christ?

---

[49] T. Watson, *Body of Divinity* (London: Banner of Truth, 1958), 153.

Chapter 10

Reflections on Determinism and Human Freedom

JEREMY A. EVANS

Introduction

In a discussion about the problem of free will and the nature of salvation, especially in a Christian context, the discussion parties need clarity about the real problem set before them. The question pertains not to the compatibility of divine sovereignty and human freedom, rather to whether we can make sense of the idea that human freedom and causal determinism are compatible. Libertarians, that is, persons who *do not* think that freedom and determinism are compatible, defend the view that "some human actions are chosen and performed by the agent without there being any sufficient condition or cause of the action prior to the action itself."[1] For libertarianism, in order for a person to be free, certain conditions must be present, namely, that genuine alternatives are open to the person while deliberating on a course of action, no coercion is present, *and* the person

---

[1] W. Hasker, *Metaphysics: Constructing a Worldview* (Downer's Grove, IL: InterVarsity Press, 1983), 32. See also the excellent work of R. Kane, *A Contemporary Introduction to Free Will* (Oxford: Oxford University Press, 2005), 32–39.

is still deemed free. Libertarian views of freedom focus on the *person* (i.e., a personal agent) and take seriously the idea that in the nexus of events the agent is a contributing cause of certain things (not necessarily all) that happen. Libertarian freedom holds that the person is a cause, *does* certain things, and *does not* merely undergo a series of events. For example, suppose when I return to visit friends in New Orleans, they take me out to my favorite New Orleans restaurant. At lunch I deliberate over what I will eat and eventually choose the paneed chicken pasta, as I have many times before. While I deliberate about ordering chicken pasta, at least two options avail themselves: either I will or will not order it. After making *that* decision, several options arise (e.g., if I choose not to eat the paneed chicken, I then deliberate over what I, in fact, will eat—perhaps catfish Lafayette). This example illustrates (not perfectly) the libertarian view that in order for people to be free, genuine options must be open to them as agents.[2] If people's choices are determined either from external or internal causes, then they cannot claim in any meaningful sense that the choices were free. Both internal and external factors influence their decisions but do not determine them. Hence, libertarians describe causal determinism and human freedom as *incompatible*.

Determinists respond to the problem of free will in a different way. Generally speaking, determinism claims that for every event that happens "there are previous events and circumstances which are its sufficient conditions or causes, so that, given those previous events and circumstances, it is impossible that the event should not occur."[3] If we return to my deliberation at the New Orleans restaurant, the determinist will claim that factors beyond my control govern my decision to choose or not choose the paneed chicken pasta. Thus, due to any number of psychological causes, strongest desires, or other determining factors, my decision at the restaurant is causally necessary. So how can a compatibilist claim that my decision is relegated from internal and external causes but that I am still free in a meaningful way? Robert Kane explains that at this point the determinist will ask people what they mean by saying actions or choices are free—for example, free to eat the paneed chicken pasta. For those holding to determinism, the first condition of freedom is that I am free to order

---

[2] Important note: this does not mean that alternate possibilities are required for every decision an agent makes. Libertarianism takes seriously the idea that our decisions shape our character and bring about a progressively narrowed range of possibilities when we persist in certain courses of decision making and action.

[3] See Hasker, *Metaphysics*, 32. See also Kane, *Contemporary Introduction*, 12–23.

paneed chicken if I have the power or ability to choose it, should I want or decide to do so.[4] Indeed, freedom does require a power or ability to choose a course of action, or this may be a power I choose not to exercise. The second condition for a compatibilist understanding of freedom is that there are no constraints or impediments "preventing me from doing what I want to do."[5] I would not be free to eat paneed chicken if circumstances prevented me from doing so—for example, due to time constraints, we did not have the time to travel to the restaurant, or if I had a sudden attack of paralysis, or if the restaurant were not open on that day. As long as I have the ability to eat paneed chicken and no constraints prevent me from choosing the paneed chicken, then from a compatibilist perspective, I am free regarding that decision.

How does this view of freedom differ from the libertarian account of freedom briefly explained above? First, neither of these two conditions stipulates that genuine alternatives are required for the agent to be free. If we suppose that the restaurant is open, that I do not suffer from paralysis or a tight speaking schedule, and I want to eat paneed chicken, then I am free to do so. Further, I am still considered to be free in compatibilism even if the past determines what I will or desire. So, even though this construal of human freedom affirms that determinism is true, it finds no problem in saying that human freedom is *compatible* with determinism. As it were, although my desires are beyond my direct control (in fact, they control me), they are still *my* desires. Often this kind of freedom is called *freedom of inclination*, where I can do whatever I want but have no power over my wants. I am free insofar as I am unhindered in exercising these desires through choices. Admittedly, this strand of "compatibilism" is one of many,[6] but it will be the center of our discussion in this chapter since it dominates the landscape of theological thought on the problem set before us.

Is compatibilism, or theological determinism as some call it, the best way to understand free will both biblically and philosophically? Calvinists answer in the affirmative, and libertarians are less than convinced. This chapter aims to provide some thoughts on why endorsing a strong Calvinist view of human freedom is unnecessary even when taking the problem of sin seriously. Again, I affirm the comprehensive sovereignty

---

[4] See Kane, *Contemporary Introduction*, 13.

[5] Ibid.

[6] The type of determinism holding that free will and determinism are incompatible is often called "hard determinism" or "fatalism."

of God, which is compatible with human freedom, and deny the claim that *determinism* is compatible with human freedom.[7] The structure of this paper does not attempt to make one long connected argument against Calvinism; it offers food for thought ranging over a number of issues, hopefully providing some insight for future discussion and reference. Hence, this chapter has the title "Reflections on Determinism and Human Freedom."

A Brief Treatment of Sin and Its Effects— Biblically and Historically

Most Christians affirm that Adam's sin drastically altered the course of human events; it altered humanity and the natural world. One of the supposed alterations occurred in the nature of human agency, the problem of free will. In light of the fall of Adam, the effects of sin on human agency must receive serious consideration—is it within everyone's capacity to accept the offer of salvation in Christ, given the radical change in human character and environment? After all, Scripture describes humanity after the fall as spiritually dead (Eph 2:1) and unable to accept the things of the Spirit of God, which are spiritually discerned (1 Cor 2:14). Further, unbelievers are under a yoke of slavery to sin (Gal 5:1), gratifying the desires of the flesh (Gal 5:16). Understandably, the greatest sin is the rejection of what God has accomplished in Christ *via* His passion and resurrection (Mark 3:28; 1 John 5:16–17). Scripture categorizes this last sin as unpardonable, yielding eternal judgment (Rom 6:23). In short, human beings are in need of grace and salvation.

Given this short sketch of the human condition, seeing how one might endorse determinism is not hard. The doctrine of the perversity and universality of sin[8] cannot be denied. "All we like sheep have gone astray; we have turned—every one—to his own way" (Isa 53:6).[9] We find in Proverbs: "Who can say 'I have made my heart pure; I am clean from my sin'?" (Prov 20:9). Consider the affirmation in Ecclesiastes: "Surely

---

[7] This chapter intends to offer a critique and, at least for now, leaves it to others to make the positive case for libertarian accounts of freedom. Some works worth reading include H. McCann, *The Works of Agency: On Human Action, Will, and Responsibility* (Ithaca: Cornell University Press, 1998); T. O'Connor, *Persons and Causes: The Metaphysics of Free Will* (Oxford: Oxford University Press, 2000); R. Kane, *The Significance of Free Will* (Oxford: Oxford University Press, 1998); and R. Clarke, *Libertarian Accounts of Free Will* (Oxford: Oxford University Press, 2003).

[8] Universal except for Christ, of course.

[9] All scriptural references are from the English Standard Version.

there is not a righteous man on earth who does good and never sins" (Ecc 7:20). In his sermon on Mars Hill, the apostle Paul made a universal appeal for sinners to come to repentance: "The times of ignorance God overlooked, but now he commands all people everywhere to repent, because he has fixed a day on which he will judge the world in righteousness by a man whom he has appointed; and of this he has given assurance to all by raising him from the dead" (Acts 17:30–31). So serious are the consequences of the fall, Jesus tells Nicodemus that unless one is "born of the Spirit" or "born again" he cannot enter the kingdom of God (John 3:5–8). Jesus even speaks of our being slaves to sin: "Truly, truly I say to you, everyone who commits sin is a slave to sin. The slave does not remain in the house forever; the son remains forever. So if the Son *sets* you free, you will be free indeed" (John 8:34–36; italics mine). Certainly, more can be said about the problem of sin, but consideration of the implications of sin on human beings' ability to choose God next will receive attention. More specifically, is human depravity so comprehensively destructive in both human minds and wills that we must affirm a complete inability to understand and accept Jesus?[10]

Armed with biblical narrative describing humans as self-seeking and in need of deliverance from the bondage of sin, Bruce Ware concludes:

> Probably the single most important biblical conception relating to the question of human freedom is the notion that we human beings perform our choices and actions out of what we desire in our hearts. That is, what we want most, what our natures incline us most strongly to—this is the pool out of which the stream of our choices and actions flows.[11]

Consider the claims of Augustine in his influential work *Grace and Free Choice* (426 CE):

> But clearly, once grace has been given, our good merits also begin to exist, but through that grace. For, if grace is withdrawn, a human being falls, no longer standing upright, but cast headlong by free choice. Hence, even when a human being begins to have good merits, he ought not attribute them to himself, but to God.[12]

---

[10] Sin denotes both an intellectual and volitional failure; it is not merely a matter of the will.

[11] B. Ware, *God's Greater Glory: The Exalted God of Scripture and the Christian Faith* (Wheaton, IL: Crossway Books, 2004), 79.

[12] See Augustine, "Grace and Free Will," in *Answer to the Pelagians IV*, part 1, volume 26 (trans. R. Teske; Hyde Park, NY: New City Press, 1999).

Interestingly, Augustine does not claim here that humanity's affections are determined from forces beyond their direct control. Later in the same work, he claims that it is "certain that we will when we will, but God *causes* us to will what is good" (16.32; italics mine), and says, "I think I have argued enough against those who violently attack the grace of God which does not destroy the human will, but changes it from an evil will to a good will, and once it is good, helps it" (20.41). Moreover, Augustine not only holds that persons of good will have that good will from above, but he also implies that God's will *controls* the wills of those who do evil as well. Although he writes in *Grace and Free Will*, "The almighty produces in the hearts of human beings even the movement of their will in order to do through them what he himself wills to do through them, he who absolutely cannot will anything unjust" (21.42), this sentiment is predicated on an earlier statement that God "does what he wills even in the hearts of evil persons, repaying them, nonetheless, according to their merits" (21.42). Some instances of God causing evil wills (notes Augustine) are the hardening of Pharaoh's heart and the betrayal of Christ by Judas (20.41).

These previous statements are hard to reconcile with Augustine's earlier works, where he seemingly taught that the voluntary movement of the will is required for any meaningful account of personal responsibility.[13] By "voluntary" he seems to mean the content of people's will that is not made through "some violence which compels against one's will" or an "irresistible cause" (3.18). Nonetheless, Augustine later saw that if he commends a view of human freedom that is deterministic, then certain results follow from this commitment. Concerning the darkened mind, God illuminates it to understand who He is and what He has done in the person and work of Jesus. As for the will, the illumination of the mind enables the will to choose that which is truly good (God), for after humans *understand* what the true good is, and insofar as they choose according to perceived goods, they then choose God.

John Calvin, in his famous *Institutes of the Christian Religion*, concurs with Augustine, noting that in Adam human beings all lost their original abilities and can do nothing good (2.2.1).[14] As Calvin describes it, the effects of sin are exhaustive; nothing remains of the *imago Dei* (2.1.9), including the original freedom that He endowed to Adam for its proper

---

[13] See his famous work *On Free Will*, especially books 2 and 3.
[14] J. Calvin, *Institutes of the Christian Religion* [ed. J. McNeil; Philadelphia: Westminster Press, 1960), 22.

use.[15] Though people's sinful nature compels them to choose all and only evil, they still sin voluntarily. So long as the relationship is one of constraint on humans' ability and not necessitating what humans choose, then they are significantly free and morally responsible (2.3.5; 2.2.6). As a counterpart explanation, Calvin argues that God Himself, being perfectly good, cannot do anything but the good (His nature demands that He act only in ways that are good). Again, persons may be morally praised or blamed so long as they act freely, where freedom is to be understood as choosing according to one's greatest desire.[16]

Irresistible Grace/Effectual Calling: Biblically and Logically Unnecessary

Classical compatibilism leads to the idea that when God works a saving grace in persons' hearts, they will come to faith in Jesus. As the mantra affirms, regeneration precedes faith. This relationship is intended to be understood logically, not temporally. Temporally, the cause and effect relationship occurs simultaneously; logically, regeneration occurs before faith. The mechanism of God's saving work is the inner call to man, which is a special call to the elect that elicits the gifts of faith and repentance. Sometimes this view is referred to as the effectual call, as opposed to the "outer" or "general" call to everyone unto faith and repentance.[17] According to Calvin, the Holy Spirit "causes the preached Word to dwell in their hearts."[18] The manner of God's activity in such a work is irresistible, hence often referred to as irresistible grace. The famous Calvinist R. C. Sproul notes, "We do not believe in order to be born again; we are born again in order to believe."[19]

On the face of it, such a view may appear to have biblical support. In John 6:44, Jesus says that "no one can come to me unless the Father who sent me draws him." Traditionally, in order to solidify this point, the word

---

[15] This claim to original freedom, which is often argued as libertarian freedom, is controversial. Admittedly, some argue that Adam's sin was determined in eternity past by God, and that God causally brought about the sin in Adam by giving him his desire for sin, thus compelling the fall. I disagree but reserve that discussion for another time.

[16] Another controversial point is that God, under this construal, is causally determined to do what He does as well. That is, His nature determines His desires.

[17] That the reference here is to the general call, rather than the ineffectual call, is interesting. For reference in Calvin to this distinction, see the *Institutes* 3.24.2.

[18] See the *Institutes* 3.24.8.

[19] R. C. Sproul, *Chosen by God* (Wheaton, IL: Tyndale, 1986), 72–73. See also his work *Willing to Believe: The Controversy over Free Will* (Grand Rapids: Baker Publishers, 1997).

for *draw* is equated with being "dragged" (*helkuō*). Admittedly, in some instances, the word has this exact meaning (see Jas 2:6), but in matters of salvation the picture is not so clear. James was not speaking of salvation but of the sin of partiality; hence, these are different categories with different applications. To clarify the point, Jesus, speaking of His crucifixion, says, "And I, when I am lifted up from the earth, will draw (*helkuō*) all people to myself" (John 12:32). This text is about Christ's saving work, which falls in the same category as what is found in John 6:44. The difference between John 6:44 and 12:32 is not the term *draw* but whether to understand it as "being dragged." Extending the application of Jesus' statement in 12:32— He draws all people to Himself—produces Christian Universalists, but this conclusion will not work with any number of passages that indicate most people will not enjoy eternal beatitude with God (Matt 7:13).

Richard Cross asks, "Suppose we do adopt . . . that there can be no natural active human cooperation in justification. Would such a position require us to accept the irresistibility of grace?"[20] Cross gives us reason to think not. Consider his example:

> Suppose . . . I wake up to find myself traveling in an ambulance. Suppose too that I have, all the time that I am conscious of being in the ambulance, the option to not be there. Perhaps I can simply ask the driver to stop and let me out. If I do not do this, then I do not impede the action that is done to me—being brought to the hospital, or whatever. But—by the same token—I do not causally contribute to it, other than counterfactually (i.e. by not impeding it). Does not impeding *a* amount to wanting or doing *a*? Not generally, given the coherence of the notion of an interior act of will, for given this it is possible to accept that there are many things that I, for example, neither impede nor want—even in the case that I can impede them. If I do not do something, I remain in the ambulance. But it would be odd to describe this as a case of my going to the hospital (as opposed to my being brought there).[21]

The analogy is clear and certainly applies to our discussion. Strong Calvinism cornered the market on monergism as entailing irresistible grace,

---

[20] R. Cross, "Anti-Pelagianism and the Resistibility of Grace," in *Faith and Philosophy* 22:2 (2005), 204.

[21] Ibid., 207. Ken Keathley uses Cross's analogy in his excellent work *Salvation and the Sovereignty of God: A Molinist Approach* (Nashville: B&H Academic, 2010). Moreover, Keathley offers a much more extensive biblical treatment of the concepts deployed than does Cross, which is an invaluable asset to theologians who are not of a philosophical bent. I highly recommend this work.

but Cross's model offers an account of monergism and resistible grace. In doing so, it overcomes many of the concerns traditionally ascribed to synergism. If the only contribution humans make in salvation is negative, then this contribution can hardly be considered an act worthy of praise—in fact, it hinders God's activity to bring humans to a right relationship with Him. Instead, believers receive no personal credit, for in and through the work of God, the persons come to repentance and faith.

As previously noted, libertarian accounts of freedom require that ultimate responsibility must rest on the agent in some way and that morally this requires that at some point the agent had it within his or her ability to choose otherwise. This account of saving grace means the only contribution the person makes is not of positive personal status, as strands of Pelagianism and Semi-Pelagianism hold. Indeed, the work done in salvation is wrought by God (Eph 2:8–9) and does not result from the individual's "pulling himself up by his own bootstraps." The believer's faith is a gift freely given from above and does not reside in any natural capacity of the person (Phil 1:28–29). Holding to monergism and resistible grace also helps explain how God desires that none perish (1 Tim 2:3). Last, a more promising ordering of events obtains. Rather than saying a new life leads to a saving faith, a saving faith brings about new life. Jesus provides forgiveness of sins for those who believe in Him (Acts 13:38); the one who hears the words of Christ and believes passes from death to life (John 5:24). Notice that the verse does not say "the one who passes from death to life believes" but the "one who believes passes from death to life." The New Testament is replete with other instances where new life is brought from faith (John 20:31; 1 Tim 1:16). Suffice it to say, even holding to monergism does not biblically or logically entail that irresistible grace necessarily follows.

The rest of the chapter will give some attention to other concerns that surround endorsing classical compatibilism as a viable model of free will in Christian theism. The scope of these objections centers all and only on views that replicate ideologically the tenets explained before in the writings of Augustine, Calvin, and Edwards.

The Responsibility Objection

In an attractive way, compatibilism provides sufficient conditions (or causes) to explain why one event occurs rather than another. Further, since the cause of persons' choices are derived from their character, this account of freedom does not undermine personal responsibility. Thus, the important question to ask is, "What are the sources of these sufficient conditions?" Consider my choosing paneed chicken pasta. All of the conditions for responsible action are met. Nothing forced me to choose paneed chicken; I ordered it because I wanted to do so. According to determinism, immediately before I chose the paneed chicken, a series of events and circumstances occurred such that they guarantee my choosing paneed chicken. These events and circumstances are the "proximate causes" of my choice.[22] My desire to have paneed chicken conjoined with my belief that I could have it brought about by my choosing it. So where did this desire and belief come from? Both are the byproduct of previous causes, for "since *every* event, according to determinism, has prior sufficient causes, we can go on tracing the chain of causes backward until we have arrived at a set of events and circumstances which together constitute a sufficient condition for the occurrence of the proximate cause."[23] Pressing the concern one step further, all of this occurred *before* I was born, and as for sin, this may be traced in our human lineage back to Adam.

These distinctions prepare for considering the implications of causation on personal responsibility. If grounding moral responsibility on the immediate cause of the event appears sufficient, then clearly the determinists have made their case. The wishes, desires, objectives, or intentions of the agent explain the immediate cause of the action. The concern is whether the agent is responsible for the *prior cause(s)*, not the *immediate cause*. The moral corollary then shifts from "is Judas responsible for his rejection of Jesus" to "is Judas responsible for the events that determined his rejection of Jesus?" How Judas could be responsible for the prior cause, given that he did not exist when the causal loop was being formed, is difficult to see.[24] Judas's act of betrayal was causally necessitated by circumstances grounded in prior causes, to which he made no contribution at all. Where there is no contribution, there is no moral responsibility.

The best scenario a determinist can offer is that punishment becomes one link in the causal chain of human behavior—in effect becoming a prior cause of future intention formation and choosing. But this construal does not help our discussion on matters of salvation because the only

---

[22] See Hasker, *Metaphysics*, 35.
[23] Ibid.
[24] Ibid.

future referent open to this discussion is in glory, when the effects of our choices are rendered unto judgment. So I concur with Robert Kane, that ultimate responsibility (UR) resides where the ultimate cause is.[25] If I am *never* the original force behind my choices, then I am not responsible for the contents of my choices. At some point in the causal chain, I must have contra-causal freedom (the ability to do otherwise). My responsibility for my current volitional state may be the result of previous decisions that I have made, character-forming decisions that perhaps narrowed the likelihood that I would ever choose differently in the course of my natural life. My previous choices as a part of the narrative of personal responsibility are significant. Only then can prior causes become connected with current choices (immediate causes), and personal responsibility makes sense. According to Kane, so long as the agent's current decision has some standing to a previous free decision, then persons are ultimately responsible for their current decisions.

The Emptiness Objection

Is there any evidence that humans always choose according to their greatest desires as Calvinism states? Some passages of Scripture indicate otherwise. Paul says, "*For I do not do what I want*, but I do the very thing I hate," and "*I have the desire* to do what is right, but not the ability to carry it out" (Rom 7:15,18). One might claim that this passage is about Paul's sanctification and not about his salvation since clearly he was already saved. But this argument misses the point. The strong Calvinist's claim hinges on the notion of complete psychological determinism—that humans *always* act on their strongest desires or motives. Otherwise, no sufficient reason can account for choosing one course of action rather than another. The normal response to this concern is that humans misperceive what their greatest desire or strongest motive actually is. Concerning Paul's desires, compatibilists have two possibilities. First, they can remain true to their position and explain Paul's choosing against what he wants as Paul's misunderstanding what his strongest desire actually was. Rather than taking Paul as saying, "I have the desire to do what is right," he must have meant, "But I have a greater desire for something else." Clearly, however, Scripture

---

[25] See R. Kane, *The Significance of Free Will* (Oxford: Oxford University Press, 1998), 35.

does not make this statement but provides the opposite one—he does the things he hates.

In addition, this proposal reduces the strongest motive as the motive leading to action, which results in the trivial claim that we "always act on the motive which we act upon."[26] Not only is this proposal uninformative; it is also question-begging. No element of this discussion has been reducible to self-evident propositions about human willing and action, but strong Calvinists make this exact move—determinism becomes a rational truth, on par with "all bachelors are unmarried men." Stipulating that strongest motive governs action is a far cry from proving it.

The second option for the compatibilist (which I will not give much attention) is to shift views of agency midstream and argue that after salvation God works with (synergism) our wills in sanctification but does not causally control our wills. Instances such as Romans 7 may suffice to ground such a claim—that internal and external factors influence people's decisions without determining them. Experience also gives reason to make such a claim. Although justification is complete in Christ, humans continue to work out their salvation with fear and trembling (Phil 2:12). Humans continue to sin, though they are not under the curse of sin. However, attendant with this shift in agency are all of the concerns that supposedly plague it. The same compatibilists who argue that libertarian freedom fails to supply a sufficient cause or reason now must provide a response to their own objections. What is more, if they explain how to choose between alternative courses of action, then they have undermined their previous claim that no such reason(s) for human willing exist in a libertarian construct. I await anxiously their contribution to our discussion on sanctification.

The Self-Sufficient God?

God is worthy of worship. He is the self-sufficient, self-existent Creator of every contingent being. The Triune God lacks nothing and requires no other to fulfill or explain the completeness of His being. In fact, the Trinity has at its disposal great power to explain *how* God may be understood as self-sufficient and independent. Before creation the Trinity exemplified a unity of will and purpose, loving-kindness, and even justice from one

---

[26] Hasker, *Metaphysics*, 44.

member to the next. These relational properties were expressed with perfection and depended on no other to be manifest in His nature. Our commitment to the self-sufficiency of God is without compromise. However, according to James Beilby, the Calvinist assertion that God's fundamental purpose in creation is to "demonstrate his glory" seems to "entail that God have an 'other' to whom his glory must be demonstrated."[27] As Beilby notes, if this relationship is the case, then God is dependent in some sense "on this *other* for the demonstration of his glory, and ironically, less sovereign than in a theology where the demonstration of God's glory is less central."[28] The heart of the problem is that this dependence relationship not only undermines the claim that Calvinism best explains what God's sovereignty and glory means, but it also threatens a pivotal theological belief—God's *aseity* (self-existence).

Beilby distinguishes two types of aseity. The first type is *ontological aseity*, which affirms that "God is uncaused, without beginning, not dependent on external person, principle, or metaphysical reality for his existence."[29] The second type of aseity is *psychological aseity*; there is no lack or need in God. God is "fully self-satisfied, not needing anything outside himself to be happy or fulfilled."[30]

Making this distinction underlines what is truly advantageous to Trinitarian theology. Given the Trinity, God did not need creation to fulfill anything lacking in Him (psychological aseity). Without creation, the Father, Son, and Spirit held a relational unity that was perfect, not only in lovingkindness but in justice as well. Justice needs mentioning because much can be made of the idea that humans are "vessels of wrath" and that making the fullness of God's properties known requires that He manifest both His mercy and His wrath. But this suggestion misconstrues what Scripture means by God's wrath. Wrath is *not* one of God's properties; justice is. Wrath is only a manifestation of what justice demands. If humans freely reject Jesus, then God's wrath falls rightly upon them (John 6:33); but there is no need for God to exemplify wrath in order for Him to be perfectly just. Justice existed before creation in the Trinity; hence God does not need any human to be fully satisfied in His justice.

---

[27] J. Beilby, "Divine Aseity, Divine Freedom: A Conceptual Problem for Edwardsian-Calvinism" in *Journal of the Evangelical Theological Society* 47/4 (December 2004): 647.

[28] Ibid., 647, italics mine.

[29] Ibid., 648.

[30] Ibid.

But another problem lingers after challenging the self-satisfaction of God. If God needs creation to exemplify these properties, then humans can rightly question whether God was free in His act of creation. Divine aseity logically requires that God's choice to create the world be free. But discerning how God can be free to create or not create is hard if we posit that *in creating* He was intending to accomplish the task of bringing glory to Himself, a task that He cannot accomplish without creation.[31] Beilby rightly notes that no tension exists between divine aseity and *our* purpose in creation to give glory to God, or even for God to be glorified by His creation.[32] Each of these concepts is right. God's glory was complete without creation; nothing that occurs in creation can add to or take away from His perfection and holiness. He does not *gain* glory when He is praised—His glory is *recognized* in praise. Humans should expect as much when they recognize that their chief end in life is to know and enjoy God. Indeed, a tension does exist between "aseity and the claim that *God's* purpose in creating was to bring glory to himself."[33]

The more pressing aspect of this issue concerns God's freedom. Consider the previous discussion about God's psychological aseity. Divine aseity requires that God's decision to create must be free from either internal or external governing factors. Given God's status as the only self-existent being, pinpointing any external cause that could determine His act of creation would be difficult. Determining internal factors requires understanding that the completeness and perfection of God's being keeps the notion at bay that something is being fulfilled in Him as He creates the world. Beilby correctly points out, "If it [creation] was internally necessitated, then God's nature would be such that he needed to create the world to be who he was. By implication, while God has the capacity to create, being a creator is neither one of his essential properties nor is it entailed by any of his essential properties."[34]

At this point it simply will not do to say that God has the type of compatibilistic freedom mentioned in this discussion. If God is choosing according to His greatest desire, and something in His nature determines his greatest desire is to communicate His glory, then the revelation of God's glory in creation is internally determined, and His self-sufficiency is once again undermined. By logical extension, if God's act of creation

---

[31] Ibid., 649.
[32] Ibid.
[33] Ibid.
[34] Ibid.

is necessary, then every state of affairs in creation is also necessary.[35] Such concerns are more than a nuisance; they challenge the concept of the perfection of God. But there are further implications that deserve consideration.

On the Is/Ought Principle and the Best Possible World

Something has gone wrong in creation. To sin means to miss the mark, to fall short of perfection, or to fail to meet an obligation. In biblical terms, sin deceives (Heb 3:13), which indicates that the human mind is not as it *should* be. Sin is also described as doing what is morally wrong (Ps 51:4); humans do not do the things they *ought* to do (Romans 7). Sin is not merely a condition that humans have, it is something humans do, and *de facto* involves a failure on their part to meet a standard of evaluation. Sin indicates the world is not as it should be.

Emphasis lies on the words *should* and *ought* because they are normative terms; they do not merely describe events; and this distinction brings up an interesting problem for the Reformed view of the will. To state the problem concisely, anyone who wants to grant God the type of sovereignty proposed by strong Calvinism, which is a causal account of human willing and acting, yet wants to say that the world is not as it should be (sin) is under a particular burden to explain how they can make these claims in conjunction with one another.[36] To avoid issues less than crucial, let us focus on the rejection of God. As previously noted, the condition of fallen man is one of separation from God. Further, as Augustine, Calvin, and Edwards claim, without the assistance of God, human beings are unable to come to accept Jesus as Lord and Savior. Given their commitment to irresistible grace, the only viable conclusion for them to make concerning why persons reject Christ is that God chose not to work a saving grace in their hearts.

Why did God not work a saving grace in their hearts? Admittedly, Calvinists typically defer to the distinction between the sovereign and moral wills of God, and postulate that human beings can only know the moral will of God—those principles of Scripture that govern our moral well-being, and commands uttered to bring about actions of positive moral

---

[35] On this point see T. Flint, *Divine Providence: The Molinist Account* (Ithaca, NY: Cornell University Press, 1998), 28–30.

[36] I am indebted to my good friend John Ross Churchill for his invaluable insights in this discussion.

value. The sovereign will of God remains a mystery. Why He chose some for salvation and not others is a mystery. But this suggestion raises an interesting point. On biblical grounds the rejection of God is a moral failure, and the conditions under which human beings make amends with Him are met in Jesus. None of these ideas are mysterious. An argument might be raised that since human beings are dead in Adam, God did not cause humans' rejection *per se*, and any act of grace on His part (even on one person) displays His loving-kindness. Further, God has no obligations to save any person, and so all the more the gratuity of His saving work.

Perhaps such claims have merit if only God were free. When Augustine, Calvin, and Edwards proposed that God's works were of necessity, the implications go beyond His determined act of creation but must also be applied to the persons He elected to regenerate unto faith. That God has no obligation to save is not the point. That God could not have elected otherwise *is* the point. On this Thomas Flint offers a helpful suggestion, that when humans deny that God has libertarian freedom, and He creates because He has to, then the human world is the only possible world. As a result, the contrasts between contingency and necessity are absolved, and along with it the graciousness of His creation and our existence.[37]

The second point relates to the first but centers on a discussion about Best Possible Worlds (henceforth BPWs). Much could be said about BPWs, but in general, of the array of possible worlds available to God before He created, one of the worlds is the best. The strong Calvinist view claims the present world is the BPW. As the writings of Augustine and Calvin have displayed, God's involvement in the events of the world is a direct byproduct of His willing them to be exactly as they are; the salvation of Peter and not Judas is unilaterally derived from the decree and causal control of God. Moreover, every last detail of the universe goes into making the cosmos exactly as God intended it to be. If God's sovereignty and control are taken as exhaustive, this world cannot be anything other than the BPW; any other world would indicate that God acted in a way that manifests His attributes with deficiency. So, even though there may *conceivably* be an array of worlds that God could have created, He is morally constrained to create the best. What is more, if every detail of creation

---

[37] See Flint, *Divine Providence and Human Freedom*, 26–30. A gratuitous person gives from abundance, not out of necessity. In fact, the term *gratuitous* denotes *uncaused* giving; uncaused means not "without reason" but "without necessity."

goes into making the portrait of the BPW, then any change would mean less than the best. If this suggestion is the case, then it becomes difficult to determine how the strong Calvinist can say that certain things that are, ought not to be, which includes sin. If God's providence governs causally down to the last detail (as the strong Calvinist insists), and we say the world is not as it ought to be (which is conceptually entailed by sin, and in this case the rejection of Jesus), then we are explicitly saying that God should not have caused the world to be as it is. Again, these ideas are not mysterious; they are contradictory.

One concern about the BPW issue still remains. Suppose one argues, along the lines of Ephesians 1 and Romans 9, that God's directing of the course of human events exactly as He does is good because that direction manifests all aspects of His glory, including His wrath. This direction may not avoid the BPW issues discussed in the previous section. If it is best for the wrath to be manifest and if sin is a necessary condition for wrath, then ultimately sin ought to be in the BPW. If one denies that a best possible world exists, this concern still does not go away. Even if it is good for God's wrath to be manifest, and sin is necessary for wrath, sin still ought to be in the world, even though it is not the BPW. Even if one could prove that no explicit contradiction has occurred, the relationships that are being simultaneously affirmed here are at best bizarre.

Speech-Acts and Calvinism[38]

The previous charge in Paul's sermon on Mars Hill needs further consideration: "The times of ignorance God overlooked, but now he *commands* all people everywhere to repent, because he has fixed a day on which he will judge the world in righteousness by a man whom he has appointed; and of this he has given assurance to all by raising him from the dead" (Acts 17:30–31, italics mine). In examining this passage, a good question to ask is, "What is the relationship between God's will and His commands?" Undoubtedly, He has commanded humans to repent, that they are to move from their state of unbelief to one of belief (Heb. 11:6). Yet this brings up an interesting question for the Calvinist: if God has willed to pass over many of the lost to enable them in belief, what sense can be made of His *commanding* their repentance and belief, especially *knowing*

---

[38] The subject matter in this section will necessarily be more technical than in the previous sections.

that He has not enabled them to believe? Earlier this discussion centered on the is/ought principle. People rightly wonder how they are responsible for something that they cannot do (ought implies can). This section will draw attention to issues involving divine discourse, more specifically the implications of Calvinism on speech-acts.

To do this task, what speech-act theory proposes must be understood. Generally speaking, discourse between persons involves more than words but includes actions (or proposed actions) built into the contents of the words. Through speech people can inform, command, persuade, or *do* any number of things. Pertinent to this discussion on biblical imperatives is realizing what God commands must have a logical connection with what He *intends to accomplish* through His act of commanding—thus creating a difficulty for Reformed views of the will. In proper speech-act parlance, an utterance's perlocution and illocution differ. Though the discussion is nuanced, the *illocution* will be treated as the speaker's intention that is revealed in his speech, and the *perlocution* as the effect or intended effect of the speech on the speaker and/or the listener.[39]

With this in mind, consider God's commands to repent and believe. If God has inspired the words of Scripture to reveal His salvation plan, then it is reasonable to believe that He intends in each of these commands to bring about an action of morally positive status for the one to whom the command is directed—He intended to command human beings to repent. People use commands to motivate other persons to act, namely to do that which they were not going to do but that they *should* be doing. Luke clearly says that God has commanded *everyone* to repent. For whom is this command morally binding? Biblically, the answer is everyone. But when a line of thought akin to Calvinism is followed, every last detail of creation manifests the purposes and sovereign control of God, including the damnation of some for His good pleasure.[40] How then are human beings to understand the imperatives quoted above, where it seems God has commanded something (repentance and faith from everyone) that He has not willed? The only tenable suggestion is that a wedge splits God's commands from His will, and human beings are morally accountable for the content of God's will and not His commands.

---

[39] See J. L. Austin's famous work, *How to Do Things with Words* (London: Oxford University Press, 1962), 101–3.

[40] See Calvin's *Institutes*, 3.21.7.

What grounds such a claim? The *illocution* is the speaker's intention in the performative utterance. When God commands repentance, He is intending to speak the truth of people's need to turn their hearts toward Him. But clearly this turning involves more on people's part than mental assent; it involves a complete change in the perspective on the real meaning of life. To love God means hating what is evil, holding Him in a unique place of esteem (the *perlocution*). Consider how this applies to our previous discussion on the general and special calls of God. The general call, as previously discussed, is given to every hearer of the gospel, but the special call is an inward call directed only to the elect. In essence, the message, though with two distinct divine illocutions, is the same. If God elects some to salvation, then He does not intend for His speech to change the moral standing of non-elect persons before Him. According to Calvinism, God elects some to salvation. Therefore, God does not intend for His speech to change the moral standing of non-elect persons before Him.

Imagine a 1970s Billy Graham crusade where 50,000 people fill Shea Stadium in New York. Suppose 5,000 receive a special call, and 45,000 receive a general call. The message delivered was the same in content (probably John 3:16); the only difference was how God intended each of the hearers to understand what was said. From this example the implications on divine perlocution follow. God intended the elect to be illumined unto salvation; for the non-elect He did not intend a transforming work in their lives. The same message, but two divine perlocutions, was given.

This conclusion about the illocution of divine commands is particularly problematic, for if God commands in order to inform human beings and direct their steps away from sinful thoughts and actions, then, as expected, He *intends* to command human beings for the purpose of change. Not only is this postulate not true for Calvinism; it is equally true that God will still hold persons accountable for patterns of thought and action that He never intended to correct by His command. Indeed, if God knew that He had not elected many, then His intention in the illocution for the non-elect would not be for a corrective course of action. If divine commands are not intended to correct a course of thought and action, then the non-elect are not morally obligated to that course of action (God never intended them to change their status).

Similar problems plague the perlocution of divine discourse. J. L. Austin and John Searle thought that a correlation exists between the illocution and the perlocution; that is, the speaker's intention in the speech and the intended or desired effect on the hearer from the speech, especially in cases where the language is directive (imperative) in nature rather than suggestive (which may include elements of persuasion but nothing resembling the force of a command). But there is good reason to question the viability of this relationship. If God's intentions in speech cannot be connected with the intended effect of the utterance, then working out a solid account of moral obligation becomes exceptionally difficult. Remember, the trouble here pertains to election, not the permissive will of God—which would not escape the fact that the rejection of God (a moral failure) is the source of all other *moral* failings.

Admittedly, the thoughts in this section are not as fully orbed as desired—a fuller explanation goes beyond the space limits of this article. The fruits of this concern are particularly helpful in several areas. Most Calvinists use speech-act theory to ground their account of inspiration, especially those who hold to a verbal plenary theory of inspiration. One might object to the proposal here by altering the model of divine discourse, for example, from speech-acts to expressionism, but such a move would be unwise. It would undermine the most profitable model of speech available and would undo most accounts of how human beings have the inspired Word of God. Here the prevailing model of Reformed theorists has been used, so the foundation of his inquiry is not *ad hoc*. In this section the relationship between God's intention in speaking and God's intended effects in His speech is open for discussion, especially as it concerns the doctrine of election. Elements of this concern pertaining to this key doctrine have not been adequately addressed.[41]

This essay has as its aim to elicit concerns about Reformed views of the will and provide food for thought as to why it should be reconsidered. A positive model of divine discourse awaits non-Reformed theorists—and I am refraining here from arriving at libertarianism simply because Reformed theology is found inadequate to explain human willing and action. A positive model must be provided for the libertarian model, but such a task will be left for another time. Suffice it to say that if Richard Cross's model of monergism and resistible grace receives consideration, then the problem in divine discourse is *prima facie* less pressing. When

---

[41] See K. Vanhoozer, *God, Scripture, and Hermeneutics* (Downer's Grove, IL: InterVarsity Press, 2002); and Vanhoozer, *Is There Meaning in This Text?* (Grand Rapids: Zondervan, 1998). See also N. Wolterstorff, *Divine Discourse: Philosophical Reflections on the Claim that God Speaks* (Cambridge: Cambridge University Press, 1995).

Billy Graham preaches at Shea Stadium, the call of God is to all persons equally, so the issue of special and general calls has no purchase. No finessing is required between the illocution and perlocution. God intends to command the listeners to repent, effecting a complete change in the heart of the hearer toward the saving message of our Lord Jesus.

Conclusion

The issues addressed in this chapter are significant, and undoubtedly this work will not be the last on the topic at hand. Sincere believers who love the Lord and serve Him diligently may be found on both sides of the aisle (or walking down the middle of the aisle). We cannot afford to lose our bearings on issues of primary significance. When it comes to the topic of Calvinism, the discussion is in-house (within the church); believers need to consider these issues because even a cursory reading of God's Word elicits the questions discussed here. Passages like the hardening of Pharaoh's heart or concepts like predestination and election simply cannot be avoided. All of these, and more, permeate Scripture and beg for explanation. For several reasons this discussion is an in-house one. First, persons who are not of the faith are not only generally disinterested in this issue but also can easily perceive it as another instance of Christian bickering and division. Attempting to discover the deeper matters of Scripture must not lead to forgetting the primary commands in them, namely to love God and one another (Matt 22:37). Difficult matters, whether personal or intellectual, must be handled with charity; but they must be handled. An approach can be direct, but it must be motivated out of love. Second, this discussion is for the church because it centers on *how God works in salvation*, not on who God has worked through to provide the necessary means of our salvation—Jesus. When we witness, the person of Christ is made much of. We lift up His sacrifice as the focus of our message and for good reason. We do not have to explain the *mechanism* of salvation when we witness, only the *message* of salvation to those who do not know Jesus as their Savior. These are practical concerns but concerns nonetheless.

This chapter has aimed to provide useful insight into the nature of human agency and the richness and texture of this problem. No matter which view of human freedom one espouses, problems will arise. In deterministic theories about human freedom, God's relationship to sin and evil will always surface. Libertarians have their own demons to cast out, including providing a satisfactory treatment of the passages that Calvinists love to quote and on the surface seem to support their view.

I moved from a Reformed view of the will to a libertarian view during my time as a seminary student. Interestingly, the move occurred not because of my professors; most of my professors were admittedly Calvinists. Instead, I grew to consider libertarianism as the view with the least pressing problems ranging over the most significant areas of inquiry. It was hard enough reconciling determinism with a meaningful account of human freedom and even harder to understand how God, knowing that everyone is in need of a Savior, would not enable everyone to accept the offer of new life in Christ. I felt the intellectual transition away from Geneva was needed to avoid what I considered to be problems bigger than those faced by non-Reformed views of the will. Ken Keathley makes an excellent point here in his defense of Molinism (a libertarian view of freedom):

> If Molinists have to appeal to mystery . . . they do so at a better and more reasonable point. I'd rather have the Molinist difficulty of not being able to explain how God's omniscience operates than the Calvinist difficulty of explaining how God is not the author of sin. In other words, Molinism's difficulties are with God's infinite attributes rather than His holy and righteous character.[42]

These same sentiments provided the impetus for my journey away from Geneva.

---

[42] See K. Keathley, "A Molinist View of Election, or How to Be a Consistent Infralapsarian," in *Calvinism: A Southern Baptist Dialogue* (ed. E. Ray Clendenen and B. Waggoner; Nashville: B&H Academic, 2008), 214.

{ Chapter 11 }

Evil and God's Sovereignty

BRUCE A. LITTLE

On the clear autumn morning of September 11, 2001, I was straightening up my office (having moved in only a few days earlier) when a news bulletin caught my attention. My small desk TV was tuned to the *Today Show* when a news flash announced that a plane had just crashed into one of the World Trade Towers. Troubling as that was, it seemed that the immediate danger or threat was limited to those in the immediate vicinity of the event. Soon, however, it became clear that this crash was not a small-scale accident but a premeditated act of terror involving much more than the World Trade Towers. It would be hours later before the magnitude of the destruction and the cost of human life bound up in this epoch-making event etched its reality upon the fleshy memory banks of America citizens as well as the watching world. On that day thousands of lives were lost, and many thousands more would never be the same. Where was God? Or was there a God at all, at least the Christian God?

The unthinkable had happened. Staring in the face of a nation was the reality that evil exists in a concrete way. Diplomacy and technology had not banished it to faraway places. The event startled the hearts of millions with a renewed sense of human finiteness and impotency (if only for a time) resulting in an intuitive reaction to call out to God. Instinctively, people prayed and talked of God. This reality once again raised the age-old dilemma: If God is all-powerful and all-good, how could such horrific evil[1] be permitted in this world created and maintained by this God? On the one hand, there is the instinctive need for God in such times; yet, on the other hand, if God is all-powerful and all-good, how did He allow something like 9/11 to happen? That is, if God is all Christians claim He is, why does evil exist in a world created and maintained by this sovereign God? Furthermore, this event underscores the need of the human heart to have real answers regarding the question of the relation of God to evil. However the question of evil's existence is answered, this response must consistently offer an answer concerning suffering (evil) caused by moral agents (such as rape), suffering caused by natural disasters (such as tsunamis), and physical suffering (such as cancer). Any answer that fails to take into account these three areas has not yet faced the scope of the question and will be found wanting. If Christianity's claim as a superior worldview is to have any intellectual currency in the marketplace of ideas, it cannot ignore the question of evil. Of course, many have attempted to answer the question of evil, and their answers have only raised other questions.

It is not that Christians have not offered answers over the past, for they have. This set of answers is often referred to as a theodicy.[2] In clarification, not everybody who deals with the question of evil would subscribe to the concept of theodicy. This essay, however, does not develop or defend a theodicy.[3] In particular, this essay examines answers given by those in the theological tradition called Calvinism.[4] The moment the word *Calvinism* surfaces, it may produce an instinctive reaction in some persons to prepare for a fight. That reaction, at least not here, is not so. This critique hopefully will be evenhanded and fair-minded, conducted not as warfare but thoughtfully. Intellectual honesty presses me to disclose that I do not

---

[1] The word *evil* is used in a broad sense in this discussion. Its use includes moral evil, which is evil caused by a moral human agent, as well as natural evil and physical evil. Its use here assumes a connection between evil and suffering. I would argue that not all suffering is evil (for example, that which comes from God when He disciplines His children as in Heb 12:6–11). Nonetheless, all suffering has its roots in evil.

[2] The word "theodicy" (*theos dikē*) signifies the justification of God and enables one to argue for the existence of God in the light of evil.

[3] This topic receives treatment elsewhere: B. A. Little, *A Creation–Order Theodicy: God and Gratuitous Evil* (Lanham: University Press of America, 2005).

[4] Other books look at this issue from different Calvinistic perspectives: J. Feinberg, *The Many Faces of Evil* (rev. and exp. ed.; Wheaton: Crossway Books, 2004); U. Middelmann, *The Innocence of God* (Colorado Springs: Paternoster, 2007).

consider myself a Calvinist or an Arminian, but my theological position beyond that is irrelevant to what is going on here.

Clarification on several points hopefully will eliminate misunderstandings that can be all too common to a discussion of this nature. First, not all Calvinists[5] are in view here, as I am sure there are exceptions to the rule in any theological position. Second, I do not use the term *Calvinist* in a pejorative sense; it is simply a matter of using a traditional classification regarding a theological position. Third, it is readily acknowledged that the difference between theological positions must not be portrayed as a distinction between those who love God and want to glorify Him and those who do not. Each position must stand or fall on the merits or strengths of the particular arguments supporting the position. Unfortunately, too often important discussions of this nature degenerate into unhelpful rhetoric which unnecessarily creates division between Christian brothers and sisters. The principle of charity is important at this point. It would be silly to think that a person claims a belief he knows is biblically wrong simply because it comes with the theological system he has adopted or because he wants to be different. While theological systems play an important role in doing theology, at the end of the day, one's commitment must be to come to the truth, not simply defend a system.

Lastly, to my knowledge, no one propositional statement in the Bible sets forth an unambiguous full-orbed answer to this question of evil. Therefore, constructing an answer involves drawing inferences from what the Bible states clearly, a procedure not foreign to the Church. In drawing these inferences, the theological inference must neither deny what God affirms nor affirm what God clearly denies; it must strive for internal consistency. Any answer to the question of evil will touch many different doctrines, but however the answer is framed, it must reflect (1) consistency within one's theological system, (2) avoidance of logical fallacies or inconsistencies, and (3) a balanced application of all the acknowledged attributes of God. Method, or what is known as hermeneutics, is, therefore, important, as are all prior theological assumptions with which one comes to the discussion.

Although this essay begins with the event of 9/11, other events beg for an answer as well and possibly even more so. Hundreds of evil events

---

[5] Some within the Reformed tradition take sovereignty to a different level than others. See, for example, R. C. Sproul Jr. in his book *Almighty over All: Understanding the Sovereignty of God* (Grand Rapids: Baker, 1999).

causing great suffering occur every day around the world; however, they often receive far less publicity because they involve much smaller numbers. Many of these events are cases of horrific evil and suffering that rip families apart and wound human beings in the innermost part of their being because the principal sufferer is a child. Fyodor Dostoevsky's *The Brothers Karamazov* wrestles with this matter, as does Voltaire's *Candide*. In a natural or intuitive sense, the suffering of small children offends people's moral sensibilities no matter who they are or what their religious beliefs are. Not only are children seen as defenseless, but the Christian perspective introduces another existential difficulty. What sense is to be made of the abusive cruelty directed toward children when Jesus says they are special in God's sight?

The Gospel of Matthew records the words of Jesus regarding God's view of children: "Assuredly I say to you, unless you are converted and become as little children, you will by no means enter the kingdom of heaven. . . . Whoever receives one little child like this in My name receives Me" (Matt 18:3,5).[6] Later Jesus said concerning the little children: "Take heed that you do not despise one of these little ones, for I say to you that in heaven their angels always see the face of My Father who is in heaven" (Matt 18:10). Jesus rebuked the disciples when they attempted to prevent the little children from coming to him: "But Jesus said, 'Let the little children come to Me, and do not forbid them; for of such is the kingdom of heaven'" (Matt 19:14). At the least these texts indicate that children are special in God's sight. Jesus, who was God, says so. Such texts do not give an answer for why children suffer; they only acknowledge that mistreating children is an offense to God. The suffering of children not only offends God; it offends the moral sensibilities of humanity almost universally. This suffering must be understood as set against the words of Jesus. Therefore, however one answers the question of evil, it must not only address the scope of evil in general but the suffering of children in particular.

Consider the situation of the little girl Jessica in Florida a couple of years ago, whom a convicted sex offender abducted, raped, and then buried alive in his yard. She was nine years old when taken from her bedroom. She is chosen here not for any particular reason but merely as a representative of hundreds of little children, many younger than Jessica, who are subjected to horrible torture every year. Not only did Jessica suffer such inhumane torture, but those related to or associated with her have and

---

[6] All Scripture references come from the New King James Version unless otherwise stated.

will suffer for years to come. Most think that if there is a God, surely He would intervene on behalf of little children, that is, if He were to intervene for any, especially in light of what Jesus says. If God is the God of the universe, why would He allow such things to happen to the innocent ones?[7] Of course, this example does not, on the face of it, serve as a sure defeater of the claim that God exists. Nonetheless, the suffering of children does present a serious challenge to those attempting to provide an answer to the question of evil. Where is God in all of this?

While this discussion has mentioned the matter of children and their innocence, Calvinists such as John Piper claim that no one is innocent. Commenting on US Airways flight 1549, which on January 15, 2009 experienced an exceptional landing on the Hudson River, Piper makes this comment: "God can take down a plane any time he pleases—and if he does, he wrongs no one. Apart from Christ, none of us deserves anything from God but judgment. We have belittled him so consistently that he would be perfectly just to take any of us any time in any way he chooses."[8] This viewpoint means that when Jessica was tortured and buried alive, God had injured no one. After all, as it is argued, Jessica is a sinner and deserving of the wrath of God, so God owed Jessica nothing. Of course, it is true that God owes human beings nothing and only in Christ is there security from the penalty of sin. Christ died for the sins of the world (1 John 2:1–2), and only those in Christ are delivered from the second death. However, Piper seems to confuse suffering in time with suffering in eternity. If Christ has died for the sins of the world, then the Father has been satisfied on that account. So why claim that because Jessica is a sinner, God can justifiably ordain her torture? In addition, if He ordained her death the way things turned out, then in reality it is the only way it could turn out if sovereignty means anything. It is not that it just happens this way; it is ordained to be this way because God is sovereign—or at least that is how sovereignty is applied to the situation. It means more than simply saying God allowed it to happen.

According to Calvinists such as Piper, God is not blameworthy even though He ordained it. God ordains the evil He commands humans to refrain from doing. Either God orders the world under moral principles

---

[7] When I speak of children being innocent, I am not suggesting they are not corrupted from birth. I am not using the word in its theological sense, but rather in a sense of personal moral culpability for personal actions.

[8] J. Piper, "The President, the Passengers, and the Patience of God," http://www.desiringgod.org/ResourceLibrary/TasteAndSee/ByDate/2009/3520/; accessed March 21, 2009.

different from those He gives mankind, or there is a contradiction in the nature of God. What logically follows if one accepts the idea that God ordained Jessica's horrible end even though the rapist bears the responsibility? Since God ordained the particular act, God also must have ordained the pedophile to act (although according to this view, the pedophile bears the full responsibility for acting the way he does). Understand the logical force of this view: there is no way for Jessica to be raped except for *someone* to rape her. If the rape is ordained, then so is the *rapist* ordained to act.

Jessica, however, is not alone in all of this suffering; many others suffer as well. The parents, grandparents, and other relatives must live with the knowledge of the torture as well as with the loss of a dear daughter. One can now only conclude that God also ordained this grief. But Jesus does not seem to reflect an indifferent attitude toward suffering and loss, even though Jesus revealed the Father to humanity (John 1:18). What about the widow of Nain? It appears that Jesus had compassion on the widow when He came across the funeral procession taking her only son to be buried. On that occasion no one begs Him to do something, and no one prays. According to the text, "He had compassion on her" (Luke 7:13). Jesus simply reaches down, touches the coffin, and says, "Young man, I say to you, arise" (Luke 7:14). The boy's life comes into him again. The Calvinists' view of the same God ordaining the torture and hideous death of a child like Jessica and dispassionately watching her parents grieve seems curious in light of this passage. Furthermore, according to Luke, Jesus proclaims humanity is living in "the acceptable year of the LORD" (4:19) because "God was in Christ reconciling the world to Himself, not imputing their trespasses to them, and has committed to us the word of reconciliation" (2 Cor 5:19). Surely, this passage has something to say to us regarding the way God is now interacting with the world, which seems at odds with the Calvinist's view. One must agree that God, in one sense (apart from His grace), can do as He pleases with any human being. Still, it must not be ignored He has laid something on Himself for these days, namely to be "longsuffering toward us, not willing that any should perish" (2 Pet 3:9). While it is right to affirm God can, in one sense, do as He pleases, His commitments (promises) to His creation constrain Him, and this constraint in no way detracts from His sovereignty. In addition, Christians are commanded to do good to all people, especially those of the household of faith (Gal 6:10). Should God do less—especially the sovereign God?

The doctrine of divine sovereignty looms large in this discussion and rightly so. If Christians did not claim that God governed as the omnipotent sovereign One over His creation, the question of God and evil would assume a considerably different shape. The doctrine of God's divine sovereignty stands at the center of the Calvinist position on evil. However, that others may apply divine sovereignty somewhat differently is not the problem but rather how Calvinists understand sovereignty in relationship to the question of evil in the larger context of God's sovereign control.

The other side of the argument focuses on free will. The term *free will* is an unfortunate one since it does not precisely mean what is suggested by the term, for man is not free to will just anything he wishes. Libertarian freedom is a much preferred term.[9] Many of those who affirm libertarian freedom also affirm a high view of divine sovereignty. That both human free will, which is roughly interchangeable with libertarian freedom, and divine sovereignty have support in the Scriptures, explains why many Christians hold to both. The controversy develops over how to understand the relationship between sovereignty and free will. How one understands the relationship goes to the heart of how the question of God and evil is answered.

With that said, the subject at hand—how Calvinists typically answer the question of evil—can move forward. Generally, many Calvinists[10] (as well as any who reject the notion of free will), in explaining evil in this world, appeal to some form of a greater good, which finds its beginnings in Augustine of Hippo. This approach argues that God allows into this world only that evil from which He can either bring about a greater good or prevent a worse evil. Whereas there is no way to know if a worse evil was preempted or not, part of the explanation can probably be dropped. Regarding Augustine's position, Richard Middleton notes: "whereas Augustine's explicit position in *De Libero Arbitrio* is that the world is no worse for all the evil in it, due to God's providence (technically, that all

---

[9] There are some slight nuances in definition among those who affirm libertarian freedom, however. Thomas Flint offers the following general definition: "A theory of agent causation, according to which the ultimate cause of a free action is not some set of prior conditions, but the agent herself who performs the action" (*Divine Providence* [Ithaca, NY: Cornell University Press, 1995], 32.). I would add that antecedent events/conditions may incline or influence a person in making the choice, but they neither determine nor cause the choice.

[10] While I use the term *Calvinist* and quote those committed to Calvinism, the critique applies to any who would answer the question of evil in the same way. I will quote from two well-recognized spokespersons for this position: John Piper and Gordon H. Clark. These Calvinists are quoted to avoid the charge of merely responding to a straw person. Quoting these men in no way intends to ridicule their person or Christian beliefs.

evil is 'counterbalanced' by good), by the time we get to his later *Enchiridion* Augustine boldly claims that 'God judged it *better* to bring good out of evil than not to permit any evil to exist.'"[11] For Augustine, it was better for persons to have free will than not, even though free will made evil possible (not necessary) in God's creation. Augustine argued that it was God's goodness that led Him to create persons with free will, for he said it is better to be a moral being than a nonmoral being: "Such is the generosity of God's goodness that He has not refrained from creating even that creature which He foreknew would not only sin but remain in the will to sin. As a runaway horse is better than a stone which does not run away because it lacks self-movement and sense perception, so the creature is more excellent which sins by free will than that which does not sin only because it has no free will."[12]

Augustine affirmed that sin came by human free will and that God in no way ordained or forced humans to do evil. In fact, evil was not necessary even though God knew about it. Augustine wrote:

> Your [God's] foreknowledge would not be the cause of his [man's] sin, though undoubtedly he [man] would sin; otherwise you would not foreknow that this would happen. Therefore, these two are not contradictory, your foreknowledge and someone else's free act. So too God compels no one to sin, though He foresees those who will sin by their own will.[13]

For Augustine the will is free, and, therefore, persons are truly morally responsible for their acts. Furthermore, Augustine maintained that the will is culpable for its own turning or that it is its own cause. He noted that the will's turn from good to evil "belongs only to the soul, and is voluntary and therefore culpable."[14] However, he believes that God in His providence, brings good out of the evil He allowed, thus justifying the evil being allowed. Augustine has a robust view of God's providence, which understands God's work in history to bring good out of all evil; in fact, that evil is the only evil God would allow into the world. Today, many within the Calvinistic tradition argue that the greater good is the glory of God (Augustine argued for particular goods in this life) and deny the idea of free will. Furthermore, there is a subtle shift from God *allows* to God has a *purpose* in the evil.

---

[11] R. J. Middleton, "Why the 'Greater Good' Isn't a Defense," *Koinonia* 9 (1997): 83–84.

[12] Augustine, *The Problem of Free Choice* (ed. J. Quasten and J. Plumpe; trans. D. M. Pontifix; ACW; Westminster, MD: The Newman Press, 1955), 3.4.15.

[13] Ibid., 3.4.10.

[14] Ibid., 3.1.2.

Some claim that God has a purpose in all evil that He allows, but they give some room for human free will. Others, such as Piper, maintain that God has a purpose and actually *ordains* or wills the evil for this purpose. In the latter case the purpose of evil is to glorify God and is solidly constructed on God's sovereignty. In other words, either God controls all things in the strong sense, or He controls nothing. To be truly sovereign means that whatever happens on earth, if it is for His good purposes, is willed by God; otherwise, there could be no assurance that His purpose would be accomplished. Two questions surface from this view: (1) Does divine sovereignty require this strong view in order to maintain a biblical view of sovereignty? (2) If God ordains or wills all things, in what way do persons, not God, stand morally responsible for their acts? Greater-good approaches differ, for in the case of Augustine, God's providence allows evil, whereas in more recent Calvinistic views, God actually ordains or wills the evil. In the case of Jessica, then, according to one view, God *allowed* her to be tortured to death for no reason other than pure wickedness on the part of the perpetrator, and God would bring some good from it. I do not mean to say that this view does not raise other questions as well, but I am only pointing out the difference. According to the other view, God *ordained* it for the greater glory for Christ, which is His good purpose.

Those who take what might be considered a moderate Calvinism (often referred to as compatibilism) rest their answer to evil on Rom 8:28: "And we know that all things work together for good to those who love God, to those who are the called according to His purpose." This text, however, only affirms that God works "together for good to those who love God, to those who are called according to His purpose." A casual reading of the text reveals that this working together applies only to those who "love God," which excludes the majority of earth's population and says nothing about natural disasters. This verse, while it provides comfort for the believer, does not provide a foundational position from which to answer the question of evil. Asserting that God allows evil because He will bring about some good from it finds no support in this verse. A cursory examination of the greater-good explanation for all evil reveals serious weaknesses.[15] Because this explanation plays a part in so many Christian responses to evil, considering briefly some of those weaknesses will be

---

[15] The questions from evil are difficult and complex. All views have some weaknesses to them. In the end one should go with the answer that embraces the largest amount of biblical material consistently and with the least amount of appeal to mystery.

helpful. The critique will also show how these weaknesses apply to the Calvinist position under consideration in this essay.

First, it seems rather obvious (at least to me) that something happens in this world either because God has *allowed* it or *ordained* it. I envision no objection on that point except maybe from those who hold to an open theism. The point of concern arises over *why* He allows it. That He allows it because His sovereign hand will bring some good (particular good things or the good of God's glory) from the evil, faces some serious challenges. This challenge does not say that God cannot bring good from evil. The challenge is whether the good that obtains morally justifies God in allowing evil. For the moment set aside that Rom 8:28 does not explain much of the suffering in this world; it actually says nothing about why God *allows* suffering. It affirms that God will bring some good from certain kinds of suffering. These are two different matters—why He *allows* suffering and what He might *do* in the suffering. To suggest that one can move from what God might do with suffering to why He allowed the suffering makes one a consequentialist, in which the end justifies the means. That is, justifying the cause by looking at the effect is tantamount to allowing the end to excuse or justify the means. The text says nothing about why God allows the suffering.

Still, if God *ordains* or *allows* evil, a couple of practical matters come to light. If God allows or ordains evil to bring about good (regardless of what the good is), what does that say about the Christian's responsibility to uphold social justice? If God allows or ordains evil in order to bring good, then it would seem that Christians should not be engaged in standing against social injustice (that which the Bible calls evil). Should they stop it, they would keep the good from obtaining—a good necessary to God's plan. If God is really sovereign and He ordains the evil, it would be impossible for mere humans to stop it, so standing against social injustice would be an exercise in futility. Apply this to the matter of abortion, an act that can be properly put in the category of evil (taking of life). Since abortion presently occurs, then God either allowed or ordained it for some good. Therefore, logically, to attempt to eliminate abortion would, in fact, be frustrating (or at least attempting to frustrate) God's plan to bring some good. In addition, if God allowed evil, the good must be necessary, which in turn makes evil necessary.

The second concern pertains to the relationship between good and evil within the plan of God. The good (whether the good be some particular good or the glory of God) must in some way accomplish God's purposes; therefore, the good must be necessary to His purposes. If the good can only come from the evil, then the evil also must be necessary to God's plan. Avoiding this conclusion seems difficult:

> God cannot bring about certain goods without particular evils, for if any evil will do, God should pick the least of the sufferings. Also, if God can bring about the good without the evil, then He should for if He can and He does not, then He is not the good God being defended. One could argue that if God needs particular evils to bring about certain goods, then God is not omnipotent. In this case, the all-good, all-powerful God is unable to bring about a good without the help of evil. Immediately one can see how theologically convoluted this becomes. It diminishes God and makes evil a necessary part of His plan.[16]

If evil is necessary to God's plan, then since it is God's plan, God is the one responsible for evil, which John seems to contradict clearly by claiming that "God is light and in Him is no darkness at all" (1 John 1:5b). In the case of Jessica, her torture then was necessary to some good in the overall purposes of God regardless of whether He allowed it or ordained it.

Once the move has been made making evil part of God's design within His larger plan, the direct line to God as the cause of evil becomes straighter and stronger. If the sovereign God is in control of all things, then what happens on this earth must fulfill the particular purposes of God. Furthermore, either all things have a purpose, or all things are chaotic or left to chance. Since chaos and chance are incompatible with God's sovereignty, it supposedly follows that all things must have a purpose, and the guarantee of this purpose is God's will. There seems to be, however, a mistake of logic at this point. The suggestion cannot be sustained that if all things in life are not part of God's purpose, then all things are left to chance. This argument fails because it does not distinguish between reason and purpose.

Undoubtedly, or so it seems to me, if God is truly sovereign, then for everything that happens (at least on earth), there is a reason but not necessarily a purpose. Often the Bible provides the record of God's reason for something happening but not necessarily His purpose. Consider God's relationship with Israel as expressed in Deuteronomy 28. God is not giving His purpose in what He says but rather expressing the reason the

---

outcomes in Israel's life will differ depending on her choices. Giving that explanation is not, however, the same thing as saying that everything that happens must have a purpose. An illustration will display the difference. If, when you ask me why I did not pay my electric bill, I say because I did not have the money, then what I have given you is a reason. Should I, however, reply that I did not pay my electric bill because I am protesting the recent hike in the price of electricity, then I have given you the purpose for which I did not pay my electric bill. As the examples illustrate, the reason and the purpose for an action differ. Therefore, it is perfectly consistent to affirm that because God is sovereign, nothing happens on this earth by chance as there is always a reason. That God has purposes regarding history cannot be denied. Many things happen because God has a purpose, such as sending His Son to be the Savior of the world (John 3:16), but that explanation does not account for all things.

In a larger sense, it is the difference between contrivance and order. One can contrive certain things to indicate purpose. Other things, however, happen by order within the universe, which supplies the reason these things occurred. If people fall off a high building, it is not a matter of chance that they hurt themselves since that would be predicted because of the way the world is structured. That example illustrates a reason flowing from natural order. If on the other hand people jump off the building in order to take their own life, they are depending on natural order to accomplish their purposes. The two events differ not in that one is chaotic and the other not since both are predictable. Both have a reason, but a purpose is involved only in the latter case. God surely has sufficient reasons for allowing things to happen on this planet within the established natural order of creation, but that does not require claiming that He has a purpose in all things. Sometimes things happen because of the ordering of the universe: "Whatever a man sows, that he will also reap" (Gal 6:7). Furthermore, sometimes God purposes something, but because of the human agent's disobedience, it does not reach fruition (Isa 5:4). Israel's disobedience gives the reason things turned out as they did. God's purpose is to produce fruit. When that does not happen, He judges His vineyard (Isa 5:5-7) that Israel might repent. That explains the purpose of the judgment. Israel suffered, but that was not God's purpose in planting the vineyard. In the end God's purpose for Israel and the world will come to pass in spite of disobedience because of His providential hand in history. He is the sovereign One who works through His providence to bring history to its final appointed place. In light of this, it is possible to maintain a robust view of sovereignty and order in this world while maintaining that evil in this world is not necessarily the work of God's purposes.

A second, related matter concerns how to understand sovereignty. The idea of sovereignty can be understood in two ways. One way to understand that God has control (sovereignty) is by thinking of a man controlling his vehicle. If he turns the steering wheel left, the car (under normal circumstances) goes left. That is, there is a direct connection between the direction of the vehicle and the will of the driver. This form of sovereignty, as previously spoken of, is *strong sovereignty*. Another way to understand God's control is that of the man who is in control of his family. He ensures that everybody follows the established rules. This form is called *simple sovereignty* and is the one displayed in Ancient Near Eastern texts referring to the suzerain and his vassal. There is, moreover, more than one legitimate way to understand God as being in control (sovereign). In fact, the latter view of sovereignty is precisely how John Piper sees God's control when speaking about Satan. Piper writes, "God has given him [Satan] astonishing latitude to work his sin and misery in the world. He is a great ruler over the world, but not the *ultimate* one. God holds the decisive sway."[17] Surely, the same sovereign God who deals with Satan also deals with human beings. In Piper's theology, God does not give man the same latitude that He gives Satan.

The writings of John Piper display the view of strong sovereignty. Piper, an evangelical leader, has brought much spiritual encouragement to the community of faith. Therefore, the following interaction is only to see how, as a Calvinist, he answers the question of God and evil in light of a strong sovereignty. In a recent Internet posting by Piper, he refers to the event others dubbed the "Miracle on the Hudson" as a parable on our nation. The event unfolded on January 15, 2009, when US Airways flight 1549, shortly after takeoff, encountered a flock of birds (geese), some of which were sucked into the plane's engines and shut down both. Captain Sullenberger, an experienced pilot, chose to land the plane on the Hudson River rather than attempt a landing at an airport several miles away. By all accounts, it was one of those events where training, outstanding judgment, and right circumstances came together, resulting in all passengers surviving. The nation rightfully celebrated Captain Sullenberger as a hero.

---

[17] J. Piper, *Spectacular Sins: And Their Global Purpose in the Glory of Christ* (Wheaton: Crossway, 2008), 44.

Piper, however, had a little different take on the event. He writes: "Two laser-guided missiles would not have been as amazingly effective as were those geese. It is incredible, statistically speaking. If God governs nature down to the fall (and the flight) of every bird, as Jesus says (Matt 10:29), then the crash of flight 1549 was designed by God."[18] He goes on to say, "If God guides geese so precisely, he also guides the captain's hand."[19] In other words, God in His sovereignty is even responsible for the movement of the pilot's hands. Furthermore, according to Piper, this entire event was "designed" by God. This assertion can only mean that God in His sovereignty designed it before the world began to fit His purposes. If that is so, God does not merely *allow* this; God designs and executes it. In His omnipotence He executes the plan by, among other things, guiding the flight of the geese and the hands of the pilot to bring about an event that will, as Piper says, give a parable of His power to the nation. There is no way for things to turn out differently. Who is responsible for this event? According to this view of things, God is, right down to guiding the geese into the engine and guiding the hands of the pilot. God is responsible but not morally culpable. The logic of this view means He also designed all events that preceded that event. This view includes making sure those precise geese were there at that particular moment as well as ordaining everything in Sullenberger's life so he would be on that plane on that day. Notice God did not providentially intervene at the moment in response to some prayer or by His own mercy. According to this view, God designed it in order to serve His purposes, purportedly to show His power to a new president and to a nation.

Only a few days after "Miracle on the Hudson" happened, another airplane mishap occurred, but this time 50 people died. According to reports, "Continental Connection Flight 3407 from Newark, New Jersey, came in squarely through the roof of the house, its tail section visible through flames shooting at least 50 feet high."[20] As the Continental commuter plane was coming in for a landing, it slammed into a house in suburban Buffalo, sparking a fiery explosion that killed all 49 people aboard and a person in the home. Although the investigation is unfinished, the preliminary investigation concluded that "pilot commands—not a buildup of ice

---

[18] J. Piper, "The President, the Passengers, and the Patience of God," http://www.desiringgod.org/ResourceLibrary/TasteAndSee/ByDate/2009/3520/; accessed March 21, 2009.

[19] Ibid.

[20] "Buffalo Plane Crash: Continental Connection Flight 3407 Crashes into House, Kills 50," http://www.huffingtonpost.com/2009/02/13/plane-crashes-into-house_n_166609.html.

on the wings and tail—likely initiated the fatal dive of the twin-engine Bombardier Q400 into a neighborhood six miles short of the Buffalo, New York, airport, according to people familiar with the situation."[21]

Applying Piper's theological explanation of the Hudson episode, it logically follows that in this case God guided the pilot of flight 3407 to misjudgment in order that God "would bring the plane down" killing 50 people. It might be argued that He only guided the hand where safety resulted and that flight 3407 was just an accident. Yet, if Piper maintains that all evil occurs to give glory to Christ, then one can reasonably conclude that in both situations God was involved in bringing His design to pass, which includes this evil. Furthermore, whereas God owes no one anything, He has not harmed the 50 people killed. In his book *Spectacular Sins*, Piper writes in the section titled "All Things *for* Jesus–Even Evil":

> This book is also meant to show that everything that exists—including evil—is ordained by an infinitely holy and all-wise God to make the glory of Christ shine more brightly. The word *ordained* is peculiar, I know. But I want to be clear what I mean by it. There is no attempt to obscure what I am saying about God's relation to evil. But there is an attempt to say carefully what the Bible says. By *ordain* I mean that God either caused something directly or *permitted* it for wise purposes. This permitting is a kind of *indirect* causing, since God knows all the factors involved and what effects they will have and he could prevent any outcome.[22]

Later Piper claims:

> So when I say that everything that exists—including evil—is ordained by an infinitely holy and all-wise God to make the glory of Christ shine more brightly, I mean that, one way or the other, God sees to it that all things serve to glorify his Son. Whether he causes or permits, he does so with purpose. For an infinitely wise and all-knowing God, both causing and permitting are purposeful. They are part of the big picture of what God plans to bring to pass.[23]

Notice the words "purpose" and "purposeful." It may be simply a poor choice of words, but it seems that it is not. Piper carefully uses his words to say that in all the evil on this earth, God has a purpose: to make the glory

---

[21] "Pilot Action May Have Led to Buffalo Crash," http://www.foxnews.com/story/0,2933,495267,00. html.

[22] Piper, *Spectacular Sins*, 54.

[23] Ibid., 56.

of Christ shine more brightly. If it is for the purposes of God and purpose reflects the will of God, then the will of God is not perfect if any evil fails to materialize. Jessica's torturous death is part of this will. This position not only makes evil necessary to the purposes of God; it makes God the one morally responsible for the evil.

Addressing this matter, Piper agrees that God seems blameworthy, but he claims that He is not. In fact, Piper argues that in all of this, God is not blameworthy; we just do not understand how it is this way, but it is. Piper explains his claim regarding the "sovereignty of God over sin" by adding a footnote to demonstrate how he squares that view with Jas 1:13–15. He writes:

> Thus it seems to me that James is saying that *God* never experiences this kind of "being dragged away" or "being lured." And he does not directly (see Chapter Four, note 1) produce that "dragging" and that "luring" toward evil in humans. In some way (that we may not be able to fully comprehend), God is able without blameworthy "tempting" to see to it that a person does what God ordains for him to do even if it involves evil.[24]

In the end Piper concludes that though people may not understand it, God ordains evil but at the same time is not blameworthy for the evil. What does this say about the torture of Jessica and her abductor and all the events surrounding that horrible day? Could Christ's glory not shine brighter with a lot less trauma to Jessica and her friends and family? So, God does not just love the glory of Christ more than Jessica; He is actually willing to ordain the evil that befalls her that Christ's glory might shine brighter.

It is not that the glory of the Lord is unimportant, because it is (1 Cor 10:31), but to say that God ordains evil in order to magnify the glory of Christ seems to confuse the difference between good and evil. That is, God ordained Jessica's suffering for the purpose of making the glory of Christ shine brighter. Yet if a righteous life glorifies God (1 Cor 6:20), how does evil also glorify God? How do the contraries, one commanded and the other forbidden, both glorify God? That Christ *will* be glorified is not debated. It is not whether Christ *will receive* glory, because it seems that in the *eschaton* He will. As Paul says, "Therefore God also has highly exalted Him [Christ] and given Him the name which is above every name, that

---

[24] Ibid., 24.

at the name of Jesus every knee should bow, of those in heaven, and of those on earth, . . . and that every tongue should confess that Jesus Christ is Lord, to the glory of the Father" (Phil 2:9–11). But Paul's statement is an affirmation of a different sort. It only tells what the end will be and is silent on the issue of necessity or causality. The statement says only that in spite of the evil, God has the last word and glory will come to Christ even though at one point He was rejected. To say that all of this particular evil was necessary to Christ's glory says something quite different.

With little doubt, the idea of God's glory in history fills the pages of Scripture. The point of concern is whether the triumph over sin makes Christ's glory shine brighter. The night of Christ's betrayal (just before going to the cross), He prays, "And now, O Father, glorify Me together with Yourself, with the glory which I had with You before the world was" (John 17:5). The glory for which Jesus prays is the glory He had with the Father before the world was. Jesus is not referring to a glory that comes because He is about to defeat evil on the cross but rather the glory that was before creation. Undoubtedly, Christ's work on the cross demonstrates the redemption by the incarnate Son crucified for the sins of the world; that, however, does not seem to be the argument. The argument is that God ordains all individual events of evil as part of His plan so that Christ's glory might shine brighter. In the end, when the words used are understood in the common usage, sin is made a part of the plan of God. It is, as Piper says, "part of the big picture of what God plans to bring to pass." For the sovereign God, He has only one big picture.

To be clear at this point, the question is not whether God will bring glory to Himself in the end. He will. The concern is that in Calvinist theology God ordains the evil along the way in order for the glory of Christ to shine brighter. But how many acts of evil does it take to show that Christ has power over them? Does each act of evil result in the glory of Christ shining brighter? If this is the case, then it seems that people need the ugly in order to appreciate beauty. That would mean that the beauty and glory of God could not be fully appreciated until there was the ugly—evil. So Adam in the garden could not appreciate the beauty and glory of God. Does that not necessitate the fall in the garden? The necessity of the fall, which has resulted in horrible evils of human torture, to say nothing of thousands going to hell, is now justified on the grounds it was needed for Christ's glory to shine brighter. The logic of this argument says that the more evil there is, the brighter Christ's glory will shine. The Bible, though, does not command people to order their lives in such a way; in fact, it commands just the opposite: "What shall we say then? Shall we continue in sin that grace may abound? Certainly not!" (Rom 6:1–2). Therefore, that God would order His creation this way seems curious. At the end of the day, that sure looks as though in the Calvinist system God not only ordained evil but actually needs evil if Christ is to get the greater glory. In fact, it makes the fall in the garden necessary, which in the end means Adam had no choice. So why is God not the one morally responsible even if for a good cause—the glory of Christ?

Gordon H. Clark, arguing for what he calls the Calvinist position on God and evil, writes, "As God cannot sin, so in the next place, God is not responsible for sin, even though he decrees it."[25] In fact, in responding to an Arminian position, he writes, "I wish very frankly and pointedly to assert that if a man gets drunk and shoots his family, it was the will of God that he should do so. . . . In Ephesians 1:11 Paul tells us that God works all things, not some things only, after the counsel of his own will."[26] Notice here, Clark says it is God's will and earlier says it is *decreed* by God and yet maintains that God is not the cause of sin or evil. Piper says evil is *ordained* by God, but God is not blameworthy. The verse Clark quotes only says what God *does* with all things; it does not say that God *wills* all things. It says that God works all things in light of the counsel of His will. This verse seems to say only that the providential work of God in human history keeps the plan of God for humanity on course. Notice this verse is saying something quite different from what Clark says.

In the midst of all of this discussion lies the question of moral responsibility. Those of a Calvinistic position often disavow God's moral responsibility for evil.[27] Both Clark and Piper maintain that their deterministic explanations for evil do not shift the moral responsibility to God. Instead, both claim that God is not blameworthy and man is responsible. Still, apart from assigning moral responsibility, according to the Calvinist's position, the evil in this world would not be here if God had not ordained or willed it. In other words, in the final analysis, Jessica (and the hundreds like her) suffered her end because of God. The Holocaust, the millions slain by Stalin, Pol Pot's killing in Cambodia, every baby beaten to death, and every cancer could not be here if it were not for God willing it or ordain-

---

[25] G. H. Clark, *God and Evil: The Problem Solved* (Unicoi, TN: The Trinity Foundation, 2004), 40.

[26] Ibid., 27.

[27] R. C. Sproul Jr. may be an exception; however, one might argue that he is the most consistent with the Calvinist position.

ing it. At the end of the day, it seems hard to escape the conclusion that God is morally responsible, although arguments are offered to deny this conclusion.

Gordon Clark presents one way of responding to the charge that the Calvinist position leaves God morally responsible for evil even though He ordained it. Clark seeks to smooth out the contradiction by crafting the notion of God's secret will and His revealed will. In the context of Genesis 22, Clark writes:

> One may speak of the secret will of God, and one may speak of the revealed will of God. Those who saw self-contradiction in the previous case would no doubt argue similarly on this point too. The Arminian would say that God's will cannot contradict itself, and that therefore his secret will cannot contradict his revealed will. Now, the Calvinist would say the same thing; but he has a clearer notion of what contradiction is, and what the Scriptures say. It was God's secret will that Abraham should not sacrifice his son Isaac; but it was his revealed (for a time), his command, that he should do so. Superficially this seems like a contradiction. But it is not. The statement, or command, "Abraham, sacrifice Isaac," does not contradict the statement, at the moment known only to God, "I have decreed that Abraham shall not sacrifice his son." If Arminians had a keener sense of logic they would not be Arminians.[28]

For the moment, the Calvinist-Arminian debate will be put aside in order to consider Clark's argument on its own merit. The logic of all of his argument may not be as clear as he affirms. He claims the contradiction is removed by affirming God's secret will is that Abraham must not sacrifice his son, while the revealed will is that he should sacrifice his son. Suggesting that God knows which will prevail hardly resolves the contradiction. That is, it is difficult to see how appealing to God's knowledge solves the problem. In fact, appealing to God's knowledge seems to strengthen the problem. The conclusion is that God has two apparently incoherent wills since He knows two contraries simultaneously. If God is sovereign, how does He have two wills (secret and revealed) regarding the same event, especially when the wills affirm contraries? Clark admits that there is an apparent contradiction in the text, but he thinks he has solved it. However, I think his solution fails on logical grounds. Of course, undoubtedly

---

[28] Clark, *God and Evil*, 28.

there is a solution to this apparent contradiction, but I suggest it is not Clark's solution.

Clark's explanation of Abraham's situation as involving God's secret will and the revealed will must also be applied to the drunk who kills his family. It was God's secret will that he not shoot his family, but it was God's revealed will that he should shoot his family. Yet it is the revealed will that is actually accomplished in time and space. So what happens in this case is just the opposite of what happens in the case of Abraham. The secret will in the case of the drunk is that he should not murder (Exod 20:13), yet when he murders, Clark says it is God's will. Is this the secret will or the revealed will? Surely Clark cannot be saying that murder is the secret will of God. The killing of the family, since Clark affirms it is God's will, then, must be the revealed will of God. Still, this argument puts the revealed will and the secret will of the sovereign God in conflict, so that apparently one is a sovereign will and the other is not. The command "do not murder" appears to be the sovereign will of God. Therefore, when Clark affirms the murder of the family as God's will, it cannot be the sovereign will, which is the affirmation he seeks to argue. Accordingly, in the case of Jessica, both her torture and her nontorture were God's will. At the end of the day, this view can only be called incoherent. God is presented as willing what He does not will, and yet He is not guilty of contradiction, nor is He found to be blameworthy in the murder.

If God is not blameworthy, who is? Only one other agent is involved, namely man. According to Calvinism, man does not have free will, so how can he be morally responsible? Both Piper and Clark agree that God ultimately is the cause of evil—either directly or indirectly. Piper uses the term "ordained" (either direct or indirect causation), and Clark affirms that God wills the evil. If God wills or ordains the evil but is not blameworthy and persons do not have free will, then who is morally responsible? Both Piper and Clark maintain that the individual bears the moral responsibility for his evil even though he do not have free will. Clark attempts an answer to this question:

> Perhaps the matter can be made clearer by stating in other words precisely what the question is. The question is, Is the will free? The question is not, Is there a will? Calvinism most assuredly holds that Judas acted voluntarily. He chose to betray Christ. He did so willingly. No question is raised as to whether or not he had a will. What the Calvinist asks is whether that will was free. Are there factors or powers

that determine a person's choice, or is the choice causeless? Could Judas have chosen otherwise? Not, could he have done otherwise, had he chosen; but, could he have chosen in opposition to God's foreordination? *Acts 4:28* indicates he could not.[29]

Clark's point is that one cannot choose other than he did although he could have done differently but only if God had willed differently.

Clark separates the idea of "free" from the idea of will. Of course, the will is never free in the absolute sense, but for Clark it is not free in any sense. According to Clark, the human will cannot choose in any sense. The will becomes merely the channel through which what God has willed is actualized. In the case of the man who raped Jessica, he could only have chosen otherwise if God had willed otherwise. Still the rapist is responsible. Clark affirms man has a will because of its association with a human action, not because it functions as a will in the normal sense of the word (that which chooses between one thing and its contrary).

For many, including Augustine, the will meant it had the freedom to move itself. Augustine notes:

> So what need is there to ask the source of that movement by which the will turns from the unchangeable good to the changeable good? We agree that it belongs only to the soul, and is voluntary and therefore culpable; and the whole value of teaching in this matter consists in its power to make us censure and check this movement, and turn our wills away from temporal things below us to enjoyment of the everlasting good.[30]

Therefore, Augustine maintains that the will is at least culpable for its own turning prior to the fall (and for some time he also believed it was true after the fall). In fact, Richard Swinburne claims that this view persisted in the church for the first four centuries. He writes,

> My assessment of the Christian theological tradition is that all Christian theologians of the first four centuries believed in human free will in the libertarian sense, as did all subsequent Eastern Orthodox theologians, and most Western Catholic theologians from Duns Scotus (in the fourteenth century) onwards.[31]

---

[29] Clark, *God and Evil*, 31.
[30] St. Augustine, *The Problem of Free Choice*, 3.1.2.
[31] R. Swinburne, *Providence and the Problem of Evil* (New York: Clarendon, 1998), 35.

Most often theologians believed that libertarian freedom was the only way humans could be morally responsible for their actions, just as the Bible affirms clearly. Actually, the notion of will carries with it the idea of the ability to choose between this and that—between contraries even. To say the will is not free is to render what is called a will to be something other than a will, at least in any common understanding of the word.

Clark anticipates another question, namely, how can something be called a choice if it is a necessity? That is, if God wills something (actually all things), in what sense could a person be said to have a choice? Clark answers that by saying:

> Choice and necessity are therefore not incompatible. Instead of prejudging the question by confusing choice with free choice, one should give an explicit definition of choice. The adjective could be justified only afterward, if at all. Choice may be defined, at least sufficiently for the present purpose, as a mental act that consciously initiates and determines a further choice. The ability to have chosen otherwise is an irrelevant matter and has no place in the definition.[32]

He is emphasizing that the will is only something that initiates and determines a further choice. The will is not a kind of self-determiner as Augustine and many of the church fathers taught, but rather the will only initiates what God has willed. It is how the will of God gets into history. Of course, one is not sure which will, the secret will or the revealed will. Clark seems to be saying that man has the ability to choose but not the freedom to choose. It is curious how this comports with the idea of moral responsibility. It sounds something like, persons can have any color car they want as long as they want black. It is true they can choose to have a car or not have a car, but they cannot in any legitimate sense say that they have a choice regarding color. In the end the will in Clark's terms is no will at all.

The logical end of the Calvinist position on the question of sovereignty leads to a strong form of determinism, which is not the necessary outcome of biblical sovereignty. In addition, moral responsibility for sin must find its final causal agent to be God. The protest against drawing this

---

[32] Clark, *God and Evil*, 32.

conclusion involves an argument that commits the fallacy of equivocation (particularly with the word "will") and the fallacy of explaining by naming—just saying it is so makes it so. Yet the Bible seems to say something different. In the Scriptures humans can choose between contraries such as life and death (Deut 30:15–19; Josh 24:15; Isa 56:4). The Old Testament is a story of God's responding to the checkered history of Israel in which at one time she is acting faithfully and the next minute she is playing the part of the harlot. The book of Judges is a sad story revealing a pattern where Israel freely chooses unfaithfulness against God's command, and how God intervenes. Consider the review of God's curses and blessings in Deuteronomy 28. There, if Israel obeyed, blessing followed (v. 1); but if Israel disobeyed, the curses would come upon Israel (v. 15). Either this account is real history, or God makes it look as though the people have real free choices when, in fact, they do not, if the Calvinists are right. If it was not a free choice, then moral responsibility cannot be imputed. Whereas definite, different outcomes resulted, depending on whether the people of Israel obeyed or disobeyed, the common sense understanding is that they freely chose between the contraries. Otherwise, the whole episode is meaningless. In the end their choices may be worse than meaningless—more likely illusionary and deceptive as far as the record goes. To say they chose but were not free is to void the meaning of "to choose," and then language means nothing. Not only that, but it destroys the entire notion of justice. The man who raped Jessica and buried her alive could not have chosen to do differently. In the plain sense of language, that choice means he should not be held accountable. On the other hand, to affirm that God ordains but is not morally responsible cannot be solved by simply appealing to mystery.

While Calvinists such as John Piper can be respected for their desire to honor the Lord, in this issue, they are simply wrong and their position incoherent. Unfortunately, being wrong in this area has some serious implications for areas of theology beyond the question of evil. At the end of the day, if they wish to hold to their view of sovereignty, they should be willing to accept the logical conclusion of their position and acknowledge that God is morally responsible for evil. Then they can attempt to build a case for why that does not directly conflict with the clear teaching of Scripture. If my critique has any legitimacy, at the end of the day, this position logically affirms that God is both causally and morally responsible for

9/11, the drunk murdering his family, and the rape and torturous death of Jessica. As I write this concluding paragraph, I have just received a news item on my computer reporting that a man fatally stabbed his 17-year-old sister and decapitated his five-year–old sister during her birthday party before police shot him. These acts were also ordained by God if Piper and others are right.[33] Is that what the Bible teaches?

---

[33] Other general books on the problem of evil include W. Dembski, *The End of Christianity* (Nashville: B&H Academic, 2009); D. Geivett, *Evil and the Evidence for God* (Philadelphia: Temple University Press, 1993); C. S. Lewis, *The Problem of Pain* (New York: Touchstone, 1996); M. Peterson, *God and Evil* (Boulder, CO: Westview Press, 1998); A. Plantinga, *God, Freedom, and Evil* (Grand Rapids: Eerdmans, 1974); and N. T. Wright, *Evil and the Justice of God* (Downers Grove, IL: InterVarsity Press, 2006). Other books tend to deal more with answering the existential questions arising from evil: D. A. Carson, *How Long O Lord?* (Downers Grove, IL: InterVarsity Press, 1990); J. Feinberg, *Deceived by God?* (Wheaton: Crossway, 1997); C. Plantinga Jr., *Not the Way It's Supposed to Be* (Grand Rapids: Eerdmans, 1995); R. Zacharias, *Cries of the Heart* (Nashville: Word, 1998).

{ Name Index }

❴ Subject Index ❵

{ Scripture Index }